INSIGHT GUIDES

MALAYSIA

Directed and Designed by Hans Höfer
Produced by Geoffrey Eu
Revised by Susan Amy

APA
PUBLICATIONS

MaLaYSIa

Thirteen Edition
© **1990 APA PUBLICATIONS (HK) LTD**
All Rights Reserved
Printed in Singapore by Höfer Press Pte. Ltd

ABOUT THIS BOOK

This edition of *Malaysia* represents a milestone in Apa Publications' award-winning *Insight Guides* series. Some 20 years have passed since Apa writers and photographers first ventured forth and discovered the many pleasures of this beautiful land. Since then, the forces of change and progress have left their indelible mark, but the Malaysia of the 1990s retains the same exotic appeal that first attracted modern-day travellers to its tropical shores. Its people, of course, still treat visitors with the same blend of friendly generosity and native charm. In much the same way that old friends from different countries keep in touch, Apa has revisited Malaysia several times, noting with keen interest the many significant developments that have taken place. The result is this memorable new version of *Insight Guide: Malaysia*, which features new text and photos that put the country into a modern-day context.

The original *Malaysia* helped set the pattern for the entire series of *Insight Guides*. Conceived by Apa founder **Hans Höfer**, the series has received kudos for providing the broad perspective to a destination needed to give visitors a complete travel experience.

The Right Staff

Freelance writer **Susan Amy** is a much-travelled native of the United Kingdom and has lived in the South-East Asian region for several years. She has developed into something of a specialist on Malaysian topics. For this book, she traversed the length and breadth of Malaysia, visiting villages and towns, holiday resorts and some of the more remote areas. Her copious notes have been incorporated into the travel section of the guide. She also updated the history section and revamped the culture sections of the book. Amy is now focusing her attention on a guidebook to the East Malaysian state of Sarawak, having spent several months researching in the rain forest.

Helping to guide this book through the

Black

Stephens

Amy

various stages of production was Apa Editorial Director **Geoffrey Eu**, who had earlier written the Malaysia section of *Insight Guide: East Asia*, which features 10 Asian destinations. One of his first tasks was to locate picture sources to illustrate *Malaysia*, and a formidable team was happily secured. The line-up of photographers includes newcomers **Joseph Lynch**, who is a recent arrival in Asia, and Singapore stalwarts **Wendy Chan** and **Jill Gocher**. Their work was complemented by, among others, veteran Apa contributors like **Philip Little**, **Bill Wassman**, **Marcus Brooke**, **Manfred Gottschalk**, **Ingo Jezierski** and **D & J Heaton**. Also contributing nature and wildlife photos was Singapore-based bird specialist **Morten Strange**.

With a Little Help From Our Friends

Most of the original material in the guide was gathered by Höfer, American journalist **Star Black** and veteran adventurer and author **Harold Stephens**. Their collective voice is still very much heard from in this book, as is that of **Sharifah Hamzah**, a Malaysian who conducted a comprehensive historical study of the country. Thanks also go to **Desmond Tate**, a long-time resident (and converted Muslim) who has periodically kept us up to date with events in Malaysia.

Apa also acknowledges the collaborative efforts of writers **Annabelle Morgan**, **Linda Agerbak** and the Tourist Development Corporation of Malaysia. Particular thanks to **William Trower** for coordinating the TDC effort.

Finally, thanks go to the people of Malaysia who helped bring about this book with their inimitable hospitality, generous nature and warm smiles. Special thanks to **Tan Sri Mubin Sheppard**, whose willingness to share his extensive knowledge of Malaysian culture was invaluable.

To these and countless others, *terima kasih banyak*.

— Apa Publications

Brooke

Tate

Hamzah

CONTENTS

MAPS

TRAVEL TIPS

"Selamat Datang Ke Malaysia"

"Welcome to Malaysia!" is the sign greeting you from inside the pristine corridors of Subang airport, Kuala Lumpur, complete with air-conditioning and all modern airport facilities.

"Welcome to Malaysia!" will also most probably be echoed by the smiling Malay, Indian or Chinese taxi driver who takes you from the airport to your first destination, the capital city of Kuala Lumpur.

Or even if you enter Malaysia by road and arrive first at a small Malay *kampong* (village), this same friendly greeting will be offered to you.

Over the centuries, Malaysia has been open to millions of visitors from all over the globe, and its people have changed, absorbed and adapted customs and traditions from far-flung countries to suit the Malaysian way of life.

What do you picture when you think of Malaysia? If you have read the travel brochures, you will imagine a land of beaches and coconut palms, sands as fine as flour, lost idyllic islands, fabulous coral reefs. If, on the other hand, you have pored over the pages of Somerset Maugham's short stories, you will imagine colonial bungalows set in the heart of a tea or rubber plantation, with tea served on the verandah by a young Malay boy, while the Indian *punkah wallah* moves the fan into action to keep the *orang putih* (white man) cool in the heat of the tropics. Or if you have peeked between the covers of naturalist Alfred Russell Wallace's *Malay Archipelago*, you will see ancient jungles, screaming with monkeys, brimming with butterflies, and hiding legendary animals such as the famed most intelligent of primates (next to man), the *orang-utan*.

These accounts are not contradictory; indeed you will find aspects of all these visions of Malaysia in the real country. But what you will find is also much, much more. Expect some surprises!

In Malaysia you will find yourself in many incongruously different scenarios. Your first day in Kuala Lumpur might find you changing money at a bank, the ultra-modern architecture of which rivals those being built in the West. Or you may be gliding up and down the escalators of a glass and steel shopping centre, crammed with shops and offering American hamburgers as snacks.

Preceding pages: tribal carving, Kuching; "The Pinnacles", Mulu National Park; traditional kite, Terengganu; top-spinning is a popular Malaysian sport. **Left**, village girl reflects the face of Malaysian youth.

Next, you might be in Chinatown, with its bustling streets and old shophouses. In the market, voices are crying out their wares in a myriad of tongues: Malay, Tamil, Hokkien, Cantonese, Punjabi – or even English. Since colonial days, the English language has always been important to the peoples of Malaysia.

Driving out into the countryside, you will find Malay *kampong* lying in a bliss of a relaxed life and traditional forms of work and leisure. Apart from the odd Mercedes parked outside the house of a villager who has made good in the city, and the numerous plastic items in daily use, you could imagine yourself back in the last century. But this is the point: Malaysia binds its past closely with its present in a unique amalgamation of cultures and customs.

Then you might find yourself in the central jungle of the peninsula, where travel is principally by river, and where aboriginal people choose to live, in spite of enticements to join the rat race, a nomadic life, living on the treasures of the jungle.

Venturing across the sea to the island of Borneo, you might climb South-East Asia's highest mountain, or stay at a remote longhouse in Sarawak. There are surprises everywhere in Malaysia.

Some of Malaysia's secrets will be unlocked from between the pages of this guide; others are waiting for you to discover for yourself. You will find those idyllic beaches and islands, those rubber plantations (with the *punkah wallah* replaced by electric fans and air-conditioning) and you will, if you venture out, find yourself in age-old jungles. But no matter how strange the sights are to you, there is an innate sense of being in a land that welcomes you to explore it – Malaysia beckons, as it has done for countless centuries.

In the introductory sections of this book, the varied landscapes and faces that make up Malaysia are described. A comprehensive history may answer many of your questions about why Malaysia is as it is. And then you will be introduced to the different racial groups that make up Malaysia's population, with some insight into their cultures and customs.

After this you will be ready to explore Malaysia in the central sections of the book, which give details of some of the fascinating sights you will be able to see.

For practical information on travel and accommodation around the country, turn to the Travel Tips at the back of the book. We hope you will enjoy exploring Malaysia with us – "Selamat Datang!"

Right, bashful Muslim schoolgirls in Kelantan.

THE JUNGLE – SHADES OF GREEN

More than two-thirds of Malaysia is jungle. The green cover begins at the edge of the sea and climbs to the highest point of land. Along the coastline, there are extensive areas of mud swamps and mangroves. Behind the mangroves are the lowland dipterocarp forests which extend up to an altitude of 600 metres. Trees grow to majestic heights of 60 metres or more, with the first branches 30 metres above ground. This is called the triple canopy forest. Commercially, this region is the most important; from here comes the timber for the sawmills.

Huge lorries with 15-ton loads of giant logs chained to the back are a common sight on Malaysian country roads. Hundreds of logs float downriver from inland camps in Sabah and Sarawak, down to the river mouth where they are loaded onto ships bound for Japan and Hong Kong. Sawdust is everywhere in peninsular Malaysia's industrial towns. Sawn timber is becoming Malaysia's main export, and timber exploitation has to be controlled so that the immense fecundity of the Malaysian jungle will assure the timber industry a green future.

The next level of forest is mostly oak and chestnut, and above 1,500 metres, it becomes a kind of never-never land with elfin forests consisting of small gnarled trees, 3-5 metres high, covered with folds of hanging mosses and lichen. The highland forests, for the most part, are left untouched and unlogged as catchment areas, ensuring the fertility of the soil.

The world's oldest jungles: The rainforests in this region are the oldest in the world, making those in Africa and South America seem adolescent in comparison. While creeping ice fronts were swelling and shrinking across the northern hemisphere, the Malayan jungles lay undisturbed through an estimated 130 million years. Some of the most unique and diverse species of animal and plant life were evolved here, and some of the most primitive and remote tribes still inhabit the jungle world and live much as their ancestors did in the year 1000.

A glimpse of tropical sky is visible through this canopy of green.

The Malayan jungles, on the peninsula, and in particular in Malaysian Borneo, have excited much scientific interest and continue to do so, as the jungle holds many secrets barely accessible to man. Optimists believe that the plant life in these jungles may hold all the cures for all human diseases, but this is still a mystery left to be solved. Much of the flora and fauna of the forests is hard to discover if you are just "passing through", and scientists sometimes search for weeks for rare species of plants and animals.

The diversity in flora and fauna is truly staggering. In Malaysia there are over 8000 species of flowering plants, including 2000 trees, 200 palms and 800 species of orchids,

Another world's first is the towering *Tualang* tree, tallest of all tropical trees. It can reach up to 80 metres in height and over 3 metres in girth. The famous pitcher plants can be seen everywhere on the slopes of Mount Kinabalu in Sabah, their honeyed jaws stretched open, waiting for a careless insect to "drop by".

Malaysia's jungles also hold thousands of species from the animal kingdom, many unique to the region, others introduced from mainland Asia. More than 200 species of mammals live here, including elephants, rhinoceros (though sadly, their numbers are greatly diminishing), tapir, tigers, leopards, honey bears, several kinds of deer, including

most exotic of flowers. The world's largest flower, the *Rafflesia*, is unique to the region. The entire plant consists of just the flower-head, which can measure up to 1 metre across and weigh up to 9 kilos. Being a parasite, it sucks its food from the roots of the *Cissus Liana*, and starts life as a red bulb. It grows in size and finally bursts open, revealing its pink, red and white interior. And if the size of the flower doesn't catch your eye, its odour, often described as that of rotting flesh, will certainly reach you from 50 metres or so away. The *Rafflesia's* glory only lasts a week, after which it shrivels up into the earth from whence it was born.

the region's tiny mousedeer, wild forest cattle (*seladang*), and many kinds of gibbons and monkeys. Borneo is also the home of the extraordinary *orang-utan* (meaning in Malay "forest man"), treated like another tribe by the jungle peoples, and the proboscis monkey, with the males of the species parading their humorous pendulous noses.

Other strange animals include the scaly anteater (*pangolin*), and the various seemingly-land-bound animals which leap or "fly" from tree to tree! Amongst their numbers are frogs and lizards, which have developed a leathery "sleeve", allowing them to "fly" great distances between trees. As well as "flying" squirrels, there are tree snakes, who spend their whole lives in this environment and get around by flinging themselves off a branch and spiralling down to a perch below. Infamous leeches are also to be found in the jungle canopy and on the forest floor, as many a dismayed jungle walker has found. Ways to get these creatures off the skin abound: two of them are to burn the head with a cigarette, or to let them suck their fill, after which they will part company with you!

Whether you venture into the jungle or not, you will be sure to see anywhere in Malaysia some of the 450 species of birds, and quite a few of the 150,000 species of insects! Alfred Russell Wallace, who spent more than 10 years in the Malay archipelago, had a particular fondness for insects, and often described himself as "trembling with excitement" when he caught a new species of butterfly or beetle.

With conservation gaining importance in Malaysia, the government has set aside tracts of land as national parks or game reserves, where strict hunting laws are enforced. These laws are taken very seriously by both game wardens and even remote tribes in the Borneo jungle, who used to shoot the prized and sacred rhinoceros hornbill for its "ivory" beak, but now allow it to sit above them in the trees while they wait for other game. This state of affairs has come a long way from the days when animals were killed, not just for food, but also for their skins, horns or feathers.

Sunken cities and giant men?: Although much research has been done on Malaysia's tropical rainforests and jungles, there is still much which seems intent to remain a mystery. Rumours tell of a lost sunken city beneath Lake Chini in the Pahang wilds. Aerial photographs suggest that an ancient city might have existed, but all that is known of it are Orang Asli stories about a walled palace on an island, and old records of the existence of a Khmer city in the area. About 15 years ago, a British engineer working in the area swore he saw a strange water beast "with a red eye the size of a tennis ball".

More recently, two Americans on a fishing trip up the Endau River, came upon what appeared to be human footprints that meas-

ured 45 centimetres long. Their Orang Asli guides explained that they were left by "Big Foot", a sub-human giant covered with hair who roams the deepest parts of the jungle.

Whether there is any more to "Big Foot" than an enigmatic footprint is an open question. Large parts of the Malaysian jungle are only minimally recorded on maps. Many trails have been left totally deserted since the state of emergency more than two decades ago, and there are many more dark corners of the jungle that remain totally unexplored, except, perhaps, by the nomadic tribes that live there.

With the growing international consciousness of depleting world forests, Malaysia is

facing pressure to decelerate logging concerns in Borneo. With criticism from outside nations and angry factions amongst local tribes with their sympathisers from the peninsula, Prime Minister Dr Mahathir has chosen to take the problem head on. At the Commonwealth Heads of Government Meeting in Kuala Lumpur in late 1989, this concern was the main topic of discussion. With increased consciousness in the industry, and with perhaps the help of developed nations, together with large reforestation projects already underway, there is still some hope that the Malaysian jungle will be allowed to keep some of its great mysteries.

Left, Strangling Fig provides sculptural form.
Right, sap flows from a rubber tree.

THE COUNTRYSIDE EVERGREEN

A smooth, well-maintained highway unrolls through green hills. Rubber trees flash by in never-ending even rows, monstrous tipples of tin mines appear where plantations leave off. Freshly-planted oil palms stitch the land in a patchwork of deep green against cleared and cultivated red earth. In the northern and coastal areas, fields are rich with stalks of golden rice.

As far as the eye can see, the lush green vegetation of the tropics smothers the landscape. Yet, contrary to its looks, Malaysia is not suited to agriculture. Unlike the Nile River Basin or the Ganges Valley, where seasonal rains flooding the land bring new fertile soil, the torrential downpours in Malaysia wash away the thin but valuable top soil. In many places, only red mud remains.

Erosion is one of Malaysia's oldest problems. Geologists believe that the Malay peninsula and Borneo were once one rugged landmass, joined to and running the entire length of the Indonesian and Malayan archipelago. For millennia, the sun, the wind, and torrential rains reduced the mountains to hillocks and outcrops. Precious soils were washed into the sea and fingers of land became cut off by subsidence and erosion. The meticulous work of nature continues today. The extent and speed of this erosion can best be seen in Malacca. If you stand on the ramparts of St John's Fort in Malacca town, you may wonder how the old cannons could have shot so far out to sea. Maps of that early period show that the area, including the present parade ground, was then covered by the sea. Alluvial soils washed down from the hills have reclaimed it in less than 400 years.

Despite the shifting landscape and annual monsoon rain, Malaysia's early settlers were basically food growers as well as fishermen. As far back as A.D. 500, Malays were growing crops for export: sugarcane, bananas, pepper and coconuts.

Control of the land in centuries past was based on a strictly feudal system, where the sultans held the powers of life and death, in theory at least, over their people. Their

The gently rolling hills of a Malaysian tea plantation.

realms were administered by district chiefs and compulsory labour and slavery were regal institutions.

The *Rakyat*, or common people, lived only to serve and obey their ruler, who was invariably as far away from a village as a one-month river trip. Few of the power struggles among the ruling class penetrated the rural *kampong*. With enough food and a warm climate, life in the village remained the same for centuries.

Malay *kampong* are still peaceful enclaves, with small, wooden communal homes, shaded by a green awning of coconut palms, banana and papaya trees. *Kampong* houses are propped up on stilts above a soft mud and warm water behind buffalo and a single-blade plough. The activity of the day begins in the early morning, before sunrise, when the day is at its coolest. By midday, there is time for more leisurely pursuits, and village men congregate beneath the trees to discuss the harvest or the latest news from the city. Towards evening, the television attracts the entire family back to the home.

Both men and women are traditionally engaged in the cultivation of rice, a crop introduced to these lands over one thousand years ago. Rice, the staple food and prime source of income for the rural Malay, is a recognised and respected necessity. The tempo of *kampong* life has quickened with

neatly-swept courtyard. Chickens wander freely in between and under the houses, picking up anything that was left behind by the household broom. The aroma of curry and salted fish wafts from the kitchens at the backs of the houses. A central meeting house stands empty, waiting for a feast or ceremony to be served. The village mosque wakes up several times a day to call the faithful to prayer. Photographs of the King and the Prime Minister hang prominently on living room walls together with other more personal mementos.

Beyond the village, a path leads towards the ricefields, where farmers trudge through the introduction of double cropping, using new hybrids of rice which reap a second crop each year. Malaysia produces 85 percent of the rice it consumes, with additional imports from Thailand and China. Self-sufficiency in rice is high on the list of government objectives, and more and more fields are yielding to modern rice growing.

A fortune in a tin pan: Malaysia is not exceedingly rich in mineral deposits, with the exception of tin, and there the country knows no rivals. Tin mining led to new settlements that sprang up from a few prospectors' shacks and became cities as large as Kuala Lumpur. This industry gave the British the revenue to build roads and railways through the jungle terrain, and it also introduced the Chinese pioneer to Malayan soil. The all-male mining townships were rough and risky to live and work in. Malaria and cholera wiped out hundreds of prospectors who sweated in the intense heat. Those who survived did so under a constant threat of tiger attacks, recorded at one time as a daily occurrence. Thousands perished in Chinese secret society feuds. Others made a fortune.

To maintain a semblance of government in the early mining communities, the Malay chiefs appointed a civil governor or *Kapitan China*, usually a man who commanded some respect amongst his compatriots, and this

ticism by the coffee planters.

The man inspired by the rubber tree was Henry Ridley, Director of the Botanic Gardens in Singapore, where some of the first trees were planted. "Rubber Ridley", as the planters called him, was convinced that his crop had great possibilities, and he was known to journey around the country with seeds in his pocket, looking for anyone he could convince to plant them. Ridley's was a far-sighted and lonely crusade, until John Dunlop invented the tyre, and Henry Ford put the automobile on the assembly line.

The rubber tapper continues to set out before dawn to collect the cups of latex that make up 42 percent of the world's rubber

practice continued under British rule. For decades, the Chinese held a virtual monopoly on the tin mining industry, and for more than 70 years, Malaysia has been producing over one third of the world's tin.

Rubber seeds – a reckless gamble: But what stands out on the green scene far more frequently than the cumbersome tin tipple is a plant first grown in the soil of Brazil – the rubber tree. This plant, which now takes up more than three-quarters of all the developed land, was originally viewed with great scep-

Left, a familiar sight in Malaysia – working the rice fields. **Above**, a typical countryside abode.

supply, but now he stops short of the old boundaries of the estate to view a field planted with oil palms. The government encourages farmers to diversify their crops by growing coconut, coffee, tea, fruits, nuts, spices – and oil palm. Palm oil increased in dollars earned in the late 1970s by 20 percent a year, bringing Malaysia's share up to nearly half the world's palm oil production. With the recent threat of a US ban on palm oil, Malaysia is now having to look more closely at its other industries, timber in particular, to bring in the dollars, and to take Malaysia's presently prosperous economy into the 21st century.

TIDES UPON THE SEA

The sky, a misty grey umbrella, releases streaks of rain that splash down on a white-capped sea. Along the coast fishermen have built barriers of thatched palm leaves to meet the winds sweeping inland from an unsettled surf. Their wooden huts are bleached silver from the intense sun and heavy downpour. The willowy casuarina trees that line the shore bend low in wind-blown curves. Fishing *prahu*, deprived of their buoyancy on turbulent seas, wait empty-handed on the beach. Tyres squeak on the film of water covering the coastal roads. The rivers run quick and high: it is the monsoon season in Malaysia.

Three months in a year, Malay fishing folk who live in the small villages along the East Coast of the Malay peninsula, store away their fishing nets, dock and repair their boats, move their fishing huts far up the beach, and settle down in the shelter of their wooden houses to wait for the winds to change. They cannot sail their *prahu* against the force of the monsoon. During the rains, time is spent following more leisurely pursuits: repairing fishing nets, spinning enormous and heavy tops, or making a trip to the city, perhaps even to Mecca, if the year's fishing trade has been prosperous. When the winds drop, they will again venture out to sea in search of the wide variety of big fish and small, as well as other tasty and much sought-after seafoods to take to the marketplace. This pattern of life has characterised Malaysia's eastern shores for centuries.

Nowadays, however, the sea's importance as a highroad has been somewhat diminished in favour of faster land and air travel, and the oceans no longer bring in the traffic of the seafaring days. In the days of antiquity, the seas of all of South-East Asia were highways for tradesmen and explorers, adventurers and pirates, seeking the wealth centred in the Malay and Indonesian archipelago.

While the indigenous Malays were content to remain close to the shore, having a primitive and deep-seated fear of deep oceans from which it was once believed sea

Lush tropical Island provides a stunning backdrop to this fishing *kelong*.

monsters rose, other nations were turning their eyes to this part of the world in search of rare goods and possible prosperity. They came from India with the southwest monsoon, in search of gold nuggets, camphor, cloves, pepper and sandalwood. They came also from China, in primitive junks loaded with silks and porcelain, blown across the China Sea by the northwest monsoon.

Almost completely surrounded by water, Malaysia was where the monsoons met, where the tides of the Indian Ocean and the South China Sea flowed together into the Straits of Malacca. Seafaring merchants travelling in either direction stopped along these coasts to wait for the winds to change

The spice trade also caused Malacca, on the west coast, to become the centre of trading, as it was from here that the seaways to the Spice Islands were commanded by powers, constantly fighting one another for this control. Trade, however, was a hazardous business. Traders sailed on merchant ships carrying up to 200 men who endured violent storms and a constant fear of pirates.

Greatest seaport in the world: "Malacca is the richest seaport with the greatest number of merchants and abundance of shipping that can be found in the whole world," wrote a Portuguese sailor in the 16th century. It was also a great centre for languages, and business was conducted in no less than 84

in their favour. Malaysia was the halfway point in this ancient interchange, linking China to India and India to the Spice Islands.

It was the Spice Islands, a small cluster of islands in the Indonesian archipelago, that set Asian maritime kingdoms against one another, and in Europe sparked off the Age of Discovery in the 16th century, impelling Columbus to cross the Atlantic and Magellan to circumnavigate the globe. In time, the spice trade to Europe became so lucrative that a vessel loaded with spices from the Far East could make enough profit to pay ten times over the cost of the voyage, including the value of the ship.

tongues. Small wonder that the Malay language is replete with words adopted from Arabic, Sanskrit, Persian, Portuguese, Dutch and English. An ancient dialect of Portuguese is still spoken by the Portuguese-Malay descendants of old Malacca.

Piracy on the high seas was a widespread, lucrative and once honourable profession, attracting merchants, noblemen, tribespeople and fishermen alike. For centuries, sailors trembled at the thought of passing unarmed through Malaysian waters at night.

The most formidable pirate bands were the Lanuns from Mindanao. Sometimes these men would recruit head-hunting warriors from the Borneo interior, and while the captains pillaged the cargoes, the crew collected war trophies.

Malaysian seas today hold untold riches from ships wrecked by storms or plundered by pirates. Rumours still circulate of hidden treasures buried in caves on islands off the East Coast of the peninsula.

Malaysia's seas are also famous nowadays for the Vietnamese boat people, who have been fleeing this way for several years. There are still hazards at sea, to be found in the form of Thai and Indonesian pirates, who hold sway out in the open seas beyond the reaches of Thai and Malaysian police. Occasionally, the modern pirates, armed with

their home here. Until recently, the seas were thought of only as a source of food, but today, there is a growing interest in underwater discovery, and the number of scuba-diving and marine clubs is steadily growing.

Above water, a steady stream of 200,000-ton oil tankers and cargo vessels, replacing silks and porcelain with black gold, oil and tin, sails through the Malacca Straits. This section of water between the Malay peninsula and Indonesia's island of Sumatra still has the same strategic importance that spurred ancient kingdoms to war. Control of the Straits remains an international controversy, because both Malaysia and Indonesia claim rights to supervise all traffic sailing

lethal weapons and not swords, are caught and newspapers herald the victory over these bloodthirsty bandits.

Whether there are treasure troves of sunken boats loaded with gold and silks and buried chests hidden in caves or not, there are certainly other underwater treasures in the beautiful and varied marine life of the Malaysian waters. Much of the coast is surrounded by coral reefs of vivid colours and creatures both beautiful and curious find

Far left, bringing the day's catch home. **Left**, sparkling waters off the west coast. **Above**, idyllic cruise.

within their territorial waters. The recent increase in offshore oil exploration has greatly enhanced the value of sea territory, and the trading posts established by the British are now the leading commercial centres of the region.

While the west coast is fringed by thick mangrove swamps in many areas, and by pretty beaches marred by murky waters, the east coast has found profitable possibilities for its long stretches of beach and coral islands, as tourists, eager for sunshine and palm-fringed coral sands, flock to coconut beach huts and developed holiday resorts all along the coast.

THE CITY – FROM 'WILD WEST' TO THE BIG TIME

Half of Malaysia's population is engaged in agriculture, but the once isolated and self-sufficient village is now linked by paved road and outstation taxi to the nearest town, where a farmer can stock up on Guinness Stout and rubber boots as well as dried fish and batik *sarong*.

Peoples from the remotest longhouses or *kampong* know all about the capital city with its gleaming skyscrapers and air-conditioned shopping centres, from the omnipresent television set, given pride of place in city apartments and longhouses alike.

If most Malaysians do not live in the big city, enough is heard about it to make like under neon signboards and revolving restaurants the topic of long conversations. Country youths let their imaginations glide up the escalators and down the jet runways of the cities where possibilities seem boundless. The lure of big city life enters the daydreams of more and more teenagers in rural Malaysia. Many young men leave the family and the farm in pursuit of other worlds, for towns and cities spell to them ambition, prestige and opportunity. *Kampong* grandparents listen in wonder, but such places are beyond their scope of imagination, for knowledge of faraway places outside the village area is still something relatively recent.

Pioneers in Wild West Malaysia: The origins of the large cities and towns are very different from one another. Some, like Johor, were established by powerful sultans as capitals to their empires. Others were first trading settlements set up by foreigners such as the Portuguese, the Dutch or the British. These became centres of administration in British colonial days. Others grew up quickly by trade, and some dwindled back down into villages again.

Kuala Lumpur grew from a supplies centre for local tin mining in nearby Ampang, and many other towns emerged during the tin mining boom. Malacca had its big moment in history when it became the centre of trade for all Asia, serving traders from Europe, the Near East, India and China. Kota

Reflections of old and new. Masjid Jame, the "Friday Mosque" and modern high-rises.

Kinabalu was originally a British trading settlement for rhinoceros horn and birds' feathers. From these varied origins, the towns and cities of Malaysia are now moving closer together in their quest for a modern way of life that rivals the West.

Tin trading towns were originally unplanned and more or less grew up shop by shop as competition increased. Towns such as Kuala Lumpur developed into shockingly filthy, diseased and violent places, plagued by fires, floods and feuds. Chinese secret societies warred over tin holdings; nightfall became a dangerous time.

Colonial town planning: British administrative centres, however, were the epitome of native populace. By the end of the 19th century, however, this had become a positive concern of the British, and even landscaped gardens were laid in many cities.

The town today: Nowadays, Malaysia's towns reflect both their notorious and colonial past as well as the future of glass and steel. Colonial buildings nestle between modern office blocks and traditional Chinese shophouses. These shophouses, two-storied terrace houses with shops below, are the pervasive architecture of all Malaysian centres. The business of the day goes on under the shade of the famous "five-foot-ways", arcades in front of the shop entrances.

Stallholders sell lottery tickets, change

bureaucracy, law and order. The centre of town was planned around a *padang* (literally a field, but meaning a stretch of closely-cropped grass), where official ceremonies took place and cricket was played. Around the *padang* would be several administrative buildings, the City Hall, a post office perhaps, a law court and often a church.

This arrangement can still be seen in Kuala Lumpur, as well as in many other towns and cities throughout Malaysia. Graceful colonial houses were usually built as far away as possible from the swamps and shanty towns. But proper drainage and public utilities were slow in arriving for the

money, sell flowers or tell fortunes. Restaurants and coffeeshops open directly onto the five-foot-ways, and Chinese cooks stand at the entrance, in undershirts and drawers, tossing noodles, sprinkling spices and taking orders all at the same time. Indian restaurants have a free "show" included with their meals: the *roti canai* (Indian bread) is cooked at the front of the shop. The bread is first flung and pounded before being cooked on a large griddle, heated by glowing charcoal.

Around the back of the shophouses are the small alleyways where children play improvised football and badminton, and where washing is hung out on bamboo poles extending from upstairs windows.

Besides the more traditional living accommodation, more and more urban Malays are now moving into planned surburbs, equipped with shopping centres, supermarkets, community centres, mosques, temples and churches.

Tomorrow's city: Despite sporadic signs of the stereotypic metropolis, there are Asian overtones in Malaysia's towns totally undiminished by the concrete cosmetics favoured by urban planners. Festivals, markets and bazaars crowd the streets, Malay love songs and Chinese opera singers wail out from radios, car horns blare and streetsellers call out their wares in several languages.

thay. Signboards spring out from shophouses, painted with elegant calligraphy (and sometimes transcibed into roman lettering): "Everlasting Harmony Shoemakers", or "Virtuous Accomplishment Goldsmiths" or "Mercers of the Thousand Prosperities".

In the last two decades, there has been a boom in the building industry. To match its fame in tin and timber, the country also wants to be known for its architecture. In recent years, public buildings have departed from colonial and western styles, and skyscrapers now have Chinese domes, Moorish arches or traditional Menangkabau roofs, the ends of which curl upwards like a pair of bull's horns.

On Sundays in Sabah's and Sarawak's rural towns, the central square forms into a Borneo bazaar, down to which barefoot tribeswomen trudge from the hills, carrying baskets of bananas and betelnut. The marketplace, where fishermen dump their catch and farmers' wives collect the dollars, remains the prime link binding countryside and town.

The Chinese assert the culture of their ancestors by combining pioneer stamina with the romantic memories of ancient Ca-

Even within the more anonymous modern buildings, arrows on the ceilings indicate the direction of Mecca for the followers of Mohammed, and tucked round behind the staircase of 30-storey buildings, small Buddhist shrines smoke with incense and glitter with golden Buddhas.

Cities also have neighbourhoods completely Malay where the urban squeeze and the suburban sprawl compromise with neat rows of bungalows on stilts, so that the Malay bureaucrat can still spend the day at his air-conditioned office and return home to cultivate fruit trees outside his living-room in the evenings.

Left and **above**, city on the move: the ever-changing Kuala Lumpur skyline.

43

Bingen
Junsalan
ISOLA DI
UNSALAN

SIAM

Lespera Patanor P.Sangori
P.Cornan

CAMBODIA

C.Scebo
Foyes
Bay

Cornan
Along

Pulo
Way

GOLFO

Clao

Pulo Cara

Pulo Panjag

Pulo Ubi

Pulo C

DI

Ligor

I. Ligor

DI

Bondelon
Wanting

Cabo Patane

SIAM

STRETTO

Pendaon
P.Boulon
P.Iado

Singor

Keidab

P.Coffin
Luaro
S.P.Rou

Pinaca

Queda
Vechio

Patane

Pulo Ridang

F.Secco
F.Kalantan

DI

P.Pisang

Tarano
P.Serga

Pulo Capes

Bazuas

Poncan
Bassan
Kedaor
F.Basset
F.Dongon
F.Palano

MALL

Lago di Diamanti
delli Olandesi
P.Sambila

Soengei
Boroas

Salom
ngri

P.Iara

I. del
Aqui

Soengei
Pao

Pontigaran

Gors

P.Barbala

MALACCA

Ugly
Casang
Brama
Porto Besaar

I

Petra
Selongor F.
Pulo
Pracelar

Tinaram

Pahang

P.Verella

Col. di Logue
Col di S.Anna

Behack

Meselan

P.Aru

C.Rachardo

Malacca

P.Timon
P.Pisang
P.Laor

Utiel I.

P.Medang

Sincapura
Strait

Djohor
Passi

P.Tingi

Cincel
Boere
Ita

I.Pedms

I.Naos

Sensang

C.Romania

Bancalis

Cincon

P.Boby Balaban
P.Baton Sickerban

I.Pantou

Siasqua

Strello di Sincaporea

Carimon
Saban

Camper

Bilitan

Domines

Passaman
com

Andavasa

Lingen
Uclgote

Equinozia

Priaman
Catatenge

Drop

Sojo
Fratelli

Zelanda

la buona For-
tuna

Padang
Tellekan

Manacabo

Saleda

Andragari

Olandesi

Tique

Speriamo
Baros

Liz

Jutuu

Billeto

ISOLA BANCA

Petten I.

Pietra di Guvin

I.Cocos
I.Willems

Indrapou
Rentapou
Mochomacho
Lamanta

Bantal

Lamby

Telombuan
Salecar

Palambam

La Punta

La 2.Punta
La 1.P.mo Punta

Nasson
Mosquiten I.
I.Tartaruga

I.Bassa

I.Cocos
3.Monti

Tamang
Cattam

Ipoe
Bencolen

F.Giovanni

Monte Sillebar

F.S.Clara

Laucapar

Sorbres

Dampin

met Recif

Fort
Martebou

Sillebar

Sanjon Siande

Pongon

Dolce

Cabo Desst

Setten

Sorelle

ISOLE

Pisang I.

Assomaon
Mortalle
Baubon

Goudan

Engano I.

Salnamento

La Fortuna I.
Cantone Basso

Cracalno

STRETTO DI SUNDA

TRA

44

Gentle, young and growing – Malaysia is all this. But peel away the layer of modern-day life, and the kaleidoscope of Malaysia's history unfolds with a cast of Malays, Portuguese, Dutch, Chinese, Indians, Ibans, Englishmen and others. The legacy of the land abounds with ancient temple ruins, impregnable Portuguese fortresses, Malay krisses, native blowpipes and imposing British colonial buildings. It all started in 35,000 B.C.

Prehistoric Malaysia: The beginnings of human habitation in Malaysia are enveloped in shadows as deep as those cast by the equatorial rainforest, pieced together from ancient Indian, Chinese and Arab sources and archaeological discoveries. This origin is still rife with theories and speculations.

In Sarawak's Niah Caves, the skull of a *Homo sapiens* dating back to 35,000 B.C. was discovered, providing the earliest evidence of human habitation in Malaysia. In the Malay peninsula itself, the earliest remains to have been excavated are only about 10,000 years old.

There is evidence that during the period of the Middle Stone Age (about 8000 to 2000 B.C.), Mesolithic men lived in rock shelters and caves in the limestone hills of the Malay peninsula. They used stone implements for cutting and grinding, as well as for hunting wild animals. A typical tool of these people was the hand axe, made by chipping a rounded pebble until a cutting edge was formed on one side. These people may have been the ancestors of the Negrito aborigines, today known as the Semang and Jakun.

Around 2500 B.C., the Proto-Malays spreading south from Yunnan in China made their way to the Malay peninsula and the islands beyond. They were also Stone Age people, but their stone implements were more sophisticated than those of the Negritos. Besides being hunters, they were also cultivators and sailors and thus lived a more settled life. Eventually they forced the Negritos into the hills and jungles.

But around 300 B.C., a new wave of immigrations in turn pushed the Proto-Malays inland. They were the Deutero-Malays and had advanced to using iron weapons and tools. The Deutero-Malays were in fact Proto-Malays who, through intermarriage, were mixed with Chinese from the Chou period, Indians from Bengal, as well as peoples of Arabic and Siamese blood. The Deutero-Malays and the people from Java, Sumatra and other parts of Indonesia are the ancestors of the Malays of today.

Indian influence: Through trade, the early inhabitants of the Malay peninsula were exposed to older civilisations. Located at the convergence of two major sea routes linking the great markets of India and China, the peninsula was a convenient stopover for Indian ships travelling further east.

The first Indian voyages made to the peninsula were estimated to have occurred early in the Christian era. In order to prepare for the long voyage, some of the ships carried not only a big crew, but also a year's supply of food, including live chickens as well as a vegetable garden at a corner of the vessel.

In the peninsula, the ships waited for the monsoon winds to change before continuing their journey. The Indian traders discovered that they could obtain gold, aromatic woods and spices here. They also discovered that by transporting their goods overland, from one side, they could minimise the threat posed by pirates rampaging in the Straits of Malacca.

Soon, many settlements developed along the Straits. Through contact with Indian traders, many native inhabitants became Hindus or Buddhists and built temples. The remains of some of these have been discovered in the state of Kedah. Some of the settlements grew to become Indianised kingdoms in which various features of Indian culture were adopted. The local rulers came to be known as *rajah*, and many Brahministic rituals were adopted in the courts.

Even today, this early Indian influence can still be seen. Some Malay words are borrowed from Sanskrit, and Malay wedding rites contain numerous Indian customs.

The Chinese also had trading contacts in the Malay peninsula and in northwest Borneo. In particular, the Chinese sought a

Preceding pages: Sultan Abdul Samad of Selangor and his retinue in 1874. **Left**, Italian map of the peninsula, circa 17th century.

✢ AFOSO·DALBOQVERQVE ✢

prized delicacy – birds' nests – from which they made soup. But their influence on indigenous culture was minimal.

The founding of Malacca: The Indianised kingdoms of the Malay peninsula were constantly subjected to the dominance of stronger Indianised kingdoms in South-East Asia. First the kingdom of Funan in Cambodia, then the Sumatran power of Sri Vijaya, exerted influence. Borneo was under the control of the Javanese kingdom of Majapahit. However, a quiet village in the Malay peninsula soon rose to prominence as a major centre of power.

The *Sejarah Melayu* or *Malay Annals*, written in the 16th century and comprising legends based on historical events, traces the transformation of a small coastal village into a famous trading centre.

The island of Tumasek (now Singapore), at the tip of the Malay peninsula, was ruled by Iskandar Shah, also called Parameswara. When the Javanese attacked the island, he and his followers were compelled to flee to Muar in the peninsula. Monitor lizards drove him onward in 1403. One day, when he was hunting near a fishing village, one of his hounds was kicked by a white mousedeer. The king, always appreciative of spunk, exclaimed, "This is a good place! Even the mousedeer are full of fight!" Taking a cue from this good omen, Parameswara decided to build a settlement on the site. As he happened to be standing near a *melaka* tree, he decided that the settlement should bear the name of that tree. Under his rule, Melaka grew to be a thriving centre.

Parameswara and his followers planted new crops in Malacca and discovered inland deposits of tin. Gradually, as the community grew, passing ships stopped at Malacca for replenishment. News of this flourishing settlement began to spread and within two years, the population had increased to 2,000.

Meanwhile, the emperor of China was expanding his maritime activities. In 1409 he sent his famous admiral, Cheng Ho, to Malacca to proclaim it as a city and a kingdom, and to present Parameswara with Chinese tiles for the roof of his palace. In 1411, the admiral took Parameswara on a visit to China – a trip which confirmed Parameswara's status as an independent king owing fealty to China alone.

Parameswara's readiness to accept China's protection was a clever diplomatic move, for it not only guaranteed protection against the Siamese, but also added prestige and respectability to Malacca.

Not only did Malacca lie geographically at the confluence of major trade routes extending eastward to China and westward to India and Europe; the city was also ideal as a port. The harbour was free of mangrove swamps and deep enough for safe passage. It was fortunate also to have the monsoon winds blowing in the right direction twice a year. The northeast monsoon brought the Chinese, Siamese, Javanese and Bugis vessels early in the year; in May, Arab and Indian vessels arrived with the southwest monsoon.

The port was a colourful sight with vessels of various shapes and sizes, from Chinese junks with eyes painted on the bows in the belief that it would help the vessels to "see", to the robust three-masted Bugis schooners.

The city was an equally exciting bazaar with an exotic range of goods – silks, brocade and porcelain from China, carvings and precious stones from India and Burma, spices and pepper from the East Indies archipelago, and tin, gold and jungle produce from Malacca's hinterland.

Another reason for Malacca's success was its ability to assure the safety of traders. The rulers of Malacca commanded the allegiance of the *Orang Laut*, or sea gypsies, who managed to curb the pirate menace in the Straits of Malacca. In Malacca itself, four *shahbandars*, or harbourmasters, were appointed, each representing a group of nations. The duties of a *shahbandar* included overseeing affairs and disagreements among sailors and merchants in his group.

The coming of Islam: Towards the end of the 13th century, Muslim traders from India brought Islam to the Malay archipelago. By the 15th century, Malacca had embraced the religion. The rulers took the title of "Sultan" and the Jawi script – the Malay language written in Arabic – evolved. By 1488, the kingdom of Malacca included the west coast of the Malay peninsula, Pahang and much of the east coast of Sumatra. These subsidiary states eventually embraced Islam too.

In about 20 years, Malacca had risen from obscurity to become the strongest state in

Left, Alfonso de Albuquerque led the Portuguese conquest of Malacca in 1511.

South-East Asia. Its population at the zenith of its power was 40,000 – mainly Malays, but also including Indian and Chinese settlers. The city was located at the mouth of a river and was divided into two halves. The sultan's palace and the Malay *kampong* or villages were situated south of the river, while on the north bank the houses and stores of the merchants provided the cosmopolitan bustle and activity of the city. The two halves were linked by a bridge over the river. Everyday, the population moved to and fro across the bridge; some enterprising merchants built their shops on the bridge itself.

The palace was the centre of life. Peasants, traders and noblemen had the right to present

umbrellas were to be used only by rulers, and yellow umbrellas only by princes. Only royalty could wear gold anklets.

The ruler was assisted by a *bendahara* (chief minister), a *temenggung* (chief of police), and a *laksamana* (admiral) in his administration. Below them were the various titled nobles. The royalty, the common people and the traders abided by this system. Apparently, it worked for Malacca.

The shapers of Malacca: Parameswara died in 1414, leaving behind him a prosperous trading port. When his grandson died in 1444, there was a power struggle in the court. The Malay chiefs supported the younger heir, as his mother had royal blood, while the

their petitions to the sultan in his *balai*, or audience hall, at his palace. The sultan sat on a raised platform, surrounded by richly embroidered cushions, flanked by his ministers, two or three steps below him.

The ruler's power was in theory absolute, and the people believed in the concept of undivided loyalty to the ruler; no one could disobey him even if wronged. There are many tales of Malaccans who would rather kill their friends or relatives, or suffer in silence, than incur the ruler's displeasure.

Royal power also took the form of other privileges. No commoner could wear yellow clothes, as it was the colour of royalty. White

elder heir was the son of a common Muslim-Tamil consort. But 17 months after the younger son was installed as ruler, he was killed and replaced in a Muslim-Tamil coup.

Sultan Muzaffar Shah was a fervent Muslim who declared Islam as the state religion. He was also an able ruler, remembered for his code of laws. And he received undivided loyalty. On one occasion, his *bendahara* observed the sultan's door being slammed by the wind, and wrongly believed that it had been slammed by the displeased sultan. Dismayed by the thought of having incurred his ruler's wrath, he went home and committed suicide by taking poison.

In 1456, Tun Perak became the new *ben-dahara* and successfully repelled a Siamese invasion. Tun Perak was to be the brains behind Malacca's expansion, and a leading figure in Malaccan politics for 42 years. During the reign of Sultan Mansor Shah, who succeeded Muzaffar Shah, Malacca was at the peak of its glory. But the glory was largely attributed to Tun Perak, who built a formidable fighting force and honoured brave warriors with the title of *Hang*, or captain. He led expeditions and conquered many other states.

One of Tun Perak's fighting men was a young warrior named Hang Tuah. He was so handsome that he turned heads wherever he went. When he joined a Malaccan mission to visit Majapahit in Java, the womenfolk there were so struck by his beauty that they composed many songs, like this one:

"Here is betel leaf. Take it to allay the pangs of a whole day's love – but you will still yearn for him!"

A famous episode tells how Tuah killed his best friend to prove his loyalty to the sultan. Mansor Shah had ordered Tuah to be killed but the sympathetic *bendahara* imprisoned him instead. Meanwhile, Tuah's friend, Hang Kasturi, had an affair with one of the sultan's concubines; he was discovered and surrounded in the palace, but no-one dared go in and attack him. Told that Tuah was still alive, the sultan immediately summoned him to kill Kasturi. In the ensuing duel, Kasturi three times permitted Tuah to free his kris when it stuck in the wall. But Tuah refused his rival the same privilege, instead stabbing Kasturi in the back. In his dying moment, Kasturi cried, "Does a man who is a man go back on his word like that, Tuah?" To which Tuah coldly replied, "Who need play fair with you, you who have been guilty of treason?" And he stabbed Kasturi again and killed him. Tuah was appointed *laksamana* for his deed.

Sultan Mansor Shah was an admirer of beautiful women. He married many Javanese and Chinese princesses, and at one time the object of his admiration was the exquisite princess of the mountain of Gunung Ledang. He sent an expedition to scale the mountain,

where his men met the princess – who had disguised herself as an old woman. They told her of the sultan's desire to court the princess and she in turn laid down her conditions: bridges of gold and silver from Malacca to Gunung Ledang, seven trays each of mosquitoes' and mites' hearts, vats of areca-nut water and of tears, a cup of the sultan's blood and a cup of his son's blood.

When this message was relayed to the sultan, he answered sadly: "All that she demands we can provide, save only the blood of our son; that we cannot provide, for our heart would not suffer to take it."

Sultan Mansor Shah was succeeded by Sultan Alauddin Riayat Shah. He was an

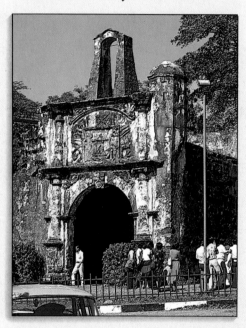

able ruler who had the habit of walking the streets at night to check the enforcement of law and order. One night he personally caught two robbers, and reprimanded the red-faced *temenggung* the next day. His independence made many jealous enemies. He died when he was only 26, apparently poisoned. In contrast, the next sultan was heavily influenced by his chiefs and his days on the throne were also numbered.

The invasion of the 'Franks': The 15th century was Portugal's Age of Discovery. The Portuguese were eager to expand to the far corners of the world for a number of reasons – a search for the mythical priest-king

<u>Left</u>, a Dutch bridge over the Malacca River. <u>Right</u>, the gateway of *A Famosa* is a remnant of the Portuguese era.

Prester John, believed to live in a Christian kingdom in Africa; a crusading spirit against Muslims; and a desire for Asian spices.

Spices were the most important commodity in the trade between Europe and Asia. Portugal wanted to divert the trade route from Muslim traders via a new trade route around Africa's Cape of Good Hope. Malacca was one of their targets as it was the collecting point for spices from the Moluccas, also known as the Spice Islands. As the Portuguese writer Barbosa put it, "Whoever is Lord in Melaka has his hand on the throat of Venice."

The Portuguese went to Malacca to seek permission to establish a trading post. The thick of battle, riding on caparisoned elephants. But most of the non-indigenous population were either apathetic or on the side of the Portugese.

On 24 August 1511, Malacca was captured. The sultan and his followers fled to the interior. Malacca had lost its independence, and under a string of foreign rulers, it never regained its days of glory.

The victor and the vanquished: De Albuquerque set up a Portuguese administration and built a fort. He called it *A Famosa* ("The Famous"), and it was so impregnable that none of its enemies could penetrate its walls for 130 years. Within a walled area, a mediaeval Portuguese city developed with a town

locals were excited to see the foreigners, whom the Malays nicknamed the "Franks". Backed by the Indian Muslim traders, the *bendahara* attempted to capture the Portuguese fleet. Warned by a Malaccan woman, the Portuguese escaped. But 20 of their men were left behind and taken prisoner. This gave them a reason to return in force.

In 1511, a large Portuguese fleet, led by Alfonso de Albuquerque, the architect of Portuguese expansion in Asia, arrived at Malacca. They concentrated their onslaught on the bridge over the river. The Malaccan defenders put up a courageous resistance and even Sultan Mahmud and his son were in the hall, offices and homes for the Portuguese civil servants. The other races lived outside the town wall.

The trade that the Portuguese established in Asia was extremely lucrative. For instance, pepper bought in the East for US$45 could be sold in Portugal for US$1,800. Malacca also became the centre for Catholic missionary work, and in 1545 Francis Xavier, the well-known missionary, arrived to spread the Christian gospel.

But Catholicism did not appeal to the local population and the arrogant Portuguese were not well liked either. They attempted to obtain a monopoly on the spice trade; all ships using the Straits of Malacca had to obtain passes from them, and arbitrary duties were imposed at the port of Malacca. This aroused strong anti-Portuguese feelings. The Europeans found themselves continually fending off attacks from other Malay states; in many cases, *A Famosa* proved to be the saving factor.

After his flight from Malacca, Sultan Mahmud established himself at Bintang in the Riau Archipelago. He made two unsuccessful attacks on Malacca, but he died in 1528. His elder son established himself at Perak, while his younger son started a sultanate in Johor. The new sultan of Johor continued to harass Malacca. Meanwhile, in North

closed to Dutch and English merchants. So the northern Europeans were compelled to turn to the East for spices and other goods.

Dutch trading companies combined to form the "United East India Company" in 1602. Although their main interest was focussed on the Spice Islands, they considered control of Malacca necessary – not only because of the geographical position of the Straits of Malacca, but also as an expression of their antipathy towards the Portuguese.

In July 1640, after blockading the port of Malacca and bombarding *A Famosa*, the Dutch encircled the town. As the siege continued, the Portuguese garrison and the people trapped in the fort ate whatever came

View of Chinese Mills, Penang, 1817—18
From a lithograph by William Daniell and based on a sketch by Capt. Robert Smith.

Sumatra, Acheh was an ambitious power that was growing in strength. It launched attacks on Malacca and also waged wars against Johor and other Malay states. This Acheh-Malacca-Johor power struggle for political and economic supremacy dragged on through the 16th century.

The siege of *A Famosa*: The arrival of the Dutch and the English in South-East Asian waters was the result of certain events in Europe. In 1580, Spain had annexed Portugal; in 1594, the trading port of Lisbon was

Left, Malacca was once a bustling trading port.
Above, view of life in early 19th-century Penang.

into sight – rats, dogs, cats and snakes. It was reported that a mother even ate her dead child. The acute hunger was aggravated by diseases such as malaria, typhoid and cholera. Finally in January 1641, after a seven-month siege, the Dutch forces stormed into *A Famosa* and fought on to victory.

The Dutch government had decided that Batavia (now Jakarta) should be their capital. Malacca was acquired principally to prevent another power from using it; it was to be just another outpost in the Dutch Empire.

As the only traders then buying spices in the East, the Dutch were able to offer low purchasing prices. To maintain their monopoly, any Indian or English trader who wanted to trade in South-East Asia had to obtain permits from them. This monopoly made many enemies for the Dutch, and although they held Malacca for 150 years, they did not leave behind any significant influence.

Meanwhile, the other states in the Malay peninsula continued the saga of prosperity and decline. When the Dutch occupied Malacca, many merchants diverted their trade to Johor, and the sultanate there grew stronger. But after an attack by a Sumatran state in 1673, Johor began to decline. Perak also grew in strength, as it was rich in tin.

Other settlements on the peninsula were founded by immigrants. Menangkabau

people from west Sumatra brought a matrilineal social system to Negri Sembilan. The Bugis, who migrated from the Celebes in the 17th century, possessed exceptional navigational and commercial skills. They infiltrated and occupied positions of power in the Malay states and established an independent state in Selangor.

The arrival of the English: The East India Company was an association of merchants who were granted a charter by Queen Elizabeth in 1600 for the monopoly of all English trade in the regions east of the Cape of Good Hope. A very important trading contract that belonged to the Company was the export of tea from China to Europe. Not only was this trade very profitable for the Company, it provided Great Britain with substantial revenue from tax on tea imports.

The British displayed an active interest in South-East Asia primarily to establish a port on the sheltered side of the Bay of Bengal for replenishing supplies and refitting ships along the China trade route.

In 1785, the sultan of Kedah allowed the Company to establish a settlement on the island of Penang. He saw this as a golden opportunity for obtaining protection against his enemy, Siam, in exchange for trading rights granted to the Company. Francis Light landed in Penang in July 1786. The Union Jack looked rather odd on the sparsely populated, jungle-smothered island.

Light had promised to assist the sultan of Kedah against Siam, but it soon became obvious that the Company had no intention of fulfilling this vow. The sultan felt that he had been deceived and assembled a fleet to recapture Penang. But Light was swifter, and attacked the sultan's fleet before it even began the offensive. This time, Light made sure that everything was in black and white. A treaty guaranteed the sultan $6,000 a year, while the Company got Penang.

Light cleared Penang's jungle and made it into a free port. To the annoyance of the Dutch, ships from throughout South-East Asia and India began to trade in Penang. The population grew rapidly and Light followed the Malay and Dutch practice of appointing *kapitans* – community leaders with authority to hear all minor crimes committed by members of their representative communities. For major crimes, Light himself tried offenders with his rough-and-ready sense of justice. He died of malaria in 1794.

In 1808, "civilisation" arrived in Penang when the Charter of Justice introduced English law to the settlement. Penang prospered for a while, but it was too far from the Spice Islands to become really important.

The French Revolution led directly to the British occupation of Malacca. The revolutionary armies of France had overrun the Netherlands, and the Dutch naval bases were due to come under French control. To fore-

Left, Sir Thomas Stamford Raffles of the East India Company. **Right**, James Brooke, the first "White Rajah" of Sarawak.

stall French use of the bases, Britain and the Dutch government-in-exile agreed that the British would take over the Dutch possessions during the war and hand them back when the war was over. That was how Malacca was transferred to the British in 1795.

The British were determined that when Malacca was returned to the Dutch, it should be of as little use as possible. The plan was to destroy *A Famosa* and transfer its population to Penang. For about a year, the historic fort was systematically disassembled. But ironically, the city was never abandoned, and the fort need not have been destroyed at all. The Dutch reoccupied Malacca for only six years, and in 1824, under the Anglo-Dutch

Malays and *Orang Laut*. Raffles established a trading post on the island and in 1824 succeeded in getting the sultan and *temenggung* of Johor to cede Singapore outright to the British.

With its free port status and its strategic geographic position, Singapore achieved phenomenal success. Ships from India, China and the Malay archipelago filled the port with a wide range of goods. By 1824, the population had increased to 11,000 with a mixture of Malays, Chinese, Indians, Bugis, Arabs, Europeans and Armenians.

In 1826, Singapore and Malacca were joined with Penang to form the Straits Settlements as trading centres and protectors of the

Treaty, peacefully ceded it to the British.

The Straits Settlements: The Dutch had returned to Asia when their war with France ended, and reoccupied their former bases, including Malacca. By 1818, they had extended control over parts of the East Indies. This alarmed a number of British officials, one of whom was Stamford Raffles. He convinced the East India Company authorities that another settlement in the Straits of Malacca would establish British supremacy and would also serve as a port of call for British ships en route from India to China.

In 1819, Raffles landed on the tiny island of Singapore, then populated by about 1,000

trade route to China, and had no intention of becoming involved in the Malay states. More territory meant more expenses; hence, the official policy was one of strict non-intervention. But there were a few occasions when this rule was bent. The Menangkabau people of Naning paid annual tithes to the Dutch but refused to make similar payments to the British. This led to the Naning War, in which armed British troops were sent through thick jungle to capture Naning and make it a district of Malacca. On another occasion, the first governor of the Settlements, Robert Fullerton, though lacking authority to make war, sent the Penang forces to scare off the Siamese, who were planning an attack on Perak.

The white *rajahs* of Sarawak: While the Malay peninsula was prospering, the territories on the northern shore of the island of Borneo were undergoing a separate development – Sarawak with its "white *rajah*", Sabah under the British North Borneo Company.

James Brooke was born and raised in India where his father worked for the East India Company. As a young man, he was an ensign in the Sixth Native Infantry in Bengal, but resigned from service in 1830. When his father died in 1835 and left him a sum of money, Brooke used it to buy a schooner. He named it *The Royalist* and set sail to explore the East. Little did the dashing adventurer realise that he would gain a kingdom!

Sarawak was the westernmost province of the Brunei sultanate. The sultanate's decline in power had brought about greater independence among the Malay chiefs. Brooke landed in Sarawak in 1839 and found the Rajah Muda Hashim, a relative of the Sultan of Brunei, trying to quell a rebellion against the misrule of the Governor of Sarawak. A year later, Brooke returned and helped Muda Hashim bring the four-year rebellion to an end. For his contribution, he was awarded control of Sarawak.

In 1841, against a backdrop of Malay guns firing a salute, James Brooke, then 38, was installed as the Rajah of Sarawak. It marked the beginning of over 100 years of rule by the white *rajah*.

With the help of local chiefs, Brooke tried to establish peace and order in Sarawak. He made no attempt to introduce new laws, but based his administration on existing customs and consultation with the chiefs. Brooke was not strong on finances, and his administration was always in the red. But he refused to introduce foreign capital because he believed that "the activities of European government must be directed to the advancement of native interests...rather than...aim at possession only." Under Brooke's rule, the population grew, more territories were brought under Sarawak's control and peace and order were restored. An 1857 revolt by Chinese gold miners was quickly suppressed. In 1863, the ailing *rajah* left Sara-

wak to retire in England, where he died five years later. His dream of a voyage of adventure really had come true.

Brooke's successor was his nephew, Charles Brooke. The second *rajah* was a better administrator than his uncle. He brought Sarawak out of debt, reduced headhunting, expanded trade, and brought greater prosperity. Whereas James was debonair and charming, Charles was reserved, preferring solitary recreation like tending his private betel-nut plantation. The English ladies in Kuching did not fancy his lack of social graces, and he must have created quite a stir when he declared that the most suitable population for Sarawak would be derived

from intermarriage between Europeans and the native races! But he himself married a European lady 20 years his junior.

Sovereignty over North Borneo (present-day Sabah), meanwhile, was obtained in 1877 by Overbeck, the Austrian Consul-General in Hong Kong, in partnership with the British company of Dent Brothers. In 1881 Overbeck withdrew, and the remaining partners formed the British North Borneo Company under a royal charter. While the Company agreed to provide facilities for the British Navy, it was allowed to "borrow" various senior officers from the Straits Settlements to assist in administration.

<u>Left</u>, British officials strike a pose. <u>Right</u>, Sir Hugh Low.

But the North Borneo Company was not as successful as the Brookes in fostering recognition of white rule. It encountered recurring resistance, the most significant of which was the Mat Salleh Rebellion of 1895-1905. The introduction of new taxes had created general discontent, and Mat Salleh gathered many supporters in his revolt against the Company. Prestige and mystique enveloped Mat Salleh. He carried flags and the umbrella of royalty, and it was said that his mouth could produce flames and his *parang* (cleaver) lightning. In 1900, Mat Salleh was killed, but the rebellion was not quelled until five years later. Today, he is still regarded as one of Sabah's most famous heroes.

tion caused the export of tin to drop to a slow trickle. What was even more stressful to the Straits Settlements merchants was that the demand for tin began to exceed its supply.

Meanwhile, officials of the British Colonial Office were fearful that if Britian did not intervene in these states, the merchants who had invested in the mines would obtain assistance from another power, particularly Germany. A new governor, Andrew Clarke, was sent to investigate the situation.

Clarke went one step further. He met the Malay chiefs on his ship, anchored near the beautiful Pangkor Island. In January 1874, both parties signed the Pangkor Agreement. The treaty settled the dispute of the Perak

The Pangkor Agreement: The Malay peninsula had always been rich in tin. The ore had been mined and sold in the peninsula for centuries, but after 1861 – with the growth of the canning industry in America – there was an increased demand. Merchants from the Straits Settlements invested money in the new mines in Selangor and Perak, and petitioned for British intervention in these states to safeguard their commercial interests.

Selangor and Perak were plagued by unrest. There were power disputes among the Malay chiefs. Chinese miners had formed rival secret societies that constantly fought against one another. This unsettled condi-

throne and the new Sultan of Perak agreed to accept a British Resident whose advice "must be asked and acted upon on all questions other than those touching Malay religion and custom." By August, Clarke had made a similar agreement with Selangor, and British influence began to spread to the Malay states. Meanwhile, in 1867, the Straits Settlements had become a Crown Colony under the direct control of London, and no longer ruled from British India.

The British residents: The government-by-advice procedure in the Malay states was carried out by appointing British "residents" to advise the rulers on how to improve the administration of their states. This control by indirect rule was dependent on how well the resident could exercise his influence.

In Perak, the first resident was J.W.W. Birch. He was intolerant and tactless enough to lecture the sultan in public. He had little regard for local customs and wanted to change immediately anything that displeased him. Birch wanted to abolish debt slavery but failed to see its lack of similarity to the Western concept of slavery. Debt slavery involved a person mortgaging himself in return for financial assistance from his creditors. In bad times, debt slavery was the only way a peasant could raise finances. If he was unable to redeem his debt, he was absorbed into the creditor's household to carry out his orders until the debt was paid off. The locals resented Birch's interference.

There were additional sources of friction. The introduction of a centralised tax-revenue collection system took away the rights of the sultan and his chiefs to collect taxes. Then in 1875, the new governor of the Straits Settlements proposed that British officials should govern directly on behalf of the Sultan of Perak. Birch exerted great pressure on the sultan to have him agree to this proposal.

Birch began to post notices announcing the British government's intention of directly administering Perak. But he was killed while bathing in a floating bathhouse at a Perak village. Those found guilty of conspiracy against Birch were hanged, while several chiefs were exiled for their involvement in the assassination plot.

Perak's third resident was Hugh Low. He made no attempts to interfere with Malay customs and was friendly with the local population. Consequently, he was more successful than Birch. He brought the revenue from the tin mines under his control and constructed roads, a railway and a telegraph line for Perak.

Elsewhere, things were less problematic than in Perak. In Selangor, the resident, Frank Swettenham, was doing well. He spoke good Malay and was quick in winning Sultan Abdul Samad's approval. Swettenham often accompanied the sultan on game-hunting and snipe-shooting expeditions. In

1889, Negri Sembilan also accepted the appointment of a British resident.

In each of these states, indirect British rule was exercised through a state council which discussed the policies to be implemented. The members of the council were the resident, the sultan, major chiefs and one or two Chinese leaders. While the council provided a useful sounding-board for public opinion, the resident alone was the real policy-maker. He nominated all council members who met only about seven times each year.

Resistance in Pahang: Reports of "great wealth" in the large eastern state of Pahang whetted the British appetite to gain control. By 1887, Pahang's ruler, Sultan Ahmad, was

persuaded to accept a British agent. But the first agent, Hugh Clifford, found the sultan and his chiefs unwilling to relinquish their rights. The atmosphere in Pahang grew tense with the lack of understanding between British and Malays. Rumours began circulating of an impending British attack on the sultan's palace. In 1888, when a British subject was murdered in Pahang, the British enforced a demand that Sultan Ahmad write a letter requesting a British resident.

The Pahang chiefs resented the interference of the resident and their subsequent loss of power and income. In 1891, Dato' Bahaman, an angry and defiant tribal chief, openly declared rebellion against the British. This rebellion became known as the Pahang War, and proved to be an expensive and arduous affair for the foreigners.

Bahaman's men were acknowledged guerilla fighters, and many stories and legends are told of the rebellion and its leaders. Even now, the Pahang War symbolises the struggle for Malay independence. One of its famous fighters, Mat Kilau, is a hero of Malay nationalism. (In 1969, there was great excitement when an old man in Pahang identified himself as Mat Kilau. The Pahang government conducted an extensive investigation to confirm his claim.)

In 1892, a general amnesty was issued.

control over the residents. But the sultans did not regain their lost authority. On the contrary, the resident-general now became the initiator of policies, and greater administrative control was exercised by the resident without any reference to the sultan. In effect, "federation" meant centralised power. The original aim of indirect rule was swallowed up as the states came to be run almost entirely by British officers.

Meanwhile, the northern states of the Malay peninsula recognised the general overlordship of the King of Siam. This suzerainty was demonstrated by the sending of the *Bunga Mas*, or golden flowers, to the Siamese capital. But the power that Siam had

Most of the rebels surrendered while others fled to Terengganu. In 1895, a force led by Clifford chased the rebels north to Kelantan where they were eventually arrested.

The Federated Malay States: In 1896, the Federated Malay States were created. The federation consisted of Selangor, Perak, Negri Sembilan and Pahang, with its capital at Kuala Lumpur. A resident-general was appointed with jurisdiction over all other residents. To ensure uniformity of the civil service, all laws, except those of a local nature, were drawn up in Kuala Lumpur.

The sultans had agreed to federation under the belief that they would exercise more

over these states was somewhat vague and differently interpreted from one generation to another.

In 1909, the British made a treaty with Siam whereby the latter handed to Britain whatever rights and power it possessed in the northern states of Kedah, Perlis, Kelantan and Terengganu. These states became British protectorates, and British advisors with similar status to residents were appointed.

'Mad' Ridley's 'miracle crop': At the southern end of the peninsula, Johor was pressed to accept a British advisor in 1914. British control over the Malay peninsula was complete, although three different groups of states existed – the Straits Settlements, the Federated Malay States and the Unfederated Malay States. "British Malaya" was born.

In the latter half of the 19th century, new technology brought about an increased use of tin-plate in the West. This affected the demand for tin ore and more mines were opened in Selangor and Perak, leading to an influx of Chinese immigrants to Malaya. By 1904, Malaya was producing half of the world's tin.

More spectacular was the success story of rubber, which arrived in Malaya as a foreign "stranger" but grew to become the mainstay of its economy. Rubber seeds had been transported from Brazil to London's Kew Gardens for experimentation as an Asian crop. When the seeds germinated, a handful were sent to Malaya. They were immediately planted in Singapore and in the garden of Hugh Low's residency in Kuala Kangsar. From these seedlings developed the millions of rubber trees in Malaysia today.

The development of rubber was slow until H.N. Ridley was appointed to direct the Singapore Botanical Gardens in 1888. Ridley had no doubts about the future of rubber and persuaded coffee estates to experiment with the growing of this new crop. Soon, planters and estate managers sat on the verandahs of their bungalows, nursing their gin-and-tonics, and talked about "Mad Ridley" and his enthusiasm for this new crop. But those who sniggered at him had the tables turned when, at the beginning of the 20th century, the increased popularity of the motorcar brought about a high demand for rubber. By 1920, Malaya was producing 53 percent of the world's rubber. Many fortunes were made in the great rubber-boom years from 1910 to 1912.

Indian labour was brought into Malaya to work the rubber estates. Many Malays became smallholders, although the British tried to discourage them from holding this new economic role. The rubber industry went through gluts and slumps, but it survived and remains a thriving industry.

Revenue from tin and rubber was used to build up the government infrastructure of communications and social amenities. At-

tention was focussed on the mining and estate areas, however, at the expense of the less economically profitable areas.

At the same time as tin and rubber were booming, Malay's plural society had developed. In 1931, the population of Malaya excluding Singapore was 3,788,000. It comprised 49 percent Malays, 34 percent Chinese and smaller groups of Indians and other races.

The Japanese invasion: The first sparks of World War II reached Malaya in 1937. That was the year the Japanese launched military attacks on Peking and Shanghai after having occupied Manchuria six years earlier. By 1941, the Japanese were making no more

than slow progress in their conquest of China. This sluggishness was aggravated when the Americans, British and Dutch governments froze the shipment of all essential raw materials and oil supplies to Japan. Japan was forced to look to South-East Asia, which produced these important materials, to guarantee its supply. Already the Japanese had occupied Indochina, and the threat of Japanese invasion loomed over Malaya.

Meanwhile, Britain was preoccupied with defending itself against the threat of German invasion and the possible capture of the Suez Canal. It could not do much to protect Malaya. Besides, Britain and the United States

Left, Japanese troops sweep through the streets of Kuala Lumpur, 1941. **Right**, an occupation newspaper reports on Tokyo's successes, 1943.

had secretly agreed that Europe was to be the area of first defence priority.

On 8 December 1941, at around 1 in the morning, Japanese warships began shelling the beaches of Kota Bharu in the north-eastern state of Kelantan. The forces landed almost without opposition. At 4:30 a.m. bombs were dropped on the sleeping island of Singapore. Within 24 hours, the Japanese had mastery of the air and had seized the British airfields in north Malaya. On 10 December, Japanese bombers sank two British warships off Kuantan and established naval supremacy in Malayan waters.

The "little men" drove relentlessly down the Malay peninsula with their tanks and bicycles. Lt.-Col. F. Spencer Chapman, in his book *The Jungle Is Neutral*, wrote that he saw the enemy pouring in and noted:

nese infiltrated and outflanked the British defensive positions. One by one, they fell to the invaders. By 31 January 1942, the remaining Commonwealth troops withdrew across the causeway that linked the Malay peninsula with Singapore.

Singapore was invaded on 8 February and there was fierce fighting. Many civilians perished in the bomb raids, and the island was also choked by a water shortage. After a week-long siege, on 15 February 1942, General Officer Commanding Malaya Lt.-Gen. A.E. Percival surrendered Singapore – the "Gibraltar of the East" – to the Japanese.

Troops defending Sarawak, meanwhile, were hopelessly outnumbered. Kuching was

cycles. Lt.-Col. F. Spencer Chapman, in his book *The Jungle Is Neutral*, wrote that he saw the enemy pouring in and noted:

> The majority of them were on bicycles...They seemed to have no standard uniform or equipment and were travelling as light as they possibly could. All this was in very marked contrast to our first-line soldiers, who were at this time equipped like Christmas trees...so that they could hardly walk, much less fight.

The Commonwealth troops defending Malaya were poorly trained in jungle warfare and lacked ammunition. They staggered back from defeat after defeat while the Japa-

captured by the Japanese on Christmas Day 1941. By 16 January 1942, North Borneo fell. For the next three and a half years of Japanese occupation, natives of these outposts suffered a brutal existence. Some broke down, while others demonstrated bravery and resilience.

Life in 'Maraiee': The Japanese pronounced Malay as "Maraiee" and came with promises of a "Co-prosperity Sphere" and an "Asia for Asians". But they ruled with an iron hand and imposed hardship on the population.

The brunt of Japanese brutality was directed against the Chinese. The war in China had made many of them especially hostile towards the Japanese, who in turn accused them of being British sympathisers. Thousands of Chinese were executed or put away in prisons.

Food was extremely scarce. The Japanese currency was useless, and there was spiralling inflation. Trouble-makers and suspected criminals were treated harshly and often tortured by the *Kempetai* or military police. Paranoia was rampant. Young women blackened their faces and hands to avoid being ogled by Japanese soldiers who might drag them away as "mistresses".

The entire European population became prisoners-of-war or civilian interns. Conditions in the prison camps were squalid, and

an atomic bomb. Three days later, Nagasaki was obliterated. On 14 August, Japan finally surrendered and the war ended peacefully in Malaya. In September 1945, British forces landed in Malaya and reestablished their authority as the British Military Administration. The Administration began the gruelling task of restoring the country to normality.

The doomed Malayan Union: In 1945, as the British were reoccupying Malaya, the British Cabinet approved a plan to incorporate the Federated and Unfederated Malay States – as well as Penang and Malacca, but excluding Singapore – into a Malayan Union. The Union was intended to embody a unitary state with a central government and a

the prisoners were made to do heavy manual work. Those who disobeyed the guards or who were found committing the "heinous" crime of keeping a radio were brutally tortured. Many of them, together with Indian labourers, were sent to construct the infamous railway in Burma where many died from diseases and ill-treatment.

On 6 August 1945, the United States devastated the Japanese city of Hiroshima with

Left, Japanese leaders surrender their swords in 1945. **Above**, communist caricatures (left) and British jungle patrols (right) were features of the emergency.

governor. Sovereignty was to be transferred from the sultans to the British Crown. The effect would be tantamount to turning Malaya into a colony. Eager to prove their loyalty to the British, having questioned it during the Japanese occupation, some sultans agreed to sign the Malayan Union treaty. Those who were reluctant to sign were subjected to British "persuasion".

When the plan was announced, certain ex-Malayan civil servants like Swettenham protested and petitioned Downing Street. Even stronger protests came from the Malays, who took a united stand against this plan. In March 1946, delegates representing

41 Malay associations met in Kuala Lumpur to form a national movement against the Malayan Union. Differences in philosophy were cast aside as the United Malay National Organisation (UMNO) was born. UMNO was inaugurated with Dato' Onn Jaafar as its leader. It declared the treaty signed by the sultans null and void, and demanded a repeal of the Union.

The British went on to inaugurate the Union in 1946, but opposition was so strong that the plan was never brought into effect. It was finally revoked on 1 February 1948, when the Federation of Malaya was created.

The Federation was accepted by all parties because it provided for the sovereignty of the Peoples' Anti-Japanese Army (MPAJA), recruited many supporters for a republic in Malaya after the defeat of the Japanese.

The MPAJA was disbanded after the Japanese occupation. The communists began to infiltrate trade unions and in 1946 and 1947, organised strikes to disrupt the economy. Internal problems plagued the Communist Party, however. The Secretary-General, discovered to be a double agent, absconded with the party's funds.

The infamous Chin Peng became the new communist leader. He reorganised the party and moved all its activities underground. When violence escalated after a spate of murders and attacks on European miners and

sultans, as indicated by the appointment of a high commissioner instead of a governor, the states had jurisdiction over a number of important departments.

Meanwhile, in July 1946, Sarawak and North Borneo became Crown Colonies. The cost of post-war reconstruction was beyond the resources of the Brooke government or the British North Borneo Company.

The 'War of Nerves': During the Japanese occupation, guerilla groups of British officers, Malays and Chinese had lived in the jungles and organised resistance forces to harass the Japanese. Chinese Communist guerillas, calling themselves the Malayan planters in June 1948, the Malayan government proclaimed a state of emergency throughout the country. The tense situation came to be described as the "War of Nerves".

The communists planned to attack the estates and mines in order to disrupt the economy. They organised themselves into regiments and lived in camps in the jungle. These camps were well-screened from the air, and had escape routes and well-organised living quarters. A camp could often accommodate

Above, Tunku Abdul Rahman gives the "Merdeka" salute. **Right**, the Proclamation of Independence.

300 men. Political indoctrination was a major activity.

Communism quelled: During the emergency, high wire fences were built around tin mines and rubber estates to keep out communist attackers. People who lived in remote villages were in constant fear that the communists would appear and force them to supply food and money. Travelling was risky as the danger of a communist ambush lurked behind every roadside bush.

There was not much coordination between the various security forces until the appointment of Lt.-Gen. Sir Harold Briggs as Director of Operations in 1949. Briggs, a veteran of the Western Desert and Burma cam-

These forces were soon able to concentrate on jungle operations to destroy the communists and their camps.

Nationalism and Merdeka: In 1953, areas from which the communists had been eliminated were declared "white areas". Their food restrictions and curfews were relaxed, inducing the people to cooperate more fully with the government. By 1954, a large number of the communist guerillas had been destroyed. Many more surrendered in 1958, and the few remaining guerillas retreated deep into the jungle. The state of emergency officially ended on 31 July 1960.

Merdeka means "freedom" in the Malay language. Stirrings of nationalism were felt

paigns, immediately put on his military thinking cap. His war executive committees coordinated emergency operations, and his settlement plan created 500 new villages for Malayan citizens who lived in remote areas beyond government protection.

The latter plan succeeded in removing to safer places the people who were most vulnerable to coercion by the communists, thereby depriving the insurgents of their crucial sources of supplies and information. As Briggs anticipated, the communists began to attack the new settlements. But the security forces, now fighting on their own ground, proved to be too strong for them.

throughout the country soon after World War II. With the communists virtually wiped out by 1955, Malayans began to clamour for independence.

In 1951, the Malayan Chinese Association formed a political partnership with UMNO. The Malayan-Indian Congress joined in 1954, and the political grouping – called the Alliance – came to represent the interests of the various races in Malaya. It was to play a major role in the path to independence.

The Alliance demanded that elections be

Dato' Seri Mahathir bin Mohamad, Malaysia's fourth prime minister.

held for the Federal Legislative Council. The wish was granted, and in 1955 Malaya's first national election determined 52 of the 98 members of the Council. The Alliance won 80 percent of the votes cast. Tunku Abdul Rahman became the Chief Minister. For the first time, Malayans had real influence in the government. Tunku Abdul Rahman, born into a royal family, was a son of the Sultan of Kedah. From 1930 to 1941, he worked as district officer in Kedah and was very popular with the people there. After securing a law degree, he surged along with the tide of Malayan nationalism and entered politics. "Tunku", as he soon became known, took over the leadership of UMNO in 1951.

In 1955, Tunku's government offered amnesty to the communist terrorists. He met communist leader Chin Peng for talks to end the emergency. The meeting was unsuccessful, however, and Chin Peng went back into the jungle. Tunku's government also turned its attention to the question of national unity in Malaya's multi-racial society. A common syllabus for schools of all language streams was implemented.

The Malayan constitution: In 1956, Tunku led a delegation to London to negotiate for independence. Britain was ready to grant Malaya its freedom. The Reid Commission was assigned to draw up a constitution; the draft document was based on a memorandum submitted by the Alliance, and was accepted by the sultans and the British and Malayan governments.

The Malayan constitution was a federal constitution. While the states retained certain rights and powers, the central government held supreme power in all important matters. The government was set up as a constitutional monarchy. Sultans from the nine ruling families were to elect among themselves the paramount ruler or Yang di-Pertuan Agong, who would reign for five years. The Agong would rule through a Parliament composed of a fully elected House of Representatives and a Senate of nominated members. Executive power would lie mostly in the hands of the House, while the Senate would have the power to delay legislation for one year. Each state would have its own fully-elected State Assembly. Malay was the national language of independent Malaya.

At midnight of 30 August 1957, huge crowds gathered at the Selangor Club in

Kuala Lumpur to witness a historic occasion. The Union Jack was lowered for the last time. Among the crowd, many experienced mixed feelings – a certain sadness about the end of a familiar era, and uncertainty.

The next day, crowds gathered again at the Merdeka Stadium to witness the handing over of the formal instrument of independence to Tunku – Malay's first Prime Minister. The nine states and two settlements had become the independent Federation of Malaya. Amidst impassioned shouts of "Merdeka!" that vibrated throughout the stadium, the people felt a new sense of pride and were certain that whatever lay ahead, they were ready for the challenge.

Malaysia…and 'Confrontation': Independence brought with it a new period of vitality and reform. Rural development improved and a national industrial policy was formulated. The Alliance continued to win popular support; in the 1959 federal elections, it took 74 of a possible 104 seats.

In 1961, Tunku proposed a political association – called Malaysia – which would include Malaya, Singapore, North Borneo, Sarawak and Brunei. There was considerable enthusiasm in Singapore; Brunei, however, decided to stay out ot it. A commission of Malayan and British members set up to determine the reaction of the inhabitants of the Borneo territories, discovered that more people were in favour of the idea than against it. Thus, the British and Malayan governments agreed that the new states of Malaysia, minus Brunei, would come into being on 31 August 1963.

Meanwhile, the Indonesian government voiced strong opposition to the Malaysia plan, alleging that the inhabitants of the Borneo territories had not been consulted and that the whole thing was a British plot. In January 1963, Indonesia announced a policy of "Confrontation" against Malaya. Many suspected that the real reason behind the antagonism was that Indonesia President Sukarno's dream of a Greater Indonesia, to include Malay, Sarawak, North Borneo and Brunei, would be frustrated. Meanwhile, the Philippines also opposed the creation of Malaysia, claiming that North Borneo belonged to them.

The Confrontation took the form of armed Indonesian invasions across the borders of Sarawak and North Borneo from Indonesian

Kalimantan. Indonesia and the Philippines both repudiated a United Nations survey which confirmed that the Borneo territories wanted to be a part Malaysia.

When the Federation of Malaysia was officially inaugurated on 16 September 1963, both countries severed diplomatic ties with Malaysia. Indonesia intensified its "Crush Malaysia" campaign. Attacks along the borders of Sarawak and North Borneo (now renamed Sabah) increased, and Indonesian terrorists began landing on the coast of the Malay peninsula to carry out acts of sabotage. But they were quickly killed or captured by the security forces.

In 1966, Sukarno was ousted from power by a new army-dominated administration. This new Indonesian government was not keen on continuing the Confrontation, and a peace agreement brought the conflict to an end. The Philippines also dropped its claim on Sabah and recognised Malaysia.

Meanwhile, political differences had surfaced between Malaysia and Singapore. On 9 August 1965, Singapore left the Federation and became an independent nation.

Nationhood: In 1969, the Alliance again won the federal election. More attention began to be paid to the pressing problem of unifying the nation's diverse peoples. In 1970, Malaysia's population stood at 10.4 million – Malays forming 46.8 percent; Chinese 34.1 percent; Indians 9 percent; Dayaks 3.7 percent; Kadazans 1.8 percent; other native groups 3.2 percent; foreign immigrants 1.4 percent.

Bringing this "anthropological museum" of people under one national flag was not an easy feat. In 1969, a Department of National Unity was set up to formulate a national ideology and social programmes. Today, Malaysians live and work by the *Rukunegara* (Articles of Faith of the State):

Belief in God
Loyalty to King and Country
Upholding the Constitution
Rule of Law
Good Behaviour and Morality

When the British left Malaysia, economic roles were rigidly defined and unequally divided amongst the ethnic groups. Although the nation's constitution allowed for the Malays to have considerable political and religious power, with a specified number of state leaders to be selected from the Malay race, and with Islam as the state religion, their participation in the country's trade and commerce was virtually non-existent. The Chinese had the monopoly in that realm. To prevent the indigenous Malays from becoming economically depressed, the New Economic Policy was set up to encourage a fairer distribution of wealth. This involved setting up corporations and share ownership schemes to elicit greater Malay participation in diverse areas of the economy.

Naturally, this caused much concern amongst Malaysia's other ethnic groups, especially the Chinese, who felt that the pro-Malay constitution which promoted Malay religions and cultural values, and the selection of share ownership schemes on the basis of racial issues and not on merit, would seriously undermine their own economic, political and cultural position in Malaysian society. A powerful Chinese opposition was set up to represent Chinese concerns.

In 1981, Malaysia's fourth Prime Minister, Dato' Seri Mahathir Mohamad, took office. A controversial figure in politics in his younger days, the new Prime Minister excited Malaysians with his brand of dynamism, pragmatism, forthrightness and genuine concern for the people. Mahathir is often described as the Kemal Ataturk of Malaysia. Whatever his policies, Mahathir's position as Prime Minister has been for the last decade of his office, a delicate balancing act, with pressure from the Chinese opposition, followed by the witch hunts of 1987, during which there were many arrests under the Internal Security Act. Pressure is also on the Prime Minister from the other side, from the Islamic party, to press Malay and specifically Islamic issues to the fore. The recent wave of Islamic revivalism throughout the world has convinced many Malays that a return to a purely Muslim society is the only way to remain true to the faith.

However, Dr Mahathir had demonstrated his strength as a political leader of a multiracial country, and has refused to cede to either side. The present concern in Malaysia is with forging an identity for the Malaysian, regardless of race, based not so much on a merging of cultures, but on an understanding of the different faces of Malaysia, and a pride in the country as a whole.

Right, a young Malaysian patriot.

THE MALAYS –
SONS OF THE SOIL

The Malays, long linked to the land as *Bumiputra*, or Sons or Princes of the Soil, generally prefer the sound of a cock crowing in the morning and crickets at night to noisy traffic horns and congested sidewalks. As farmers and fishermen living in close-knit neighbourhoods, rural Malays cherish the simplicity of an uncluttered outdoor life. *Kampong* life nurtures a provincial conformity laid down centuries ago. The ultimate in travel is a prestigious journey to Mecca, but other than the great pilgrimage, few *kampong* dwellers wander far.

The inherent talents of the Malays, however, find outlets far from the countryside. Malay businessmen and civil servants in the cities dress Western style, drive cars and speak English fluently. Urban youths pick up the latest in clothes imported from London or Tokyo. Some young men, though dressed traditionally in their praying clothes, sport a fashionable tuft of hair which peeps out from under their *songkok* hats. Many of them own an electric guitar and rig up elaborate wiring systems in their *kampong* houses, where they and their bands beat out imitations of Mick Jagger or Michael Jackson.

Islam – The binding spirit: Though the rift between the farm and the city widens as years go by, it does not threaten the strong unity the Malays derive from a common faith. The laws of Islam immediately set a Malay apart from his fellow Malaysians. Pork, a food relished by the Chinese, is forbidden to the Muslim Malays. Intermarriage between races is uncommon, though Malays will accept a foreigner into the family if he or she is a Muslim.

Yet Islam in Malaysia has little of the rigid dogma of the Middle East, for historical reasons. But also because of the character of the Malay people. They are an easy-going, shy people with an abhorrence of open conflicts and clashes of words. Their way of life and their faith is marked by a tolerance and self-control that have largely contributed to the peace Malaysia now enjoys.

Most Malays are Muslims, and are identi-

Right, Muslims are called to prayer five times each day.

fied by Arabic names, from whence Islam first came to these shores, through Indian traders. All are married by Islamic law and guided by the moral precepts revealed in the Koran. Sultans, though with much less power than previously, are still regarded as traditional rulers, and have combined spiritual prestige with political power. Today, Islam is *the* religion of the state, Friday the day of worship and Islamic bonds the basis for diplomacy with the Muslim world.

Cleanliness is next to godliness for the Malays and it is said that the brighter the house the more blessings God will bestow. Houses in *kampong* are kept spotless and a basin of water is placed at the bottom of the

even today, although most of these traditions are only to be found in villages.

The all-embracing spirit *semangat* is the ancient Malay life-force present in all things, from human beings to stones. All things are interconnected and belong to one another. It is still believed in some areas that the way to win a girl is to find one of her possessions, a piece of jewellery, a lock of hair or even the sand from her footprint and to steam it, meanwhile uttering incantations from a mixture of animist, Hindu and Islamic sources.

Women have been known to let their hair loose at rice harvest time in order that the crop will be bountiful.

Central to these animist beliefs are the

entrance stairs for the washing of feet before entering. Unclean things such as pig meat and the saliva of dog are never touched. Muslim food or *halal* food is specially prepared and many Muslims will only eat food prepared by Muslims. The *ustaz*, or religious teacher, guides Malay children in the recitation of the Koran in Arabic, long before they are able to say their multiplication tables, and Koran reading contests are held on television. The big celebration of the year is the Prophet Mohammed's Birthday and festivities are held throughout the country.

Older spiritual origins: There are many instances of the previous beliefs of the Malays,

pawang or medicine men, who is still expected to be present on important national days to ensure that no rain falls to spoil the festivities. More feared and disapproved of by orthodox Muslim Malays are the *shaman*, magicians who fall into trances in order to exorcise illness or to divine forthcoming events. Séances are rarely held nowadays, but *shaman* are still treated with awe and respect in their local areas. Western education and medicine, on the other hand, have done a lot to discredit them.

Sacrifices are less common now, but a chicken may still be killed when a new house is built. Ancient practices have dwindled into mere superstitions; for example, spilling salt is still considered unlucky although the original meaning is forgotten.

Hindu influences can still be seen, the most evident being the wedding ceremony, where bride and groom sit in state on thrones all day as prince and princess. A name is whispered into the baby's ear on the 10th or 12th day after birth, and the head is shaved except for one lock. Other prayers and incantations live on but now contain additions declaring the supreme power of Allah and his Prophet, while Indian gods have been relegated to the level of demons or saints who may still be called upon in times of need.

Although Islam is *the* religion for the women may buy and own property, manage their own money and businesses and make decisions for their families.

Although there is little differentiation in status between men and women, there is still some class difference between the nobility and the commoners. They may have much less power than previously, but sultans still occupy an important position in Malay ceremonies and official occasions, especially in their own states. There are eleven sultans in Malaysia (with the heads of Penang and Sarawak being governors) and a king is elected from amongst them every five years. The official residence is the *Istana*, or the palace in Kuala Lumpur, although all sultans

Malays, it was already mixed with Hinduism before arriving in Malaysia, as the Indian traders who brought it also had a multi-layered approach to religion. They taught the new faith by blending and adapting local beliefs, much as the early Christians converted the English.

Women in Malaysia, in spite of the laws of Islam, have considerable power in Malay society, and more freedom than their sisters in the Middle East. This is due to the influence of older matrilineal societies, and

Left, dressed for the beach in Pangkor. **Above**, dressed for a museum outing in Kota Bharu.

have their own palaces in the capital and only use the *Istana* for official functions.

Malay cultural traditions: In Malaysia, there are many sports, games and festivities whose traditions stretch back for centuries and are still taken as, seriously today.

Silat is the ancient Malay art of self-defence, once actively used in battle. Today unarmed fighters mimic a *kris* (dagger) duel unto death, but once it was for real. During the lawless years of World War II, Malay leaders revived the martial art by creating a uniform system of teaching *silat* as a means of promoting godliness, loyalty, self-defence and self-discipline. Modesty and secrecy are among the basic precepts of a *silat* fighter. Like karate and other martial arts, expertise in *silat* involves mediation and spiritual powers, believed to help ward off evil blows. The most popular form of *silat* is merely a refined dance that epitomises masculine grace. It is also a very thrilling and breathtaking experience for the audience.

Sepak raga is a versatile national sport that can be played almost anywhere, as long as there is the small, woven ball made of *rattan*, and a wide open space.

Sepak raga traces its origins to the Rajah of the Moluccas Islands, who held his audience spellbound by sending this ball skyward with foot, heel, sole, instep, calf, thigh,

mythical origins. No-one knows when they first started spinning in Malaysia, but Semang aborigines who live in the jungles insist that lightning is the flashing of top cords in heaven, where dead medicine men compete in a game; and thunder is the murmuring of the tops as they spin.

The record time for spinning is one hour and forty-seven minutes. Requiring great strength to spin, tops vary from a simple wooden cylinder to fantastic streamlined discs, their spindles trimmed with inlaid gold. With the harvest completed and all the rice stored, farmers settle down to watch and bet on the top local team. Contests feature either the long-time spinners or the warlike

knees, shoulders, head, in fact every part of the body but the hands, without letting it touch the ground until it had risen and fallen more than 200 times.

Other South-East Asian nations play variations of *sepak raga*. The game was standardised in 1965 for championship purposes, and became known as *sepak takraw*. Malaysia walked off with the first medal, and has dominated the game ever since.

Tops and Kites: Throughout most of the country, top-spinning is a teenage pastime, but among the Malay communities of the northeast coast, a champion spinner is the village folk hero. Tops (*gasing*) there have

strikers who spin down 7-kilogram fighting tops faster than a speeding bullet. Attackers need as much skill as muscle, since the defending team contrives sinister spinning formations designed to eliminate an attacker's top from the tiny playing circle.

As tops twirl, kites climb the skies under the command of some skilful manoeuvring at the far side of the field. East Coast kites are beautiful creations – moon kites, bird kites, cat kites – all completely covered with miniscule designs cut out of thin, translucent coloured paper. Some have a bow-like device fixed to the neck so that they hum in the sky. When the weather is good and the moon full, they are often left flying all night so that a pleasant humming sound will lull their owners to sleep.

According to *Malay Annals*, kite-flying as a sport dates back to the reign of Sultan Mahmud of Malacca in the 15th century, but probably kites were introduced from China a century earlier, along with paper umbrellas and painted masks. Competitions nowadays are keen. The kite which attains the greatest height is the winner.

Poems, dances and drums: Important national ceremonies in Malaysia almost always call upon the artistic expertise of the East Coast states, in particular those of Kelantan and Terengganu. On these occasions,

Menora has an all-male cast.

A less official festival is sure to include some other traditional dances. The *Ronggeng* with its catchy rhythm is the most typical of Malay dances and has many variations. Probably the most popular form is the *Changgong*, a lively courtship dance in which no physical contact is allowed whilst the dancers sing impromptu verses in praise of their partners. *Tari Piring* is a graceful dance symbolising the offering of gifts to the gods, usually in the form of food served on small *piring*, or plates. Another version of this found in Negri Sembilan, is performed with lighted candles. Two dances of Arabic origin are the *Hadrah*, a slow, graceful dance

dances are performed to mark the occasion. Those most commonly seen are the *Mak Yong* and the *Menora,* but you may be lucky to catch some more unusual ones. Both the *Mak Yong* and the *Menora* are more correctly termed theatrical plays or dance dramas, since dance seems to play a small part in the performance. Both are similar in that they tell magical tales of old about beautiful and divine princesses and the princely adventures of their suitors. In *Mak Yong*, all but three of the roles are played by women whilst

Faces of Malaysia. Left to right, rubber tapper, *songket* weaver, cultural dancer and fisherman.

in praise of the Almighty, and the more dignified *Zapin*. Following Arabic custom, both dances are performed only by men.

Drums and percussion instruments play an important part in traditional Malay music. Apart from a shrill wind instrument, the only other instrument usually played with the percussion is the *rebab* or Malay violin. Drums are also played on their own, for the exciting rhythm they create and for the skilful movements of the drummers.

The *kertok* is a drum fashioned from a coconut with its top sliced off and a piece of *nibong* wood fastened across the mouth to form a sounding board. To show which village they represent in inter-village competitions, *kertok* team members attach colourful pennants onto their drums.

More impressive in terms of size and volume of sound are the *rebana*, fashioned out of a log hollowed out and brightly decorated. On one side of the drum which is turned on its side to be played, is a wheel of spokes, enabling the heavy instrument to be moved. The *rebana* drums are used sometimes as accompaniment during ceremonial rites, but more often for recreation and competitions. At the end of each harvest, villagers challenge each other in the art of drum-beating.

Skilful hands: Of all the cloths woven on the Malay peninsula, Terengganu's *kain*

Weaving mats from screw-pine or *pandanus* leaves is a more down-to-earth craft, though still requiring great skill, which is practised from Mauritius in the Indian Ocean down to East Timor in Indonesia. Weaving begins at the centre of the mat and moves outwards, using dyes to produce simple criss-cross patterns. More professional weavers (all weavers being women) fashion hexagonal boxes of *pandanus* or *nipa* palm leaves. These women usually set up shop right in their own living rooms.

The East Coast is also famous for its batik, a cloth decorated by patterns produced by the use of dyes and wax. It was a method practised by the Javanese at least 2,000 years ago,

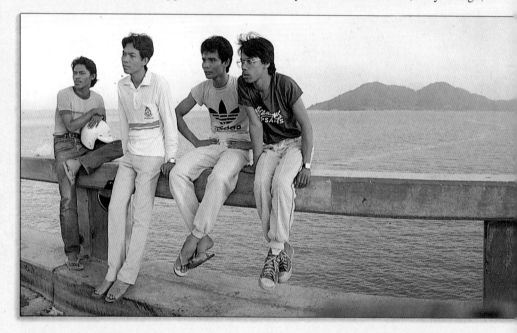

songket – deep blue, forest green, maroon or purple silks studded with silver and gold thread – is the most highly prized. One piece of cloth can require the talents of five different weavers, each specialised in a certain pattern interwoven into the overall design. Malay women cultivate a hierarchy of weavers, the most experienced arranging the warp threads on the loom and the least experienced flicking the shuttle. The body of the cloth is usually plain with an ornate border of stylised floral and geometric motifs. In former times, the entire *kain* was a melody of silver thread on silk and the finest of all were sent for inspection at the sultan's palace.

but evidence also shows that it was not unknown to the ancient Egyptians. Although much of the batik available today is produced in batik factories, prized pieces are still created by hand. The best Malaysian batik comes from Kelantan where artisans use metal stencils to stamp cotton with wax designs. The cloth is then dipped again until the wax is removed, revealing a dazzling cloth with its pattern emboldened by the empty wax-covered areas.

Malaysians favour more modern motifs than their Javanese neighbours, although even these are interspersed with stylised birds, flowers and plants that were found on batik centuries ago. With the onset of tourism, batik is no longer confined to the graceful *sarong*. Batik tablecloths, purses and bags, and even batik wallpaper fill shops in Kuala Terengganu and Kuala Lumpur.

The traditional centre of the silversmith's craft in Kelantan at Kampong Sireh is nowadays full of small workshops where smiths hammer out designs onto silver plates. The filigreed work is fine and delicate, and reflects cosmopolitan inspiration. Some patterns of the *bunga raya* (hibiscus flower) were found on Majapahit jewellery 600 years ago. Other pieces are inspired by shadow play figures with Siamese inflluence, while the conventional lotus blossom

loyalty to one's brethren. The *Wayang Kulit*, literally leather puppet play is unabashedly moralistic. The characters are either immortalised heroes, or infinitely doomed villains. Everyone knows, however, that Prince Rama, personification of godly grace, will eventually prevail over the hideous ten-headed demon called King Rawana. The excitement lies in the way that the tale is unfolded. This is up to the expertise of the *To' Dalang*, "Master of the Mysteries".

The *To' Dalang*, working behind the shadows, has an almost superhuman task to memorise, conduct and sing all the parts of as many as fifty different puppets. He also leads the orchestra which provides the back-

is Indian in origin.

The flickering screen: A thousand years ago, puppeteers of the shadow theatre were entertaining imperial hosts in the courts of China. Otherworld figures punched out of buffalo hide have appeared and flickered in the lamplight for centuries, in Turkey, India, Burma, Cambodia, Java, Thailand and Malaysia. Malaysia's shadows tell the immortal tales of the great *Ramayana* Hindu epic – tales revealing the heavenly virtues of filial piety, marital devotion, valour in war and

Study in symmetry: keeping a watchful eye on the Penang Bridge.

ground music, and directs the action on the screen at the same time. This single-handed performance can last for six hours without stopping. His repertoire of personalities includes strange animals in warriors' clothing, princes, priests, sages, giants, ghouls, and the inevitable monkeys.

But his favourite characters, as every shadow enthusiast knows, are two slapstick clowns named Pa' Dogah and Wak Long. Using parochial jokes and well-known personalities, the puppeteer is at his most improvisational with this pair and their wit and acrobatics can keep a village audience howling until their eyes water.

THE CHINESE – ANCIENT AND MODERN

The Chinese population makes up only 35 percent of the country's total, yet their presence in and control of major industries such as rubber and import and export companies would seem to make their numbers far greater. They can be found in any trading centre from Kuala Lumpur to the smallest isolated "shop" far up the Rejang River in Sarawak; in fact anywhere where there is trade to be had and fortunes to be made.

It was for fortunes and also for adventure that the Chinese first headed for *Nanyang* (The South Seas). From the 13th century onwards, the Chinese were frequent traders throughout the Indonesian and Malay archipelago. The famous Cheng Ho, Admiral of the Ming Emperor Yongle's navy, first visited Malacca in 1403, and many Chinese traders afterwards followed his example and set up warehouses there.

But the majority of the Chinese arrived in the 19th century during the period of the Manchu dynasty. Problems were rife in China at that time: the class structure was disintegrating, corruption amongst officials was widespread and the country was overrun by flood, famine and rebellion. An edict was issued making it virtually impossible for Chinese to travel abroad, but some, mostly out of necessity or encouraged by reports of wealth and employment in the *Nanyang*, risked their lives and escaped. These peoples were mostly from the coastal areas of Amoy and Canton, and included dialect groups such as Hokkien, Teochew, Cantonese, Hakka and Hainanese.

Tough jobs in the Nanyang: They came to Malaya and took on many of the toughest jobs the local population spurned. Unlike the easy-going Malays, the Chinese workers played as hard as they worked, and opium and gambling were the popular pastimes of the forerunners of players at Genting! The Chinese were involved in tin-mining, road and railway building in which they earned sums of money that folks back home would have wondered at. Most put their wages aside for a triumphal return to the homeland, for it was for wealth and not for settlement

The eyes have it: pretty playful in Penang.

that the majority of them came, and their thoughts and loyalties always lay with China.

Mainland China is still important to the Chinese and the older generations still send parcels of clothes back to relatives there. Some elderly folk save up their money in order to be able to return and die on their mother soil. China provides the tradition for the Chinese Malaysian community; it is the focal point for family ancestry and worship, and its customs are continued through its languages and religion. Younger generations of course, are more caught up with modern Malaysian life, and express more nationalistic feelings than their elders.

particularly the area around Malacca. The men are called *Babas* and the women *Nonyas*. The *Peranakans* are extremely proud of their heritage, and with their background of wealth and luxurious living, consider themselves a race apart from the other Chinese. *Nonya* women wear *sarong* and their language is a mixture of Malay with many Chinese colloquialisms thrown in.

Of dragons and incense: The Chinese tend to be more serious and less easy-going than the Malays; they have always worked tremendously hard, hard work being a traditional virtue, and this has brought them fame, success and fortune. There is a strong belief in self-help, but also in close family and clan

The Chinese community of Malaysia has less integrated with and absorbed Malay culture than put its own traditional stamp on the land. Through the educational system, all Chinese must now learn Malay, but at home Mandarin and local dialects are spoken. However, on a street level at least, there is harmony between the two races, and with all children attending the same schools, this is likely to increase.

A new culture: There is one exception to integration between the Malays and the Chinese and that is the *Peranakan* culture which was first forged when Chinese men married local Malay women from the west coast,

ties. Their philosophy is shaped by their history of hardship and pioneering, but also by the three important Chinese ethical strands: Confucianism, Taoism and Buddhism. Even if they have converted to Islam or Christianity, this background is still not forgotten and many of the associated festivals are still celebrated.

Most of the Chinese population are Tao Buddhist, and splendidly colourful temples display their curled and embellished roofs and walls in town and city. The temple, before the clan house, is the centre of the community. Both religious and secular festivals are celebrated here, and classes for the education of the young are held on the premises. Orchestra practice is also held in the temple, and during festival times, stages are often set up in the grounds of the temple for an opera or drama performance or sometimes for a puppet show, which makes Punch and Judy look positively staid. Drums and cymbals can often be heard and add to the activity and vitality of the occasion.

Ang pows and lion dances: The major Buddhist festivals are celebrated not just in the temples but in the clan houses and in homes as well. The biggest and most famous festival is the Chinese Lunar New Year, where non-Chinese are welcome to join in the festivities. Everywhere *Nien Koay*, "cakes of

the year", are on sale as well as oranges and tangerines. Younger or unmarried members of the family receive *ang pows*, small red and gold packets containing a gift of money. Street calligraphers paint with gold on red paper lucky mottoes or the astrological sign of the year. Much of New Year's Day is spent visiting relatives and friends and eating snacks at each house. The latest movies from Hongkong are shown at the cinemas and public shows such as lion or dragon dances

Left, dragon boat races are a popular part of the Malaysian calendar. **Above**, Peranakan culture in Malacca.

are held in public places.

The strange-looking lion houses two or more energetic dancers who twist and turn the half-fierce, half-humorous lion with its fluttering eyelashes and flapping jaws while cymbals clash. The lion is the guardian of the legendary empire and protector of the faith, and its image is to be found on many a balustrade of a Chinese Buddhist temple.

Hungry ghosts: Two other notable festivals are *Qingming*, festival for the departed ancestors, and *Yulan*, festival for the hungry ghosts, where great feasts are laid out for the restless spirits, and fantastic paper houses, paper Mercedes cars, and other material possessions, together with stacks of "hell bank notes" are burnt, the ashes and their benefits rising to the appeased ghosts. In recent years, spirits have also been receiving "Hell" cheque books and even credit cards!

Every day is important: Of all the events in a Chinese person's life, the wedding is the most important, and whether it is celebrated in the traditional or the modern way, great banquets are held in flashy Chinese restaurants attended by relatives, friends and even business associates.

Almost every day in the Taoist Buddhist calendar has some festival, and every day has some significance, some days being luckier than others. Birth anniversaries of the well-known deities are celebrated both at home and in the temple.

If you enter one of the large modern business buildings in a Malaysian town or city, you are quite likely on the ground floor to stumble upon a small Buddhist shrine, some elaborate, some rather makeshift, with sticks of incense and candles burning. Seemingly incongruous in a modern world, yet Chinese Buddhism is unabashedly practical and materialistic.

On the streets, Chinese fortune tellers set up shop along the five-foot-ways, guiding clients on the most auspicious day for a business transaction or for a wedding. Temple mediums may offer a more otherwordly interpretation of their prospects. Grandmothers are often familiar with divining and the occult, and consult their *tongshu* or Chinese Almanac for their family. Whatever their profession, the Chinese combine their modern way of life with the knowledge and wisdom of their ancestry and look to the future with confidence and optimism.

THE INDIANS

Although Indians had been visiting Malaysia for hundreds of years following runours of fortune in a land their ancestors knew as the "golden peninsula", it was not until the 19th century that they arrived and stayed in large numbers, employed mainly as rubber tappers. Many of the original rubber tappers returned to their homeland, and Malaysian Indians still maintain strong home ties with their former villages, sometimes even taking wives from there and bringing them to live in Malaysia.

Indians make up less than 10 percent of the population of Malaysia today, but their culture is pervasive in towns and cities. With few exceptions they all came from South India, and approximately 80 percent are Tamils and Hindus. There are small numbers of Sikhs, Malayees, Telugus and Parsis. Indian Muslims came to Malaysia and opened restaurants, textile and other businesses. Some of them married Malay women, especially in Penang. The majority of the Indian population is concentrated in the states of Selangor, Perak and Penang.

The rural culture of South India they brought with them left a rich and colourful stamp on Malaysian life as vivid as a saffron silk sari, and what they lack in numbers they make up for in festivities and temples. Indian weekly magazines, the astrologer's calling card and the indomitable prevalence of the Hindu faith that continues to absorb change like an ink blotter have all become part of the Malaysia. The Indians also introduced the banana leaf curry which is now a popular local dish. Rice, vegetables, curried fish and meats are ladled out generously onto the leaf, and it is traditional to eat with the fingers, though only with those of the right hand, as the left is considered unclean.

Fulfilling the holy vow: The Hindu religion pervades every part of an Indian's life, and there are festivals and celebrations all year round. Hindu temples are splendid affairs with every piece of wall and ceiling brightly decorated. The main entrance is crowned by a soaring archway, crowded with figures of

The Thaipusam festival brings a throng of people to the Batu Caves.

Indian deities, and along the top of the temple walls, sacred cows sit placidly observing the goings-on in the street below.

There are many kinds of Indian Hindu festivals, and they come from a mixture of backgrounds. Some celebrate the rice harvest and other agrarian events, although the Southern Indian rice fields are now far away and most Malaysian Indians live in towns and cities.

Others celebrate the weather and the stars, while the body of the festivals are purely religious. The two most spectacular of the latter type are *Thaipusam* and *Deepavali*.

Thaipusam is a very popular festival in Malaysia, celebrated by Hindu Indians of all

bullocks. The chariot is a work of art made out of carved wood, plated over with silver and decorated with statues of gods, goddesses and animals, and decked with flags, tinsel and streamers.

On the following day the festival proper begins. Up to 200,000 people may throng up to the caves, walking from the temple in the capital, chanting and singing. The most extreme form of devotion is the carrying of the *kavadi* for the deity. It represents the fulfilment of a vow that the devotee has taken in furtherance of some desired object in his life or as recompense for the avoidance of some calamity.

The prospective *kavadi* bearer must pre-

classes and groups. The day of its celebration is determined by the Hindu calendar on a day which is auspicious for Hindu worshippers. It is dedicated to Lord Subramanya, son of Siva. There are a few special temples in Malaysia where celebrations draw people from all over the country, notably the Batu Caves, just outside Kuala Lumpur, and the temple at Waterfall Road in Penang. Also the Thandayuthapani Temple in Tank Road, across the causeway in Singapore.

The festival generally lasts for three days. On the first a splendid statue of Subramanya is mounted on a chariot surrounded by expensive jewels and finery, and drawn by

pare himself spiritually for the event by abstinence for a period before the date of the ceremony. He must live on a fully vegetarian diet and must not indulge in physical pleasures. The *kavadi* is a wooden arch on a wooden base decorated with peacock feathers and paper, and carried by the devotee on his shoulders. It supports on this base ritual objects like a pot of milk or special fruits. All these are offered to the deity at the end of the journey. From the *kavadi* extend metal spokes and hooks which are attached to the skin of the devotee, who is in a state of trance. The holes are said never to bleed if the bearer is truly committed. Some devotees pierce their cheeks with needles. The chanting on the way to the caves maintains the trance and many of the women chanters often become possessed themselves.

Within the hallowed destination is a dim sea of lightbulbs and candles, scattered fires and a throng of pilgrims. In a deep grotto framed with stalactites rests the image of Lord Subramanya. A dozen white-clad priests tend to thousands of worshippers and bestow blessings and sacred ash upon the spent *kavadi* carriers. The burden is lifted, water is sprinkled on them and the trance subsides, although they are dazed for some time afterwards and remember little of what they have done. A coconut is dashed to the

people were ended when Lord Krishna conquered the evil Narakasura and thus brought hope and happiness to the populace. Other Hindus believe that the festival celebrates the defeat of Rawana by Rama, the symbol of goodness as depicted in the Hindu classic *Ramayana*.

This is a time for indulgent feasting, especially on sweet cakes and candies, and their colour, shape and taste are a sweet-toothed celebrant's delight. Traditional Hindus start the day by having an oil bath before sunrise and saying their prayers. New clothes are worn and worshipping is done either in the temple or at home. This is followed by a show of respect to the older members of the

ground and camphor is burned. The holy vow has been fulfilled.

Festival of Lights: *Deepavali*, with its emphasis on lights, is like an early Christmas. The lights lit in Hindu homes celebrate the triumph of good over evil, and nowadays Christmas lights are preferred to the traditional oil lamps because of their brightness and variety of colours. The darkness signifies the misdeeds of the ruler who ruled over the people unwisely. The miseries of the

family. Afterwards it is open house for friends and relatives, and non-Hindu friends are invited to join in the celebrations, being pressed to eat just one more curry puff or another delicious *mysore pahu*!

Enterprising shopkeepers always do well during the *Deepavali* holiday, as presents and decorations are in hot demand. Many decorate their shops with Christmas decorations, which in fact are hardly taken down at all, as they are kept up for their Christian customers over December, and some even leave them until Chinese New Year, binding all the faiths together with their commercial ingenuity.

Far left, newsstands are a common sight. **Left**, roadside *rojak* stall and **right**, local hardware vendor.

THE ORANG ASLI – THE ORIGINAL MALAYSIANS?

Whether you are venturing up to the Cameron Highlands for some cooler weather, driving along the Johor coast or exploring Malaysia's National Park for the first time, it is equally possible in all cases that you will meet with the comment from a Malaysian friend: "Ah, but then you will see the *Orang Asli* there."

Who are the *Orang Asli*? The question is not so simply answered. The Malay term means "original people" and covers three more or less distinct groups and a score or more of separate tribes. *Orang Asli* has become a convenient term for explaining those groups of people who do not belong to the three predominant races of peninsular Malaysia. Undoubtedly, one group, the *Negrito*, are the oldest inhabitants of the Malaysian peninsula, but other groups only arrived here as recently as 100 years ago. Inaccurate as the term is, it is also to some extent harmful, for it has come to denote amongst other Malaysians a "primitive" or "backward" people, a generalisation which cannot possibly be backed up. The *Orang Asli* can only perhaps be grouped together in the sense that economically and educationally they are the poorest of the land. But as you move from one area of the peninsula to another, you will gradually learn more about what is behind this blanket term.

The British were perhaps the first to group the *Orang Asli* together, using the term "*sakai*" or debt-slave to define them. With independence, a special government department was set up to administer to the needs of these peoples, and through this body, much useful and clarifying information about them has come to light. Yet their origins still remain something of a mystery. What is known is that the different main groups vary from one another in racial, cultural, linguistic and economic dimensions. There are of course many overlaps between the three groups through intermarriage and adoption of a superior tribe's language, but academically a division of three is a convenient way

These Negrito aborigines are very much at home in their jungle encampment in the north of the peninsula.

84

of studying these fascinating peoples, some of whom are the forerunners of the modern Malay.

Of the estimated population of 60,000 *Orang Asli*, 60 percent of them are jungle dwellers, while the other 40 percent are coastal peoples, many of them fishermen. The largest group in number are the *Senoi* (embracing the *Temiar, Semat, Semok, Beri, Che Wong, Jah Hut, Mah Meri* tribes), the second largest are the Proto-Malays or *Orang Melayu Asli* (whose various tribes include *Temuan, Semelai, Temok, Jakun, Orang Laut* [another sub-group comprising several tribes living close to one another], *Orang Kanak* and *Orang Selitar*), and the

is thought that they arrived in Malaya 8,000 years ago. Nowadays, the *Negrito* mostly inhabit the northeast and northwest, and are the only truly nomadic tribes of the *Orang Asli*. Practising little or no cultivation, the *Negrito* tribes pride themselves on their mobility, and possessions are thought only to be a hindrance to their lifestyle.

Although several *Negritos* have left the protection of the forest and sought a modern education, the majority of the tribes have spurned government help in settling them into specially-built villages. The *Negritos* do not have a written language, but demonstrate their sharp intelligence by being competent linguists, often speaking up to a dozen tribal

smallest and oldest of all are the *Negrito* (including the *Kensiu, Kintak, Jahai, Lanoh, Madrik* and *Batek* peoples). As you read this, the names will not mean much to you, but as you travel around the peninsula, you will hear the various tribal names mentioned rather than just "*Orang Asli*".

The oldest and the youngest Malaysians: The features of the *Orang Asli* are strikingly different from tribe to tribe. In general, the *Negritos*, as their name suggests, are mostly dark-skinned and frizzy-haired, and their features, though unique, remind you of Papua New Guinean or east African peoples.

Their true origin, however, is unknown. It

dialects, as well as Malay and Thai. They are an extremely shy people, and if frightened, are more likely to flee than fight. Social order is more or less unspoken and relaxed, with the oldest or the most suitable senior man being the chief. Respect for one another and for all living things dictates their code of behaviour. Fear of the spirits of dead ancestors and hunted animals is very strong amongst them, and it is an unwritten law that all animals caught in the forest should suffer no pain.

The *Negrito* forefathers were also hunters and gatherers who lived in caves and rock shelters. They knew the use of fire and cooked their own food with the aid of crude instruments hewn from stone. Their migrations to the Malay peninsula were hardly a conscious effort. Children born into a family, grew up, mated, needed more space for the family, and shifted to the next cave. In 20 generations they may have moved only 200 kilometres.

Some of the darker people of the *Senoi* group could be mistaken for *Negritos*, while some of the fairest, walking down the street in Kuala Lumpur in jeans and a tee-shirt, look almost exactly like Malays. However, in the Cameron Highlands, with a *Semai* youth wearing his traditional loincloth and carrying a blowpipe, his handsome features

reflect a different ancestry. The *Senoi* are thought to have common ancestors with the hill peoples of northern Cambodia and Vietnam, arriving in present Malaysia between 6 and 8,000 years ago. Most of the tribes are shifting cultivators, moving from a settlement when the land is exhausted. Their land is marked and within their *saka*, or territory, they will return to abandoned villages once the soils have become more fertile. Many *Semai* in the Cameron Highlands have become wage earners, working on the tea es-

Left, inside an *Orang Asli* home. **Above**, raising a family in the jungle is no easy task.

tates. Others have headed for the city lights, finding jobs as varied as government employees and taxi drivers.

The Proto-Malays were the latest group to arrive, having been in the peninsula no earlier than four thousand years ago. This group is perhaps the least connected, however, and many of the tribes arrived from the Indonesian island of Sumatra only a few generations ago. The Johor *Orang Laut* were still in the islands south of Singapore a century ago. Many of this group also have a distinct resemblance to the Malays, not surprising, as modern Malays have a common ancestry with many of them. Others have decidedly Polynesian features. The Proto-Malays of Pahang are semi-nomadic in the main, while other groups in Johor and Selangor live in settled fishing villages. With the adoption of Islam and the easy-going life of a fishing community, their lives hardly differ from the Malays who live by the sea.

Spirits in the trees: The majority of the *Orang Asli*, however, have chosen not to take on world religions such as Islam and Christianity, and have animistic beliefs, making them acutely aware of the benevolence of the natural world – and its occasional wrath. The tribal medicine man is known as the *shaman*, the *bomoh* or the *pawang* (depending on the tribe), who mediates with the spirit world to cure sickness through incantations, and has a knowledgeable use of herbs collected from the forest.

The *Orang Asli* beliefs, their diverse and sometimes difficult languages and their oral tradition of tales of old, are little known outside their tribes. For the jungle dwellers, the isolation has set them apart from city life. Many exchange jungle products such as *rotan*, to be found in the deepest parts of the jungle where only they dare go, for their basic necessities such as iron objects and salt. With government support, the Department of Orang Asli Affairs is providing land settlements, schools, hospitals and medical training in an effort to provide channels of integration with Malaysian society should the *Orang Asli* want them. Many also live in clearings on the jungle's fringe where they cultivate hill rice, maize and tapioca. But the bonds which have sustained a self-contained inland conmmunity are not easily broken, and the identity of the *Orang Asli* remains strong.

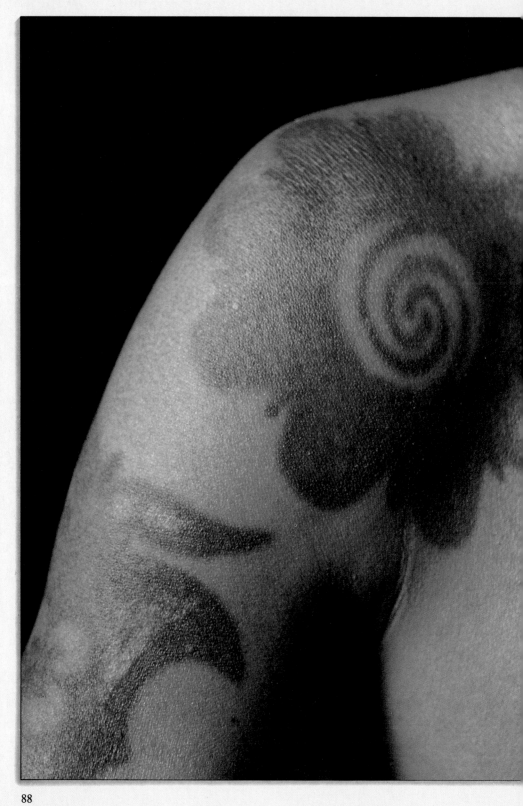

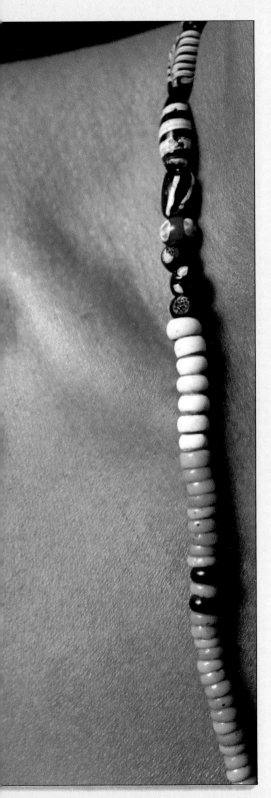

TRIBES OF SABAH AND SARAWAK

The two easternmost states of Sabah and Sarawak, situated in the north of the island of Borneo, have the most diverse racial groups of all Malaysia. As there are so many different groups, it is impossible to document all of them here, but some of their origins and many of their cultural traditions are similar to one another. Most of them are of Mongoloid extract and moved here from Kalimantan (Indonesian Borneo). They generally live in the interior along the jungle rivers, although some live near the coastal regions, while others who have received state education have found work in towns, commercial centres and national industries.

With its cultures so different from that of the Malays, Chinese and Indians, Malaysian Borneo has the feeling of being a different country, and it is for the most part accessible only to the intrepid traveller willing to venture up rivers and along the jungle trails.

In Sabah, the largest group comprises the *Dusun* or *Kadazan* tribes, followed by the *Muruts* (hillpeople, and the last of the tribes to renounce head-hunting), the *Bajau* (Muslims and famous cowboys and seafarers of Sabah), the *Rungus* (with their beautiful coiled armbands and black costumes), and *Bisaya*, *Suluk*, *Lundayeh* and *Kedayan* in smaller numbers.

In Sarawak there is an even greater diversity of peoples and languages: the *Dayak* include *Ibans*, who make up the majority of the Sarawak population, and the *Bidayuh* or land Dayaks. The *Melanau* are also a large community and then there are many tribes lumped together under the name of *Orang Ulu*. This term, meaning "interior people", has become somewhat derogatory in the sense that it denotes a primitive and ignorant people and most tribes prefer to be known by their own names. The *Orang Ulu* group includes the nomadic *Punans* and *Penans*, the highly structured *Kayan* and *Kenyah* communities, the *Kajang*, *Kelabit*, the *Lun Bawang* and *Bisaya*. Even these names house several different tribes who have their own special names.

Tattooed patterns decorate the arm and shoulder of an *Iban* tribesman in Sarawak.

The majority of the indigenous tribes have traditions and ways of living in common, but each group has some unique belief or activity that sets it apart from the rest.

A house for all: Most of the peoples live traditionally in *longhouses*, a large building that houses the entire community under one roof, and may contain up to 60 families or more. The Malaysian government is attempting to move longhouse communities into villages with separate houses, meeting with much resistance from the longhouse dwellers. Living in the longhouse is naturally very communal, and society organisation ranges from the very stratified system of the *Kenyahs* to the egalitarian life of the

ing, but nowadays permanent ladders are also used. The longhouse is usually built entirely of different kinds of wood, although longhouses further downriver with easy access to industrial and commercial centres now sport corrugated iron or plastic roofs and concrete walls and steps.

There are four main areas in a longhouse: the first being the much-used *ruai*, or communal verandah which takes up about half the space of the longhouse. This is where the men like to sit and chew betel; visitors are entertained here and meetings and ceremonies take place on its wooden or bamboo boards. The *bilik* are the family apartments, whose doors open onto the *ruai*; each one has

Iban. Each longhouse has a headman, traditionally an inherited position, but nowadays elected by the people, and his job is mostly to settle disputes and arrange ceremonies.

All longhouses are situated next to rivers or streams, which are used for washing, fishing, and waste disposal, and are their main form of transport and contact with other longhouse communities. The longhouse is raised on stilts for security and airiness and also to prevent flooding when the river level is swollen during the monsoon.

A notched pole is the traditional mode of entry to the longhouse, as it could be drawn up at night to prevent intruders from enter-

its own kitchen. The third area is the *tanju* or outer verandah, attached to the *ruai* and used for drying rice and sometimes for ceremonial occasions. Finally there is the *sadau* or attic, which is used for storing grains, weaving baskets and cloth, and also as an extra bedroom for village maidens!

River trade and hospitality: As the longhouse usually faces the river, it is open to river travellers who may stop for a night's rest before continuing their journey, and also to Chinese traders who barter commercial goods for the much sought-after baskets and beadwork of the longhouse women. Most tribes and especially *Iban*, are extremely hospitable and guests are welcomed with a glass of *tuak* (rice wine) before being offered a bed. It is customary for visitors to bring gifts of food, money or clothes to pay for their stay, but they are more than repaid in kind. Staying at a longhouse is really just a matter of arriving there and asking to see the village headman for permission to stay.

However, there may be a time when you see a special sign at the entrance of a longhouse or even down on the path by the river. This is a longhouse taboo and is marked by a stick with green leaves, a piece of white cloth or areca blossoms placed on the top. This signifies that some bad luck or unfortunate event such as death, a curse or a crop

have been grown. Fishing and some hunting is also undertaken. Several tribes also build their own boats and canoes.

The myth of the headhunters: Religious practices are almost as varied as the peoples of Sarawak, but since the spreading of Christianity, many tribes have given up their old superstitions and instead of incantations to the forest god or gods, now sing hymns on their communal verandahs. There are many communities who have embraced Christianity but also continue to observe some of their old customs. Those who have not been converted display a variety of beliefs, the most important being the observance of forest omens, and the traditional ceremonies

failure has befallen the longhouse, and visitors may not stay until the sign has been removed. For a death this taboo can last from two weeks to three months. A hat placed outside a *bilik* door signifies that just that household has a taboo because of a death and visitors may stay in any *bilik* but that one.

Most longhouses are self-sufficient in rice and also in fruit trees, both of which are cultivated around the longhouse land. For a long time now, cash crops, such as rubber, cocoa and sago for sale at markets downriver

Left, an *Iban* musician in traditional dress. Above, *Kadazans* in colourful costumes.

conducted to ward off evil spirits or encourage prosperity for the community.

Borneo is perhaps most famously known as the land of headhunters, a term which seems to conjure up a cruel and aggressive people. Contrary to this misconception, the people of Sarawak are gentle, law-abiding people and in the days of head-hunting, the taking of the heads of one's enemies only occurred when the community was suffering some plague. The heads of enemies were thought to bring protection from danger and sickness. Taking a head was also a way of proving one's manhood. Only the heads of warriors were coveted, and the women and children of the enemy eventually became integrated into the victor's community.

Beautiful long-lobed women: Today headhunting is outlawed, and the skulls to be seen hanging in longhouses are those that have been inherited by families. Other items such as rhinoceros horn and hornbill feathers are also coveted for charms of protection for the longhouse. Both men and women receive many tattoos, both for protection and decoration, with each tattoo arrangement and combination of designs suited to the wearer. Many tribes place long weights in the ears of children or simple wooden plugs in order to stretch the earlobe, but only women wear the heaviest ones so that their lobes may eventually stretch down to the chest, long lobes being considered a sign of great beauty.

There are many interesting customs practised by Borneo tribes, but perhaps the most attractive to Westerners is one that they will probably never see, as it takes place in the dead of night in Iban longhouses. Should a young Iban man wish to marry a girl, he undertakes a form of courtship whereby he may be allowed by the parents to visit the girl under her mosquito net at night, a purely innocent affair, since the girl's parents will be awake and alert under their mosquito net only a metre or so away! The young man may visit the same girl three times in this way after which he has to make a proposal to the girl and to her parents. Marriages can be very elaborate ceremonies in some communities, usually made to coincide with harvest and a full moon, while in other communities, it is simply a matter of telling the headman that you are shacking up together.

Of bird omens and rice harvests: Omens are of particular importance to Borneo tribes, and some Dayak groups' entire rice cultivation rests on whether a certain bird should call, heralding a good harvest, or dreading an unlucky bird adding its voice, forewarning of crop failure. On special occasions, a pig may be killed and its liver carefully studied for signs both favourable and unfavourable. Chicken sacrifices are more common, and heads used to "go flying" if someone in the village fell ill. Amongst the protective cover of the jungle, many of these age-old traditions continue, although now wrist-watches adorn Iban men along with tattoos, and Guinness Stout may be offered as an alternative to rice wine.

With the migration of the younger members of the communities to towns, however, it may not be long before this serene and simple way of life dies out forever. Many of the young do return to the longhouse, but the numbers are diminishing as opportunities in commerce and industry increase.

Civilisation moves in: On the brighter side, the present communities are still fairly successful with their cash crop cultivation, and the women add to the income by weaving blankets and making baskets of rattan, bamboo and beadwork, items much coveted further downriver on the coast. Practical lightweight baby carriers are one of the most prized works of art, being covered entirely in a colourful beadwork. These items as well as crude woodcarvings (traditionally made as protectors for the sick) are now being produced for the tourist industry, the rate of their demand causing the craftsmen to produce poorer handiwork than they are known for.

Advancing stealthily through the jungle, armed with a blowpipe and a spear, the nomadic *Penans* and *Punans* are mostly unaffected by these changes. Government attempts to make them settle permanently in one place have largely failed, as their love of freedom and inherent self-possession lead them to pursue their traditional ways of life. Extensive logging in Sarawak is threatening this traditional lifestyle, and Punan and Penan men have joined forces with the Iban to set up barricades at logging roads as a form of passive resistance. Despite accidents and arrests, the nomads are still committed to protecting their home: the jungle.

While other tribes prefer to remain in the proximity of their longhouses and to travel by river, the nomads have an uncanny knowledge of the jungle and its inhabitants. Some use special signs, marks carved on tree trunks or strips of leaf tied in a certain manner to pass on messages to others in the forest. These may indicate how many people are travelling, where the next settlement is and whether there is good food to be had in the area. Others know the jungle so well that they do not need to read these signs for direction. They are one with the pulse of their natural surroundings and move as silently as the animals of the forest.

A Kenyah Dayak woman has traditional ornamental elongated ears.

Peninsula Malaysia

80 km/ 50 miles

South China Sea

Andaman Sea

THAILAND

Yan Ta Khao
Palian
Rattaphum
Songkhla
Ban Pakbara
Hat Yai
Khlong Ngae
Chana
Pattani
Panare
Satun
Sadao
Dung Na Ma **616**
Yala
Sai Buri
PERLIS
Kangar
Jitra
Kuala Nerang
Ban Nang Sata
Narathiwat
P. LANGKAWI
Alor Setar
1145
Buket Bubat
Tumpat
KEDAH
Sungai Ko-lok
Kota Bharu
Peringat
Pangkal Kalong
Sungai Petani
Gerik
Batang Merbau
Kuala Kerai
George Town
Ayer Itam
Butterworth
Bukit Mertajam
Tasek Temengor
G. Chamah 2171
Kuala Kerai
Kampong Buloh
G. Lawit 1519
Kuala Terengganu
P. PINANG
Kubu Gajah
G. Besar 1749
KELANTAN
Kampong Lalok
Marang
Parit Buntar
Port Weld
Taiping
Sungai Siput Utara
Limau Kasturi
Kampong Merchang
Kuala Kangsar
G. Korbu 2183
Gua Musang
TAMAN NEGARA
TERENGGANU
G. Mandi Angin 1459
Dungun
PERAK
Ipoh
Batu Gajah
MALAYSIA
Kampong Surau
Kerteh
Pengkalan Baharu
Kampar
NATIONAL PARK
Kampong Ayer Puteh
Lumut
Tapah
Jelai
Kuala Lipis
G. Tapis 1512
Kemaman (Chukai)
Kuala Perak
Benta Seberang
Jerantut
Kampong Balok
Telok Anson
Selim River
Raub
G. Benom 2107
PAHANG
Manis
Kuantan
Sungai Besar
Tanjong Malim
Bentong
Mentakab
Pahang
Kampong Cherok Paloh
Kuala Kubu Baharu
Temerloh
Kampong Kuala Lepar
SELANGOR
Ampang
Kampong Kerayong
Tenassi
Nenasi
Tanjungbalai
Kuala Lumpur
Petaling Jaya
Kajang
Tasek Dampar
Leban Chondong
P. TIOMAN
Cape Pertandangan
Kelang
Telok Datok
Morib
NEGRI
Bahau
Keratong
Rompin
Kampong Telek
Labuhanbilik
Seremban
Rembau
Kuala Pilah
Segamat
G. Tiong 1014
Mersing
Port Dickson
SEMBILAN
Labis
Rantauprapat
Masjid Tana
MELAKA
Tangkak
JOHOR
Kotapinang
Bagansiapiapi
Melaka
Muar
Keluang
Langgapayung
RUPAT ISLAND
Batu Pahat
Simpang Rengam
Kota Tinggi
Gunungtua
Sungaisahir
Simpangyam
BENGKALIS ISLAND
Pontian Kecil
Kulai
Pujut
Sintong
Dumai
Bengkalis
Ketamputih
Kukup
Tanjungmedan
Duri
PADANG ISLAND
Pisang
Johor Bahru
Singapore
Pasarsibuhuan
Daludalu
Tasikserai
Lemang
RANGSANG ISLAND
Pangke
BATAM I.
Sagulung
Pasirpengarayan
Balaipungut
Selatpanjang
Timun
KUNDUR ISLAND
Hutanopan
SUMATERA (SUMATRA)
Buatan
TEBINGTINGGI I.
Siaksriinderapura
MENDOL ISLAND
Tanjungbatu
Rau
Aliantan
Pakanbaru
Pelalawan
RIAU
Kampar
Sungaiguntung
INDONESIA
Bangkinang

Strait
of
Malacca

102

THE PERFECT TRAVEL CURE

The tourist brochures modestly claim that "only Malaysia...has it all." And so it does. Picturesque fishing villages, cosy hill resorts, unexplored tropical forests and miles of empty white sand beaches. Mix into these scenes the cultural pastiche that is the Malaysian people, and the result is an irresistible combination of rural charm, intriguing lifestyles and a slight but ever-so-appealing hint of adventure that's guaranteed to send expectant visitors to travel heaven.

And that's just the tip of the coconut tree. Malaysia's multitudinous attractions also include traditional arts and crafts, colourful religious festivals and copious amounts of comestibles to pacify even the most epicurean tastes. In fact, sampling some mouth-watering Malaysian food comes close to being a religious experience in itself.

Situated smack in the middle of South-East Asia, with a total land area of 342,000 square kilometres (132,000 sq miles), Malaysia is about the size of Japan, but with only a fraction of the population (about 15 million compared to Japan's 121 million). Peninsular Malaysia accounts for 40 percent of the land area, and 86 percent of the population. The East Malaysian states of Sabah and Sarawak are separated from the peninsula by 640 kilometres (400 miles) of the South China Sea, but each of the 13 states has a charm and character of its own. Malay and indigenous tribes make up over half the population while Chinese, Indians and others also come under the broad spectrum that is covered by the term "Malaysian".

The country's economy is based mainly on agricultural commodities, and it is one of the world's major suppliers of tin, palm oil and rubber. Since achieving independence from colonial rule in 1957, Malaysia has faced a series of internal and external economic and political pitfalls. It has emerged each time with the same clear-eyed determination to succeed.

Despite some physical changes, the inevitable outcome of living in an age of rapid development and high technology, Malaysia is still very much a land of *kampong* (villages), jungles, beaches and rice fields, made that much more appealing by a friendly, deeply religious and uniquely diverse group of peoples. Malaysia really does have it all.

Preceding pages: Sarawak snapshots take pride of place on a longhouse wall; little boys all in a row; farmer reflects on the day's work; launching a fishing boat in Kuala Terengganu.

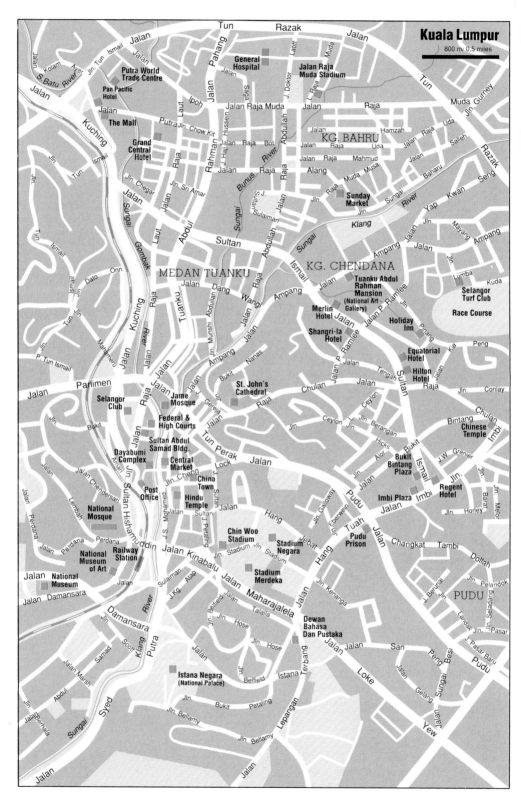

Kuala Lumpur

800 m/0.5 miles

Putra World Trade Centre
Pan Pacific Hotel
The Mall
Grand Central Hotel
General Hospital
Jalan Raja Muda Stadium

KG. BAHRU

Sunday Market

Klang

MEDAN TUANKU

KG. CHENDANA

Tuanku Abdul Rahman Mansion (National Art Gallery)
Merlin Hotel
Shangri-la Hotel
Holiday Inn
Equatorial Hotel
Hilton Hotel

Selangor Turf Club
Race Course

St. John's Cathedral

Parlimen
Selangor Club
Jame Mosque
Federal & High Courts
Sultan Abdul Samad Bldg.
Dayabumi Complex
Central Market
China Town
Post Office
Hindu Temple

Bintang Chinese Temple
Bukit Bintang Plaza
Imbi Plaza
Regent Hotel

National Mosque
National Museum of Art
Railway Station
National Museum

Chin Woo Stadium
Stadium Negara
Stadium Merdeka
Pudu Prison

PUDU

Dewan Bahasa Dan Pustaka

Istana Negara (National Palace)

FROM SHACKS TO BOOMING CAPITAL

A mining outpost 100 years ago, a big city today, **Kuala Lumpur** is the capital city of Malaysia, with a population of 1.5 million people. To the newcomer, Kuala Lumpur – or "KL" as it is affectionately known – is a fascinating mixture of old and new, with skyscrapers and temples, and a colourful scene of multi-racial activity, with Malay mosques of Moorish design, elaborate Chinese temples and crowded shophouses, Hindu temples with towering gates and Indian restaurants, not to mention the impressive municipal buildings and shipshape British order.

On the green of the *padang*, a cricket match is in progress and its players include a British businessman, a Chinese bank clerk, a turbaned Sikh schoolboy and a Malay government official. A hospital in town announces: "Western medicine in the mornings, Chinese medicine in the afternoons"; shop signs form a chequered pattern of Chinese, Arabic and Roman scripts. There are stately mansions of eclectic style, traditional mosques and temples squeezed between modern office blocks, and supermarkets vie with well-stocked shophouses selling everything from hairspray to incense sticks. KL's restaurants and open-air stalls offer food for every palate, from delicious noodles and satay to pepper steaks and irresistible seafood.

Bare beginnings: Various stories tell of how Kuala Lumpur got its name. The best one is the simplest: the miners and traders who first came in search of tin poled up the river to where the Klang and Gombak rivers converge. The Gombak estuary was the highest point upstream that the miners could land their supplies for prospecting the tin of Ampang, a few kilometres further inland. The first party of 87 men to do so, however, fared badly, and within a month 70 had died from fever. But others soon followed and persevered, building shelters and opening trading posts. They named the settlement Kuala Lumpur, which means "Muddy Estuary" in Malay. By the 1860s the miners' landing place had become a flourishing village.

Kuala Lumpur was founded in turbulent times, when fierce rivalries over mining claims and water rights led to civil wars. Gang clashes, feuds and murders went hand in hand with an ever-present threat of devastating fires and pestilence. Essentially a rambunctious pioneer mining settlement, KL was predominantly Chinese, with its brothels, gambling booths and opium dens. It was put under the leadership of Yap Ah Loy, the *Kapitan China* or Chinese headman, who was supposed to keep some semblance of order in this wild, all-male settlement. He played a major role in the civil wars and continued to direct the affairs of the town till his death in 1885. The Kapitan warred against crime, built a prison and quelled revolts. Under his guidance KL was rebuilt, but the damage done during the civil wars was more than skin-deep, so that by the time of Yap Ah Loy's death, the town remained nothing more than a jungle outpost of wooden huts huddled along narrow lanes.

Then Frank Swettenham, the British Resident of Selangor, made his entry and moved his administration here. KL began to assume its modern shape as Swettenham encouraged local businessmen to build brick kilns, and street by street the old town was pulled down, reconstructed with wider thoroughfares and stone and brick structures. A rail line from Klang to Kuala Lumpur, connecting the capital city to the sea, was opened in 1886.

KL's development was rapid from this time onwards. With its establishment as the state capital of Selangor, more and more people from surrounding villages moved there. It quickly grew in size and population to become an administrative centre and the hub of all business and trade. By the end of the century it was the colonial capital of the then newly-created Federated Malay States, and graduated in 1946 to become the headquarters of the Federation of Malaya.

After independence in 1957, the pace of KL's progress became even more rapid. Kuala Lumpur came of age on 1 February 1974, when it was formally detached from its mother-state of Selangor and made into a unit of its own called the Federal Territory. Today, it is the seat of government for all Malaysia with its own administration headed by a minister of cabinet rank. Over the past 15 years, the skyline of the city has changed out of all recognition as new high-rise buildings continue their upward thrust.

A tour on wheels: In order to get an idea of the different faces of KL, it is a good idea on your first day to take one of the tours offered by local travel companies, often running from major hotels. Or make up your own tour by hiring a taxi for the day (negotiate the price before setting off). This will give you a chance to see some of the fascinating sites which are more spread out, so that you can save your feet for a stroll around the vibrant streets of Chinatown.

You might do well to start at **Jalan**

Benteng, although there is very little to see there nowadays. This is the site of the first KL settlement, next to the confluence of the Gombak and Klang rivers, where tin mining supplies were first unloaded and taken to Ampang. Behind Jalan Benteng lies the area that was originally Yap Ah Loy's empire, now the business centre with towering glass and steel blocks, and blending into this area are the old streets of Chinatown.

If you cross the rivers, you will come to the old centre for British colonial rule, with its Moorish administrative buildings, still important today. The Old City Hall and a British colonial Club face the **Padang**, a stretch of green which can be found in most towns influenced by British rule, notable examples being in Singapore and Ipoh.

It was here that the strangest of all British games, cricket, was played, and the crack of bat against ball can still be heard today. This was the centre for the British community, and games could be watched from the verandahs of the British Selangor Club on one side of the Padang. Other games such as hockey, football, rugby and tennis have also been played here, although nowadays these are more likely to take place in KL's modern stadiums. The Padang saw the British flag lowered for the last time on 31 August 1957 and the new Malaysian flag replaced it. The Padang is still used as a venue for national events, and parades on National Day start here. After nightfall, a different kind of parade takes place here, as local transsexuals and transvestites take over the green. In 1989, the Padang was dug up to make way for an underground carpark to help alleviate KL's parking problems.

The imposing **Sultan Abdul Samad Building** casts its shadow on the Padang. The core of colonial KL, this building was once the colonial secretariat headquarters, and now houses the **Supreme Court**. It was the first building to be built in a North Indian-cum-Moorish style, a trend brought to Malaysia by two architects, A.C. Norman and A.B. Hubbock. Both men had spent some time in India, and deemed that an

Grandoise architecture features heavily in KL's railway station.

architectural style featuring Moorish, Indian and Arabic motifs would best suit a predominantly Muslim country, apparently ignoring the fact that the Malays already had a very highly developed and practical building style of their own.

The Supreme Court is now the most photographed building in the city, with its 40-metre-high clock tower, the Big Ben of Malaysia, topped with a golden dome and flanked on either side by two dome-topped towers. On state occasions, coloured lightbulbs light up the arches of the Supreme Court, making it look like a setting for an Arabian night tale. Its foundation stone was laid in 1898. Sir Charles Mitchell, the Governor of the Straits Settlements at the time, thought the building a ridiculous extravagance, and was heard to say: "The tin won't last for ever, you know." He was right, of course, but tin was later replaced by other resources, now the backbone of Malaysia's economy.

On one end of this building is **Infokraf**, or the Handicraft and Informa-tion Centre, where there are exhibitions of local and also an art gallery.

A white man's club: On another side of the Padang is the **Selangor Club**, built in 1884 in mock-Tudor style, with a more recent extension which blends in well with the older and smaller building. The club was sometimes known as the "Spotted Dog", a derisive allusion to the club's emblem of a running leopard. It was once the watering hole for colonial officers and a white man's club, but now its members represent the changing faces of Malaysia and senior government administrators and prosperous businessmen prop up the long bar where the British once sat over their *setengah* (literally half, meaning half a peck of liquor). A.C. Norman was responsible for the building of the Club, and if you look closely, you may find some more Malay architectural styles incorporated into the building's design.

On the third side of the Padang is **St Mary's Church**, built in 1894 also by A.C. Norman. Colonial families once trooped across the Padang on Sundays

The Sultan Abdul Samad Building houses the Supreme Court.

in their Sunday best, to listen to and sing with the magnificent pipe organ built by Henry Willis, a renowned British organ maker during the 19th century.

Minarets of Islam: The Church has somewhat taken a back seat since Malaysia was declared a Muslim state, and behind the Padang, on the tongue of land at the meeting of the Gombak and Klang rivers, lies the serene and elegant **Jame Mosque**. It was designed by A.B. Hubbock, and adapted from a Moghul mosque in North India. Until the opening of the National Mosque after independence, the Jame Mosque was the principal Muslim centre for prayer in the city. Its onion domes and minarets rest on the level of the palm trees in its gardens, and its pink and white walls are especially spectacular at sunrise and sunset. It is accessible from Jalan Tun Perak from which you enter the mosque grounds through the *sahn* or walled courtyard. It is open to visitors, but shoes must be removed before entering and women should be well dressed. At sunset a mirrored glass skyscraper nearby gives a mystical reflection of the mosque, linking old and new Kuala Lumpur together.

There are other buildings in the area around the Padang built in Moorish style, and these buildings have influenced more recent edifices since built with Islamic inspiration. On the same side of the river as the Padang but further down, and connected to the Central Market and business district by a pedestrian bridge is the towering white **Dayabumi Complex**. Fragile Islamic arches raise this 30-floor skyscraper, reputedly the most expensive building in Malaysia, and built entirely from imported materials. It was completed in 1985 and is fully computerised. It houses government offices and is the headquarters for the government-owned Petronas company, which exploits Malaysia's oil reserves.

Below are shops and restaurants and the equally impressive **General Post Office**. On Saturdays there are excursions to the top of the Dayabumi building which start from the fountain be-

The Padang's green expanse fronts the venerable Selangor Club.

tween the Dayabumi and the General Post Office. It is an excellent way to get a bird's eye perspective of Kuala Lumpur and its surroundings, and inspired one artist so much that he painted his version of the view on the wall at the top of the building.

Beyond these modern buildings on Jalan Hashamuddun, lies the KL **Railway Station**. To arrive by rail in Kuala Lumpur is a fantastical experience as turrets, spires, minarets and Arabic arches greet the eye in every direction, although inside, its design is that of many large Victorian railway stations in England. This was so much the case that construction was held up because the roof design did not meet the then British standards which stipulated that the station roof must be able to support one metre of snow! It was completed in 1911 and its platforms have been crowded ever since. Within the railway station there is a post office, a selection of restaurants and a hotel. The wonderfully old-fashioned **Station Hotel** underwent renovation in recent years,

although it still retains an air of faded grandeur. The original lift is still in operation for a leisurely ride upwards, the lobby and restaurant downstairs have lofty ceilings with spinning fans, and the bedrooms are enormous, with large balconies and attached cavernous bathrooms with Victorian bathtubs.

Opposite the station is the **Malaya Railway Administration Building** with the same Moorish design. Along from this giant building is the old Majestic Hotel, which formerly provided lodgings for important colonial officers and their families. It has now been converted into the **National Art Gallery**, which exhibits permanent pieces as well as temporary exhibitions in rooms once the lobby and restaurant of the old hotel.

Just next to the Art Gallery is the **Balai Kuala Lumpur**, a tourist information centre, open from Monday to Friday from 8.30 a.m. to 4.45 p.m., and from 8.30 a.m. to 1 p.m. on Saturdays, closed on Sundays. It has few brochures but the staff are helpful and will be able

to give you directions. Upstairs is the **Sang Kanchil craft shop** which has a selection of handicrafts, carpets, pots and clothes for sale.

Just up the road from this Victorian enclave is the ultra-modern **National Mosque** or *Masjid Negara*. Completed in 1965, the jagged 18-point star roof and the 73-metre-tall minaret catch the eye. The 18 points of the star represent the thirteen states of Malaysia and the five pillars of Islam. This was one of the country's first post-independence constructions and is one of the largest mosques in the region. Its Grand Hall, busiest on Fridays, can accommodate 8,000 worshippers.

On the roof there are 48 smaller domes, their design and number inspired by the great mosque in Mecca. It is an impressive building with cool marbled halls, long galleries and reflecting pools in the courtyard. The minaret rises from the centre of one of these pools. The mosque is set in 13 acres of gardens. One area of these gardens is reserved for the tombs of Malaysia's most celebrated dignitaries, the former Prime Minister and other pioneers of independence already at rest there. The mosque is open from 9 a.m. to 6 p.m. and 2.45 to 6 p.m. on Fridays. Decorous clothing and behaviour is recommended, with shoes removed before entering. Scarves and covering robes are available for women, who should also use a separate entrance.

A garden retreat: Downtown KL is crowded with buildings, both old and new, and you may begin to wonder if there are any green spaces in the city apart from the Padang. A recent upsurge of interest in the greening of KL now allows it to boast 30 public greens, from roundabouts planted with bougainvillea to spacious parks. The best-known and most popular of these are the **Lake Gardens**. Seventy hectares (170 acres) of undulating green with magnificent trees and flowering plants prove that the jungle can be tamed. The park owes its existence to A.R. Venning, a British official who managed to persuade Swettenham in 1888 that the young Kuala Lumpur needed a public park. The largest lake, **Tasek Perdana**, once known as Sydney Lake, has boats for hire by the hour. The gardens are popular with locals and visitors alike and are especially crowded at weekends when in the early morning or evening, joggers puff their way around the humid paths, families sit amongst a lavish picnic, lovers seek more secluded spots, and old Chinese men go through their *tai c' hi* routine. The park is open from 10 a.m. to 6 p.m. (Mondays to Saturdays) and from 8 a.m. to 6 p.m. on Sundays and public holidays.

Within and around the park are several interesting buildings. Seventy-six metres (250 feet) above the lake, stands the gleaming white **Parliament House**, a mixture of modern architecture and traditional motifs. The building consists of an 18-storey tower and a transcepted chamber, housing government offices, committee rooms, a banquet hall, restaurants, bars and a library. In use since 1962, the building is also open to visitors, but respectable attire and previous appointment are necessary.

The National Mosque is the spiritual centre of Kuala Lumpur.

On a smaller hill but in an imposing position stands the **National Monument**, erected to commemorate those who died in the struggle against communist insurgency in the 1950s. The galleries at the base of the statue record the names of all the units who fought including British, Australian, Fijian, Maori and Malay troops. The statue itself may seem surprisingly familiar to some visitors, as it is a model of the famous Iwo Jima memorial in Washington DC. This statue caught the eye of the late Tunku Abdul Rahman, Malaysia's first Prime Minister while on a visit to the United States. Felix de Weldon cast the Malaysian model in bronze in Italy, and the statue now has a purely Malaysian symbolism.

The topmost figure holds the Malaysian flag, symbolising unity and strength, two men on either side of him denote strength and vigilance; a man comforting a wounded comrade on the centre front of the group stands for the suffering and sacrifices made by soldiers of all ranks. The base of the statue

Answering the call to prayer.

is moated by a pool with a cascading fountain and pewter water lilies, pewter being one of Malaysia's prized metals. Access to the monument is by a small bridge over the moat.

Not far away is the **Cenotaph**, erected by the British to commemorate the soldiers who died in World Wars I and II. It originally stood near the railway station.

Also in the gardens is the **Lake Club**, founded by breakaways from the Selangor Club in the early 1900s. Close by is **Carcosa**, the epitome of a colonial bungalow, which was built for the chief administrator of the Federal Malay States in 1896, and was once the residence of the British High Commissioner.

Another interesting edifice is the **Tun Abdul Razak Memorial**, the official residence of the late Tun Abdul Razak, the second Prime Minister of Malaysia. Known locally as Sri Taman, the house is now open to visitors, and houses documents and possessions belonging to Tun Abdul Razak, best remembered for his rural developments and his sense

of social justice.

Scenes of Malaysian life: On the edge of the gardens, sitting on an incline on Jalan Damansara and facing Jalan Travers, is the **National Museum**. The present museum was built on the site of the old Selangor museum, destroyed during World War II. The new museum was opened in 1963, and sports a huge Menangkabau roof, with the front walls covered with Italian mosaic flanking the main entrance. The museum is well worth whiling away a few hours in, especially for its social and cultural sections. These include an extensive section on the *Nonyas* and *Babas*, the unique culture born of a fusion between Chinese and Malay traditions.

There is also a complete reconstruction of a Malay *kampong* (village) and on the other end of the social scale, a courtly scene complete with antique attire and gold and silk adornments. Also represented are Malay pastimes and sports, and there is a detailed history of shadow puppets, with displays from Turkey, India, Indonesia, Thailand and Malaysia. There is good documentation of the *Orang Asli* cultures and societies, and displays on wildlife and natural resources, with a diagrammatic representation of an open-cast mine. Other interesting exhibits include the skull of an elephant which is reputed to have derailed a train! There is also an *amok* catcher, a frightening device once used to catch and render harmless a person who has "run *amok*".

In the basement is an extensive reference library with original manuscripts and charts, accessible to the public with permission from the curator. The museum is open daily from 9 a.m. to 6 p.m., except Fridays, when it is closed between noon and 2.45 p.m.

The **Museum of Asian Arts** is 4 kilometres down the road from the National Museum, in the grounds of the University of Malaysia, itself worth a visit if you are interested in doing research on any aspect of the country. The museum has more than 2,000 representative items on display of Chinese, Japanese, Indian, Persian and South-East

Flower shop in downtown KL.

Asian origin. The museum is open during office hours, on weekdays only.

Tai C'hi on the hill: Still on your tour on wheels, cross the river to Jalan Kinabalu which leads to Jalan Stadium, where Kuala Lumpur's three main stadiums dominate *Changkat Stadium* or **Stadium Hill**. The **National Stadium** (*Stadium Negara*), with its enormous unsupported roof, looks rather like a spaceship from *Close Encounters*.

Chin Woo Stadium, the oldest of the three, has a swimming pool, but the grandest of all is the **Stadium Merdeka** (Independence Stadium), a huge arena with a capacity for 50,000 spectators, and built in time to mark the nation's independence in 1957. The formal handing over of power from the Queen's representative to the nation's first Prime Minister took place here in the presence of the nine rulers of the peninsular Malay States.

Today the stadium continues to function as the venue for national occasions, ranging from annual international Koran-reading competitions, to military

tattoos and football cup finals. Soccer enthusiasts take the opportunity to watch a football match by floodlight, for, sensibly enough, Malaysians like to play after the sun has set.

In the early morning, on Changkat Stadium, you can catch sight of many exponents of *Tai C'hi*, a graceful and dignified Chinese martial art. Most of the performers are elderly citizens, oblivious to the sound of the city starting up the morning rush to the office. They come here almost, if not every day to gain their daily exercise and to enjoy a sense of peace.

Prisons, palaces and temples: On Jalan Pudu is the **Pudu Prison**, which has its name in the Guinness Book of Records for having the longest wall painting done by one man. This man was a prisoner who every day from 8 a.m. till 6 p.m. painted a mural on the outer walls of the prison; the murals show rural and jungle scenes, perhaps the environment the prisoners were dreaming of inside! After completing two walls, the painter stopped as he had finished his sentence,

Early morning mist shrouds the track at the KL Turf Club.

and was now free to view those scenes for himself.

Also in this part of southern Kuala Lumpur is the **National Palace**, official residence of the king. The palace began life as the town house of a wealthy Chinese *towkay* and in 1926 it was sold and converted into a palace for the sultans of Selangor. Its design with its white walls and large balconies is colonial, but on the roof a golden dome surrounded by a crown proclaim otherwise. Yellow is the colour for royalty, and only kings may walk on the welcoming yellow carpet while politicians and visiting dignitaries tread on red. Royal garden parties, investitures and receptions are held here, but normally the king lives in his own palace, every sultan having his own "mini" palace in the capital. The present King is the Sultan of Perak who succeeded to the throne in early 1989. Each sultan is given "a turn" as King, for a five-year period, and election is by rotation and consensus.

Beyond the National Palace and further south along Jalan Lepangan Terbang is a small road which climbs a steep hill (Jalan Kerayong). You will find yourself near the Chinese cemeteries, and with a commanding view over the city. On this hill stands the largest and newest Buddhist temple in KL, which was completed in 1985. It was built by several Chinese multi-millionaires who it is said each donated one pillar of the temple – count the pillars! Although it is known that the cost of building the temple was phenomenal, the exact figure remains a firm secret. This is the **Yuen Tung Tze Temple**, and the building is a complete community centre, with a large conference hall on the ground floor for clan meetings and weddings, a restaurant in the basement, youth and women's clubs and offices on the first floor and the temple itself with its many large and small roofs, right at the top. There is even a small garden in the temple, which is perfect viewed from any angle. The building is an incongruous mixture, gaudy yet impressive, mystical, yet also **Busy night market in Chinatown's Jalan Petaling.**

decidedly worldly.

Miners' mansions: There is another road which is also well worth visiting, although it is suggested that you continue on four wheels, as it is a very long road. This is **Jalan Ampang**, the road which once led to fortunes, as at the end of it were the rich tin mines of Ampang, some 10 kilometres (6 miles) away.

The tin empire gave mine-owners the money to build lavish mansions, and these were generally built along Jalan Ampang itself. They were all large and flamboyant, and served as signs of how well the owner was doing in the mines. Many have since fallen into disrepair and have been pulled down, making space for the modern version of the mansion: the skyscraper and office block. Some remain, quietly being taken over by the jungle that was once a well-kept garden; yet others have been preserved and give a glimpse back into the tin boom days when elegant ladies and gentlemen peopled the rooms, danced on the verandahs and walked in the gardens. The mansion **Chan Chin Mooi** is one of these, although it is a private house.

A house you may enter to get the feeling of the old grandeur of Jalan Ampang is **Bok House**. The house now holds a fine restaurant, **Le Coq d'Or**, in which you can sit and let your imagination wander back through the decades. The house remains as it was originally, with porticoed verandahs, Italian marble and 18th-century paintings. As well as an interesting present, the house also has a fascinating past.

Chua Cheng Bok was a poor boy who lived in Kuala Lumpur in the last century. He ran a bicycle repair shop, and was desperately in love with the daughter of a wealthy mine owner whose house stood proudly on Jalan Ampang. The mine-owner forbade the couple to marry, and so Chua put all his energies into his work, bitterly disappointed and longing for revenge on the proud man. From a bicycle repair shop to a garage to tin-mine holdings, Chua's fortune grew, until at last he was able to build his own mansion right next door to his

The art-deco style Central Market was once a vegetable market.

enemy's, overshadowing it in size and grandeur. Bok's house still stands, while the arrogant tin miner's has long since disappeared – a fitting end! In his will Chua decreed that Bok House should never be sold nor its design or decor changed; thanks to him, we can still imagine the days of fine living and feel ourselves within Chua's story.

Further up the road is the **Dewan Tunku Abdul Rahman Mansion**, which once belonged to the Eu Tong Seng family. After independence it served as a temporary parliament, then became the National Art Gallery, but now houses the Welfare department. Many of the other mansions still standing now house embassies and consulates, so that Jalan Ampang has come to be known locally as *Ambassadors' Row*. Also along Jalan Ampang is the **Selangor Turf Club** and the **Khoon Yam Buddhist Temple**, the oldest Chinese temple in KL, although extensive renovations have been made to the original. At the junction with Circular Road (Jalan Pekeleling) are several

shopping centres and the new **Ampang Park** with a boating lake and cloud-flecked mountains as a backdrop to your trip on the lake.

KL's Chinatown: Having travelled around the city by tour bus, taxi or car in order to get a general impression of the city, it is time to start walking. On foot (or by trishaw) is still the best means of discovering the heart of the old city. There is much to be missed by driving, as the old shophouse interiors conceal many fascinating sights.

Chinatown lies within the boundaries of Jalan Sultan, Jalan Bandar (now known as Jalan Tun HS Lee, once the old High Street) and along Jalan Petaling. For the inveterate shopper and connoisseur of exotic oddities, Chinatown is a paradise. Chinese apothecaries display their herbs and medicines in porcelain pots, or beneath glass counters, mixed with more familiar western brands. There are jewellers and goldsmiths, casket and basket makers, dry goods shops, petshops, optical houses, coffin makers, frame makers and haber-

Sikh fortune teller awaits a customer.

dashers. Along the "five-foot-ways", there are shoe repairers, fortune tellers, Chinese sign painters, leather workers and Indian flower sellers. Look out for a small crowd gathered in one spot and you may find a medicine man trying to sell his wares, or a snake charmer coaxing onlookers to part with their dollars.

Jalan Petaling changes its appearance constantly, depending on which time of the day you find yourself there. In the early morning, Chinese housewives visit the market stalls for fresh produce, and Chinese bakeries emit delicious aromas of traditional dumplings and sweet breads filled with red bean paste and chicken curry. As the city wakes up, traffic pours down the street, flashy Mercedes fighting for space between bicycles and trishaws.

To get away from the crowds, move into the cooler interior of the **Chan See Shu Yuen Clanhouse and Temple**, built in 1906. Inside are elaborate ceramic glazed tiles and ornamentation, and intricate wall paintings; amongst these you may find a small cat chasing a butterfly. Outside, the business of the day is under way. Shops selling pots, shoes (made to order), coffins, wedding clothes, spectacles, tinware, jewellery and medicines open up their shutters. A temple shop makes and sells paper models of servants, mansions, limousines, wads of money, all to be burnt and sent to the departed for their success in the future life.

Yoke Woo Thin is a busy Chinese restaurant further down the street, that sells delicious *dim sum* from 6 a.m. Or there is the **Seng Kee restaurant**, reputedly the oldest in Chinatown, which makes its own mooncakes for the autumnal Moon Festival. There are Chinese medicinal drinks stalls, where you can sit and sample drinks to cure all ailments. Here too, there is a shop which makes flags to order.

At 5 p.m., every evening, the mood of Jalan Petaling changes again, as many of the shops replace their shutters. A section of the street is closed to traffic to make way for a night market, which is erected with lightning speed. Here you can find all the "genuine" copies of

brand name watches and tee-shirts. Swarthy Nepalese display an exotic selection of jewellery, gems, silverware and fabrics, "fresh" from Nepal. Antiques and toys, household goods and incense sticks jostle together in this animated scene. It is said that it is still possible to barter here – try your luck! Exotic meats such as crocodile, cat and dog are for sale, or sit down for a Chinese seafood meal or a beer at one of the tables that spill out from restaurants onto the street. Music is supplied by a nearby Cantonese cassette stall.

Jalan Bandar, now re-named Jalan Tun HS Lee, and once KL's High Street, also holds treasures. At one end sits the old **Victorian Institution**, built in 1893, in an incongruous English cottage style, which has now become a drama hall. More shophouses, selling clocks old and new, cane goods, crockery and spectacles, line the street. Many have been restored in an effort to preserve some of the old KL from the onslaught of the new.

On Jalan Bandar is the **Kwoong Siew**

The wildly elaborate Sri MahamariammamTemple.

Association Temple, and, quite suddenly in this very Chinese quarter, you catch sight of the **Sri Mahamariamman Hindu Temple**, its towering gate an explosion of colourful gods entangled in an arresting design. It was built in 1873, and occupies an important place in Hindu religious life, as it is from here that the *Thaipusam* pilgrimage to the Batu Caves, just outside the centre of KL, begins. Outside, women and children sell strings of fragrant jasmine, and a man in a *dhoti* keeps a shoe stall for those wishing to enter the temple courtyard. Devotees emerge from prayer, their foreheads smeared with sacred white ash.

In **Jalan Sultan**, look for the pet shops, alive with singing birds in cages. Lap dogs, kittens, rabbits, guinea pigs are to be found inside too, as well as more unusual pets such as monkeys, mongeese and snakes, and watch out for the large turtle making its way across the shop floor! Not all these animals will end up as pets – some are destined to furbish a lavish wedding table or a showy business banquet.

At the end of Central Market is the business centre. This juxtaposition of the old and the new creates interesting alleyways. There is a shophouse complete with a tree growing out of its walls on one side, small food stalls in the middle and the stark wall of a high rise building on the other. The **Central Market** stands where the original one, according to Swettenham "a very insecure shed", once housed market sellers from out of town displaying fruit and vegetables, as well as household products and handicrafts. The present building, completed in 1936, which also began life as a produce market, was recently spruced up, its art-deco features and high ceilings renovated, repainted in pastel pinks and baby blues, and has now become a **Handicraft Centre**. Inside, there is a good selection of handicrafts at fairly reasonable prices, though bargaining is still advisable. Besides housing various shops, stalls and restaurants, the Central Market also has a programme of live shows.

Left, modern batik painting. **Right**, cultural show.

Pick up a brochure here or at the tourist office, and you may be lucky enough to catch a music, dance or shadow puppet performance.

A short alley opposite the Central Market in Jalan Hang Kasturi leads to the oldest temple in Kuala Lumpur, the **Temple of Szu Yeh** (Hsien Szu Yeh Miao). Ducking your head so as not to bang into the low-hanging awning poles, walk past the alley's food stalls to arrive at the temple gate. The temple itself is rather small and dark, its ceiling blackened by a century of incense smoke curling up from the altars below. Fine examples of wood carvings illustrate scenes from the Buddhist canon. A framed photograph of Yap Ah Loy sits on a side altar, looking more like a kindly saint than the tough and exacting leader he really was.

Temples were among the first permanent buildings on which successful Chinese pioneers lavished their wealth. When Kuala Lumpur was being rebuilt in the 1880s, much money was spent on such buildings. Built in 1884 by Yap,

Puppets depict figures from Malaysian folklore.

the **Temple of Sen Ta** became the centre of a major Chinese cult which was to last for years. The cult of Sen Ta and those of many other Chinese deities were marked by processions through the town every year, on some occasions with great wealth and splendour.

Saris, batik and steaks: Besides Chinatown, there are several other districts in which it is pleasant to stroll and enjoy the sights. Northwards from the Padang lies another area of interesting shops. The main road here is **Jalan Tuanku Abdul Rahman**, named after the country's first Prime Minister following independence. To the locals this road is often referred to as **Batu Road**. The street leads off the Padang and all along it lie the shops, both old and new; modern department stores and smaller shops, cheap hotels and many "*kedai makan*", or eating shops, some of which are very good and their food should be sampled.

The Coliseum Cinema, built in the 1920s, and one of KL's first, lies halfway down this road, and the next-door

Coliseum Cafe and Hotel is the most famous bar and restaurant in town for its past history. The Coliseum has been serving customers for more than 60 years, and behind its plain facade, it is reputed that the town's best steaks at the most reasonable prices are offered. For decades, it was the favourite watering-hole for planters, miners, government officials and soldiers, and today, its bar is still patronised by a medley of their modern-day counterparts. The decor has not changed much either, and the Chinese waiters' service is of a bygone colonial era.

For six days a week Batu Road is crowded with traffic, but every Saturday night it becomes a pedestrian mall. In place of the taxis, minibuses, cars and motorbikes are stalls offering sometimes for half the price (and certainly more cheaply) goods to be had from Batu Road's shops by day.

Off Batu Road where the Padang ends, is **Jalan Melayu**, which was the site of one of the original *kampong* lying on the outskirts of the city, now closely embedded in it. This area is principally interesting for its Indian shops selling silks, saris and handmade jewellery. After 6 every evening, portable kitchens with tables and chairs take over the street, offering food which is as spicy as you like it.

Eating *al fresco* is definitely more enjoyable than dining in a large restaurant, where often the icy air-conditioning forces you to don winter clothes. Food stalls set up under the stars are common all over the city, but the most famous are the ones here along the riverbank. Mutton and chicken soup are specialities. Noodles (*mee*) can be fried (*goreng*) to become *mee goreng*, or boiled (*rebus*) to become *mee rebus*. *Satay* (spicy meat grilled on skewers) is also served along with sugarcane juice (*tebu*) or lychee juice. Other mouth-watering treats include steamed cockles and a concoction of beans and peanuts in coloured ice (*ice kacang*).

Beyond Jalan Melayu is **Jalan Masjid India**, whose mosque sits on the spot where one of the town's first

Satay is a delicious staple of the Malaysian diet.

mosques used to be. The road leads to what was formerly the red-light district, but which now boasts shops, restaurants, business premises and moderately-priced hotels.

Where Batu Road crosses Jalan Dang Wangi, the street broadens and leads to **Chow Kit**, an area filled with cheap hotels catering to those with modest means. Here many "ladies of easy virtue" seek their livelihood. At night, this is the place for one of the most colourful and lively of all night markets, and is said to be the cheapest. Stalls by the roadside serve Malaysian delicacies; the pungent smell of durian in season pervades the air. Above the roar of the traffic the night air is rent with the raucous sound of pop music. This is Kuala Lumpur's low life.

In the heart of all this activity stands the **Chow Kit Market** which is reputedly the best and cheapest food market in town. Struggle through the Sunday morning shopping brigade to witness how Malaysian housewives choose their household goods, and to capture the aroma and atmosphere of Malaysian marketing.

On the right off Batu Road on the way to Chow Kit, **Wisma Loke** poses as another reminder of KL's past. Cheow Ah Yeok, a crony of Yap Ah Loy and a Chinese mine owner who made his fortune, built this charming Chinese town house with classical Greco-Roman arches and pillars, balustrades of glazed jade-coloured porcelain from China, Malaccan tiles and a "moongate" within. After Cheow's death, the house was bought by Loke Yew, who had landed penniless in Singapore at the age of 13 and went on to become one of the most colourful of Malaysia's millionaires. The first house in Kuala Lumpur to be lit by electricity, the mansion became the showpiece of the community. It is now open to the public and there is a small antique shop inside.

The other end of Chow Kit has now been renamed **Jalan Putra**, and has become an important national centre, with several attractive modern buildings. The **Putra World Trade Centre** with its 40-odd storeys was built at an infamous cost, and now houses government offices, as well as the head office for the **Tourist Development Corporation** (TDC) on the 24th to 27th floors.

Nestled in its shadow is the **Putra Concert Hall** and conference complex. The concert hall on the outside looks like an outsized traditional ceremonial hall with its Menangkabau roof. Next door is the **Pan Pacific Hotel** with its elevators riding on the outside of the building, affording an interesting view of Chow Kit, Jalan Raja Laut and the city beyond. This set of buildings itself can be seen from many other points of the city including the ring-road which brushes close to its front steps.

Across the road is **The Mall Shopping Centre**, recently opened and at present the most fashionable place to be seen shopping in. Here are modern shops with Western goods and brand names. But if this kind of shopping does not interest you, perhaps the more traditional **Kampong Bahru**, with its exclusively Malay shops and stalls will.

Saturday's Sunday Market: In 1889, 90

Local pottery bears native-style motifs.

hectares (220 acres) of land were set aside at the request of the Sultan of Selangor for a Malay agricultural settlement to meet the needs of Malays in that area. This marked the origin of Kampong Bahru (literally the new village), a large Malay enclave set back behind Chow Kit. To enter the "village" is to leave the sounds and smells of a bustling city for a rural world of quiet grass-lined roads and dignified wooden Malay homes shaded by fruit trees. Although this image is perceptibly eroding as the more affluent brick structures replace their wooden counterparts, the feeling of no longer being in a big city remains.

Sheltered under the blocks of flats found here, the *Pasar Minggu* (**Sunday Market**) springs to life, not on a Sunday, as you might think, but on a Saturday night, lasting into the early hours of Sunday morning. It is well worth a visit for an exclusively Malay market. The *songkok* (fez or cap), prayer books, hand-printed batik, and all kinds of handicrafts are on sale at the various

stalls. Ashtrays, vases, jewellery boxes, flowerpots made from shells, traditional earthware pots (*labu*), Kelantan silverware and the richly embroidered *sarong* of Terengganu are common merchandise here. All around are *sarong*-clad men, wearing their white skull caps, token of their having performed their pilgrimage to Mecca.

The ever-present *satay* and other choice dishes of the Malay kitchens are sold at many of the stalls found here, or for those who prefer greater comfort, in most of the air-conditioned restaurants. Right in the centre of all this is a permanent stage on which Malay pop songs are crooned.

KL's Golden Triangle: About 1½ kilometres away from Batu Road is an area which has become KL's Golden Triangle, a district of expensive shops, high-class restaurants, international class hotels and a sophisticated nightlife. Along **Jalan Bukit Bintang**, are the large shopping centres, **Sungei Wang Plaza**, **Bukit Bintang Plaza** and **Imbi Plaza**. Bukit Bintang Plaza, linked to Sungei Wang Plaza, is well-known for its consumer fairs and exhibitions. A fourth plaza, **Kuala Lumpur Plaza**, is famed for its electrical showroom, the largest in town. Imbi Plaza houses the couture shops of designers Cartier, Givenchy among other glamorous names.

Northeast of Kuala Lumpur Plaza, along **Jalan Raja Chulan**, is the handicraft village of **Karyaneka**. The country's 13 states are represented by 13 identical *kampong* houses in which are to be found exhibits of each state's famed artistry. Handwoven textiles, woodwork, batik, basketwork, silver and pewter goods, shellwork and pottery are on display, and there are demonstrations of cloth-weaving, batik printing and silver and copper tooling. There is also a large showroom, where some of the handicrafts exhibited are on sale, but unfortunately some of the finest and most unusual handicrafts are not for sale. A list of shopping possibilities in Kuala Lumpur is given in the Tourist Information section at the back of the book.

The Mall – a popular KL hangout.

125

SIDE TRIPS FROM KUALA LUMPUR

Some of the first trips you might make out of the capital city may involve visits to factories situated on the outskirts of KL. To the northeast on Jalan Pahang is the **Selangor Pewter Factory**, where Malaysia's famous pewter products are made and are for sale. On the road to Ipoh, near the Batu Caves is a **Batik factory**, where demonstrations are held; other tours take you to rubber plantations and tin mines. Inquire at your hotel for tour details.

One of the first things you'll notice on leaving the capital are the *pintu gerbang* or ceremonial arches which bridge the road and announce that you have left the Federal Territory and have now entered the state of **Selangor**. Even more of these arches are erected to celebrate National Day. The grandest permanent arch, with its pleasing cream and blue colour and Moorish architecture, is on the Federal Highway that sweeps south of Kuala Lumpur to the Subang International Airport and then leads down into the Klang Valley. Engraved in bold wording on the arch is the inscription "Kota Darul Ehsan" or "The Bastion of Selangor". Darul Ehsan means the Land of Goodwill in Arabic.

Petaling Jaya, KL's satellite town, takes its position immediately beyond this arch. It has grown in the last 40 years from a squatters' settlement into a self-contained urban centre, whose tree-lined avenues now house a quarter of a million people.

With the **University of Malaya** on the road to the town, Petaling Jaya, or PJ, as it is known locally, is the home for many of the higher salaried Kuala Lumpurans and for much of the expatriate community. To accommodate their leisure and pleasure needs, an active nightlife and a busy shopping area has been developed, and for visitors, large five-star international hotels await. The town boasts several popular parks and a lake garden, as well as good sports facilities. Dominating the scene in PJ is the Petaling Jaya Municipal Council

Building, the Menara MPPJ, its 27 storeys surveying the growing city. This affluence has spread to Subang where a shopping centre, Subang Parade, attracts shoppers from PJ and KL alike.

Historical Klang Valley: The Federal Highway, also Malaysia's oldest motorway, picks up its course from Petaling Jaya and cleaves its way through the **Klang Valley**, ending at the town of Klang. Coming this way visitors will pass the **Subang International Airport** on the right, the new township of Subang Jaya on the left, Batu Tiga with its circuit for car and motorbike racing fans, and the new state capital of **Shah Alam**. The capital of Selangor warrants a stopover; much construction is in progress to bring the town up to the standard of being a state capital, and the Sultan of Selangor knows best how to do this in a lavish way.

The Sultan himself resides in the **Istana Bukit Kayangan**, which contests for attention with the **Selangor State Memorial** nearby. On a hill overlooking the city, a huge building project is

Left, cavernous interior of the Batu Caves. Right, Selangor pewter makes a perfect gift.

underway, and when completed a museum, cultural centre, theatre and library will look out onto the city and its man-made lakes. These lakes are part of the **Lake Gardens** which green the city, and offer boating facilities, as well as a floating stage and restaurant. The Institut Teknologi MARA is an active centre of academia situated here.

But perhaps the most eye-catching building of all is the State Mosque, the **Masjid Sultan Salahuddin Abdul Aziz Shah**. It has some of the largest domes and some of the tallest minarets in the world, and it is certainly spectacular to view from any angle. Set in a 15-hectare (35-acre) garden, the dominant colours of the mosque are silver and blue, echoed in the giant enamel dome. It is certain that the Sultan has destined this city for great things.

Klang conceals a long, colourful and violent past. Placed in its commanding position on the river, it was soon obvious that whoever possessed the town controlled the tin trade. It became a centre of fighting during the Selangor Civil War of the 1870s. One of the protagonists, Raja Mahdi, built his fort on the hill where the municipal offices now stand. Raja Mahdi's fort overlooked the stronghold of his chief rival Raja Abdullah, whose warehouse, **Gedong Raja Abdullah** was built in 1857. It is a fine example of traditional Malay workmanship and has now been converted into a museum bringing Klang's exciting past to life. Klang is the royal capital of Selangor and is also famous for its *bak kut teh* or pork rib soup.

The road from Klang runs for another 8 kilometres (5 miles) before arriving at **Port Klang**, once Port Swettenham. Motorists do not usually stop here but if they do, it is to eat at the seafood restaurants by the quayside. Port Klang is the major seaport for Kuala Lumpur. It is also used very often as a springboard for visits to the islands in the estuary of the Klang River. A *sampan* (boat) ride to **Pulau Ketam** (Crab Island) takes only two hours. The largest island is **Carey Island**, famous for its *Orang Asli* community. The *Mah-Meri* peoples are

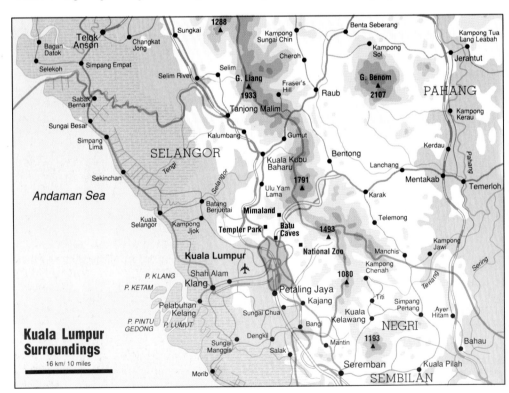

well-known for their beautiful wood carvings inspired by mystical dreams. Visits to their communities must first be arranged with the *Orang Asli* office in Shah Alam.

Morib Beach is situated south of Port Klang. It is not one of Malaysia's most beautiful beaches, but is a popular getaway for locals at weekends. Just before Morib, a side road winds its ways to **Jugra**. On the hill overlooking the village and the estuary are the graves of Selangor royalty and noblemen; the ruins of some old government buildings can be seen below. Nearby, standing alone in the padi fields are the abandoned palace built by a Selangor sultan in the 1800s and an equally elaborate mosque where the sultan used to pray.

Hilly landscapes: Geography gives **Kuala Selangor** setting, history gives it a sense of mystery. The town is 45 kilometres (30 miles) away from Klang on the coast road due north. Two small hills dominate its landscape: the main **Bukit Melawati** is the site of **Fort Altingberg**, where Selangor's first Bugis

rulers made their base in the 18th century. The fort's cannon still points out to sea, an impotent warning to traders and seafarers. A lighthouse and a wooden rest house are also to be found on this hill. There are said to be seven wells located here and also the **Batu Hampar**, once an execution block for traitors. A mausoleum of past Bugis sultans lies nearby. For company in this deserted place is the silver leaf monkey, now a protected species.

At the bottom of the hill is **Taman Alam**, a bird sanctuary where several of Malaysia's rare birds can be sighted. Close to this is a mangrove sanctuary. The second hill, **Bukit Tanjung**, is only about 2 kilometres (1½ miles) away and its peak holds a smaller fort.

There are several interesting villages around Kuala Selangor, mostly Chinese fishing villages where saltfish and fishballs are prepared. It is possible to take an evening river trip from the town to witness a spectacular sight around the village of **Kuala Kuantan**. Along the riverbank here, hundreds of *klip-klap* (fireflies) alight on the branches of the overhanging trees, looking something like multi-coloured Christmas decorations. During the day coconut processing can be observed in this village.

The neighbouring **Kampong Permatang** is famous as the establishment of the first Bugis ruler of Selangor, Rajah Lumu, in 1756. A local storyteller can recite for you the complete genealogical descent of the line of the sultanate since that date. Bugis-style kampong houses are also to be seen here.

For the return trip to Kuala Lumpur, visitors who like to travel along narrow twisting lanes can take the route which goes to Batang Berjuntai and Rawang. A kilometre or two from Batang Berjuntai you will see on the left-hand side through the surrounding trees a large wooden bungalow with a sweeping *attap* roof, a typical planter's home at the beginning of the century. It belongs to the SOCFIN who were the pioneers of oil palm cultivation in Malaysia. The house is also associated with one of their pioneer planters, Henri Fauconnier, whose book *The Soul of Malaya* is a classic on the country. The road between the two towns becomes remote as it snakes its way around the contours of the thickly jungled hills.

At Rawang the side road from Kuala Selangor joins the main trunk road which links Kuala Lumpur with the northern states of Perak and Kedah. Just off the new north-south highway can be found the **Hutan Lipur Kanching Nature Park**. There is a waterfall here with seven levels, and trekking in the forest to see the insects, butterflies and birds can be done on a tour from Kuala Lumpur or on your own by car.

Much of the land around Kuala Lumpur, particularly in the south, is scarred by the mining of tin, which gave the state its initial fortune. A few kilometres from Sungai Besi just south of KL, a little platform by the roadside provides a vantage point for looking out over what is claimed to be the largest opencast tin mine in the world. The Hong Fatt mine has been producing tin since the 19th century, and obviously its resources are still not exhausted.

Evidence of exhausted tin mines are found in the Ampang and Gombak districts to the northeast of Kuala Lumpur. Here also are several points of touristic interest. In **Gombak** itself is the Gombak Traditional House. Although occupied, it is possible to arrange a visit to this bungalow of traditional Sumatran architectural inspiration, which was built by an expert brought over from the birthplace of Menangkabau culture.

Also in Gombak is the *Orang Asli* **Museum** which is well worth a visit. **Taman Rimba Ampang** lies on the banks of the Ampang River, where rest huts, camping grounds and picnic areas have been provided for jungle enthusiasts wishing to explore the surrounding forests. Another pleasant recreational forest lies around the **Semenyih Dam**, where there are several waterfalls.

Tamed jungles: Twenty-two kilometres (15 miles) north of Kuala Lumpur just off the Ipoh road is the **Templer Park**. It was founded by the once British High Commissioner Sir Gerald Templer, a man very fond of the great Malaysian outdoors. A 1,200-hectare

(3000-acre) tract of jungle was set aside, offering jungle paths, natural swimming lagoons and waterfalls. To the north of the park are the dramatic limestone formations, **Bukit Takun** and **Anak Takun**, the latter with some interesting caves to explore.

The pride of the Malaysian forest is seen in more orderly surroundings in the green captivity of the **National Zoo**, 13 kilometres (8 miles) from the centre of KL on the Ulu Kelang road. Living in its attractive 20-hectare (55-acre) grounds is a good cross-section of Malaysia's wildlife. Plumed birds, pythons, wild buffalo (*seladang*), tapir, crocodiles and of course, tigers are on view in concrete enclosures or fenced pastures only paces away from the jungle where the creatures belong.

To the delight of young visitors, camel and elephant rides are available and boats can be arranged for a "voyage" on the lake. The nearby **Aquarium** displays more than 80 different species of freshwater fish, including the deadly and carnivorous *piranha*, which is not,

Worshippers flock to Batu Caves for the Thaipusam Festival.

however, a Malaysian fish. A reptile park has also been opened here. The Zoo and Aquarium are open from 9 a.m. to 6 p.m. every day.

For those interested in studying Malaysian flora and fauna, the **Forest Research Institute Park** is located at **Kepong**, covering an area of 600 hectares (1500 acres) of natural forest, experimental plantations and arboreta. FRIM also has a herbarium, a museum and a library on forestry. Laboratories studying chemicals, insects and timber may be visited, and there are camping gounds for those wishing to stay overnight, but you must bring your own equipment and food.

A limestone cathedral: Closer to Kuala Lumpur, only 11 kilometres (7 miles) away, on the road to Templer Park, a bold limestone outcrop lies across the scarred landscape of old tin mines. Within are the famous **Batu Caves**.

During the Japanese Occupation, only about 45 years ago, the Batu Caves were still sufficiently remote to serve as an anti-Japanese communist guerilla hideout. For centuries it was obscured by the jungle, and known only to forest inhabitants who lived nearby. Then in 1878, William Hornaday, an American naturalist was on a hunting expedition with British Commissioner of the Selangor Police, H.C. Syers, when he smelt the pungent odour of bat *guano*. His Malay guides led him to the caves. The existence of the caves was soon public knowledge, and they became a popular destination for a picnic (travelling by elephant) for the town *tuans* and their *mems*.

Years later, the local Hindu population, with their predilection for sacred caves, began making pilgrimages there to celebrate the *Thaipusam* festival. Worshippers had to scale the steep jagged cliffs to the Hindu shrine in the topmost grotto. As a sign of repentance for past sins, and to demonstrate their vows of reformation, devotees often carried *kavadi*, burdens, from a simple milk jug carried on the head to the wooden frames decorated with flowers and fruit and supported by long thin spikes pinned into the carrier's body. Today, the way to the top is paved with 272 concrete steps and is surrounded by hanging ferns and tropical flowers. The sight is never so spectacular as at the time of *Thaipusam*.

Apart from the main cave (known as the **Cathedral Cave**), there are about 20 known caves, only some of which are open to the public as there is a danger of collapse and falling rocks. Most interesting are those situated along the south face, which bear such names as Hermit's Hole, Priest's Hole, Fairy Grotto and Quarry Cave. But the main Cathedral Cave is definitely the most breathtaking. Under a huge vault pierced by stalactites that point downwards for 6 metres (20 feet), spreads an empty hollow. Eerie shafts of light streak down from gaps in the ceiling high above.

Nearby are the **Dark Caves**, now closed to the public, as limestone quarrying has made them unsafe for regular visits. However, the Malaya Nature Society conducts tours here (contact their head office in KL) of varying degrees of adventurousness. Bats,

Pain is transcended by Hindus fulfilling their vows to the son of Siva.

white cave racer snakes, scorpions and monkeys can be seen here. The Society also conducts some rock climbing expeditions. These caves have an elevator which runs parallel to the main steps, but which is temporarily closed. A small cave at the base of the outcrop houses a small museum, displaying figures of some of the Hindu gods. Amongst the sprawling tourist shops down below, good Indian vegetarian food can be obtained.

A left turn about 18 kilometres (11 miles) on the old highway from Kuala Lumpur to Pahang leads up to **Mimaland**, a man-made playground fashioned in an elevated hollow enclosed by jungle hills. Recreational facilities include fishing and boating, swimming and jungle trekking. There is also a natural swimming pool, a children's amusement centre with its own model dinosaurs, a small zoo and even a mini rubber plantation. Accommodation is available in the form of chalets, a motel by the lake and native-style *bagan* raised on stilts. The park is best visited during the week, as it can get very crowded at weekends.

Wooing Lady Luck in luxury: From a distance, **Genting Highlands**, shrouded in mists which blanket the dense jungle foliage covering the undulating hills high above Kuala Lumpur, stands aloof – here is a mystical palace of pleasure perched on top of the Barisan Titiwangsa mountain range that runs down the centre of the peninsula.

This all-modern and civilised hill station houses Malaysia's only **casino**, where Western gambling games are played amongst traditional Chinese games of luck such as *keno* or *tai sai*. Ties, which can be rented, are compulsory, or you can opt for traditional Malaysian dress. A sign over the door of the casino is a warning from the sultans of Selangor and Pahang that Muslims are forbidden to enter and try their luck here. At weekends, gambling continues around the clock but during the week the casino closes its doors between 4 a.m. and 10 a.m. Incongruously set in a lush countryside, Genting has three

Land being prepared for a palm oil estate.

modern hotels, one housing the casino, one without a casino but with similiar room prices, and one for visitors who want to save their money for the gambling tables. Outside there is also an artificial lake, a mini railway for children, a golf course and other organised games. Save your walking for the other hill stations.

A more tranquil setting: **Fraser's Hill**, at 1,500 metres (5000 feet) high, was initially created by the British as a cool retreat in the mountains. The resort takes its name from Louis James Fraser, an elusive English adventurer, who had long disappeared when the hill station was built in 1910. Stories circulated that he held a gambling and opium den here, but not much else is known of him. Fraser's Hill is a relaxing retreat for business executives seeking respite from the big city.

Scattered over seven hills that make up the resort, a series of English greystone bungalows were built, with neat English gardens blooming with roses and hollyhocks. To these have been added more modern facilities, including a 109-room hotel which unfortunately fails to blend with the landscape. More economical and old-fashioned accommodation is offered in the form of bungalows and a youth hostel. Fraser's Hill is for those who like to relax in the countryside, walk jungle paths or swim in the pool of the **Jerlau Waterfall**. For recreation there is a 9-hole golf course, tennis courts, playgrounds and pony rides.

Unfortunately, for those without private transport, Fraser's Hill is rather difficult to reach. It is a one-hour bus journey from Kuala Lumpur (100 kilometres [62 miles] to the south) to Kuala Kubu Bahru, from where you have to board a second bus which takes another one and a half hours to get to the top. The last 8 kilometres (5 miles) is up a narrow road on which a one-way traffic system operates. It was along the winding road from Kuala Kubu Bahru that Sir Henry Gurney, the once British High Commissioner, was ambushed and killed by communist guerillas in 1951.

High rollers at the Genting Highlands Resort.

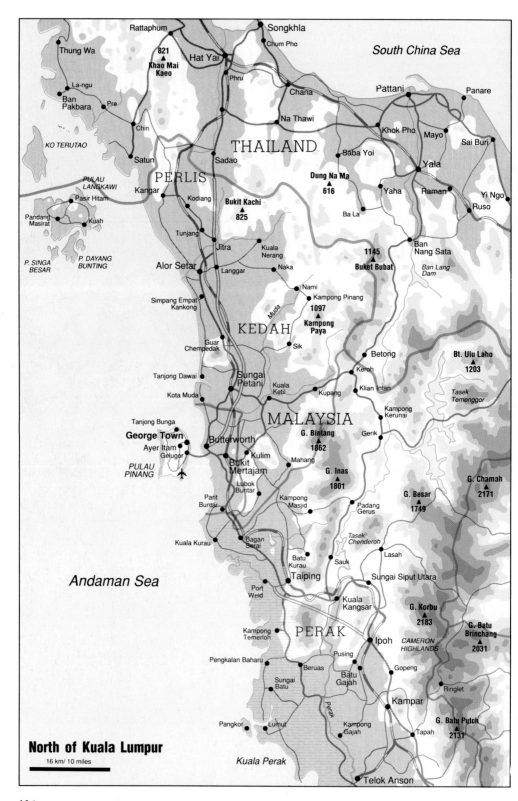

Thung Wa

La-ngu

Ban Pakbara

Pre

Chin

KO TERUTAO

Satun

PULAU LANGKAWI

Pasir Hitam

Pandang Masirat

Kuah

P. SINGA BESAR

P. DAYANG BUNTING

Rattaphum

821 ▲
Khao Mai Kaeo

Hat Yai

Phru

Songkhla

Chum Pho

Chana

Na Thawi

South China Sea

Pattani

Panare

Khok Pho

Mayo

Sai Buri

THAILAND

Saba Yoi

Yala

PERLIS

Sadao

Kangar

Kodiang

Bukit Kachi ▲
825

Dung Na Ma
616 ▲

Yaha

Raman

Yi Ngo

Ruso

Tunjang

Ba La

Ban Nang Sata

Jitra

Kuala Nerang

Naka

1145 ▲
Buket Bubat

Ban Lang Dam

Alor Setar

Langgar

Nami

Kampong Pinang

Simpang Empat Kankong

Muda

1097 ▲
Kampong Paya

KEDAH

Guar Chempedak

Sik

Betong

Bt. Ulu Laho ▲
1203

Tanjong Dawai

Kota Muda

Sungai Petani

Kuala Ketil

Keroh

Klian Intan

Tasek Temenggor

Kupang

Kampong Kerunai

Tanjong Bunga

George Town

Ayer Itam

Gelugor

PULAU PINANG

Butterworth

Kulim

Bukit Mertajam

Mahang

MALAYSIA

G. Bintang ▲
1862

Gerik

G. Inas ▲
1801

G. Chamah ▲
2171

Parit Buntar

Lubok Buntar

Kampong Masjid

Padang Gerus

G. Besar ▲
1749

Kuala Kurau

Bagan Serai

Tasek Chenderoh

Lasah

Andaman Sea

Batu Kurau

Sauk

Taiping

Sungai Siput Utara

G. Korbu ▲
2183

G. Batu Brinchang ▲
2031

Port Weld

Kuala Kangsar

Kampong Temerloh

PERAK

Ipoh

CAMERON HIGHLANDS

Pengkalan Baharu

Pusing

Gopeng

Beruas

Batu Gajah

Ringlet

Sungai Batu

Kampar

Pangkor

Lumut

Kampong Gajah

Perak

Tapah

G. Batu Putch ▲
2131

North of Kuala Lumpur

16 km/ 10 miles

Kuala Perak

Telok Anson

Perak – the silver state: *Perak* is the Malay word for silver, but the "silver" of the state of Perak is its shining tin, which has made it into one of the richest states of the Malaysian Federation. One of the oldest in the peninsula, Perak is the only state whose royal house can claim direct descent from the sultans of Malacca. Sultan Idris, today's ruler, is the 33rd of his line founded in 1528 by Sultan Muzaffar Shah, who was the eldest son of Malacca's last Malay monarch. The present Sultan was crowned King (Yang di Pertuan Agong) in January 1989, a title he will retain for five years.

The history of the state revolves closely around its abundant tin supply, but until the 19th century its civilisation was concentrated along the banks of the Perak River where state rulers made their capitals. With the discovery of tin, the wealth of the trade became of interest to these rulers who attempted to control it from their bases, as the tin was brought downstream from the mines further inland. But they had to contend with greedy outsiders – the Achenese from Sumatra, the Bugis from Selangor, the Thais from the north, as well as the Dutch and the Portuguese from Europe. The Dutch built forts at the mouth of the Perak River and on the strategic island of Pangkor in order to take a hold on the tin trade.

The tin revolution of the 19th century, however, transformed the face and the politics of the state. Mining on a large scale for the first time shifted the centre of power from the Perak River Valley to the tin-rich areas of Larut and Kinta. During the 1840s, newly discovered deposits in Larut made its Malay territorial chief the wealthiest and the most powerful man in the state. It also turned Larut into a cockpit for the struggles of rival groups of Chinese tin miners until their activities, affecting the welfare of the Straits Settlements, led the British to intervene. Within a decade of British intervention, the main interest in tin

mining had shifted to the Kinta Valley, which contains the richest tin deposits in the world. Since the turn of this century, Kinta has been the leading district in Perak, and Ipoh, the most prosperous of all its settlements.

The town that tin built: **Ipoh**, the tin centre of the world, lies on the trunk road and rail line about midway between Kuala Lumpur and Penang. It is now connected to these two centres by the new north-south highway. Like Kuala Lumpur, Ipoh started as a landing stage at the point beyond which the river was no longer navigable, and sprang up almost overnight into another Chinese miner's settlement on the ancestral land of the Dato' Panglima Kinta, the local Malay territorial chief. By the 1890s, brick buildings were replacing the fire-prone wooden shacks of the miners' town, and by the 1900s, it was *de facto* the principal town in the state, although the state capital remained at Taiping until 1937. By this time, Ipoh had emerged as the best-planned town in the peninsula, as can be witnessed today

Preceding pages: wooden scaffolding of a tin mining operation. *Right*, Perak Tong cave temple.

from its broad, regularly laid-out streets. It is now Malaysia's second largest city, with a population fast approaching half a million.

Apart from its excellent amenities, good accommodation and its convenience as a centre from which to explore other parts of the state, Ipoh does not hold too much to detain the tourist. The old part of the town lies on the west side of the Kinta Valley, and it is here that the official buildings are to be found. The railway station and the municipal colonial buildings surrounding the **padang** have a stately, dignified air. The immense new **state mosque** rises within close proximity to the **clock tower**, another colonial legacy built to commemorate the assassination of James Birch, Perak's first British resident.

The *padang* itself – surrounded by a clubhouse, St Michael's Secondary School, a convent, bank and the well-known FMS Hotel – is the epitome of every Malaysian town with a colonial past and the scene of important matches, school athletic meets, parades and public rallies. The **railway station** bears a familiar resemblance to the one in Kuala Lumpur and is known locally as the "Taj Mahal".

On the eastern side of the river is the new town of Ipoh dominated by the Majlis Perhadanan Ipoh (MPI) or Ipoh Municipal Council, which has great plans for the city's future, including making it worthy of the name, "the City of Bougainvilleas"! The new Royal Casuarina Hotel is a credit to the city. Other plans include a forest park in Jalan Tambun with a forest museum, lake, fruit orchard, playground and jungle trekking.

Attractions already established are the **Taman DR Seenivasagam Park** with its roller-skating rink and the **MBI Swimming Complex** with the first ever wave pool in Malaysia. The **Geology Museum** is worth a visit to study Perak's rock structures. Opened in 1957 on Jalan Harimau, the museum has over 600 examples of minerals, an exhibition on tin ore, including one of the best examples of cassiterite in the world, and

Temples embedded in the rockface are common sights around Ipoh.

a fine collection of precious stones.

On Gopeng Road, Ipoh's **Race Track** is set against a magnificent backdrop of craggy limestone outcrops and the more distant hills of the Main Range. Situated incongruously against this is an orderly Japanese Garden.

Temples in the rock face: The limestone formations of the **Kinta Valley** lend mystery as well as beauty to the surroundings of Ipoh city. Many of them are riddled with caves which in their time have served both as homes for Stone Age men as well as hideouts for bandits. In 1959, a British Gurkha army officer leading a patrol hunting for communist guerillas, came across the only rock paintings ever to have been found in peninsular Malaysia.

They are on the face of a cliff barely 275 metres (300 feet) from the main road to Tambun and are easily accessible with the help of a guide. While perhaps not as impressive as paintings found in European caves, they are reckoned at being at least 2,000 years old and are of great importance and value to man's early history. More recent rock artists have added their own designs to the originals!

Three kilometres (2 miles) north of Tambun are the **Tambun Hot Springs**, which are popular with Ipoh citizens at weekends and have changing and eating facilities.

The limestone caves around Ipoh, so reminiscent of similar features in the south of China, are of great fascination for both Buddhist and Hindu worshippers. Odd-looking white buildings, some with red-tiled pagoda roofs, are seen spread out flat against the rock, close to the road. These are in fact the entrances to caves which have been converted into temples. One of the largest shrines is the **Perak Tong**, 6 kilometres north (4 miles) of town on the trunk road. Traditional Chinese paintings adorn the walls and retell traditional folk tales and legends. Built in 1926 by a Buddhist priest from China, the temple has more than 40 Buddha statues, the central one being the largest one in Malaysia, sitting at 13 metres (40 feet) high.

Beyond the main altar are more Buddhas and a painting of Kuan Yin, Goddess of Mercy. In semi-darkness you can then climb a stairway (ask the caretaker for the key) to the upper reaches of the cave. After an arduous climb of 385 steps, follow a thin shaft of light to where the cave opens out to reveal the surrounding countryside. Here again Kuan Yin, now seated on an elephant, gazes out over the scene.

On the trunk road south of town, at Gunong Rapat, is **Sam Poh Tong**, 6 kilometres (4 miles) away. The biggest of the rock temples, its origin dates back to the 1890s, when Ipoh was emerging as Perak's largest town. A monk passing through found the cave and decided to make it his abode and place for meditation. He remained in the cave for 20 years until his death. Other monks followed his example. The present temple facade dates back to the 1950s, and today the cave houses a temple where a group of monks and nuns live, having dedicated their lives to the Buddha. Buddha statues are dotted everywhere

Characteristic limestone hills of Perak.

in between the stalacmites and stalactites. A stiff climb of 246 steps leads to an open cave with an excellent panorama of Ipoh and surroundings.

Hollowed out in the centre of the outcrop is an almost perfect circle of perpendicular cliff 70 metres (230 feet) high, where an old dilapidated stone house stands. Thousands of small turtles, symbols of longevity, swim in a garden pool in front of it, waiting to be fed by visitors to the temple.

Apparently, the privacy of this inner chamber has lured other people besides the clergy: on walls carved out of the cliff face is enough romantic graffiti to fill a book!

Underground riches: The Kinta Valley, whose tin production a few years ago was half that of the rest of Malaysia combined and 17 percent that of the world's total, stretches funnel-shaped for 70 kilometres (45 miles) from Sungai Siput in the north of Ipoh to Kampur in the south. The new north-south highway cuts straight across these hills joining Ipoh with the Perak River Valley and Kuala Kangsar. What was once a vast expanse of forest crossed by sluggish jungle streams and swamps has over the past 100 years been virtually denuded of all its trees, its swamps drained and even the course of the Kinta River straightened out. The land now lies open, offering vistas of deserted mining pools over the bleached scars of tin tailings; dotted here and there are the wooden *palong* (boxes) of the Chinese mines; and floated majestically in pools of their own making are the huge tin dredges.

Mining townships, occupying land once roamed by wild herds of elephants, scatter themselves over the face of this valley. Some, like Ipoh, rose with the tin industry, but when the local tin deposits were exhausted, they declined and shrivelled into villages or even became ghost towns, like Papan, Tronoh and Pusing. Some, such as Batu Gajah and Gopeng, were once greater and more prosperous than Ipoh itself.

Kampar, a very Chinese town at the foot of the Bujang Melaka on the main

Buddhist statues crowd a shrine in Sam Poh Tong.

trunk road south of Ipoh, prides itself as being the largest of these towns, while **Gopeng** has its long-gone prosperity wanly reflected in its large wooden market, its Chinese theatre and the dignified rows of shophouses.

Just south of Gopeng, a narrow side road to the right branches off to Kota Bharu, a little village on the railway. It then leads on to **Makam Teja**, the tomb of Bendahara Alang Iskandar, one of the great state officers of 19th-century Perak and a direct ancestor of the present ruler. As is often the case with the graves of distinguished Malays, the site has become a shrine (*keramat*) visited by humble folk in search of blessings or special favours. It has also become a tradition that a newly installed sultan of Perak must pay his respects at this shrine.

A pioneer's castle: Between Gopeng and Ipoh, another branch road follows the Sungai Raya, a tributary of the Kinta, across the valley to Batu Gajah. Suddenly about 5 kilometres (3 miles) before you get there, a bend in the road reveals a large ruin on the other side of the river. Until recently this building (known as **Kellie's Castle**) was overgrown with wild fig and banyan trees, spreading over and into it. An effort has recently been made to rescue this interesting structure from the encroaching foliage. It stands on the land of what was once the estate of a William Kellie-Smith, a rubber plantation owner who made his fortune in Malaya. The house was in fact his second home, and was never entirely finished, as Smith died while on a visit to his native Scotland. The house was meant to be a reminder of his own Scottish castle far away, and its fine architecture and orange-coloured bricks lying in ruins and all but forgotten, give it the air of something from a fairy tale.

Smith was an interesting man, who was evidently popular with his South Indian workers. A Hindu shrine stands nearby, erected for the plantation workers during a time of sickness. Amongst the figures of animals and gods, stands a man in a white suit and topee, pre-

Colourful wall paintings adorn the cave walls.

sumably Smith himself. A walk around the ruin is to step back into the prosperous days of colonial life. To get there visitors must first take a *sampan* across the river. Tours can also be arranged from Ipoh.

Batu Gajah itself is a small town once destined for greater things: it was designed as the administrative centre for the Kinta Valley in the early days of British rule before circumstances placed Ipoh to the fore. The evidence of what it might have been is found in the palatial government offices on top of the hill overlooking the town. Batu Gajah now hopes to attract visitors with its modern park for children, modelled along the lines of a Malaysian Disneyland.

The heart of Perak: A 20-minute drive from Batu Gajah brings you to **Parit**, which is in the heart of the historic Perak River Valley. For centuries the Perak River provided the only means of access to the state's interior and was therefore the main area of Malay settlement and the scene of some of the most dra-

matic events in Perak's history. Now good roads run along either side of its banks through villages which were once the homes of Perak's greatest heroes. At various places along the way are the simple tombs of Perak's sultans, all carefully marked and cared for by the local villagers.

Across the river at Kampong Gajah is **Pasir Salak**, where James Birch, Perak's first British resident, was assassinated in 1874. Birch was killed while out bathing in the Perak River by a group led by Dato' Maharaja Lela. The latter was later executed for his part in the assassination plot and a stone slab declaring "let this place be desolate for ever" was placed just outside the village mosque. The slab has now been removed to the state museum at Taiping, but an obelisk commemorating Birch still remains at Pasir Salak. A state memorial is also planned in honour of Lela. Around the village of Pasir Salak are many attractive *kutai* houses of very fine workmanship.

The road on the left bank from Pasir Salak eventually crosses the Kinta River near its confluence with the Perak River and continues across the broad rice fields of Sungai Manik into Telok Intan. **Telok Intan**, formerly known as Telok Anson, is the chief town of Lower Perak and the market for the local produce, particularly pineapples. Its main claim to fame is its century-old **clock tower**, with its distinct tilt, which was originally used for water storage. Telok Intan was earmarked as the main outlet for tin of the Kinta Valley, which was why the railroad was extended to it. But the north-south highway, built for the benefit of Penang and Port Klang, has passed Telok Intan by and reduced it to a backwater.

Island of princesses and pirates: **Pangkor** lies off the coast of Perak, and is the most popular beach resort in the state. To get there, you need to take the road from Ipoh to Sitiawan and Lumut. The broad Perak River is crossed at **Bota Kanan**, where there is a hatchery for river terrapins. After the town of Sitiawan, head for the coast at Lumut, the principal base for the Malaysian Navy.

Fishing boat off Pangkor Island.

Their offices, ships and apartments can be seen from Pangkor just across the bay.

Many locals do not even make the crossing to Pangkor, but make for **Telok Batik**, a pleasant beach resort 6½ kilometres (4 miles) from Lumut. Others go to the **Wilderness Adventure Camp**, accessible from Lumut, where activities are arranged to exercise the body and to teach adults and children alike about life in the forest. The *Pesta Laut* or Sea Festival is held in Lumut in August every other year, and sea-sport competitions, funfairs and food outlets attract the crowds. Pangkor can also be crowded during this time, and during any of the Malaysian school holidays, so if you like the beach to yourself, make sure you choose the right month.

Twelve kilometres long and four kilometres wide (7½ by 2½ feet), Pangkor is one of the few places on the west coast to offer palm-fringed beaches that reflect those lone stretches of sand on the east coast. Unfortunately, the sea on this side of the peninsula is never as crystal clear as it can be on the other coast.

Legend tells that once a Sumatran warrior fell in love with a beautiful princess, and to win her favour he sailed north to distinguish himself in battle. When he failed to return after many months, the princess set out to find him. She searched high and low and upon reaching Pangkor Island learned the tragic news that he had died in battle and was buried there. The villagers led her to the grave, whereupon, distraught and heartbroken, she climbed a cliff and flung herself onto the rocks below. **Pantai Puteri Dewi** (The Beach of the Beautiful Princess) is named after her.

Ferries run to several parts of the island all day until early evening. The ferry slides down the Dindings River with mangroves on one side and the huge Navy Base on the other, out of the kilometre-wide channel into the Malacca Straits and the island of Pangkor lies directly ahead. The trip takes about 35 minutes.

The eastern side of Pangkor has

Rock depicts the coat of arms of the Dutch East India Company.

changed little over the years. Until tourism arrived, the island's economy depended on the sea and its two main *kampong* (**Kg Sungai Pinang Kecil** and **Kg Sungai Pinang Besar**) are fishing villages with narrow streets which extend on stilts far out over the water. **Pangkor Village** further south, has not changed much either.

On the road south of the village are the remains of a **Dutch fort** built over 300 years ago in an attempt to control Perak's tin trade. It was also a stronghold against the many pirates of the Malacca Straits. The fort was abandoned after it was attacked by a local warrior, Panglima Kulub, and although later regained, it was by then no longer of any great importance. If it looks remarkably well-preserved it is because in 1973 the National Museum undertook its reconstruction. Chiselled on a boulder close to the fort is the Dutch East India Coat-of-Arms. Later adventurers have since added their own messages! In the vicinity of the fort there is said to be a famous snake man, who, for a small fee, will demonstrate his fearlessness for poisonous snakes.

The name of Pangkor is as familiar to every Malaysian schoolchild as that of Gettysburg to an American teenager, for it was on board a warship anchored off the island that the historic Treaty of Pangkor was signed in January 1874, granting the British entry into the Malay states of the peninsula for the first time. Before that the island had long been notorious as a pirate base and stronghold.

The western side of the island is primarily a beach resort. It is a short taxi ride or walk of twenty minutes from the main village to **Pasir Bogak**, where most of the tourist accommodation is to be found. Pasir Bogak is by no means the prettiest beach on the island, but luckily far more beautiful beaches are easily accessible by the small road which encircles the island. Rent a bicycle or motorcycle and pedal round. Sometimes the road dwindles into nothing more than a sandy track, and cycling can be difficult but rewarding.

The accommodation at Pasir Bogak

is sadly rather run-down but the area makes a good base from which to explore the island. The main road from the village runs directly to the **Seaview Hotel** and the **Beach Huts Hotel**; both have boats that can take you out to nearby islands. Along the side road that follows the west coast is the spacious but dilapidated **Rest House**, and a string of tidy little A-frame hut resorts. These are cheap and relaxed places, and the owners will make you feel welcome.

Continuing past the **Minivillage**, small huts much favoured for their low prices by impecunious Malaysian students, the road climbs up a hill to allow lovely views of both sea and jungle. Birds and butterflies abound here. The road slopes down again onto a string of deserted beaches, which very often you can have completely to yourself, but for a few villagers passing by. **Telok Ketapong Beach**, which sometimes has turtles coming ashore to lay eggs, is followed by the beautiful **Telok Nipah Beach** and finally the loveliest of all, **Coral Bay**. Coral Bay is off the road and is reached by following the beach. Here the water is very clear, even during the monsoon, and the water deliciously warm. Save a set of small beach huts behind Telok Nipah, where a Malay family will take care of your needs, there is no accommodation all along these beaches.

Moving back towards civilisation, the road now cuts inland at a narrow point of the island and comes out at **Oyster Bay** where there is a small jetty. This jetty is the entry point for visitors patronising the fairly new **Pan Pacific Resort** on the Beach of the Beautiful Princess, or more popularly called **Golden Sands Beach**. The resort has chalets spread along the beach which incorporate traditional building styles, and a swimming pool right next to the beach. The beach is pleasant and all water sports can be arranged here. The hotel charges M$30 for day visitors wishing to make use of their facilities. Included in their grounds is a 9-hole golf course. But if you want to be alone, Coral Bay is a 40-minute walk back along the road.

Left, the glittering gold domes of the Ubadiah Mosque.

For the energetic, the road now moves along the eastern side of the island and a tough walk up the hills surrounding Bukit Pangkor will bring you out at the coast near a fishing village (Kg Sungai Pinang Kecil).

Off the coast of Pasir Bogak is Pangkor's second resort situated on **Pulau Pangkor Laut**. The French-owned **Pansea** has chosen the best spot for its pleasant hotel and probably the best beach around is held by the hotel, the famed **Emerald Bay**. Even if you do not wish to stay here, day trips can be arranged to the island, and as with the Pan Pacific Hotel, the entrance fee is about M$30. Ferries also run from Lumut directly to Pansea.

Accommodation in Lumut is in the form of Chinese hotels or the **Government Rest House**. The latter has a mini museum with an excellent collection of seashells, corals, ancient weapons and other items of historical interest.

Golden dome, royal town: About 35 kilometres (20 miles) upstream from Parit and on the new north-south high-way which crosses the Perak River over the graceful 50-year-old Iskandar Bridge lies the attractive town of **Kuala Kangsar**. The **Government Rest House** here overlooks the river and is worth a night's stay both for its own quiet beauty and as a convenient centre for exploring the countryside.

Kuala Kangsar, the residence of the Sultan of Perak, is a royal town and is famous for three other things besides – for possessing one of the first rubber trees to be planted in the country; for its spectacular golden-domed mosque; and for its Malay College, the earliest of residential schools in Malaysia.

A plaque on **Government Hill** near the Old Residency (where the British Resident lived but which is now occupied by a girls' school) marks one of the few surviving original rubber trees, originating in Brazil, then cultivated in Kew Gardens, London, and finally sent to Singapore for experimental purposes in the the late 1870s. The seeds flourished but it was almost another generation before British planters took the cue

The landscape features jagged outcrops and hidden valleys.

and began to plant rubber seriously. Another of these pioneer trees is situated near the agricultural office in town.

The road which winds along the riverside past the Old Residency and the Rest House ends up on **Bukit Chandan**, where the huge golden dome of the **Ubadiah Mosque** gleams. This must be one of the most photographed Muslim buildings in the country, and justly so, if just for its striking and symmetrical domes and minarets. The construction of the mosque began in the reign of Sultan Idris Murshidul Adzam Shah, but was interrupted a number of times: once, when two elephants belonging to Sultan Idris ran over the imported marble floor and again during World War I.

Beyond the mosque, which was finally completed in 1919, the road arrives at the compound of the Sultan's palace, the **Istana Iskandariah**. Conspicuously placed on a hill overlooking the river valley, the stone vulgarity of the palace is clearly shown up against the much smaller but more dignified

and graceful **Istana Kenangan**. Its name means the Palace of Memory and it was previously known as Istana Lembah. Built as a temporary residence while the Istana Iskandariah was under construction, the Istana Kenangan is an extraordinary architectural achievement, being built without a single nail or any architectural plans. The Palace has now become a Royal Museum and contains an interesting collection of mementos and photographs connected with the Perak Royal Family.

The **Malay College** is near the main part of town, set back in its own spacious grounds. Founded in 1904 as a residential school for the sons of the *rajah* and of the Malay aristocracy, its doors are now open to all Malay boys of talent. A good cross-section of Malaysia's establishment today received their education under this roof.

A 30-*sen* trip in a *sampan* across the river at Kuala Kangsar takes you to **Sayong** on the opposite bank, also once the home of sultans. A walk of three or four kilometres (get a guide in town to show

Paddling on the calm waters of Tasek Chenderoh.

the way) brings you to the place where Sayong pottery is made – in particular, the grey-black *labu*, water pitchers distinguished by their broad bases and tall narrow spouts. Other kinds of potteryware are available for sale at low "warehouse" prices as well: ornamental tortoises, elephants, birds, practical ashtrays, vases and bowls.

The uncrowned king: From the highlands of the interior the waters of the Perak River, the second largest river in the peninsula, pour southwards. Formerly this river flooded the towns and villages along its banks every year. Nowadays, however, its water is controlled by Malaysia's largest dam constructed across the tributary of Temenggor, which lies deep in the jungle 150 kilometres (95 miles) upstream from Kuala Kangsar.

The region in which the dam is built is known as **Upper Perak**, a district which is still largely covered by mountainous jungles and which has only in modern times formed part of the state of Perak proper. In the 19th century, Up-

per Perak belonged to the Malay principality of Reman, whose territory extended into Southern Thailand and whose rulers paid homage to Bangkok. In 1909 Reman was formally transferred by treaty to Perak and the story goes that Perak gained a few extra square miles of territory as a result of what Hubert Berkeley did: the British district officer at Gerik, with his men, moved the jungle boundary stones outwards in the dead of night to increase the size of the conquered land.

For the next few years, Upper Perak continued to be so remote from the rest of the country that Berkeley, who was its district officer for almost 20 years, ruled like an uncrowned king. Many are the stories told about him by the district's old folk; he identified with the local people and by the time he retired he had become a living legend.

On the map, a solitary road winds from Kuala Kangsar into this domain until it reaches the Thai border at Keroh before swinging back into Kedah. The scenery is picturesque and becomes increasingly wilder. Not far from Kuala Kangsar, it crosses **Tasek Chenderoh**, a man-made lake formed by the dam of the same name built across the Perak River. At Kota Tampan near Lenggong, the road passes caves once occupied by Stone Age men who left behind their tools and utensils as evidence. As it continues northwards, the land becomes wilder and more lonely, with only occasional clearings in the hillside jungle for patches of tobacco and *Orang Asli* crops.

Gerik is a self-contained colony in this jungle wilderness, important not only as an administrative centre but also as the starting point of the east-west Highway on its way to Kelantan and the East Coast. There is a **Government Rest House** and some other smaller hotels in town. On the way to the East Coast, the road crosses the spectacular **Temenggor Dam**, where the waters are enclosed by the wild hills and dead and dying trees are blackened by the water and shrouded in mist, adding to the feeling of eerie mystery. On the shores of the Temenggor at **Banding** is an iso-

Towering trunks of the lowland forest make an impressive sight.

lated retreat for fishing enthusiasts.

From Gerik the road makes its way to Keroh in the west, through *Orang Asli* villages and impressive scenery, eventually climbing past the open-cast tin mine that sprawls across the slopes of the hills above **Klian Intan**. This mine was sending tin to Malacca in the days of the sultanate, but its resources might have been long exhausted if mining had not been inhibited by the fear of offending the jealous spirits of the hill. After Klian Intan comes **Keroh**, the small and pleasant frontier town about 5 kilometres (3 miles) from the Thai border, with a **Rest House** and Customs and Immigration offices if you wish to enter Thailand from this unusual entry point.

Town of everlasting peace: A narrow pass at Bukit Berapit separates Kuala Kangsar and the Perak River Valley from the plains of Larut and Matang and the north. Both road and rail go through this gap, first passing the impressive rock of **Gunung Pondok** which stands like a sentinel to moving traffic. While the railroad burrows through the hill-side, the highway runs above, and as it goes down the other side it crosses a cold, fresh mountain stream which is a favourite spot for picnickers.

From there it is a quick 20-minute drive to **Taiping** (peace in Chinese), the chief town of Larut and Matang, and for 50 years capital of the state. Taiping has the heaviest rainfall in the peninsula and the peace referred to in its name was first acquired at the end of the bloody struggles between rival Chinese mining factions in Larut, when the Treaty of Pangkor was signed. The town seems to have been left undisturbed ever since.

In the 1890s, long before the word "ecology" was in common usage, an abandoned tin mine on the edge of the town was landscaped to create the beautiful **Lake Gardens**. The creation of these gardens owed much to the generosity of the *Kapitan China* of Perak at that time, Chung Ah Kwee, on whose concession the gardens lay. Situated in the gardens is a nine-hole golf course and a zoo which covers an area of about 50 hectares (125 acres).

A tree-lined Taiping street.

Here too is the **Government Rest House**, built in the Sumatran Menangkabau style but supported by a row of classical Doric columns, demonstrating the Malaysian genius for marrying different traditions. More architectural gems include the colonial town hall and the government offices standing not far away in a corner of the gardens. At the foot of the hills is an extensive war cemetery. Also in the gardens is a prison used by the Japanese during the war, and was later a rehabilitation centre for communists during the emergency.

The **State Museum**, the oldest in the country, is housed in a venerable Victorian building, placed, perhaps not so appropriately, opposite the prison. The museum has a wide variety of displays, many of which were gathered at the beginning of the century, and are now no longer obtainable anywhere else.

Taiping was also the starting point for Malaya's first railway, which went as far as Port Weld, but the trains no longer run here.

The **Ling Nam Temple** in Taiping is the oldest Chinese temple in Perak and there is a model of a boat within, dedicated to the Chinese emperor who built the first canal in China.

On the coast east of Taiping at Gula is the **Kuala Gula Bird Sanctuary**. Over 100 species of birds, some of them rare and thus protected, have been sighted in this area. Amongst the mammals to be found there are the smooth otter, the dusky leaf monkey, the long-tailed macaque and the ridge-back dolphin. The months between August and December are the best time for watching the thousands of birds which flock to this place. Information on the park can be obtained from the Wildlife Department in Batu Gajah.

Privacy in a rose garden: Rising above the town, and largely responsible for Taiping's reputation as the wettest place in the peninsula, towers **Maxwell Hill,** now re-named Bukit Larut. On the slopes of this 1,020-metre (3350-foot) hill is Malaysia's oldest hill station: here there are no golf courses, fancy restaurants or swimming pools, but limited

Maxwell Hill is the country's oldest hill station.

jungle walks and a badminton court. However, the cool air and moist clouds hanging low over the jungles below, the ever-changing view as the clouds wash off the Straits of Malacca from Penang to Pangkor, and the comfortable bungalows with their English names and fireplaces give Maxwell Hill the simplicity of a natural hideaway that sets one's heart and mind delightfully at ease.

The first road to the top of the hill was constructed after World War II with the "help" of Japanese prisoners-of-war and was completed in 1948. Before that anyone who wished to reach the top but did not fancy hiking had the choice of going by pony-back or on a sedan chair. In the early years the trail was lined with porters carrying heavy loads of fragrant tea down the hill. Now tea growing is no longer practised here and only a handful of Indian labourers remain to keep the all-powerful jungle at bay and the gardens neatly manicured.

Although the road is paved today, access is prohibited to private vehicles. Government-owned Landrovers which operate from the far end of the Lake Gardens in Taiping serve as mountain taxis departing every hour between dawn and dusk. The one-lane road is steep and narrow; at sharp bends the jungle suddenly parts to reveal the green land below divided into a pattern of roads and fields. The air turns brisk and the sun becomes lost in a bow of mist and clouds.

At the **Tea Gardens House**, traffic halts until the Landrovers coming down the hill have passed. The 12-kilometre (7½-mile) journey takes 40 minutes. Landrovers will deliver a traveller to the front step of his bungalow and leave him to the privacy of this delightful retreat. If he is feeling energetic, at the foot of the hill, a stone's throw away from the Landrover station, there is a large freshwater swimming pool, fed constantly by a waterfall.

Back on the plain, the trunk road pursues its course northwards to Penang, Kedah and the Thai border. At Simpang, the crossroads for Taiping, a branch road bends off in the other direc-

Malaysia's hill resorts are richly endowed by nature.

tion to go to **Port Weld** which was the terminus for Malaysia's first railroad. Opened in 1885, the line runs for 12 kilometres (7½ miles) between the port and Taiping, but is now no longer used.

On the way to Port Weld the road passes at **Matang**, the old fort of Nagah Ibrahim, named after the Malay territorial chief of Larut who became rich through the tin trade but who was unable to control the turbulent Chinese factions who produced the wealth. Later it was used as the first teacher-training college in the Malay States.

The trunk road rushes north through towns with fanciful names like Bagan Serai (Lemon Grass Quay) where the rice-growing Krian district begins; Parit Buntar (The Bulging Dyke) and Nibong Tebal (The Stout Nibong Palm). Another half hour and you are on the shore facing Penang.

Deer parks and waterfalls: In the south of the state, close to Tapah, and on the way to the Cameron Highlands, are a number of small parks of interest to the nature lover. Situated in Menderang,

Sungkai, and about 82 kilometres (50 miles) from Ipoh, is the **Sungkai Deer Farm**. The park provides space for around one hundred deer to wander freely on the 100-hectare (250-acre) breeding and conservation site. There is also a bird sanctuary. Closer to Tapah, about 13 kilometres (8 miles) away is the **Kuala Woh Jungle Park**. Facilities are made available here for picnickers, fishermen and walkers, and there are a number of waterfalls to visit. Other waterfalls around this area include the **Lata Iskandar waterfalls** on the way up to the Cameron Highlands, the **Ulu Kinta waterfalls**, 16 kilometres (10 miles) from Ipoh, and the **Batu Hampar falls** near Taiping.

Golf clubs and blowpipes: The **Cameron Highlands** are not part of Perak but of Pahang, but they can only be reached through Perak. The road to the Highlands branches off the main trunk highway 60 kilometres (37 miles) south of Ipoh at Tapah. It shoots off toward the hills and for 90 kilometres (56 miles) winds and twists its way to the

Panorama of the Cameron Highlands.

top. As cool air funnels down the mountain pass, the temperature drops. Palms and banana trees give way to deep jungle growth. Coniferous trees appear, thick ferns line the road and clusters of bamboo add the touch of a Chinese scroll painting. *Orang Asli* wearing loin cloths and carrying blowpipes amble along the road.

The Cameron Highlands are actually spread out over three districts. For the newcomer it can be a little confusing, and at first somewhat disappointing, especially when, after 45 kilometres (28 miles), he arrives at **Ringlet**, the first district and a rather ugly little settlement. Better to push on! Four kilometres (2½ miles) later comes the pretty **Sultan Abu Bakar Lake**, a man-made body of water formed by the damming of the Bertam River, and extensively covered with lush green plants. Fifteen kilometres (9 miles) further on lies **Tanah Rata**, the principal township in the Highlands. The scenery becomes superb – cool and clean air, streams, lakes and a view of rolling green mountains which fade into distant greys on the horizon.

The scenery has not always been so charming. Steep, hostile, seemingly impenetrable and infested with spirits and demons, the Cameron Highlands were unknown even to the Malays until 1885, when William Cameron, a government surveyor on a mapping expedition reported finding "a fine plateau with gentle slopes shut in by the mountains."

Tea planters hastily claimed the plateau, and before long the Chinese discovered that the high altitude was ideal for growing vegetables, and began farming the valley floors. To carry their produce to market they built a road. A wealthy rubber planter came looking for a place of leisure and built a house for use by his family at weekends. The mountain resort of the Cameron Highlands has not stopped growing ever since, and tea and vegetables continue to be cultivated there.

It seems somewhat incongruous to arrive from the tropical lowlands at Tanah Rata where the single street is

The Merlin Hotel overlooks the golf links at Cameron Highlands.

lined with shops and restaurants, many of which advertise "Cream Teas" and "English Breakfasts"! But strawberries and strawberry jam are part of life in the Camerons. Amongst Chinese hotels, are several very good Indian restaurants, serving simple snacks and meals that agree very well with the climate here. Shops sell mounted butterflies and scorpions for tourists alongside more practical household goods.

At the end of this street is a park, and the **Government Rest House** and the **Garden Hotel** are both placed on its edges, the quiet setting making both their pretty gardens a haven of peace. It is possible to arrange a visit to the Agricultural Research Institute, and also to the **Blue Valley Tea Estate**, where tours take visitors around the various processes involved in making tea. Everywhere in the Camerons' many teashops and restaurants, the tea seems to taste fresher and its perfume sweeter than when drunk in the lowlands.

Tanah Rata has become a popular destination for Malaysian college students and diplomats alike. Local boy scouts with knapsacks on their backs thumb rides up the winding hills, while expatriates from Singapore lounge on colonial verandahs, munching fresh strawberries and cream.

The **Smokehouse Inn** towards Brinchang has these delicacies on its tea menu, and you can sit there in the evenings beside a roaring fire and not find it difficult to imagine you were in England, so perfect is this copy of an English inn, both on the outside and also within. The Smokehouse is situated between Brinchang and Tanah Rata, and behind it is the Highlands' 18-hole golf course with a cosy pavilion equipped with a bar and a restaurant. If golf is your reason for being here, then you can stay at the nearby Golf Course Inn or at the Merlin Inn. There is cheaper accommodation in Brinchang, the third district of the Camerons.

In Tanah Rata, buy a map from one of the shops and decide on your walking capabilities. The map gives advice on which trails are family strolls and which are tough hikes. These trails lead to tea plantations, waterfalls, *Orang Asli* settlements and, for the energetic, to the summits of the surrounding mountains, with **Gunung Brinchang** as the ultimate goal. It is the Highlands' highest mountain reaching 2,000 metres (6500 feet), and on clear days, Ipoh and other west coast towns, as well as the Malacca Straits are visible.

The jungles of the Highlands are deceptively dense. Information booklets cautiously advise visitors hiking into the interior to tell someone which way they are going and to stick to the paths. Probably the most famous person to have gotten lost here was the Thai silk entrepreneur, Jim Thomson. The American-born Thomson with his silk empire in Bangkok, was on holiday in the Cameron Highlands on 26 March 1967, when he announced his intention to go for a pre-dinner stroll. He never came back, and his strange disappearance without a trace has invited many explanations for the mystery, amongst them suggestions of a kidnapping or a tiger waiting for his dinner!

Left, living conditions have changed little for the *Orang Asli*, despite the pylons of progress. **Right**, picking tea leaves.

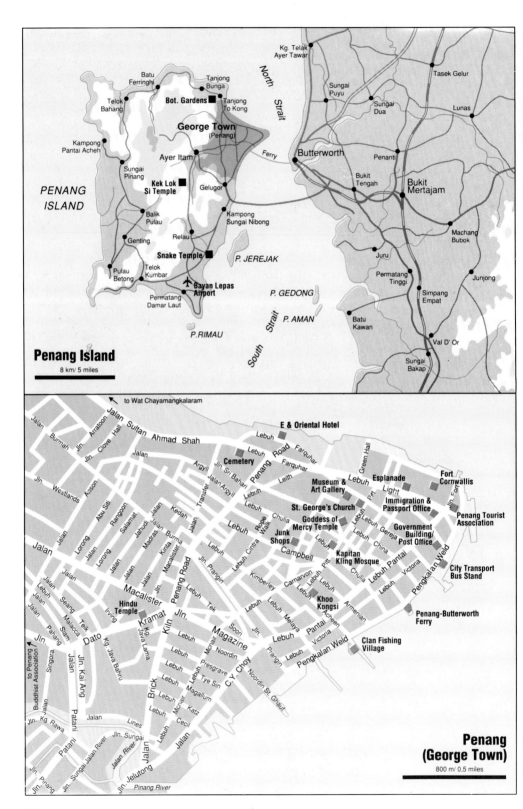

Penang Island

8 km/ 5 miles

Kg. Telak
Ayer Tawar
Tasek Gelur
North Strait
Sungai
Puyu
Lunas
Batu
Ferringhi
Tanjong
Bunga
Sungai
Dua
Telok
Bahang
Bot. Gardens
Tanjong
To Kong
George Town
(Penang)
Penanti
Butterworth
Kampong
Pantai Acheh
Ayer Itam
Ferry
Bukit
Tengah
Bukit
Mertajam
PENANG
ISLAND
Sungai
Pinang
Kek Lok
Si Temple
Gelugor
Balik
Pulau
Kampong
Sungai Nibong
Machang
Bubok
Genting
Relau
Juru
Junjong
Snake Temple
Pulau
Betong
Telok
Kumbar
P. JEREJAK
Permatang
Tinggi
Simpang
Empat
Bayan Lepas
Airport
P. GEDONG
Permatang
Damar Laut
P. AMAN
Batu
Kawan
Val D' Or
P. RIMAU
South Strait
Sungai
Bakap

Penang (George Town)

800 m/ 0.5 miles

to Wat Chayamangkalaram
Jalan Sultan Ahmad Shah
Jalan Burmah
Jln. Clove Hall
Jln. Sri Bahari
Jalan Arratoon
E & Oriental Hotel
Lebuh
Penang Road
Farquhar
Cemetery
Farquhar
Jalan
Leith
Jln. Sri Bahari
Green Hall
Esplanade
Fort
Cornwallis
Jalan Argyll
Lebuh
Museum &
Art Gallery
Light
Jln. Westlands
Anson
Abu Siti
Rangoon
Transfer
Lebuh
Chulia
Pitt
Immigration &
Passport Office
Penang Tourist
Association
Kedah
Salamat
St. George's Church
Lebuh Gereja
Jahudi
Jalan Argyll
Lebuh
Rope
Walk
Goddess of
Mercy Temple
Government
Building/
Post Office
City Transport
Bus Stand
Madras
Burma
Jalan
Cintra
Lebuh China
Junk
Shops
Lorong
Jalan
Kinta
Jalan
Macalister
Jln. Prangin
Campbell
Kapitan
Kling Mosque
Lebuh Pantai
Pengkalan Weld
Jalan
Lorong
Seang
Teik
Macalister
Penang Road
Kimberley
Carnarvon
Lebuh Pitt
Chulia
Victoria
Penang-Butterworth
Ferry
Hindu
Temple
Kramat
Jln.
Lebuh Tek
Soon
Khoo
Kongsi
Acheen
Armenian
Lebuh Pantai
Malacca
Irving
Kg. Java Lama
Magazine
Mcnair
Noordin
Lebuh Meliya
Pantai
Victoria
Pengkalan Weld
Clan Fishing
Village
to Penang
Buddhist Association
Singora
Pahang
Siam
Dato
Jln. Kai Ang
Kg. Java Baru
Brick
Presgrave
Tye Sin
Jalan
C. Y. Choy
Noordin St. Ghaut
Lebuh
Prangin
Jln. Kg. Rawa
Patani
Lines
Jln. Sungai
Jalan River
Lebuh
Magallum
Lebuh
Katz
Lebuh
Cecil
Jln. Sungai Jalan River
Jalan
Jelutong
Pinang River
Jln. Pinang

160

THE ISLAND
STATE OF PENANG

In fact, Penang is no longer an island. Since August 1985 it has been joined to the mainland opposite by the Penang Bridge. The toll at M$7 per car is higher than that of the ferry but the 7-km (4½-mile) drive across gives you exhilarating views of the harbour, and you have the satisfaction of knowing that you have just driven over the third longest bridge in the world. Because of the rather high toll, it is as yet under-used by local motorists, who prefer to take the cheaper ferry, which brings them into the heart of Georgetown.

Although once under the dominion of the Sultan of Kedah, Penang has always been on its own. Until the British came, it was largely deserted despite its strategic position. To encourage trade and commerce, the British made the island state a free port; no taxes were levied on either imports or exports. This strategy worked and in eight years the population increased to 8,000, comprising many immigrant races – Chinese, Indians and Bugis, among others.

In the beginning...there was Light: But the story of how Penang fell into British hands and developed into Malaysia's leading entrepôt port does little credit to the British themselves. It was acquired on the initiative of an English trader and adventurer called Francis Light, who lived in the area for 15 years. Light spoke fluent Thai and Malay and was a familiar figure in the Kedah court. He fully envisaged the advantages that the possession of Penang would hold for the British, who were then represented by the English East India Company. The company had an increasingly urgent need for a station on the eastern side of the Bay of Bengal in order to secure naval domination of the bay from the French. Such a base would serve to victual company ships on their long haul to China in the flourishing tea and opium trade and, also, as a headquarters from which to further British interests in South-East Asian waters. At last in the 1780s, when the rulers of

Kedah sorely needed help against the imminent threats of a Thai invasion from the north and Bugis attacks from the south, Light persuaded them to trade Penang for British protection. The Kedah Malays agreed, and in July 1786, an English East India Company settlement was formed on the island.

The company confirmed its approval of Light's action in acquiring the island but refused to honour the commitment to protect the Sultan of Kedah against his enemies. The angry Sultan tried to recapture Penang but was easily defeated and, as a result, Kedah had to surrender more land to the British – this time, the land between the Muda and Krian rivers opposite Penang island, which was named Seberang Prai by the Malays. The British called it Province Wellesley, after the Governor-General in India at the time. Today, Seberang Prai and Penang constitute the State of Penang, which is headed by a governor appointed by the Malaysian king.

Throughout history Penang has changed names like the seasons. Early

Malays called it Pulau Ka Satu, or Single Island. Later it appeared on sailing charts as Pulau Pinang, or Island of the Betel Nut Tree. The British renamed it Prince of Wales' Island, and finally, with Malaysia's independence, it reverted to Penang. There are still many appendages attached to it – "Pearl of the Orient", "Gateway to the East", "Isle of Temples". Place and street names are again undergoing a change in Penang Island as colonial names are being exchanged for more representative Malay ones. To add to this confusion, the locals themselves have their own names for certain streets. Penang is nowadays spelt "Pinang".

King George's town: Like most cities of Asia that juxtapose the glass and concrete of the new with the tile and teak of the old, Penang has several dimensions. A newcomer can arrive by ferry, be transported by trishaw to a Chinese hotel on Lebuh Kimberley or Lebuh Chulia in the heart of Chinatown, eat at the small food stalls, walk the waterfront and visit the villages set on stilts,

and after two weeks leave Penang not knowing there is a tourist complex. On the other hand, another visitor may have cocktails served at the poolside overlooking the sea and later dine in a revolving restaurant 16 storeys above the flickering lights of the city and never really know that an exciting, vibrant Chinatown exists.

Georgetown, named by the British after King George III of Great Britain but referred to by the Malays as Tanjong (or Headland), is unmistakeably a Chinese town, from crowded streets with Chinese characters spelling out mystic logos, to the thriving port from which Malaysia's exports find their way to the world's markets.

Georgetown has one of the most unusual waterfronts in Asia. Visitors arriving by ferry usually do a double take when they first see it. The area is what locals call the **Clan Piers**. It consists of villages built on stilts over the sea. The people who live there are either boatmen or fishermen and each group belongs to a clan. On Lim's Pier only

Georgetown from above, with the mainland in the distance.

members of the Lim family can live, while Chew's Pier is the sole property of the Chew clan. The houses extend far out to sea, and at low tide the fishermen's boats rest high on the mud-banks. On tiny docks that consist of no more than a few narrow planks on the sand and a ware-shed, labourers unload heavy burlap sacks stuffed with cargo brought in by the lightermen. No-one minds if a visitor strolls along the often shaky wooden piers, provided he is not a Chew in Lim's territory.

As predominantly as the port is Chinese, the countryside is Malay. Outside the city, the hustle and bustle of commerce is left behind; the noise and crowd are swapped for an agrarian, quiet and thinly populated world.

But Penang is also Indian. With the British came *sepoys* (Indian natives employed as soldiers by a European power), Indian merchants, and also Indian convicts who built the first roads and filled in the swamps on which the town now stands. Not all of them stayed, but they left behind their stamp.

The spicy scent of curry dominates the older section of Georgetown; a taxi driver speaks Tamil as well as Malay, English and some Hokkien. A Hindu temple stands on top of Penang Hill and a Hindu shrine rises next to a Buddhist image on a promontory in the south.

Traces of old Penang: Probably the most costly cannon ball in history was shot at **Kedah Point**, near Fort Cornwallis. The site Francis Light had chosen for his settlement was thick with jungle and the task of clearing the undergrowth proved arduous for the *sepoys*, who complained of hardship. So Light loaded a cannon with silver dollars and fired it into the jungle. This was enough inducement to get all and sundry to set to work to retrieve the coins; before long the land was cleared and the first camp established.

Originally, **Fort Cornwallis** was a wooden structure. Between 1808 and 1810, it was rebuilt with convict labour. Today, the old fort still stands, but its precincts have been converted into a public park and playground. Its ram-

Municipal building evokes memories of colonial splendour.

parts are still guarded by old cannons, the most venerable and famous of which is Seri Rambai, known to many Penang residents as "the travelling cannon". The cannon has certainly travelled. Cast in Holland, it was presented by the Dutch to the Sultan of Johor in 1606. Seven years later in a devastating raid on Johor, it was captured by the Achenese and taken to Acheh where it remained for almost 200 years. It was then sent to Kuala Selangor by the Achenese in search of a Bugis alliance, and after the British bombarded Kuala Selangor in 1871, it was brought to Penang. For several years, it was left lying in the sea off the Esplanade until it was hauled out and placed at its present location. Like most ancient cannons, Seri Rambai is attributed with magical powers; it is believed that women desiring children will have their wish fulfilled if they place flowers in the cannon's barrel and offer prayers.

At the heart of history: Next to Fort Cornwallis lie the town *padang* (green) and the **Esplanade** (Jalan Tun Syed Sheh Barakbah) which is the heart of historical Georgetown. Handsome 19th-century colonial government offices stand at one end of the *padang*; at the other, near the entrance to Fort Cornwallis, traffic circles the city **clock tower** presented to Penang by rich Chinese *towkay*, Cheah Chin Gok, in commemoration of Her Majesty Queen Victoria's Diamond Jubilee. The dignified and well-designed **St George's Church** built in 1818 on nearby Lebuh Farquhar, draws much attention as the oldest Anglican church in South-East Asia. Francis Light lies buried in the adjoining, frangipani-shaded cemetery, along with a host of other notables of old Penang, many of whom succumbed early in life to the rigours of the climate and life in the tropics.

In **Penang Museum**, on the other side of the street, visitors can peer into a Chinese bridal chamber created in the lavish style of the 19th century when Malaysian-Chinese girls took great pride in the quality of beadwork on their slippers. One room, dedicated to a **Feet fit for a food stop.**

glimpse of yesteryear, is hung with old paintings and etchings from the days when Fort Cornwallis was the centre of town. Another is an opulent showcase of bejewelled krisses, the dagger-like weapons Malays used for protection and for prestige. **Penang Art Gallery** upstairs displays batik paintings, oils, graphics and Chinese ink drawings. Most of the techniques are new but the solemn, moody sea scenes and village portraits recapture a way of life that is little changed from the pioneer days.

Georgetown streets: On arrival, visitors are usually intrigued by the narrow, congested streets of Georgetown and its pulsating waterfront. It is here, on the waterfront, that Penang is linked to the 20th century by the flotilla of freighters and steamers anchored in the harbour, which cause the ferryboats from Butterworth to zigzag a 4-kilometre (2½-mile) course to reach the landing at Weld Quay. The voyage from the mainland to Penang costs 40 *sen*, but travelling in the reverse direction is free.

Penang is a Far East warehouse for everything imaginable, from electronic gadgets to plastic toys. There are silks from Thailand and India, fabrics from England, cameras from Germany and Japan, textiles from America and from Malaysia, brocade and *sarong*. **Jalan Pinang** is the main shopping bazaar. Shops open in the early morning and do not close until the bars are empty and the late moviegoers have cleared the streets.

Lebuh Campbell, just off Jalan Pinang, is the main "Chinese" shopping centre where Nepalese street vendors sell nylon shirts, fake alligator-skin shoes, laughing jack-in-the-boxes, and precious stones, guaranteed to cut glass.

Perhaps the most exciting shopping in Penang is in the many "junk" shops along **Rope Walk**. Here, shoppers must literally climb over mounds of discarded gear. Those who do not mind getting their hands dirty are certain to discover a dusty thing or two. One London boutique salesgirl found a Chinese emperor's robe salvaged from the local opera stage.

Disappearing markets: One typical Malaysian institution is the ***pasar minggu*** or ***pasar malam*** (weekly market or night market). These are temporary markets which spring up in the street or an open space in the evenings or on the weekends. How and where they appear varies from place to place: in Penang, they are called *pasar malam* and move from location to location every two weeks. One Italian tourist returned to Penang after visiting the south for a week and was greatly disappointed to find that the market had apparently closed down. Only by chance did she learn that it had been moved somewhere else. The areas, wherever they might be, are well lighted and the bargains range from tiny trinkets to cheap Kelantan batik *sarong* and plastic sandals. People-watching here is especially enjoyable.

In Georgetown, walking is a delight and distances pass unnoticed. Taxis are plentiful and inexpensive but they are not allowed to "cruise" for customers. The easiest and most enjoyable way to get around is by trishaw. That way, the

Shopping cart with a difference.

city passes by in a kaleidoscope of changing colours, the way it should be in Georgetown. Even a trishaw ride in the monsoon rain can be enjoyable. The driver zips his passengers into a plastic covering, and pedals slowly through the misty streets. At night there is a special romance about riding in a trishaw, when the driver lights small lamps that adorn both fenders. The tiny lights flicker in the inky darkness like glowworms in a tree.

Nighttime niceties: The streets of Georgetown are made for nightlife. The Chinese never seem to go to bed. Their open-front restaurants are noisy gathering places where waiters shout your order to someone in a back room. A jukebox, if there is one, is turned on full volume. Hawker stalls on Gurney Drive and the Esplanade do a thriving business, whilst brightly lit stores cater to late-night shoppers. At the fashionable hotels, latecomers wait in line at the discotheques. There are rooftop restaurants where diners look down over the city lights, hills and harbour, and dark cellar cabarets with no view at all.

Those who prefer their entertainment in bars can find a few around Georgetown and on the northern outskirts of the city. Some small and friendly establishments, like the **Hong Kong Bar**, keep a "family album" of snapshots showing just about every traveller who has walked in and bought a drink. They provide jukeboxes for dancing, game machines for entertainment and good-looking barmaids for conversation. Others are more consciously sophisticated, like the 1885 Room in the **Eastern and Oriental Hotel**. The leader of the band and the pianist as well, Albert Yeoh, has been playing for varied audiences at the E & O (once sister to Raffles Hotel in Singapore) for over 40 years. He once remarked that nowadays people prefer to sit and drink while they listen to the band, whereas previously his audience was always keen to get up and dance.

Penang is undoubtedly a place that makes evening walks fond memories. One does not have to look for excite-

Despite the Penang Bridge, traditionalists still take the ferry.

ment on the streets of Georgetown. If you take a room in a Chinese hotel, you will understand why. Early morning might begin with a funeral procession through the streets: there are drums and gongs and mourners. In the afternoon it might be a lion dance, a noisy affair with more drums and gongs, where mobs of youngsters follow the lion. Come evening and it could be a Chinese opera, where people sit and watch heavily painted faces pantomime classical tales of old, or a rock band playing pop tunes on the Esplanade. You can never tell what you might find – a bargain or a baritone.

Georgetown is still a city with few skyscrapers. **Komtar**, Penang's civic centre, is one and it has the most fashionable office block and the most sophisticated shopping plaza in the city. Its lower storeys are taken up by shops, a couple of cinemas, restaurants, and right down below, a bus station. Its probing circular tower forms a landmark clearly visible from the mainland.

Dainty doorways: It is not just the shops and junk stores that make wandering through the streets of Georgetown a delight. Narrow alleyways off bustling roads lead to quiet rows of Chinese homes, whose carved lintels and doorways bedazzle passersby: the small family temple erected on Gat Lebuh Gereja (Church Street) by millionaire Chung Keng Kwee is a good example. Inside the temple, a lifelike bronze statue of Chung in the robes of a Chinese mandarin stands resplendent. Chung made his fortune from the tin of Larut and is remembered as one of the leaders of the Chinese factions in the Larut Wars of the 1860s.

Chinese immigrants arriving in Malaysia for the first time a hundred years ago fell under the protection and control of one of the clan associations, whose functions were not unlike those of mediaeval European guilds – to promote the interests of their members and to provide help to those of their number in distress. The ancestral halls of these clan associations – such as the Khoo, Ong, Tan and Chung – are called *kongsi*

The Eastern & Oriental in colonial days.

and they are scattered all over town.

But the most impressive is the clan hall built by the Khoo Kongsi. The **Leong San Tong Khoo Kongsi** at the junction of Lebuh Pitt and Lebuh Acheh, comprises two buildings standing on opposite sides; one is the ancestral temple itself and the other serves as a stage for plays and operas on appropriate occasions.

Dragons on the rooftops: Khoo Kongsi is so elaborate that it almost exceeds celestial proprieties. The clan house was designed to capture the splendour of an imperial palace with a seven-tiered pavilion, wondrous dragon pillars and hand-painted walls engraved with the Khoo rose emblem. The original design was so ambitious that conservative Khoo clansmen cautioned against it lest the Emperor of China be offended. Construction began in 1894 and it took eight years to complete. However, on the first night after the building was finished, the roof mysteriously caught fire. Clan members interpreted this as a sign that even the deities

considered the Khoo Kongsi "too palatial" for a clan house. The Khoos rebuilt it on a smaller scale and the result was one of perfection.

Entering its courtyard is like being guided out of time to a heavenly abode where dragons dance on rooftops and fairies play lutes among the clouds. Sagging eaves are transformed into enamel mosaics of celestial kingdoms. Gilded beams become curvilinear gardens where saintly immortals dwell. The outer walls are a pageant of legendary episodes carved, painted and polished by experts from Cathay. Giant guardian gods on the main doors prevent the intrusion of evil spirits, while stone lions chiselled from green granite help keep guard. Behind the altar's facade of glistening gold leaf and red lacquer stand statues of the gods of longevity, wealth, prosperity and happiness. On either side of the central shrine are ancestral halls honouring the patron saints of the clan. Surrounding their images are *sinchoos*, wooden tablets remembering deceased clansmen. Gold plaques on the walls are inscribed with the names of members who have earned a high academic degree or who have attained a position of leadership, such as Justice of the Peace.

Joss sticks for the Goddess of Mercy: Of all the Chinese temples, Penang's oldest is the **Kuan Yin Temple** in Lebuh Pitt, which is also the most humble and the most crowded. It belongs to the people in the street – the noodle hawkers, the trishaw riders, the housewives who do the daily marketing, the old shopkeepers who count abacus figures, the workers who build cupboards, repair bicycles or sell sundries. A Buddhist deity who refused to enter Nirvana as long as there was injustice on earth, Kuan Yin personifies mercy.

She is ever-present on Chinese altars, whether the worshippers be Taoist, Buddhist or Confucian. Throughout the day, people visit her temple to burden her with problems they cannot solve or to thank her for the blessings which ended their worries. The clicking of "divining sticks" ricochets throughout the halls as devotees ask her advice for **Rooftop patterns in Chinatown.**

the coming week. Men and women of Georgetown know that Kuan Yin will reply. She is perhaps the most beloved divinity of all the Chinese altars in Penang. The worshipping of Kuan Yin is a meeting-ground between traditional Chinese belief and Buddhism.

Kuan Yin's temple has a well-worn look. The halls are heavily laden with scented smoke. The floors are littered with joss-stick wrappers and discarded shopping bags. The altar looks like a banquet table with roasted chickens, sweet cakes, oranges, pineapples and cookies neatly placed as humble offerings to the goddess.

On the eve of Chinese New Year, when good luck is in highest demand, Kuan Yin's temple catches fire. Hundreds converge at her altars to burn joss sticks, light red candles, and invoke her name. Smoke billows from furnaces set up in the courtyard, as paper "joss money" is sent to Kuan Yin via the fire. Businessmen and beggars alike jam the front gates, carrying a stream of glowing joss sticks. An apparition appears amid the smoke. It is a human face transfigured by goggles and a kerchief over the nose. It looks like a space-age bandit or an air-pollution survivor behind a makeshift gas mask. Actually, it is a boy hired by the temple to collect the plethora of burning joss sticks and dump them in the furnace outside.

Set nearby, in direct contrast, is the Indian-Muslim-styled **Kapitan Kling Mosque**; built in 1800, it is the state's oldest mosque.

Penang Buddhism: The eve of Chinese New Year at the **Penang Buddhist Association** less than 2 kilometres (1½ miles) away on Jalan Anson, is a more formal affair compared to the mad rush of devotions at other temples. Women arrive in modern and simply cut *samfoos* or store-bought Western dresses, conscientiously fashionable. A teenage girl patiently leads her dignified grandfather across the wide marble floor where a seated congregation chants praises to Lord Buddha. The Association organisers busily arrange patterns of bright flowers, fruits and coloured

Ornate entrance to a Georgetown house.

cakes on a large, shiny table carved out of blackwood imported from Canton. Enthroned on the high altars are six white marble statues of Lord Buddha and his disciples. Crystal chandeliers from Czechoslovakia hang overhead and the walls are decorated with fine-lined paintings depicting Buddha's path to enlightenment. As temple bells ting, the chanting rises to usher in the new year, to celebrate an eternal rebirth for all generations. Outside the front door, beggars sit quietly chatting amongst themselves. They know benevolence is a precept of the Chinese New Year and they receive it passively.

Ordinarily, the large, luminous hallway that dominates the Chinese Buddhist Association is the most serene sanctuary in Penang. The building, completed in 1929, reflects the desire of a Buddhist priest who wanted to indoctrinate his followers with orthodox rites and ceremonies. Joss-stick hawkers or paper-money burners are not found here. Prayers are considered the essence of Buddhist worship, and the Penang Buddhist Association cherishes the simplicity inherent in its Buddhist faith.

The variety of Buddhist worship in Penang is so striking as to make sightseeing a new experience in every temple. One can enter the gigantic meditation hall at **Wat Chayamangkalaram** and find a workman polishing the left cheek of the 32-metre (105-foot) long Reclining Buddha, third largest statue of its kind in the world. Wat Chayamangkalaram, on Jalan Burma, is a Thai Buddhist monastery. Gigantic Naga serpents, mystical creatures that link earth to heaven, form the balustrades at the entrance of the meditation hall. Fierce-visaged giants tower over the doorways in the role of otherworldly bodyguards who leave little to the imagination. Monks with shaven heads and saffron robes soundlessly tread over lotus blossoms patterned on the tiled floor. All around the monumental image of slumber are smaller statues of lesser Buddhas with donation boxes on their pedestals. Inscribed on one box are the words: "To devotees who worship

Burning joss at the Kek Lok Si Temple.

this god, your wish will come true, what you wish will come to you."

Another form of Buddhist worship can be seen in the Burmese Temple on the other side of the road. A Buddha with a half haughty, half-serene expression is worshipped here. Another shrine is surrounded with a moat over which "heavenly" bridges fly. On either side is a Buddha, one refusing tempting fruits cradled in vast shells offered by a goofy-toothed man, who looks the picture of worldly indulgence. The other is accosted by two young women, and though the Buddha seems to be casting them aside, he almost looks as if he is secretly enjoying the temptation! Little shops in the shaded walkways sell little pink and green lotus flower-shaped candles to worshippers who leave the lighted candles reverently in front of the shrines.

Inspired by a vision: High above the bustle of Georgetown on a hilltop at **Ayer Hitam**, which is about 6 kilometres (4 miles) from the Buddhist Association, looms the **Kek Lok Si** or

Temple of Paradise. This temple, the largest Buddhist temple in Malaysia and one of the largest in the region, owes its existence to Beow Lean, a Chinese Buddhist priest from the Fukien province in China who first arrived in Penang in 1887. Soon after his arrival, he was appointed resident priest of the Kuan Yin Temple in Lebuh Pitt, and so impressed was he by the religious fervour of Penang's Buddhists that he decided to found a monastery to propagate the religion. He chose this site at Ayer Hitam, whose hills reminded him of his home in Fukien.

Work on the temple started in 1890, with its main buildings completed by 1904. The great pagoda tower, however, was not finished until 1930. It is dedicated to all manifestations of the Buddha, hence appropriately named the Pagoda of a Million Buddhas, renowned for the three architectural styles it contains – a Chinese base, a Thai middle section and a Burmese top.

When completed, Kek Lok Si became an instant tourist attraction as well

Chinese opera is a pleasant evening's diversion.

as a centre for Buddhist devotion. The tourism aspect dominates, however; visitors walk through arcades of souvenir stalls to the top of the pagoda and pay "voluntary" contributions for the privilege of ascending the tower.

On Sundays, Kek Lok Si witnesses a holiday parade as Chinese families spend their free afternoons strolling among the opulent gardens on the threshold of paradise. The spiritually oriented playground has an informal give-and-take atmosphere, free from the solemnity of secluded shrines.

Kek Lok Si is split into three tiers spread over a rocky incline. The three "Halls of the Great" honour Kuan Yin, goddess of mercy; Bee Lay Hood, the Laughing Buddha; and Gautama Buddha, founder of the faith. It is here that the monks pass their hour in prayer. The Tower of Sacred Books on the topmost tier houses a library of Buddhist scriptures and *sutras*, many of which were presented by the Kuang Hsu Emperor of China. An edict from the same emperor, cemented into a wall of this block, grants imperial approval to the establishment of the temple.

Neighbouring hills: In the northern direction, Jalan Ayer Hitam leads to yet another hill – the **Penang Hill**. Despite the first impression one might get about Georgetown being a busy place, it is a town of leisure beneath its facade. People who live here enjoy their city and island. They frequent the parks and gardens, take trips around the island and visit the many temples. Penang Hill is one of their favourite spots. As far back as 1897 people were struck by the scenic beauty and "the desirability of Penang Hill as a health resort".

There was only one problem: getting there. Someone finally came up with the idea of building a railway to the summit. After years of labour the line was completed. Two passenger cars mounted on tracks were attached to a thick cable, which passed through pulleys. Steam power was ruled out in favour of a Pelton wheel, propelled by water power. "An ingenious method," was the remark at the time. Everyone awaited

The picturesque Kapitan Kling Mosque.

the day when the railcars would start rolling. But when it finally arrived, the water wheels would not work. They did not even sputter.

In the next 25 years science progressed. After studying the funicular railway system in Switzerland, Penang residents opened the present line on 21 October 1923. It has been in operation ever since. The ride to the summit is one of the highlights of a visit to the island. As the cars rumble slowly up the steep incline, a panorama of sea and island, mountains and tropical valleys continuously unfolds. From each small substation along the way, paths disappear into the cool forest or gardens of private bungalows on the terraced slopes. One of the most pleasant experiences a visitor can have is to spend a day or two in the hotel at the summit. The 500 people who live on the hill have built a small Hindu temple and a mosque. The funicular railway operates from 6:30 a.m. to 9 p.m. daily. Rates are M$3 for adults and M$1.50 for children (return).

Apart from funicular railcars, Penang has much to offer in the way of recreation. Georgetown is Asia's Monte Carlo where, once a year, racing cars from all over South-East Asia career around the winding roads and along the sea front to compete in the Malaysian Grand Prix. Horse-racing is also popular and races are held five times a year at the Penang Turf Club. There is an 18-hole golf course; green fees are M$20 a day.

Penang has its share of the latest English language films. Anyone who has not seen a Chinese swordsman of old on the silver screen, wreaking vengeance against great odds, and usually winning, might find it a memorable experience.

Bliss below the waterfall: "Another very important consideration in a place proposed for a Colony is fresh water," wrote Lt. Popham of the Royal Navy. "No country can be better supplied with this valuable article than Prince of Wales' Island. Water descends from the hills and is collected into several small rivulets, the two principal of

Thai-style Buddhist statues at Wat Chaya-mangkalaram.

which empty themselves into the harbour, the one near, the other 5 kilometres (2 miles) from the town; and in the latter of these the ships' casks may be filled in the long-boats at low water."

After nearly 200 years, the freshwater springs in the hills above Georgetown continue to lure visitors up from the lowlands. Although they are labelled Waterfall Gardens, situated about 3 kilometres (2 miles) due northeast from Penang Hill, they are actually Penang's **Botanical Gardens** in the grounds of which grow some of Malaysia's most beautiful tropical plants. Monkeys inhabit the trees and delight visitors when they come down to the lawns to be fed, especially in the early mornings or late afternoons. The waterfalls start over a hundred metres above the gardens and come tumbling down through the green, where there are footpaths and small wooden bridges, much like a Japanese garden. On holidays, families round up distant relatives for a picnic lunch by the stream while barefoot children romp on the rocks or play "follow-the-tourist".

Benches are scattered throughout the gardens and provide pleasant resting spots in the shade. And, like other similar places in the world, lovers come to take advantage of blissful nature.

One of the most scenic spots on the island is **Ayer Hitam Dam**, with an 18-hectare (45-acre) lake reflecting the lush green foliage of the surrounding jungle. A 3-kilometre (2-mile) road from Kek Lok Si Temple winds its way up to the dam. The air becomes cool, especially in the evening when the breezes blow across the lake.

Beyond the dam, atop a hill and reached by a long flight of steps, is the Indian shrine of **Nattukotai Chettiar**. Here, as well as in Kuala Lumpur, is held the awe-inspiring festival of *Thaipusam*. There are those who claim that the *Thaipusam* festival in Penang is even more dramatic and interesting than the one in Kuala Lumpur. Certainly, it does not suffer in comparison.

Apart from Ayer Hitam Dam, Penang has a wealth of small reservoirs, most of them constructed not only for their

The funicular railway at Penang Hill, and the Kek Lok Si Temple.

usefulness but also with an eye for aesthetics. **Guillemard Reservoir** reposes on the peak of a hill on Mount Erskine. Its dazzling reflection is one of the first things arriving passengers see when flying into Penang. Around the reservoir are casuarinas planted in rows and trimmed to match the landscape.

Penang has numerous streams and waterfalls. Early Malays believed the water came from springs connected to Lake Toba in Sumatra. In fact it comes from rainfall, which averages 325 centimetres (130 inches) a year. Nonetheless, it remains a "valuable article" as Lt. Popham said, particularly when it runs through the gentle gardens behind the town.

Round-the-island trip: Beyond the outskirts of Georgetown another Penang begins. By starting at the waterfront in the morning, the visitor can head south, follow the winding and sometimes mountainous road for 74 kilometres (46 miles) and by the evening return to the same spot from which he started. He can visit a temple where poisonous snakes hang from the rafters, watch tropical fish swim in an aquarium, see an alleged footprint of a heroic Chinese admiral, swim in a pool beneath a waterfall, meet Malay fishermen in remote villages, have lunch in a polished teak restaurant and lounge away the afternoon on a soft, white beach.

Travellers have a variety of ways to make a round-the-island tour. Hotels and tourist offices can arrange for group tours in air-conditioned buses with guides. Private chauffeured cars with or without guides can be hired through the tourist office. There are also rent-a-car services, offering sedans for M$32 a day. Or make the trip by public bus: for less than a dollar it will take you anywhere. The only difficulty is that unless you want to hike, you cannot leave the main road.

On the outskirts of town are the mills and factories, and the Malay countryside. The roads are well marked with kilometre-stones indicating the distances from Georgetown. A road map is helpful but not essential. You cannot

Giant joss, and young temple visitor.

really get lost. There are a number of side roads, some worth exploring, but most of them end in remote villages on the coast. Where there is little traffic, the fishermen have the habit of drying their *ikan bilis* (very small fish) on the pavement. Oftentimes there may be a half-kilometre of fish laid out to dry, with slightly more than tyre room left on the road.

"Not worry, no bite," a Chinese lad insists as he probes at a small tree. Interwoven amongst the branches slithers a one-metre-long, green and yellow viper. The jaws open and red fangs hiss, "See," the boy repeats, "no bite."

The viper lives in the famous **Temple of Azure Cloud**, more popularly known as the Snake Temple. The road south from the aquarium passes the **Science University of Malaysia** (Universiti Sains Malaysia) and the 14-kilometre stone marks the serpents' shrine. When you climb the steps to the ornate temple, you may think there is nothing unusual about it. Even when you see a few snakes curled up, it does not seem too extraordinary. But then you begin to notice that poisonous pit vipers are everywhere – on altars, shrines, incense burners, candlesticks, vases, tables, underfoot and overhead. There is even a "maternity" tree where earthworms slither along the branches. In an adjoining room a photographer stands by to take your photo, if you care to pose with a snake or two curled around your arms and neck. These vipers, the photographer guarantees, have no poison fangs.

The snakes are venerated because of their kinship to the mythical dragons of Chinese folklore. It is claimed that, during the day, burning incense in the temple keeps them doped. At night they let themselves down from the ceiling and branches to suck the chicken eggs left for them by worshippers.

Sacred footprints: Having no luck with lotteries? Do you suffer from poor health, or need success over business rivals? Or is it one of the opposite sex you wish to conquer? If so, you might try joining the multitude of believers who pay their respects at a small shrine

Malay kampong house is tidy and colourful.

176

on a rocky promontory at **Batu Maung**, a fishing village on the southeast tip of the island about 3 kilometres (2 miles) from the Bayan Lepas Airport. The shrine marks the sacred footprint of Admiral Cheng Ho, the Chinese "Columbus" of Malaysia. Villagers believe that Cheng Ho called at this spot on one of his seven voyages to South-East Asia. On Langkawi Island, 96 kilometres (60 miles) to the north, is a similar footprint. The two are believed to be a pair and anyone who lights joss sticks and places them in the urns beside the footprint will have good luck and great fortune.

When it is high tide at Batu Maung, fishing boats are run up on the beach, and left high and dry when the waters recede. Ships' joiners take advantage of nature's drydock to repair vessels before the next tide ends their workday. These skilled carpenters use tools that should be museum pieces, as ancient as the result of a thousand years of handed-down experience. It was in vessels such as these that their distant ancestors explored and traded in the islands of the Malay archipelago. They have perhaps turned from traders to fishermen but their art remains the same.

Malay *kampong*: Several small roads in the south branch off to the coast. Usually they are the commercial link between a fishing village and the trunk road. It was in small villages such as these that the few Malays lived when Francis Light established the first settlement.

Malaysian architecture in cities and towns changes constantly with the times but the *kampong* houses look much the same as they did a hundred years ago. Malays take pride in their homes, the interior of which can often be glimpsed from the road. The furnishings are simple and each house will have a framed photograph of the King and Queen. Houses are elevated, making the lifestyle within cool, dry and clean. There are fruit trees in the neatly swept courtyards, bearing rambutans, mangosteens, bananas and papayas. Outside each house is a basin for wash-

Hotel pool at Batu Ferringhi.

ing the feet before climbing the stairs. Malays always leave their shoes outside to keep the interior of their houses clean. Cleanliness is one of the prime virtues laid down in the Koran and most women sweep their homes several times a day.

Winding roads to the north: The road skirts around the southern end of the island and turns north. The scenery changes from flat rice land to rolling hills. Cultivation gives way to dense, damp jungles. The road twists upward and where the foliage clears, there are striking views of the island dropping to the sea far below. Here, too, are spice plantations of pepper, cloves and nutmegs, whose yields lured Arab, Spanish, Portuguese and other Western traders to this part of the world long ago. At **Titi Kerawang**, there are waterfalls in the hills, with a serene view of the Indian Ocean. The natural freshwater pool that is filled from the waterfalls is suitable for bathing, though a big water pipeline mars the scenery.

Finally at **Telok Kumbar**, the road reaches the northern end of the island, where it again swings eastwards to run along the coast which has become the preserve of hotels and sun worshippers. As it does so, it leaves behind the rugged jungled promontory of **Muka Head** which has a lonely lighthouse at its tip. Muka Head is part of a forest reserve and there are no roads to its quiet isolated coves: however, hired boats at Telok Kumbar take visitors out to any one of them to spend the day or to camp for the night. The small forest station near Telok Kumbar itself is set in a well-laid out arboretum.

The road to Penang's north coast follows the curve of the land, twisting up and around a hill or skirting the fringe of the sea. Rocky headlands jutting out into the sea divide the shoreline into small bays and coves, each with a different character and charm. Although the waters are not as clear as on the East Coast, the beaches are still popular for swimming and sunbathing.

Most activities are centred around **Batu Ferringhi**, one of the most popular beach resorts in South-East Asia. Here are the large luxury hotels of **Rasa Sayang**, **Casuarina**, **Golden Sands** and the **Holiday Inn**. Their facilities include waterskiing, sailing, windsurfing, water scooters, and pony or horseback riding. Smaller and older, but comfortable and reasonably priced, are the **Palm Beach** and **Lone Pine**. There are also small inns and motels. Many villagers in this area, especially at Telok Bahang, also offer accommodation.

At **Telok Bahang** there is a 100-hectare (250-acre) recreational park for trekking and picnicking. There is also the country's best **Butterfly Farm**, where some of the loveliest butterflies and most awe-inspiring insects of Malaysia are bred and displayed – alive, and not pinned down!

These beaches are readily accessible from Georgetown – the road is good and the distances are short. The bus journey involves a change of buses.

Sandwiched between the Hotel Rasa Sayang and the Casuarina on Batu Ferringhi beach is the **Yahong Art Gallery**. The gallery is a storehouse of some of the finest arts, crafts and antiques of Malaysia and China. It is also the home of Mr. Chuah Thean Teng, Malaysia's foremost batik artist, whose work has won international recognition at a number of one-man exhibitions in the major capitals of the world.

There are restaurants galore, from the beginning of the beach area at **Tanjong Tokong** stretching the 11 kilometres (7 miles) to Telok Bahang. Often they consist of nothing more elaborate than a collection of rickety, wooden tables set up on the sands overlooking the distant shoreline of Georgetown to the south. Waiters approach the tables casually dressed in whatever best suits them for that day. But the dishes they suggest are something else – delicious, fresh seafood soup with sharks' fins, big, round, crisp rolls and chicken baked in seasoned black sauce. At Tanjong Tokong, the **Sayang Masmera Restaurant** serves excellent Malay food. At **Tanjong Bungah**, two of the better restaurants are the **Hollywood**, offering Muslim, Chinese and European cuisines, and the **Seri Batik**, serving authentic Malay dishes.

Watching the evening show – a golden sunset at Batu Ferringhi.

KEDAH
AND PERLIS

One of the best views in Penang is from the Esplanade, looking across the water over to the mainland where **Gunung Jerai** or **Kedah Peak** rises majestically – a bluish-grey mass which, at 1,200 metres (3,950 feet) is the highest point in the northwest of the peninsula. This same peak, standing prominently above the flatland surrounding it, was the first sight the land-hungry sailors from across the Bay of Bengal had of the Malaysian shore. It is hardly surprising that Kedah Peak served as a lodestar to early merchant voyagers and that the peninsula's first centre of civilisation should spring up at the foot of its slopes.

But Kedah's position at the cross-roads of South-East Asian trade also exposed it to constant danger. In its early years, the state was subject to the control of the great trading empire of Funan, based in Vietnam, and then of the Sri Vijaya Empire, established near Palembang in southern Sumatra. Later, Kedah fell under the shadow of the Malaccan sultanate and in the years that followed, had to fight for survival against the Portuguese, the Thais, the Bugis, the Burmese and the Dutch.

Up until the beginning of the 19th century, Kedah's rulers were remarkably successful in preserving their independence, but having put their faith in British power (and lost Penang in the process), they fell to the Thais. Kedah was under the direct rule of Bangkok for 20 years; the price it had to pay to regain its autonomy from the Thais was the loss of Perlis which became a separate principality under Thai protection in 1842. From that time until 1909, both Kedah and Perlis were vassals of Bangkok; in 1909, the two states were transferred to British suzerainty. They accepted British control but were more successful in maintaining their own way of life than most other peninsular states during the British period.

The inhabitants of Kedah and Perlis are mainly Malays, and the Malay character of the state is immediately evident as soon as their borders are crossed.

Ancient temples: A single-span steel bridge across the broad Muda River marks the entrance into Kedah. Penang island appears as a low hump to the rear and the mass of Kedah Peak looms in front. **Sungai Patani**, Kedah's second largest town, is 15 kilometres (9 miles) away, from where the road runs northwards. At **Bedong**, another few kilometres away, a turning to the left leads to Merbok and the Bujang Valley.

The whole area between the Bujang Valley and the Muda River seems to have its roots in being the outpost of the Pallava culture of South India, and it is littered with the remains of ancient Malaysia – buried temples, ancient inscriptions in Sanskrit (the sacred language of Hinduism), numerous examples of porcelain from China, Indian beads, and glassware from the Middle East. These remains paint a picture of the ancient civilisation which once flourished here, to the delight of archaeologists who, for over a hundred years

Preceding pages: The Zahir Mosque at Alor Setar. **Left**, waiting for the school bus.

now, have been uncovering them from the edges of villages, sides of riverbanks and at the foot of jungled hills.

To get an idea of what has been found, take the turning at Bedong, and go to Merbok, the village at the foot of Kedah Peak where the **Temple of the Hill of Chiselled Stone** (Candi Bukit Batu Pahat) stands beside a rushing mountain stream. The *candi* is the largest and best preserved of all those found in the area, and fittingly, nearby the Museum Department has established an **Archaeological Museum** which contains the most important finds. Other relics can be found in the state museum at Alor Setar. Because of the historical importance of the whole Merbok-Muda area, it has been designated a national park.

Beyond Merbok, the road winds picturesquely on and eventually turns south to **Tanjong Dawai**, a picture-card fishing village on the Muda Estuary, where the day's catch is laid out on concrete slabs to dry in the sun. A ferry crosses the estuary (but not for cars) to **Pantai Merdeka**, a popular beach for bathers. The beach can also be reached direct from Penang by road.

To get onto Kedah Peak, the young and energetic climb the mountain track; the older and wiser take the narrow road which winds up from its junction with the main highway near Guar Chempedak. The rooms in the small Government Rest House at the top can be booked through the government offices in either Sungai Patani or Alor Setar.

The rice capital: Leaving Kedah Peak behind, a new (toll) highway rushes northwards with hardly a bend until it reaches the state capital of **Alor Setar** about 40 kilometres (25 miles) farther on. The country through which the highway passes is flat, offering vistas over broad, green (or fallow, depending on the season) rice fields which stretch as far as the eye can see until they merge with the misty cloud-flecked hills of the Main Range in the distant background. The flatness of the landscape is only interrupted here and there by clumps of bamboo and palm sheltering a village or a small homestead.

The Crown of Kedah monument in the town centre.

If you take the old main road to Alor Setar, you will find that it is accompanied all the way from Kedah Peak by a 19th-century irrigation canal built by Wan Mat Saman, the state *menteri besar* (chief minister) of the day, in order to boost rice production.

Kedah's rice output has quadrupled in recent years as a result of the construction of a dam on the upper reaches of the Muda River and by the development of a vast irrigation scheme. Known as the Muda Irrigation Project, it is one of the few schemes financed by the World Bank which has fulfilled the aims of its sponsors and provided adequate returns. This jolted Alor Setar out of its centuries of small-town existence.

In the heart of Alor Setar is the traditional **padang** that is somewhat marred by a modern and monstrous fountain, but nothing can obscure the grace and beauty of the **Zahir Mosque** which was built in 1912 and is one of the largest mosques in Malaysia. The charming and unique Thai-style **Balai Besar** (Great Hall), built in 1898, occu-

pies another corner of the *padang*. Balai Besar was used as an audience hall by Kedah's sultans of old when they appeared in public to receive petitions and hear grievances. Today, it is still the place where His Royal Highness the Sultan of Kedah observes ceremonial, festive and other occasions.

The **Balai Nobat** opposite houses the instruments (*nobat*) of Kedah's royal orchestra. Only four such orchestras exist in Malaysia today – the other three are to be found in Terengganu, Selangor and Johor – and Kedah's is reputed to be the oldest.

According to tradition, the drums of the Kedah *nobat* were a gift from Malacca's last sultan. The *nobat* is an important part of the regalia of state: no Kedah sultan is considered a legitimate ruler if he has not been installed to the accompaniment of the *nobat*. The Kedah *nobat* is also played on other state occasions when the sultan is present, and may be heard daily during the Muslim fasting month when it is played for five minutes before the end of the

Despite some preoccupations with the modern world, Kedah is still known as the rice capital.

day's fast from the Balai Nobat. The privilege of being a member of the royal orchestra, by the way, is hereditary and has been handed down through the generations. Special permission to see the *nobat* may be obtained through the offices of the state secretariat in the modern government building nearby.

The **State Museum** near the stadium, on the road to the airport and the north, displays an interesting collection of items connected with Kedah's past as well as exhibits from the Bujang Valley. A few kilometres farther on, at **Anak Bukit**, lies the sultan's modern *istana* (palace), the grounds of which are open to the public on weekends.

Side trips: The small fishing village of **Kuala Kedah**, 12 kilometres (7½ miles) from Alor Setar, has one of the best preserved Malay forts in the country and is renowned for its excellent seafood, which is obtainable "on board" two boat-like restaurants set out on the sea. As you eat your steamed crabs with hot chilli sauce, your fried squids, and your *otak-otak* (a spicy fish concoction

of Thai origin cooked in banana leaf), watch the sun set over Pulau Langkawi 50 kilometres (31 miles) away, and savour the fresh salt air.

The fort is on the other side of the river, easily reached by an inexpensive *sampan* trip. At about noon on a calm November Sunday in 1821, "a large fleet of prows full of Siamese was observed standing into the Quedah river". The Siamese landed on the pretext of collecting rice supplies and then, without warning, turned on the Malay dignitaries who had assembled to greet them. Although the flower of Kedah's aristocracy had been killed or taken prisoner within the hour, the fort held out for another six days before it too fell. This disaster marked the beginning of 20 years of subjugation to direct Siamese rule. The fort was built in the 1770s, precisely to meet the attack which came in 1821. Today it stands, partially restored, with its handsome main gateway bearing witness to strong Western influence on its design.

From Alor Setar, other roads branch

Kuala Perlis is the jumping-off point for Pulau Langkawi.

inland to remote and less-frequented parts of the state. Along the road to Kuala Nerang at **Langgar**, Kedah's rulers lie buried in stately mausoleums. **Kuala Nerang** is a small market town prettily set at the confluence of two streams. Many of its inhabitants are of Thai descent.

Another road branching off from Pokok Sena runs to Nami, Sik and eventually, to Baling, passing through wild hilly country with occasional patches of settlement. **Nami** is the scene of the *Mak Yong* performances, a traditional Thai-Malay dance-drama which is only seen elsewhere in Kelantan. **Baling** is famous as the place where talks took place in 1955 between Tunku Abdul Rahman, the Prime Minister at the time, and Chin Peng, the leader of the Malayan Communist Party, in an attempt to find a peaceful solution to the communist insurrection. The talks failed, but communism petered out. The massive limestone hill which looms over the town is a landmark for kilometres around. From Baling, the road climbs up to Keroh and the Thai border, and from Keroh down to Gerik and the East Coast Highway or to the Perak River Valley. Another road runs from Baling to Sungai Patani and Penang.

Patrolling Perlis: **Perlis**, Malaysia's smallest state, is really an extension of the Kedah plain and of Kedah itself. The boundary between the two states is invisible except for the large signs posted. However, there is a change in the scenery; the flat rice fields give way to stark, solitary limestone outcrops which stand like sentinels on the plain. Spectacular and mysterious, these caverns hand out secrets to those who care to explore them. Many were the homes of Stone Age men.

Perlis has two main towns – **Arau** and **Kangsar**. Arau is a royal town, the seat of Perlis's *Rajah* and it has an attractive centre, but is of little interest to the tourist. Fifty kilometres (31 miles) to the north from here, is **Padang Besar** where the Malaysian and Thai railway systems meet and which has a market very popular with Malaysians during the weekends. The road to Padang

Besar also leads to **Kaki Bukit**, literally "the foot of the hill", where an interesting tunnel through the hill illuminated by electric light leads to a tin mine on the other side. A road opened in January 1984 connects Kaki Bukit with Wang Kelian and Setul (Satun), across the Thai border.

Islands of labyrinths and legends: Tucked into the northwest corner of the peninsula and nestled on the Thai-Malaysian sea-border are the **Langkawi Islands**, all 99 of them. Unlike the other islands of the west coast, the vast majority of the 30,000 people who live here are Malay. Of the 99 islands, only three are populated, and two of these very sparsely. The government in recent years has concentrated on promoting Langkawi as a tourist destination and to make this island more appealing and accessible, an airport was built, regular ferry services were organised and Langkawi was given duty-free status in 1987. There has not been the great rush that the government hoped for, and even in season, Langkawi is a quiet and rela-

Resort facilities are readily available on Langkawi.

tively unspoilt island as yet. Ferries run from **Kuala Perlis**, a small port an hour's drive from Alor Setar. The crossing takes just over two hours. Flights can be made from Penang, Kuala Lumpur, Alor Setar and Singapore.

When the islands are first seen from the ferry they appear as one, spread out along the horizon in a jagged and uncertain silhouette. But as the ferry gets closer, the view changes. The various outlines of hills and bays separate themselves into a maze of islands, amongst which are secret channels, narrows, inlets and bays. Shadowed cliffs, topped by dense virgin jungle reach up to 600 metres (1,950 feet) and drop abruptly into the sea. In the inlets, fishermen catch small garoupa which they take to fish farms where they are fattened for the market. This indeed does seem the perfect setting for the many legends that surround the island. It is also obvious why pirates and buccaneers who preyed upon the trading ships in the Malacca Straits used these islands as a place of refuge.

A day in the country is an enlightening experience.

The ferry passes the **Langkawi Island Resort**, an imposing building built in a neo-traditional style, situated at the water's edge 800 metres (850 yards) from the main quay of the main village, **Kuah**. This small village has been transformed by the island's duty-free status, and nearly every shop in town is crowded with bottles of liquor, boxes of tobacco and electronic items. Not all items are a bargain, compared to prices in Penang or Singapore, but the shopper may like to spend some time browsing in these shops. There are also one or two local craft shops, with hand-painted fabrics, shellwork and Langkawi stones with miniature paintings on them.

A few years ago, Kuah was the only area on the island where visitors could find accommodation; there are several small hotels in town, as well as the Government Rest House and TDC (Tourist Corporation)-owned Langkawi Island Resort at the other end of the scale. Nowadays however, visitors can choose from a variety of hotels, beach chalets and huts situated at pretty

beaches around the island.

Coves, corals and caves: Ornithologists and lepidopterists will delight in these islands, which have species of butterflies not found anywhere else in Malaysia. For others, the main joys are the relatively uncrowded beaches and the pretty little islands that lie offshore. The main island boasts some beautiful coves rich in corals and marine life.

Most of the accommodation on the beach can be found at **Pantai Cenang**, in the southwest of the island and an hour's bus ride from Kuah. The huge **Pelangi Beach Resort** was built here in early 1988, and its attractive two-storey buildings are built in a traditional style. Small jeeps and bicycles with little carts attached drive between these chalets, delivering passengers and their luggage, sundowner drinks on your verandah facing the sea, and fresh supplies of toiletries and towels. Although service is much the same as at many international hotels, the unique layout of the resort and its pretty setting, make this a luxurious but a relaxed place to stay.

Along the beach further south lies more modest accommodation, but many of the huts and chalets are very pleasant and the staff friendly. Some of the nicest chalets are at **Semarak**, which is located at perhaps the prettiest part of the beach.

To the west, past the airport, **Pantai Kok** has a few chalets along its beautiful beach. Other accommodation can be found in the north in **Pantai Rhu**, at the Mutiara Hotel, an unfortunately rather ugly hotel on a delightful stretch of beach. From Tanjong Rhu, fishing boats can be hired to go round the cape to the grey limestone cliffs beyond, where the legendary cave, **Gua Cerita** (meaning Cave of Legends), is inscribed with writings from the Holy Koran. To reach its entrance, climb precariously up a rickety bamboo ladder hung from stalactites.

After you have chosen your place to stay, and have tried the lovely waters surrounding Langkawi Island, you may like to take a round-the-island tour, taking in the landmarks with the leg-

Waiting for a bite, left, and for the tide to roll in, right.

ends attached to them.

A tour of legends: Hotels and shops in town rent bicycles and motorbikes, but for a really reliable and versatile vehicle, none is better than the four-wheel drive jeep hired out by the Pelangi Beach Resort (for hotel guests only) which will allow you to negotiate some of the rough roads inland. Start from Pantai Cenang with your jeep or motorcycle, and take the new road that passes the airport and leads you past **Pantai Tengah** to **Kampong Kok** and its nearby beach. After stopping for a swim, turn your eyes inland to catch your breath over the glorious mountains, swathed in clouds, their black jagged peaks cut out against the sky.

Your next destination will lead you into this range as you turn off for **Telaga Tujuh** (seven pools) on the northwest road. The rough road finishes at a *warong* (roadside café) where you can park your vehicle. A short walk uphill will bring you to a view of the pools that tumble one into the other down the mountainside. Legend has it that the mountain fairies come here to bathe and wash their long hair with tree roots and sweet plants. You will not meet any of them, however, as at the sight of a human they will vanish, leaving behind them a fragrant and lingering perfume.

The road now proceeds northeastwards, with mountains to the left and rice fields to the right. After passing the turn-off to **Pantai Datai**, drive eastwards until the road meets the coast at **Pasir Hitam**, or Black Sand Beach. The sand here is streaked with black lines, which give the beach its name. Next you reach **Tanjong Rhu**. The small town here looks more developed than Kuah itself, partly because here is the jetty where large boats used to arrive from Penang. This service has been temporarily discontinued due to lack of demand. A road which travels north will take you to Pantai Rhu and Gua Cerita.

After turning back along this road, you will meet the main road again. Turn left and after a kilometre or so, a small fenced-off area with a few huts will announce that you have arrived at **Te-**

laga **Air Panas** (Hot Water Pools). This attraction is also well sign-posted from both directions. It is not, however, particularly attractive to the visitor, being three small pools (the size of large washing-up bowls) set in concrete. But it has a marvellous legend attached to it, and is therefore worthy of some note.

There once lived two rich families on Langkawi; the son of one of these fell in love with the daughter of the other, but her parents did not approve of the match, and refused the union. The son was furious, and the disagreement between the families developed into a full-blown feud. It erupted into a free-for-all fight with all the family members taking part. In the ensuing fight, pots and pans were thrown wildly. The gravy pot with its contents landed at Kuah (meaning gravy), the jugs of boiling water formed the present Telaga Air Panas, and the water remaining poured into the ground at **Kisap** (meaning to seep). It is said that the fighting raged on until the two fathers were suddenly transformed into two mountain peaks!

Continue along this road to Kuah and a small track to the right about 5 kilometres (3 miles) from Tanjong Rhu leads you to **Durian Perangin waterfalls**. The track is deeply rutted and is only passable by four-wheel drive or with difficulty by motorbike. A trek up the side of the waterfall through the undergrowth is well worthwhile to see the pool at the top. Dense jungle lies all around and civilisation seems far away.

You will by now most probably have worked up a healthy appetite. Drive on southwards to Kuah and stop at the restaurant on the seafront, which serves excellent seafood.

To complete the tour of the island, take the road leading westwards from Kuah. A turning to the right 10 kilometres or so (6 miles) from Kuah takes you to **Mahsuri's Tomb**. This famous lady who, it is said, lived about 200 years ago, was wrongfully accused of adultery with a man she had shown kindness to. Derembang was a weary traveller who welcomed her help with much gratitude and respect. But the chief's wife became jealous of Mahsuri

and after a short battle Mahsuri was condemned to death. A soldier was ordered to plunge a *kris* (sword) into her heart, and as he did so, white blood spurted out from the wound. As she lay dying, Mahsuri raised her arms to the sky and laid a curse on the island that would last for seven generations. It is said that Langkawi lay desolate and deserted during this time. Mahsuri is now a local heroine, and her tomb has become a shrine. Gleaming white walls and resting huts now enclose the tomb.

A result of her curse can be seen inland at **Padang Mat Sirat** (Field of Burnt Rice), further inland in the rice-growing area where monsoon rains occasionally upturn strata of black earth. These darkened grains are said to remain from the time when villagers preferred to burn their rice fields rather than let their precious harvest fall into Siamese hands.

Another intriguing legend is connected to one of the islands that lies off the shores of the main island. **Dayang Bunting Island**, the second largest of the group, has a lake set in dense jungle and separated from the sea by a narrow strip of land. The freshwater lake is known as the Lake of the Pregnant Maiden. The maiden was a Kedah princess forbidden to marry her Malay prince lover. After drinking water from this lake, Telani the maiden became pregnant, and on discovering this, the King became angry and banished her to this deserted island. In her sorrow, Telani drowned herself in the lake and she became Sang Kelembai, a rock by the lake. Her child who had fallen into the lake was transformed into a white crocodile. The lake has now become famous as a place where barren women can come to drink the lake's waters, and many pilgrims claim to have conceived after the visit.

Boats from Tanjong Rhu, Pantai Cenang and Kuah will take you on a tour to this island, and also to other islands, such as the pretty **Pulau Bumbon**. Scuba-diving amongst the coral-filled waters can also be enjoyed by boat. Inquire in Kuah, the Island Resort or at Pelangi Resort on Pantai Cenang.

Heading home with the nets after a day at sea.

NEGRI SEMBILAN, NINE STATES IN ONE

Rubber plantations and tin dot the landscape heading south. Along the road to Port Dickson, travellers leave the state of Selangor behind and enter **Negri Sembilan**, which means "Nine States" in Malay. The name alludes to the loose federation of Malay chiefs who ruled these lands before they were united under British administration. Much of the countryside – small wooden homes with batik on the clotheslines and papaya trees in the front yard – is reminiscent of the quiet Malay villages that were sprinkled over Negri Sembilan centuries ago.

The state owes its existence to Malacca, which thrived and waxed wealthy as a trading port at the beginning of the 15th century. As Malacca rose and developed, Menangkabau settlers from Sumatra moved across the Straits of Malacca, and made their homes in the fertile valleys and hills behind the port.

They brought with them their unique traditions – the matrilineal system, the social order in which inheritance follows the female line; their laws; their style of political organisation; and their style of architecture. The small principalities they founded formed the nucleus of the "Nine States".

Negri Sembilan is, in fact, a federation within the Federation of Malaysia; some of the original nine states have disappeared, however, and its present ruler is not a sultan but a *Yang Tuan Besar* (translated as, "He Who is Greatest"). The first *Yang Tuan* was elected in the 1770s and his successors faced the usual problems caused by the great tin rush of the 19th century – over-mighty subjects and civil wars, which eventually resulted in British protection. Under the new dispensation, Seremban, the principal town of Sungai Ujong (the largest of the nine states), was made the administrative capital, while the *Yang Tuan* continued to reside at Sri Menanti, a safe 26 kilometres (16 miles) away.

Seremban – true to the past: The old

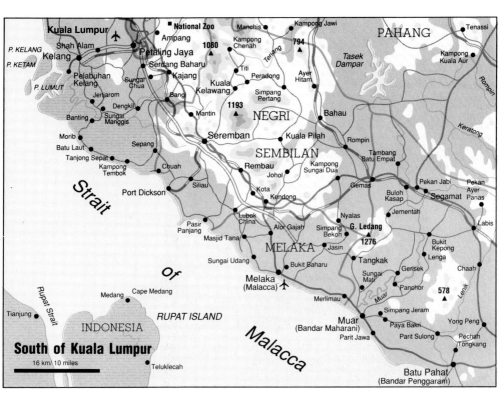

road to **Seremban** winds south from Kuala Lumpur, through Kajang and over the scenic Mantin Pass. Seremban, the state capital till today, could not be more typical of any of the Malayan-Chinese towns that sprang out of the tin mining boom a hundred years ago.

The town's Chinese kernel is represented by the regular lines of crossed streets, laid out in the commercial and shopping district. Characteristic rows of two-storey Chinese shophouses line up here although their even lines are being increasingly punctuated by taller modern buildings in between. Above the din of trishaw bells and bargain sessions, government clerks mill over their paperwork in colonial buildings set on the hills behind the town. The state council and municipal offices feature late 19th-century architecture at its best – neo-classical colonial style. They overlook the attractive **Lake Gardens**, formed by a narrow valley running down to the main town. And, true to Negri Sembilan's past, the impressive state mosque rises nearby on nine pil-' lars, symbolising the nine states of Negri Sembilan.

Seremban is in Menangkabau country, largely settled by Malays from West Sumatra. Menangkabau means "buffalo horns" and many of the town's houses have roofs that sweep up to two horn-like peaks. The **Arts and Handicrafts Centre** near the junction of the Seremban-Kuala Lumpur Highway provides a grandiose example of the Menangkabau architectural style. In its compound stand older examples of Menangkabau buildings dating back to the 19th century. One of them was once the residence of a Malay princess who lived at Ampang Tinggi, some distance away. It was dismantled at its origianl site and was brought here piece by piece to be reconstructed, and became for many years the state museum. At the centre is a fine display of ceremonial *kris*, a collection of Bugis and Menangkabau swords, and various types of royal adornments. There are also many fine examples of local woodcarving.

Seremban makes a good centre from

Ice cream break on the beach.

which to explore the surrounding countryside. Low rolling hills tuck away small villages, set amidst orchards and rice fields. These towns bear romantic names redolent of Menangkabau history – Johol, Kuala Pilah, Jelebu, Inas, Terachi and Rembau – but there is nothing spectacular about them apart from the quiet charm of their location.

About 25 kilometres (15½ miles) north out of Seremban, and **Kajang** (in the state of Selangor) is reached. If you are hungry – or even if you are not – stop awhile. Kajang boasts the best *satay* in all Malaysia. Its meat is not better in Kajang than in other parts of the country, but Kajang makes the best sauce.

Satay is the hamburger of South-East Asia. Chicken, mutton or beef is cut into bite-sized pieces, mixed with spices, salt and sugar and marinated for at least six hours. The meat is then threaded on skewers and grilled over a charcoal fire. From time to time it is basted with oil. The sauce for satay is made from peanuts, chillis and coconut milk with salt and sugar to taste.

For a hot spring dip, head for the **Pedas Hot Spring**, located just before the Pedas Village in the Rembau district, which is 30 kilometres (18½ miles) southeast of Seremban.

Carpentry without nails: A welcome neighbour to Seremban, 49 kilometres (30 miles) west, the town of **Sri Menanti** boasts the **Istana Lama** ("Old Palace"). The palace, built in the 1990s, is really not very old and was the creation of two well-known master craftsmen of the day. Not a single nail was used in its construction. Made of timber throughout, its 21-metre- (70-foot) tall tower used to house the private apartment of the *Yang Tuan Besar* as well as the royal archives and treasury. It ceased to be a royal residence in 1931, when a new stone palace was completed and today, it serves as a museum.

"Living stones": The tall irregularly shaped stones lining the wayside prove another attraction for visitors. Local villagers regard these stones with veneration and often use them as shrines (*keramat*), referring to them as "living

Promontory at Port Dickson juts into the Malacca Straits.

stones" because they believe that the stones actually grow – although there has been no evidence of growth in recent years. Also believed to mark the graves of long forgotten leaders of the distant past, the stones usually appear in pairs with a distinct north-south orientation. Thirty groups of such stones have been located in the Kuala Pilah district of the state.

But **Pengkalan Kempas**, a small village on the road between Port Dickson and Malacca, owns the most enigmatic of these stones. Popularly known as "The Sword, The Spoon and The Rudder" (on account of their respective shapes), the three stones are elaborately carved to spell their Hindu origin although one of them has the word "Allah" inscribed on it.

They lie next to the tomb of Sheikh Ahmad Majnun, another mystery in its own right. The Sheikh died a hero's death in 1467, so says the inscription, during his fight to save "the princess". But time has erased what actually happened from the memories of the local folk, although they continue to pay homage to the dead man.

The place's creepiness heightens with the "ordeal" stone, which has a hole big enough to admit a man's hand. The story tells that it will tighten around the fist of any liar brave enough to make the test.

By the blue lagoon: Thirty-two kilometres (20 miles) south of Seremban, stretches the long beach of **Port Dickson** which was planned, at the end of the 19th century, to be a new outlet for the tin of Sungai Ujong as well as a colonial health resort where tired expatriate officials could recuperate from the rigours of their work. Today, Port Dickson has become a popular weekend rendezvous for Malaysians.

Do not expect a bustling port, for it is not. Nor is Port Dickson much more than a one-street town. But the 16 kilometres (10 miles) of beach to the south, which terminates at the old **Rachado Lighthouse**, is something else indeed. That first view of the lonely sea, seen through the coconut trees, is a silent

Negri Sembilan's State Library.

196

spectacle. The sea is deep blue and seems to merge with the sky in the horizon afar. The drive southward along the uncluttered coast is so exhilarating that it's easy to be tempted to park and dive into the inviting water.

The **Yacht Club**, 7 kilometres (4 miles) out of town, encourages travellers to use its facilities but you must be introduced by a member, and its four pleasant bedrooms cannot be booked in advance. There is a swimming pool and four good, hard tennis courts, but there are no boats for rental to non-members. Across the road is the nine-hole **Garrison Golf Club**.

Boats can be obtained, however, at the **Si-Rusa Inn**, 12 kilometres (7½ miles) from the town. Next door, the first-class **Federal Hotel** completes this holiday resort with its swimming pool, its discotheque and other amenities. Other hotels along this stretch of beach include the **Ming Court Beach Hotel**, the **Blue Lagoon Village**, the **Holiday Inn** and the delightfully-named **Sunshine Rotary Club**.

Of fish and corals: Clown fish, stick fish and live coral compensate for the murky waters of the blue lagoon. Reef shrubs undulate with the tides which flow over jagged submarine landscapes sprinkled with sea urchins.

A half-kilometre winding drive from Blue Lagoon Village and a climb of 63 steps through thick jungle lead to the 16th-century Portuguese lighthouse. It was built to guide sailing ships toward the historical port of Malacca, then the most important trading station in South-East Asia. Although the lighthouse is closed to the public, a smile and a nice word will generally gain you entry. Or safer still, obtain a pass from the Malacca Tourist Office, 90 kilometres (56 miles) away. The lighthouse keeper takes you up a narrow spiral stairway to the light chamber above. The sudden view is striking. After the visit, an exciting jungle walk down to the beach can be made from the lighthouse gate.

From Port Dickson it is a 90-minute drive to Malacca, where the past of the southwest coast is very much alive.

Detail of the Menangkabau style, Seremban.

MALACCA – A
SLEEPY HOLLOW

History is everywhere in Malacca, peeping out from odd corners, hinting truths from epitaphs, yet never really telling it. It is a town with a glorious past; about four centuries ago, a Portuguese chronicler and frequent visitor said, "Whosoever holds Malacca has Venice by the throat." Even though present-day Malacca no longer holds the key to the trade by which Venice kept "the gorgeous East in fee", it still occupies the foremost place in the hearts of Malaysians.

Despite its power and glory, the history of Malacca is brief. It had hardly been in existence for more than a hundred years before it was attacked and conquered by the Portuguese. Until a Malay prince from Sumatra chanced upon the scene, Malacca was a small, unknown settlement of sea-gypsies, scraping a living as fishermen and subsistence farmers. In the 1400s, Para-meswara, the prince arrived, after fleeing from his own invaded domain of Tumasek. He proclaimed himself ruler of Malacca and proceeded to mould the obscure fishing village into a powerful centre of trade. By the end of the 15th century, Malacca had become the centre of a great trading empire and held an undisputed claim over the entire southern portion of the Malay peninsula, as well as the shores of East Sumatra opposite.

It became a rendezvous for every seafaring nation. Persians, Arabs, Tamils, Malabarese and Bengalis from the west; Javanese, Sundanese and Sulus from the archipelago; Chinese, Thais, Burmese, Chams as well as Khmers ventured to the harbour town in search of profit through trade, piracy or plunder. And each in turn left something of their own culture behind to be forged and blended into what had never been before.

The Baba and Nonya Community: The small colony of Chinese merchants, in particular, stayed behind to found the

Preceding pages: a friendly face at *A Famosa*.

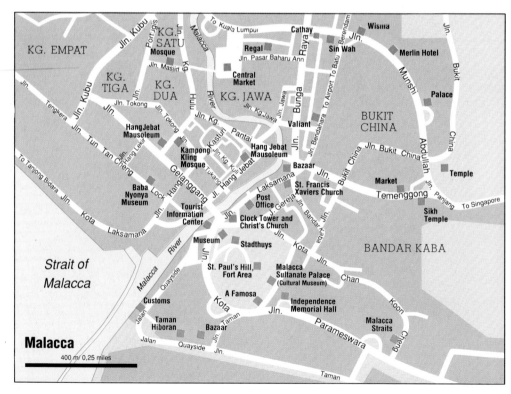

Malacca

400 m/ 0.25 miles

Baba and *Nonya* community which has become one of the most striking and colourful Chinese fraternities in Malaysia today. The *Babas* (or Straits Chinese) are descendants of the Chinese pioneers who accepted the practical realities around them but whose ideas of social relationships and religious aspirations are still derived from the traditions of their forefathers in the villages of Fukien. The womenfolk may have worshipped at a Malay *keramat* (shrine) once in a while, but that is not so much an indication of their respect for the Muslim religion as an expression of the Chinese desire to keep on the right side of all spirits of whatever origin. The Malays, for their part, seem to have been equally unaffected by the Chinese outlook on social and spiritual matters.

Islam spreads: It was also through Malacca that the Islamic faith came to Malaysia. All Malays have been Muslims since the second half of the 15th century, when rich Moorish merchants from Pasai in Sumatra settled in Malacca. From here Islam spread by conversion throughout the peninsula and its neighbouring islands.

Geography was responsible for it all. Located at the mouth of the Malacca River, astride the maritime route linking the Indian Ocean with the South China Sea, Malacca stood where the monsoon winds met. As tillers of the soil depended upon monsoons to bring them rain, so trusting sailors relied upon the winds to move their ships. Sturdy junks from the ports of China and Japan came with the riches of the East in their holds – silk, porcelain and silver – and allowed themselves to be driven up the Straits of Malacca by the northeast monsoon.

So did the traders from the islands of the archipelago arrive with various forms of crafts, camphor, nutmeg and cloves, mace and sandalwood. At the port, their cargoes were discharged and new precious wares from India and the Middle West were loaded on – cloth, carpets, glassware, iron and jewellery. When the winds changed, the southwest monsoon assisted the same vessels to return to their home ports.

It was the rich port of Malacca – the key to controlling the spice trade – that caused some of the early East-West power struggles. In 1511 Malacca fell to the Portuguese and remained their fortress for more than 100 years, before they themselves were ousted by the Dutch. After 150 years of occupation, the Dutch in turn ceded the land to the British. But Malacca's golden age was during the Malay sultanate of Malacca and these great days effectively came to an end when it fell in 1511 to the first Europeans. The place-name Malacca has now been "Malayanised" and is now spelt Melaka, but most tourist brochures retain the other spelling to avoid confusion.

Walking through history: The story of Malacca, and all Malaysia in a sense, need not come from a textbook. A one-kilometre (½-mile) walk or a leisurely trishaw ride through the town reveals the past. Trishaws are an excellent means of getting around in Malacca. The drivers know the sights and many of them speak understandable English,

Sightseeing begins in the town square.

in which case they make fine guides. You might not only learn that the Portuguese came "a much long time ago" but also that along the seafront there is a great soup stall that sells the best *mee hoon* (very thin noodles) in Malaysia.

The visitor to Malacca may find it difficult to visualise life behind the mediaeval fortress 400 years ago. But, as he or she walks the narrow streets, visits old temples and mosques, lingers among ancient ruins and epitaphs, Malacca's history begins to fall into place.

It is easy to get around and although there are many things to see, Malacca can, except for the expert, readily be "done" in one day. However, those who wish to linger awhile and absorb the atmosphere of the "sleepy hollow", as the inhabitants of Malacca love to call it, will find that they can intermingle their sightseeing with sunning and swimming 8 kilometres (5 miles) to the north, on the main road to Port Dickson.

Off the coast is a group of small islands. At weekends, there are regular boats to the largest island, Pulau Besar, from Umbai. But be warned! Legend has it that should you eat pork within 48 hours of visiting the island, your boat will sink.

Reflections of a river: The best place to begin is right in the centre of the town near the bridge built on the site where the Portuguese made their final successful assault on the town. The Malacca River itself is a history lesson. Time seems to have passed by this section of the town. Great, ancient junks, high bows and raised poop decks – reminiscent of their distant cousins that once brought Admiral Cheng Ho's dragon court entourage to Malacca centuries ago – float side by side against the wooden pilings of the dock. Their romantic cargoes of spices, silks and camphor have been forsaken, for these battered, unkempt vessels now carry bulky sacks of charcoal that fire the kitchens of Malacca. The labourers, wobbling up and down the narrow planks that join ship to dock, strain under the heavy loads, and like the

The Malacca River is Malaysian history incarnate.

sturdy junks they unload, they are part of Malacca's timeless past.

River trips can be arranged from here up river and to the Portuguese settlement. But you will not get to travel with the local fishermen, who, it is said, are very superstitious. They will not allow womenfolk on board their vessels, never speak vulgar words at sea, and will not even call each other by names, for fear that the gods will become jealous of their good catch and send them misfortunes!

Yet once the Malacca River was different. When the Portuguese colony was at its zenith, the river was a deep, bustling waterway jammed with ships of a dozen nations. Great sailing vessels, loaded onto the scuppers, vied with each other to manoeuvre up the river to tie up at the quay, while countless smaller vessels, anchored in the roads, depended upon flat-bottomed scows to load and unload their valuable wares. Ship chandlers did a thriving business selling stores to captains, and there is a story that the town was so vast that it took a cat walking over the tiled roofs a year to make the circuit. Maybe the story-tellers exaggerated but we do know that when the Portuguese captured Malacca, d'Albuquerque sailed his warships up the estuary to besiege the town.

Architecture from Holland: As you cross the Malacca River bridge onto the east riverbank, you come face to face with a neat, little square with a clock tower surrounded by salmon-coloured government buildings and a towered church, and you almost expect to see tulips growing in the gardens or a passing cyclist wearing up-pointed wooden shoes. The square obviously was built by the Dutch, and architecture is Holland's main contribution to Malacca.

The large building facing the square is the old Dutch **Stadthuys** (Town Hall). A broad flight of stone steps fronts this building constructed of incredibly thick walls and massive hardwood doors supported by studded, wrought-iron hinges. For more than 300 years after its completion, the Stadthuys served as government offices until the

administration finally shifted out in 1980. Today, it houses the well laid-out **Malacca Museum** and within its galleries, the history of Malacca unreels in a fascinating way. Its exhibits trace the city's past times from the ancient Malay kingdom, through Portuguese and Dutch rule and British occupation to its present status as a state in Malaysia. No other town in the peninsula evokes the past as strongly as Malacca, which was once one of the greatest seaports of Asia. The Museum also contains a unique collection of old coins, stamps, a rickshaw, Portuguese costumes from the 16th century, Dutch weapons, British cannons, gold and silver filigree jewellery and framed, sepia-toned photographs of sailing ships anchored in the Malacca River, as well as old Malay *kris* and shields. (The court élite carried jewel-studded golden krisses, weapons which have come to symbolise Malay royalty.)

The Stadthuys itself is an antiquity: it was erected in 1650, and it is the oldest known Dutch building still standing in

Typical
shopfront
in the
downtown
district.

the Far East.

On the embankment near the entrance to the Stadthuys is an ancient memorial whose significance has been lost in time. It stands in the shape of a much-weathered stone fish with an elephant's head. This is a Hindu relic of the period predating the glorious Malacca sultanate. The General Post Office in the Stadthuys square, is also of Dutch origin.

Hill of memories: Citizens of Malacca are very conscious of their past, so much so that the city abounds with museums. Further up the slopes of the hill, at the foot of which stands the Stadthuys, a 20th-century replica of the fabled palace of Malacca's sultans, now the **Cultural Museum**. Reconstructed faithfully from eye-witness descriptions of the original palace, it fittingly serves as a cultural storehouse dedicated to the role of Malacca as the fount of Malay culture and tradition. At the summit of this same hill (the Hill of St. Paul) lie the ruins of **St Paul's Church**. A Portuguese *fidalgo* built the chapel in 1521 in order to fulfil a vow he made on escaping death in the South China Sea. It was later taken over by the Jesuits who completed the building and painted it white so that it could serve as a guidepost for ships out on the Straits. St Francis Xavier conducted mass in the church during his several visits to Malacca. After his death near Canton, his body was interred in St Paul's for several months before being taken to Goa in India. The Dutch discontinued services in St Paul's Church when their own Christ Church was built. However, they used the burial ground around St Paul's for burial of their own noble citizens. Lining the inside walls of the old church are engraved tombstones.

Early morning or late afternoon is the best time to climb St Paul's Hill to the church. The beauty of St Paul's is the fact that it is a ruin. No restoration could make it more attractive.

Water fountain and mousedeer: As if to guarantee that the 150 years of Dutch occupation should not be forgotten, the **Christ Church** at the foot of the hill and by the old Stadthuys had its pink bricks shipped from Holland. Malaccan masons then faced them with local red laterite. The church is full of old, engraved tombstones, many of which tell a grim tale about the hardships the early European settlers faced. The immense rafters within the nave were each carved from a single tree and date back to the church's foundation. The original, solid, heavy wooden pews for Sunday worshippers still remain in use, and above the altar a wooden crucifix hangs from the iron hoops fastened to the wall. There is a story that when the church was first in use, it had no pulpit. The pastor would sit in a chair that had ropes running to the hoops. When the time came for him to deliver his sermon, his sextons would winch him halfway up the wall. Thus, he gave his sermon every Sunday without fail.

Outside the church the famous century-old tower, with the same pink brick as the rest of the square, provides a landmark. It was presented to the town by the wealthy Tan family. The small water fountain nearby was built to com-

Trishaws provide the most convenient mode of town transport.

memorate the Diamond Jubilee of Queen Victoria. Four white mousedeer (*pelandok*, in Malay) surround the fountain to remind passersby of how Parameswara came to select Malacca as the site for his new capital.

A short walk towards the seafront from the square brings you to a row of food stalls and some more permanent restaurants that cover an entire block, and are known locally as "Gluttons' Corner". Local cooks whip up Malay satay, Indian curries and fried rice, and Chinese seafood and noodles. The cool shade in these stalls is a welcome relief. The stalls used to face the seashore, but recent reclamation of land has somewhat diminished their previously fine sea-breeze position and with it some of their popularity.

Gate without a wall: The slopes of St Paul's Hill balance another historical relic besides – the ruins of the **A Famosa** fortress.

Under the Portuguese, Malacca was to see colossal changes. At first, when the town fell, Sultan Mahmud withdrew to Muar with the hope that the invaders would plunder the city and move on. But the Portuguese had other ideas; they were determined to make it one of the mightiest strongholds in the Orient. D'Albuquerque immediately ordered the construction of a formidable fortress. Hundreds of slaves and captives were put to work. Stones from demolished mosques and elaborate tombs were used to build the thick-walled fortress, which was called A Famosa. When it was completed, with cannons on the walls and soldiers standing guard, it filled the townspeople with both fear and respect.

Later A Famosa was enlarged to enclose the entire hill, including the European settlement. The city walls enclosed a castle, two magnificent palaces, a hall for the Portuguese Council of State and five churches. This fortress withstood attacks for 150 years, until it was finally breached in 1641 by the Dutch.

The Dutch arrived in 1641 as conquerors, having driven out the Portu-

The distinctive red brick buildings are a Dutch legacy.

guese after a siege that lasted eight months. But what they found was not a rich and prosperous port of the fabulous East, as they had expected. The city they struggled so hard to conquer lay in near total ruins.

But the industrious and fastidious Dutch lost no time putting things in order. As soon as they were in control, they began to rebuild the city with a Dutch flavour. The walls of the fortress were repaired and the bastions renamed. A moat was dug around the fortress and a drawbridge built. Protective ramparts were laid round the suburbs and heavy brass cannons mounted on all the walls. In a short time Malacca became a well-defended port again.

Unfortunately, when the British first occupied Malacca at the beginning of the 19th century, they decided to blow up the fortifications. The walls and gates were badly damaged and all that was left of A Famosa was the Porta de Santiago – a gate without a wall.

Visitors here are not far away from the **Padang** which lies on reclaimed land at the foot of the hill. The Padang has a special significance for modern Malaysians because it was here that Tunku Abdul Rahman, the country's first prime minister, announced Malaya's independence upon his return from negotiations with the British in London. A small obelisk records the event. The struggle for independence is more substantially commemorated by the imposing **Declaration of Independence Memorial Building**. Recently opened, it contains in the form of documents, film, video and such items as the car the Tunku rode in on his return from the successful London negotiations, materials connected with the campaign for independence. The building itself is not new; it was built in 1911 as the Malacca Club where British colonial officials and planters took their ease. Another small obelisk commemorates British soldiers killed in the Naning War, an almost farcical affair in the early 1830s when it took two military expeditions over two years to subdue Penghulu Dol Said, the defiant territory

Peranakan heritage on display at a local museum.

chief of the petty principality of Naning.

A couple of kilometres down the road southwards lies **St John's Fort**. After a short climb to the top of the hill where the concrete fort stands, you can enjoy a panoramic view of Malacca. Apart from the absence of cannons, the fort is much like the Dutch had left it when the British took over after Malacca was exchanged for Bencoolen in Sumatra. Fearing that Malacca might fall into enemy hands, the British had all the strongholds, except St John's Fort and Santiago Gate, destroyed. Now the old, vacant fort is sandwiched between a very strange-looking water tank on one side and Malacca's tallest building, a 10-storey block of flats, on the other. No matter how hard it tries, 20th-century Malacca is still an incongruity.

A Chinese princess and a magic well: On a hill at the back of the town, Chinese tombs are left unattended by relatives for generations. Hills are auspicious burial grounds, according to the Chinese geomancer, for the mass of land blocks the winds of evil and offers the spirits of the ancestors a good view over their descendants. But on **Bukit China**, "China Hill", most names and dates have been eroded by the rains. What remains is an old, half-forgotten cemetery and the story of a Ming princess.

In ancient times, Malaya and China carried on a diplomatic war of wits which grew to be legendary. Around 1460, when Sultan Mansor Shah ruled Malacca, a Chinese ship sailed into port with special orders from the Son of Heaven. The entire interior of the ship was delicately pinned with gold needles, and the message sent to the Sultan read: "For every gold needle, I have a subject; if you could count their number, then you would know my power."

The Sultan was impressed, but not dismayed. He sent back a ship stuffed with bags of sago with the message: "If you can count the grains of sago on this ship you will have guessed the number of my subjects correctly, and you will know my power." The Chinese Emperor was so intrigued that he sent his

Tombstones in the yard of St Paul's Church, dating from the Dutch period.

daughter Hong Lim Poh, to marry the Sultan. She arrived with no less than 500 ladies-in-waiting, all of great beauty. The Sultan gave them "the hill without the town" as a private residence and promised that the land they occupied would never be taken away from them. To this day, Bukit China belongs to Malacca's Chinese community. Several of the graves there date back to the Ming Dynasty; they are among the oldest Chinese relics in Malaysia.

Princess Hong Lim Poh's followers built a well at the foot of the hill, whose waters soon became as legendary as her marriage contract. The Chinese say that after Admiral Cheng Ho drank from the well, its water attained an extraordinary purity. It never dried up, even during the most severe drought, and many believed that if a visitor drank from it he would return to Malacca before he died.

Now, the **Perigi Rajah**, or Sultan's Well, is protected by wire mesh. It has not dried up and its purity has entered history. Young Malaccan students of Chinese descent come to see the land-mark and perhaps snap some pictures, but few tread the paths up the hill where their forefathers lie buried. Malacca is changing, leaving its secrets behind.

Catholic crowds: Throw a stone in a northwest direction from this spot and it will probably land on Jalan Bendahara, where **St Peter's Church** is. When the Portuguese garrison was forced into submission, the Dutch gave safe conduct to the soldiers and amnesty to the Portuguese descendants, many of whom chose to remain behind rather than take up a new life in Goa. In 1710, the Portuguese Eurasians of Malacca built this church, naming it after St Peter. Unlike its richly decorated counterparts in Goa, it is simple and relatively unimpressive. Throughout the year, except for an occasional wedding or funeral, not much goes on. Good Friday, Easter and Christmas, of course, are the big exceptions.

Good Friday services at St Peter's Church are the most elaborate in Malaysia. Thousands of people – Chinese, Eurasian and Indian – crowd the church

Traditional timber houses have tiled entrance steps, wide verandahs and carved eaves.

to attend the services and take part in a candlelight procession. A life-sized statue of Christ, crowned with thorns and draped in deep purple robes with gold embroidery, is solemnly borne above the devout Catholic congregation. The churchyard becomes a sea of flames ushered in by the mournful sound of hymns. Malacca Chinese and Portuguese Eurasian Catholics living all around the country try to return to their home town every Easter weekend and attend the ceremonies at St Peter's which they had known so well as children.

Despite the solemnity of a staunch Catholic mass, the crowds that gather outside the church after the service meet friends and cast flirtatious eyes as if it were carnival time in spring. Children, looking most reverent and pure in their Sunday clothes, romp around the lawns or negotiate coins with the Indian peanut seller. Everyone laughs, including the priest and the young girls selling religious literature, which appropriately includes a biography of St Francis

Shrimp fisherman off the Malaccan coast.

Xavier.

At the end of Jalan Bendahara, and closer to the Dutch area of town is **St Xavier's Church**, with its twin Gothic towers. It was built in 1849 by a French Father, the Reverend Farve, on the location of a former Portuguese church. It is dedicated to St Francis Xavier, known as the "Apostle of the East", who spread Catholicism in South-East Asia during the 16th century.

A 350-year-old heritage: The legacy the Portuguese left behind is far greater than their ruins. Proud descendants of Portuguese soldiers bearing such names as Sequiera, Aranjo, Pinto, Dias, D'Silva and D'Souza cherish the traditions of their European lineage. "I gave to each man his horse, a house, and land," wrote d'Albuquerque in 1604 when he reported with pride to Portugal that 200 mixed marriages had taken place. On direct orders from the king, d'Albuquerque encouraged men of the garrison to marry local girls, whom he called "his daughters". Such intermarriages flourished and girls were even sent out from Portugal to marry local men. The Portuguese were instructed to treat local folk as equals and it is said that d'Albuquerque courteously escorted local women to their seats in church as though they were noble Portuguese ladies.

As can be expected, a strong Eurasian community grew up with loyalty to Portugal through its ties of blood and religion. After 400 years the Portuguese Eurasians in Malacca, as well as in other towns of Malaysia, continue to speak Cristao, a medieval dialect once spoken in southeastern Portugal. "It is pure 16th-century Portuguese", remarked Father Manuel Pintado, a local parish priest, when asked how closely the language spoken confirms to that in his homeland. "Remarkable, but it is spoken nowhere else."

Today, the descendants of the early Portuguese live in a community of their own, 3 kilometres (2 miles) from the centre of Malacca, near the beach. There are about 500 Eurasians, mostly fishermen. The name "Portuguese Eurasian Settlement," as it is called, is

misleading. There are no cobblestone streets, white stucco walls or red tiled roofs as one might find in towns in Portugal. Instead, the dwellings resemble Malay *kampong* houses with wooden walls and tin roofs. They are all painted in pastel blues and greens, are small, unpretentious and identical to one another. "They are proud people who live within the walls," Father Pintado explained. "The Dutch occupied Malacca much longer than the Portuguese and were here after the Portuguese were expelled, yet little is left of the Dutch occupation."

Pass through the Portuguese Eurasian Settlement quickly and you will be disappointed – there is not that much to see. But linger and meet the people. Young boys still sing beautiful ballads in Portuguese and their sisters show you a dance which their grandmother learnt from her grandmother. An old man at a fruit stall tells you about a secluded tunnel from St John's Fort to St Paul's Hill, in which the Portuguese had hidden all their treasures before the Dutch overran Malacca.

The Festa de San Pedro, held each year in June, is a happy time for these remarkable people. At this time, the fishermen elaborately decorate their boats with bunting and sacred texts. A mass is usually conducted in the open and after the boats have been blessed by the parish priest, the evening is spent in merrymaking.

Another unusual custom is called "Intrudu", meaning "Introductions", celebrated on the Sunday preceding Ash Wednesday. Then the residents wear fancy costumes and throw water over one another. Even those at home are not spared. The merrymakers make a point of visiting and drenching them with water as soon as they open their doors. To show there are no hard feelings they are invited in for refreshments. Later in the day men dress up as ladies and the ladies dress as men, and go around selling cakes and fruits.

In **Medan Portugis** (Portuguese Square) and the surrounding streets, you can sample Malay-Portuguese

Tourists are not the only ones who flock to Malacca.

food, with its seafood served with spicy sauces being the most ordered items on the menu.

Streets with changing names: The main centre of Malacca's shopping and business activities is where it has always been, on the western bank of the Malacca River, away from the hills and the forts. On this side of the riverbank, visitors find themselves in a maze of ancient and narrow streets, which seem to keep changing their names. Former Heeren Street became **Jalan Tan Cheng Lock**, after a leading Baba of the community who was also an architect. His family house, as well as the town houses of several other Chinese Baba families located on this street, flaunts finely-carved doors.

At numbers 48-50 on this street, you can actually explore the interior of a Peranakan house, decorated in the rich style of the 19th century. The furniture and decor within are a gorgeous blend of Chinese furniture inlaid with Mother-of-Pearl, Victorian clocks and Dutch tiles. Within the outer gate is a small courtyard, typical of the style now called "Chinese Baroque". The family who owns the house gives guided tours around it, and can tell you fascinating stories about some of the precious and antique curios in their house.

Some of these treasures spill out into the antique shops on **Jalan Hang Jebat**, which runs parallel to Jalan Tan Cheng Lock. Hang Jebat was a Malay hero during the days of the Malacca sultanate and is believed to be buried in the mausoleum halfway down the street. It has had at least two names (Jalan Jonker and Jalan Gelanggang) before it became known by its present one.

But by any name it would still remain one of the town's most interesting streets, as well as being Malacca's main thoroughfare. Much like Kuala Lumpur's Jalan Petaling, it is a street containing every imaginable trade: spirits importers; hairdressing salons; wooden shoe stores; coffin makers; apothecaries with Chinese herbs on display; sign printers; an acupuncture clinic; a furniture factory; a dental hos-

Locals of Portuguese descent still speak an antiquated dialect.

pital with office hours printed in English, Chinese, Malay, Tamil and Thai; a photo studio; a half dozen temples squeezed between commercial enterprises; and three antique shops. Amidst the cacophony of honking horns and bullock carts thumping over hard pavements, fez-wearing tailors pedal sewing machines in open fronted shops, furniture makers hammer a table leg into place, and vendors and shopkeepers call out to passersby, "Come look around!"

There are three or four antique shops, each a mirror to Malaysia's past. Heavy brass irons with receptacles for hot coals, ornate oil lamps hanging from the ceiling, pearl inlaid nightstands, opium benches, brass urns and a Chinese wedding bed are what a typical shop offers. Rare stamps, coins in circulation during the sultanate days – recently dredged up from the mud near the estuary – and Malay *kris* are other bargains one might find. The Pakistani shopkeeper points to a carved, wooden jewellery box. "I saved it for a prime minister," he tells you, "but I don't know when he'll be back." You study the box with an unconvinced look on your face. "No matter," he continues, "I like you. You can have it."

Where the faithful flock: The streets crisscross one another to form suitable sites for three of the oldest places of worship in Malaysia; while the Cheng Hoon Teng in Jalan Tokong pays tribute to the Chinese faith and the Kampong Kling Mosque, in the same street, to the Muslim's, the Sri Poyyatha Vinayagar Moorthi Temple in Jalan Tukang Mas flies the Hindu flag.

Of the three, the prestigious **Cheng Hoon Teng** or Temple of Bright Clouds is the oldest Chinese temple in Malaysia, being founded in 1645. It was originally built by a fugitive from the Manchu conquest, and was later restored and embellished by local Chinese leaders. The temple is dedicated to three deities: the main altar being given to Kuan Yin, the goddess of Mercy; Kwan Ti (also known as Kwan Kung), the god of War who triples up as the god of Wealth and the patron saint of Tradesmen; and

The owner has added a creative touch to this bullock cart.

212

Machoe Poh, the Queen of Heaven.

The building is a beautiful example of Chinese architecture. The carved roof, ridges and eaves are elegantly decorated with exquisite Chinese mythical figures, animals, birds and flowers, all made of coloured glass and porcelain that glitter and sparkle in the sun. Step through the massive hardwood gates, and you feel you are stepping back in time. Amongst the wood carvings and lacquerwork within, all brought in from China, is an inscription cut in stone, commemorating Admiral Cheng Ho's visit to the town in 1406. An illustrious envoy of the Ming Emperor, and also an adventurer as famous in his own right as Columbus, Admiral Cheng Ho was also the city's earliest Chinese pioneer.

Monks in yellow robes move silently among the gilded pillars while Chinese worshippers with lowered heads walk from image to image, holding smouldering joss sticks reverently in their hands. The golden lions standing guard at the entrance have had the yellow worn off their heads by the countless devotees who in passing, have rubbed them for good luck.

The **Sri Poyyatha Vinayagar Moorthi Temple** was built by the Hindu community of Malacca in the 1780s. It is dedicated to the god Vinayagar, to whom is ascribed the power to remove all obstacles for businessmen who want to get rich, and for couples who want to be married to one another.

The **Kampong Kling Mosque** is the town's oldest mosque and sports a typical Sumatran design. This style of mosque, with its three or four-tiered minarets, is characteristic of the Malaccan territory. Another good example is provided by the mosque in the suburb of Tranquerah. In its cemetery is the tomb of Sultan Husain of Johor who ceded Singapore to Sir Stamford Raffles in 1819.

Surrounding suburbs: It is a delight to drive at leisure through the suburbs of Malacca town. Beyond and behind it, rice fields stretch into the low hills which continue down to the southernmost spurs of the Main Range. An area

Baba architecture: interior of the Tun Tan Cheng Lock house.

long settled, it is interlaced with numerous side roads; cutting through groves of rubber and fruit trees and past peaceful villages and compact market towns. Traditional Malay houses, with curving gables, carved eaves, wide-fronted verandahs and tiled entrance steps, are commonplace all the way from Tanjong Kling in the north to Merlimau in the south, where there is one particularly fine example you can look around.

Tanjong Kling, about 10 kilometres (6 miles) from Malacca, has a beach resort and several cheap beach huts. The sea is not very clean here, however, and is sometimes infested with jellyfish. **Shah's Beach Hotel** has its own swimming pool for those who wish to swim.

Fifteen kilometres (9 miles) from town in the same direction is **Hang Tuah's Mausoleum**. Hang Tuah was a famous Malay warrior during the reign of Sultan Mansor Shah, and south of town is a well, believed to be the abode of his soul. His soul is said to have been changed into a crocodile, but only holy people will ever catch a glimpse of it.

The waters of the well, situated at Kampong Duyong, are reputed to have medicinal values, and bring good luck to those who drink from it.

Still travelling towards Negri Sembilan, visitors pass the **Tanjong Bidara Beach Resort**, located on a pleasant stretch of beach about 20 kilometres (12 miles) from Malacca.

Kuala Linggi is at the mouth of the Linggi River, which separates the state of Malacca from that of Negri Sembilan. Here on a low hill is the tumbledown **Fort Filipina**, built by the Dutch. Named after a Dutch governor, the fort is nowadays nothing more than a pleasant place from which to view the river estuary and enjoy a picnic.

Some 12 kilometres (7½ miles) inland from Malacca town at Ayer Keroh is the **Ayer Keroh Recreational Forest**, 68 hectares (168 acres) of jungle sufficiently tamed to provide walks, deer reserves, picnicking spots and camping sites. Nearby is the **Malacca Village Resort** where visitors can enjoy pleasant accommodation. Also in the vicinity is **Mini-Malaysia**, which has model houses representing the various styles of architecture of the 13 states of Malaysia, a 50-room hotel and some 15 chalets, along with cultural and entertainment programmes. At Ayer Keroh too, is the **Melaka Zoo**, with boating and refreshment facilities, and the **Ayer Keroh Country Club**, equipped with an 18-hole golf course and its own lake and section of rainforest.

The road to Seremban and Kuala Lumpur goes through the district of Alor Gajah and passes **Naning**, the principality whose chieftain defied the British in the 19th century. Dato' Dol Said now rests in his tomb in peace close to the roadside.

Near Dol Said's grave and around this area are some 90 stone megaliths reminiscent of those mysterious stones in the Kuala Pilah district in Negri Sembilan. The **Gadek Hot Spring** is located along the route to Tampin. The restorative waters are captured in pools and are surrounded with handicraft shops, refreshment stalls and a children's playground.

Left, life still moves at a leisurely pace. **Right**, a Malaccan miss.

TAMAN NEGARA – THE GREEN HEART

Boating through swirling rapids, fishing for giant carp, shooting game with a camera, climbing mountains, watching birds, exploring caves, swimming placid river waters, going on safari through jungles 130 million years old, visiting *Orang Asli* settlements – and getting away from 20th-century traffic and pollution. Malaysia has what few countries in the world have – a great, undisturbed outdoors waiting for discovery. With two thirds of the country under jungle, where lush greenery begins at the edge of the sea and climbs up to the highest mountains, there is certain to be adventure.

Topping all accessible jungle haunts in the peninsula is the **Taman Negara**, or National Park, which spreads over the northern interior of the Malay peninsula in the state of **Pahang**. Within this area, around the central massif of Gunung Tahan, the highest peak in peninsular Malaysia, there are countless limestone hills thickly covered with forests, fast-running streams and an abundance of wildlife.

Travel within the park is chiefly by water, although visitors can make land trips from any of the posts on the **Tembeling River** with equipment, guides and porters supplied by the Park Service. Or around the headquarters at Kuala Tahan there are many trails and walks well-marked and laid out for pleasant strolls into the green interior.

A jungle trip through the National Park is the closest anyone can come to the green heart of Malaysia, and conveniently it is flexible enough to range from a leisurely two days' fishing to a two-week tropical safari. Entrance to the Park is usually by river although you can also fly there, but the river trip itself is the best introduction to the Park, as with the miles covered, you feel civilisation ebbing away.

Outboard motors of the National Park Service carry visitors the 60 kilometres (37 miles) from Kuala Tembeling Halt

Preceding pages: view to a thrill – a stretch of virgin forest. **Below**, falls at Sungai Tahan.

on the Malaysian Railway System to the Park Headquarters at Kuala Tahan on the Tembeling River.

Although the trains do not usually stop at Tembeling Halt, they will do so if prior notice is given, or you can alight at Jerantut and take a taxi to the jetty only 30 minutes away. There are also several tours to the Park that operate from major cities, and transport to and from the Park is arranged.

Boating down Sungai Tembeling: The boat journey to Kuala Tahan takes 3 to 4 hours depending on the level of the river. If the water is low, passengers are asked to disembark and walk along the banks of the river, while the boatmen negotiate the shallow waters.

After travelling 35 kilometres (22 miles), you reach the boundaries of the National Park on your left. On the right riverbank is more cultivated land, scattered with Malay *kampong*.

On arrival at **Kuala Tahan**, visitors proceed to the reception where accommodation is booked, trips arranged and information sought. There is an excellent travel guide to the Park available at the reception, priced at only M$1, which gives details of trails and river trips, as well as suggestions for fishing, and information about flora and fauna. It also contains maps of the area.

At headquarters: Visitors can stay at the **Headquarters** at Kuala Tahan in a variety of accommodation, ranging from the rest house and chalet facilities to the hostel and camping sites. At the hostel there are cooking facilities, or you can eat at one of the two restaurants. There is also a small shop selling basic supplies (vegetables, fruit, canned food), and limited types of film are sold at the reception.

Outside the Headquarters area, there are lodges at Kuala Trenggen and Kuala Kangsem and several fishing lodges further up the rivers. You can even spend the night in the thick of the jungle in one of the five jungle hides with basic sleeping facilities or in several camping sites spread out around the park.

The Headquarters have some camping, fishing and trekking equipment, but

Arrivals at Park Headquarters.

you would do well to check before-hand if it is available when you need it. The telephone number, address and booking arrangements are supplied at the back of this book in the Travel Tips section, and there is also a suggested list of the most necessary items to bring to the Park.

The Park Service has a slide show and film nightly giving background information about the Park, and explaining some of the wildlife you will see in the forest. Guides are also available from reception, should you wish for a conducted tour of the plant and animal life.

Hitching a ride to the jungle canopy: One hundred and thirty million years of evolution has produced some extraordinary plants and animals. Many plants have become highly specialised and are interlinked with other species in both parasitic and symbiotic ways. The *rattan* plant is a thick vine with huge spines; the smaller, younger rattan tendrils often taking you by surprise along the jungle trails. Other plants that "hitch a ride" include the orchid family with its several hundred varieties.

Another, more ominous "hitch-hiker" is the strangling vine, which is dropped as a seed onto an unsuspecting tree, then grows into a small appendage on the host tree, but eventually twists and twines itself around until the original tree can hardly be seen. It takes only 100 years for a strangling vine to kill off the host tree, after which its strange hollow structure stands until the weight of other epiphytes bring it crashing to the jungle floor. Fruit and flowering trees abound too.

A night in the jungle: The jungle is not a quiet place as one might suppose – it is as noisy as any big city downtown with the cacophony of insect noises, bird calls and animal cries.

Bird-watching is a delight in the jungle: a simple pair of binoculars will enable you to catch sight of the bird that arrested you with the hum of its wings. Several kinds of kingfishers, the precious hornbills, fishing eagles and osprey abound in the forest.

Noisy but shy long-tailed macaques are heard but rarely seen; more visible animals are monitor lizards, otters and the domestic buffalo which bathe in the rivers near Malay villages.

Larger wildlife is also present in the jungle, but their secretive lives deep in the jungle shades make them hard to spot. An absolute must is at least one night in a jungle hide, small huts on stilts, usually near a stream and a salt-lick, that enable you to sit quietly in the dark and observe nocturnal animals.

It is best to arrive at the jungle hides early, say around 5 p.m., bring a packed supper and a torch, and settle down to wait. Binoculars are also handy. As night falls, the forest becomes alive, and your eyes gradually adjust to the dark – moonlit nights are especially magical.

You will think your eyes are deceiving you when you see what seem to be ghostly spirits flitting in between the trees. These are fireflies and beetles with fluorescent wings and tails. On the ground, dead leaves glisten brightly in the jungle gloom, covered with luminescent lichen.

Deer are the most commonly seen

Visitors can hope to catch a glimpse of a Malayan tapir.

220

animals from the hides, but if you visit one of the hides farthest away from the Headquarters, you may be very lucky to see a tapir, and very lucky indeed to see an elephant, the quietest creature in the jungle, or a Malaysian tiger. Don't count on seeing these magnificent animals though; sightings of elephants and tigers, or even deer and tapir are to be counted as a bonus to the already thrilling experience of being out alone in the forest. You will see spiders, frogs, toads and snakes amongst the undergrowth. Most visitors take it in turns to "watch", shining the torch every 10 minutes or so.

After a night out in the forest, you will find that a new respect emerges naturally for the inhabitants of the forest, animals and people alike. The *Negrito* hunters move amongst the trees as stealthily as the animals, armed with only a blowpipe.

The park's lush setting is a nature lover's delight.

Negrito communities are a common sight around Headquarters, and it is said that the Forest Service provides food for them so that they will stay in the area. All around Kuala Tahan, you'll see their makeshift huts, which they return to from time to time, and they may even be in residence. The *Negrito* peoples have a natural dignity; don't be too quick to turn them into a tourist spectacle with the click of your camera.

Mountain hikes or river fishing: Trails around Park Headquarters range from a 10-minute stroll to a bathing place on the small **Tahan River**, to a nine-day jungle trek to the **Gunung Tahan**, highest mountain on the peninsula.

The trek up to the peak at 2,187 metres (7,175 feet) is not difficult since the ascent is not steep, but climbing through jungle can be arduous and takes time. For this trip, it is important to be well organised, and to take only what is absolutely necessary with you. You should also take a guide, as it is easy to get lost on your own, with other secret jungle paths branching off from the main one. But it is an exhilarating experience, and one that should be attempted if you are fit and healthy.

For those who prefer fishing, boats are available for hire from the Head-

quarters for access to the fishing grounds; the further you go from there, the less people and the better chance of landing a giant.

February and March, and June to August are generally considered best for fishing. The best time of day for fishing is during the middle of the day or in the late evening. Spinning is the most popular form of fishing. You can either bring your own tackle or arrange to hire some from the Headquarters.

Tackle recommended is a 2-metre rod (any longer is cumbersome in the forest), line from 6 kg as a start, moving on to finer line (3.5 kg) if the catch gets too big to handle! Line length should be a minimum of 30 metres.

Fixed spool reels are generally used, although a multiplying reel is also operable. Since most fishing here is in pursuit of predatory fish, artificial lures such as spoons, spinners, wobblers and plugs, are most commonly applied. Agreement is rare on which lure is best, but many locals swear only an "Abu Killer" will attract the big ones.

In season, local fishermen use riverside fruits for bait, cast to simulate its fall from the tree. Finally, a net or a gaff is required, the latter for its ease of transport through riverside scrub.

Riding the rapids: If fishing is not for you, then maybe just boating up the magical rivers in a narrow boat will appeal to you. Experienced boatmen, both Malay and *Negrito*, know the rivers like the backs of their hands, and stand alert, poles in hand, watching for jagged rocks and sandbanks.

Although outboard motors are mostly used, the trickier waters will require progress by pole power, and if the river is high, you can enjoy floating down the river with just the current on your return trip. The boatmen will point out basking snakes, woodpeckers, kingfishers and deer to you, so be ready with your camera. Further up the Tembeling from the Headquarters are seven sets of rapids which provide an exciting ride when the river is in full flood, but you must be prepared to get wet!

On the smaller Tahan, a waterfall or

Taman Negara is best explored by boat.

bank of rapids provides a worthwhile trip: below the rapids is a natural swimming pool, the water deliciously tepid, but still refreshing. Or climb up the rapids and find yourself in a natural jungle jacuzzi!

Bat caves: Further down the Tembeling River, a 15-minute walk inland, is the **Goa Telinga** (literally Ear Cave) where fruit and insect-eating bats cluster on the low roofs of the cave ceilings. Entry to the caves is by a tiny crevice in the rock – wear some old clothes for this adventure as you're going to have to slide through mud and bat droppings, centimetres thick on the cave floors.

Crawling along a narrow passageway, you emerge at last into a cave where you can stand up, and with the help of a torch, can pick out the two different types of bats. The fruit bats congregate near the crevices that let in a little sunlight, while the insect-eating ones gather below in darker corners.

Huge toads, bigger than the size of a large fist, survey the scene, and the cave racer, a long white snake that feeds exclusively on bats in the cave, can be seen, suspended from the ceiling, from where it disengages its jaws and entwines its long tail around the struggling bat. Large spiders and cockroaches scuttle on the floors, in a scene like something out of an Indiana Jones movie! All animals in the cave are harmless to man. A rope runs through all the caves to guide you to the narrow exit on the other side.

Two days is the minimum for a visit to the Taman Negara, and a longer stay with more extensive exploration brings rich rewards. For the more adventurous, trips can be arranged to plunge into lessknown parts of the jungle (including the areas in the north of the Park reached from the state of Kelantan), preferably with *Orang Asli* guides; but the main hindrance to such an expedition is cost – you will be told that you need several guides and porters, equipment and a boat. But if you have unlimited amounts of time and money, this would be the most rewarding and thrilling adventure you will ever embark upon.

The Lesser Mousedeer is about the size of a rabbit.

JOHOR –
A LAND'S END

The state of Johor occupies the entire southern tip of the Malay peninsula. Its west coast, facing the Straits of Malacca, is well developed with a large population, but in the centre and in the southeast of the state, the population is sparse and vast stretches of jungle separate one settlement from another. The jungle is not visible for the visitor travelling by road, however. Along the good network of roads in the state, the landscape is dominated by oil palm and rubber plantations (and in some areas pineapple farms) which stretch across the undulating hills to the horizon.

Johor is reputed to be the home of classical Malay culture; its people are known to speak the best Malay in the peninsula and its women wear the *baju kurong*, the national dress, on everyday occasions.

Many of the Malays here are of Javanese descent, and Johor is the only state

Preceding pages: the stately Abu Bakar Mosque. **Left,** looking across the causeway from Singapore.

in Malaysia where you can see the *Kuda Kepang*, a dance of Javanese origin, in which the dancer stands astride a "hobby horse" and is said to possess magical and visionary powers while under the influence of a trance.

But Johor only evolved its own identity after the fall of the Malacca sultanate to the Portuguese in the 16th century. Malacca's last ruler refused to capitulate but fled to Johor. The present royal family of Johor is related to Sultan Mahmud by a collateral line. Despite this pedigree, however, Johor's rulers never attained the pinnacle of power, prestige and influence which the sultans of Malacca had enjoyed.

Johor was basically a trading empire that had its moments of power and prosperity interspersed with the darker days of disaster. Not only did it have to contend with the Portuguese of Malacca, and then with the Dutch, but also with the new power of Acheh in north Sumatra. When Acheh weakened, the marauding Menangkabau and the Bugis began to flex their muscles. At first the

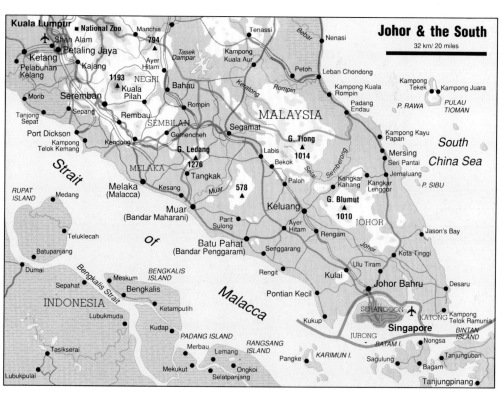

rulers of Johor had their capitals along the protected reaches of the Johor River, but later, had to settle in the Riau archipelago, which was more accessible to trade – and further attacks. Twice a sultan of Johor was taken captive to Acheh, and his royal capital was reduced to ashes. By the beginning of the 18th century, Johor sultans had become the puppets of the Bugis chiefs who held all the real power.

A turning point: The 19th century saw a decisive change in Johor's fate. At that time, Johor was the fief of a *temenggung*, an official of the sultan. Abu Bakar, who became *temenggung* in 1862, elevated himself to *maharaja* in 1868, and in 1885 he was acknowledged by Great Britain as Sultan of Johor, thereby discounting the former sultan's lineage. The present royal family of Johor are his direct descendants.

Sultan Abu Bakar was educated in Singapore by English clergy. He spoke fluent English and came to know influential Europeans in the business world. It was during his rule that the foundations of modern Johor were laid; locals today still regard him as the "Father of Modern Johor". In 1866, he moved his capital to Johor Bahru and within a few years had transformed a humble fishing village into a thriving new town. He was also responsible for founding the modern towns of Muar and Batu Pahat; he introduced a modern bureaucracy and gave Johor the first constitution ever to be written for a Malay state.

The Sultan used Western methods of policy-making and administration in his conduct of Johor's internal affairs (Britain still had control over Johor's foreign matters) and this stood him in good stead in convincing the British that his government was good and stable and so deferred the appointment of a British "Advisor" to help him rule his state. He maintained close ties with Englishmen in Singapore and in London, being the first Malay ruler to visit England and became a personal friend of Queen Victoria.

But after his death in 1895 British pressure became too strong, and his son

Malaysia is a land of gentle smiles – this one is in Muar.

and heir reluctantly accepted the "assistance" of a General Advisor (British, of course) in 1914. This made Johor the last Malay state in the peninsula to come under British control.

Sulphur springs and sultans' tombs: **Muar**, a small and pretty town lies just under the Johor/Malacca border. It is considered, along with its surroundings, as a cultural centre, and Johor *ghazal* music and the trance dance *Kuda Kepang* can sometimes be seen here.

En route to Muar, approaching from Malacca, a detour on the road to Segamat leads to **Gunung Legang**, once known as Mount Ophir. This mountain is of much interest to naturalists and in the vicinity the Sagil waterfalls cascade 2,500 metres (8,200 feet) down the rocks to the clear pools below. Closer to Muar are the **Sungai Kesang** hot sulphur springs, 5 kilometres (3 miles) off the main road. Simple changing rooms are provided.

At **Pagoh**, 26 kilometres (16 miles) from Muar, there is an old fort containing the tombs of two Malacca sultans.

Situated atop a small rise, it was constructed to protect the sultans from attacks by pirates. Nearby in the graveyard at **Kampong Parit Pecah**, stand 99 tombstones, marking the graves of an entire village which was wiped out by a single spear about 500 years ago. According to legend, this happened at a wedding party. The spear was tossed by a jealous lover into the chest of a bridegroom, removed and tossed again, eventually killing the bride and all the wedding guests.

Batu Pahat, notorious for its floods at high tides, is a conference centre. Chinese food is considered to be especially good here. There is a small beach and a legendary well nearby at **Minyak Beku**. Nineteen kilometres (12 miles) south of Pontian Kechil, which has a comfortable Government Rest House, the road ends at Kukup on the southwestern tip of the peninsula.

Chilli crabs and lobster pots: Raised on stilts above the water, the Chinese village of **Kukup**'s houses are linked to one another by plank walks, looking as

Temple on wheels, Kukup.

though they might topple into the sea. Late afternoon is the ideal time to arrive, when the sun is low over the sea and the evening breezes begin. But it is not to watch the setting sun that the hoards of visitors, especially from nearby Singapore, come to Kukup. It is to eat chilli crabs, for which Kukup with its unpretentious wooden houses is rightly famous. The restaurants do not have fancy decor, and some do not even have walls. But they do have atmosphere and great food. Since it has become popular with Singaporeans, Kukup's seafood is not as cheap as it used to be, and the drinks especially are very expensive.

Along a railing facing the sea in one restaurant is a huge square net, lowered and raised by an ancient, wooden crank. Boys wind the net up from the sea and scoop out the daily menu – eels, fish crabs, lobsters. Chilli crabs, the speciality, are eaten with the fingers; it is messy, but delicious. Choose your own style of cooking – chilli prawns, steamed fish, sweet and sour fish or chilli mussels.

On the main trunk road to Ayer Hitam, a town 93 kilometres (58 miles) from Johor Bahru or 32 kilometres (20 miles) from Batu Pahat, nobody can miss the **Aw Potteries,** proclaimed by two colossal earthenware genies. The Menangkabau showroom displays all sorts of pottery in the distinctive Aw glazes. Behind the showroom is the studio itself where you can watch craftsmen at work throughout every stage of the process. The most spectacular feature is the immense snake kiln. Forty-eight metres (157 feet) long, the brick-built kiln of traditional Chinese design is the very womb of the potteries giving birth regularly and unprotestingly to some 2,000 individual pieces of pottery at each firing. Mr Aw Eng Kwang, the founder, came from China in 1940, finally settling in Kampong Machap where there is an abundant supply of clay and firing wood. From a simple beginning manufacturing latex cups and flower pots, the Aw family, representing four generations of potters, has built up a thriving business

Nightlife in Johor Bahru is surprisingly lively.

230

of international repute.

Street shopping: **Ayer Hitam** is a dusty bazaar that has become a popular stopover point for tourists on their way to Kuala Lumpur or Singapore. This becomes evident as one sees the ubiquitous tour coaches and Singapore-registered cars parked on the sandy stretches off the road. Dark musty coffeeshops and rows of heavily laden street stalls become "a drinking hole and a shopping centre" for weary travellers, who descend on the stalls to hunt down last-minute souvenirs or snap up preserved fruits, durian cakes, peanut nougat and other typical sweatmeats, most of which are the town's local produce. So are fruits like bananas, *chempedak* and rambutans, which hang down in luxurious bunches.

Travellers familiar with Ayer Hitam head for **Claycraft Coffee House**, which is an unusual air-conditioned restaurant doubling up as a pottery shop. The place is half hidden by the street stalls but on entering, it is a different experience altogether. Patrons sit on stoneware stools and drink out of dainty ceramic tea cups. The room is taken up by tables, half of which are filled with the mishmash of arty relics and ceramic odds and ends.

Causeway connection: Johor Bahru is connected to Singapore by a causeway carrying vehicular traffic and a railroad. Its proximity to Singapore makes it a gateway for urban vacationers at weekends. Then, traffic slows down to a snail's pace. Timber lorries, tourist buses, outstation taxis, motor scooters and Singaporeans escaping city life in their Holdens and Mercedes vie for positions at the immigration gates. Whether it be to see an X-rated film banned in Singapore, to find a beach, or try the roulette wheels at Genting Highlands, the crowds flocking from Singapore to Malaysia create traffic jams. A second causeway connecting southwest Johor with Singapore's industrial centre Jurong, is on the planning table, and aims to cater to commercial vehicles, thus hoping to ease the present squash in Johor Bahru.

Unrestricted view of JB from Bukit Serene.

To the west are the **Istana Gardens** enclosing the sultan's palace. Adjoining these gardens, which include a replica of a Japanese tea house, is the famous **Johor Zoo**. Once the sultan's private animal sanctuary, it has been opened to the public since 1962.

The **Istana Besar** (the Grand Palace) displays a neo-classical Western style and was built by Sultan Abu Bakar in the 1860s. It is no longer a royal residence but remains till today, as it has always been, a venue for glittering state functions. The palace, with its halls stuffed full of antiques and Victoriana, is closed to the public but may be viewed with special permission. The present Sultan lives in a much more modern palace, called **Bukit Serene**, a few kilometres down the road. Beautiful gardens surround the building and its spectacular 32-metre (105-foot) tower is a city landmark.

The elegant **Abu Bakar Mosque** commands a conspicuous position also facing the Straits, and is a mixture of traditional Islamic and classical Italian styles. The spacious building, with marble colonnades lining its interior, can accommodate 2,000 worshippers.

Johor Bahru has several handicraft centres. Handicrafts made by the handicapped are for sale in Jalan Waterworks and at Jalan Skudai, off Jalan Abu Bakar. The craft centre offers hand-drawn batik cloths, paintings, as well as straw mats for sale. At Sri Ayu Batik Industries on Jalan Persira Satu, Taman Ungku Tun Aminah, you can watch demonstrations of batik painting, *kain songket* weaving and copper tooling.

An interesting introduction to Malaysia's wealth awaits you at **Ulu Tiram Estate**, which is 26 kilometres (16 miles) from Johor Bahru. Here you will see rubber trees being tapped and the various processes which the latex passes through before it is ready for export as either sheet or crepe rubber. Oil palm is also cultivated here and you may visit the estate factory and observe how the oil is extracted from the fruit for subsequent refinings which provide the base for soap, margarine and cosmetics.

Modern mosque has a fairytale look.

Waterfalls near the 'High Town': Kota Tinggi is a small, quiet town with a loud splash. Fifteen kilometres (9 miles) northeast of the town centre are the famous **Kota Tinggi Waterfalls** which thunder down 36 metres (118 feet) to the polished rocks below. Swimming is permitted to anyone having enough courage to plunge into the icy waters. Well-furnished Swiss-type chalets face the falls, inviting visitors to spend the night. These have cooking facilities with utensils, a gas range and a refrigerator. An open-front restaurant serves both Chinese and European dishes. In the evening the falls are gaily illuminated, making a lively, dancing spectacle for the dinner guests.

On the outskirts of Kota Tinggi, at **Kampong Makam**, on the road to Mersing is the burial ground of the 17th-century sultans of Johor, and nearby, the last resting place of Johor's *bendahara* or chief ministers during the early days. A little farther down the road, not far from the turning to Kampong Makam, another junction to the right leads to Malaysia's most modern beach resort at Tanjong Penawar (now better known as **Desaru**), 54 kilometres (33 miles) away. Before getting there – about halfway along this road – a right-hand laterite track branches off through an oil palm plantation and brings you to **Johore Lama** (old Johor) on the Johor River. It was once a great trading centre and a royal capital, boasting one of the most powerful forts in the area. That was history and until very recently, it could only be reached by river. Today Johore Lama is a tranquil sleepy village, on whose fringes archaeologists have uncovered some massive ramparts of the old fort. The road is rather hard to negotiate without a four-wheel drive. It passes through an oil palm plantation and arrival at the village is somewhat disappointing, as even the villagers seem to be deserting the area for more accessible places. The view over the Johor Straits to Johor Bahru, however, is very pretty.

At Tanjong Penawar is the **Desaru Resort**, a project in the state's overall

This local youngster waits for a ride.

development scheme designed to open up this corner of southeast Johor which was once a deserted jungled country.

The resort is much frequented by wealthy Singaporeans and Malaysians, who take up many rooms at the **Desaru View Hotel** and the **Desaru Golf Resort** at weekends. For those eager to shun big hotels, there are the delightful **Desaru Chalets** just off the beach. Between here and the Desaru View Hotel are a youth hostel, a camping site, and basic traditional huts, all occupied during school holidays.

The hotels and the chalets provide all the usual beach facilities of water sports, pony trekking and golf and tennis, and the Desaru Golf Hotel runs a **Scuba Diving Centre**.

The road northwards from Kota Tinggi pursues its lonely, undulating course, until at the 13th kilometre, a turning points the way to **Jason's Bay**, or Telok Mahkota, which was once the most popular of Johor beaches. But now the long beach has silted up and there are mud flats at low tide. There are no facilities at the beach but those who wish to get away from it all will find their solitude interrupted only by sea birds, sandflies, and no more than an occasional visitor.

Mersing, situated on the right bank of the river of the same name, is a peaceful pleasant town, except at the river mouth. Here is a large, bustling fishing fleet and there is all the excitement one associates with a fishing port. Accommodation is available in the splendid **Government Rest House** sitting on a bluff above the sea and separated from it by a simple nine-hole golf course. There are also several simple Chinese hotels, notably the **Mersing Hotel** and the **Hotel Embassy**, both with good restaurants. Around the first of May comes the annual festival of Kayu Papan in Mersing, where you may be lucky to see the *Kuda Kepang*, a trance dance seldom seen outside Johor.

Islands in the sun: Mersing is the setting off point for a group of 64 idyllic volcanic islands in the South China Sea. One of these, **Pulau Tioman**, was

There is a fair sprinkling of tropical isles offshore.

mentioned 2,000 years ago in what was perhaps the first guide to Malaysia. Arab traders then made note in their "sailing directions" that Tioman, lying about 56 kilometres (35 miles) off the east coast of the Malay peninsula, offered good anchorage and a freshwater spring for filling their casks. Centuries afterwards, the twin peaks called "Ass's Ears" at the southern tip of the island guided ships at sea. Ming pottery found in caves reveals that early Chinese traders also made Tioman a port-of-call.

Gone are the Arab and Chinese traders, their place now taken by lotus-eating sybarites. Today, Tioman is everybody's dream of a tropical island. When Hollywood was looking for a mythical island to film *South Pacific*, it chose lovely Tioman to portray the legendary Bali Hai. Lovely beaches fringe the western side of the island and the waters surrounding it are startlingly clear. But be warned: sea-urchins abound in the shallow waters. Swimming, sunbathing and fishing are the most obvious beach activities.

Tioman is on everyone's "world's best islands" list.

The more energetic may wish to trek across the island on the path that begins next to the airport and emerges on the eastern side of the island at **Kampong Juara**, taking a boat back from there to the western coast. The walk takes between 2 and 3 hours, and walkers report that it is quite easy to get lost along the path as there are sometimes several pathways to choose from. Keep your eyes open for signs!

Snorkelling should not be missed, as the coral reefs around the island have some beautiful marine life. A small islet in the bay of the Tioman Resort holds some beautiful corals and even better is **Pulau Rengis**, an hour by fishing boat from Kampong Tekek jetty.

The choice of transport to Tioman, from fishing boat to 12-seater airplane (from Kuala Lumpur or Singapore) is somewhat confusing. Travelling time is from 4 hours to 30 minutes (the latter by plane). For full details, see the Transportation section at the back of the book.

The **Tioman Island Resort** looks very much like the commercial hotels in

Desaru, and offers the usual international class hotel facilities. But to really get a feel for the island, it is much pleasanter to stay at one of the quieter and friendlier chalets ranged along the lovely beach at **Kampong Tekek** (the name means Lizard Village).

Many of the chalet owners can arrange a package tour from Mersing including transport and accommodation. Accommodation ranges from air-conditioned chalets to coconut A-frame huts and is scattered along the beaches from Tekek to **Salang Beach** in the far north. Wherever you stay, don't miss a stroll along the beach at sunset to enjoy the cooler air and the coloured skies.

Much smaller than Tioman is the pretty little island of **Rawa**, which is accessible from Mersing, just one hour away from the port. However, the rather over-developed resort can be a little crowded at weekends. Go during the week. Picnickers are not allowed on the island, and if you decide to spend the day here, you will have to eat at the island's one restaurant.

Accommodation is in the form of chalets of various styles with shared bathrooms. The staff are very friendly at the resort and will tell you where to find the best snorkelling. The resort has its own little "zoo" with monkeys, birds and small mammals.

Turn left along the beach from the resort, climb over the rocks at the end of the bay, and you will discover a sea cave with a spectacular arch, against which the waters batter, perhaps hoping in twenty years or so to bring it crashing down into the sea.

Other islands in the Mersing group include **Sibu Besar**, the "island of perilous passage" with accommodation and seasport facilities; **Pulau Babi Besar**, the closest island with basic but beautifully peaceful chalets; and **Pulau Hujong**, with private houses that have to be booked from Mersing beforehand. Offices for boat services to all the islands are located around the jetty at Mersing, or wander down to the pier and try your luck at bargaining with the men on the fishing boats.

The Endau River: Known to few along the border between the states of Johor and Pahang, lies the **Endau River**, terminating at the sea and at the small town of Endau. From Endau you can travel the river up into the remote regions of the interior, but this is not a journey for the casual tourist.

Before making the journey, adventurers must have camping and trekking equipment ready, hire guides, preferably *Orang Asli* guides, and boats. No river in the peninsula is so remote yet so close to civilisation as the Sungai Endau. At the lower reaches it is bordered by mangrove swamps, but further up you are surrounded by dense jungle in which tigers prowl and rhinoceros hide.

The interior is an extensive *Orang Asli* area, and the fierce rapids separate them from many a prying stranger, afraid to proceed beyond the frothing waters. You may visit their settlements, where you will be welcomed, but as the *Orang Asli* are a protected people, you must first obtain an entry permit from the State Security Council in Johor Bahru.

Left, an island sunset. **Right**, teeing off on Tioman.

IPOH

204

HIGHWAYS TO THE EAST COAST

After exploring the west coast of Malaysia, with its large modern cities, its countryside of rubber, oil palm and disused tin mines, most visitors to Malaysia now turn their eyes to the alluring east coast, an area specifically connected with the Malays of the country. There are to be found exclusively Malay *kampong*, traditional arts and sports, and a relaxed and easy-going way of life. Especially popular with tourists are the gorgeous stretches of beach which fringe the entire coast, and the exquisite islands enclosed in coral reefs which lie in easy reach of the coast.

Not too long ago, the east was almost entirely cut off from the west, with the **Main Range** of mountains dividing the two, and thick impassable jungle making progress so slow that the sea route was often preferred.

Nowadays, however, there are three good highways which reach out between the coasts, carrying news, business and tourism from west to east and from east to west.

The first highway runs from Johor Bahru in the extreme south to Mersing, a fishing port on the east coast of Johor state. The second highway, and by far the most used, is that which runs across the middle of the country from Kuala Lumpur to Kuantan in the state of Pahang. Taking this highway, you have an option of making a small detour to the Taman Negara (National Park) before continuing on your way.

The third highway is the most recent and to date the least used. This is the road that connects Butterworth and Penang to Kota Bharu in the northmost section of the East Coast, located in the state of Kelantan. The scenery here, along the Thai border is wild and romantic, and one of the least populated areas on the peninsula.

There are also several more unusual and less used routes to the East Coast, for those who dislike busy roads, and who wish to take in at leisure the remote

Preceding pages: a typical Malaysian highway. Below, stunning view from the East-West highway.

village life in the jungled and mountainous centre of the peninsula. You might just be the only foreigner that you'll see along these small roads, but you will be made welcome by friendly and curious villagers.

The Johor Bahru–Mersing Highway: The road from **Johor Bahru** to **Mersing** cuts through extensive rubber and oil palm plantations, some of which you will be able to visit on the way. **Kota Tinggi** (41 kilometres/25 miles from Johor Bahru) has a waterfall and chalets nearby. After Kota Tinggi, you can either turn south for **Desaru Resort**, or continue northwards to Mersing (134 kilometres/83 miles from Johor Bahru). This same road will take you up the entire stretch of the East Coast, hugging the seashore almost all the way.

The KL–Kuantan Highway: The second route, from **Kuala Lumpur** to **Kuantan**, cuts straight across the landmass from west to east. Drive out on the clearly marked highway from Kuala Lumpur and through the northeastern suburbs, passing the Batu Caves on the way. You will soon cross over into the enormous state of Pahang, shortly after which is the turnoff for the **Genting Highlands**, the gambler's paradise.

The road now crosses the Wangsa Mountains before dropping down into the plains of Pahang. After some 150 kilometres (93 miles) from the capital, you will reach **Mentakab**, a town on the Jungle Railway (which goes up to Kota Bharu and Thailand). After Mentakab is a turnoff which takes you to the small settlement of **Tembeling**, starting point for boats to the **Taman Negara**. Or you can just continue eastwards through to Temerloh.

Many small villages follow, before you arrive at **Gambang**. Here a road plunges straight down to Segamat in Johor state. Along this road, you will cross the Pahang River, directly after which is a small road leading off to the right, taking you to Kampong Kuala Chini and the legendary **Lake Chini** (see the East Coast section on Kuantan for more details).

Gambang is just 19 kilometres (12 miles) from Kuantan. From Kuantan,

you can either head south for Mersing and Tioman, or northwards for the turtle beaches, Kuala Terengganu and Kota Bharu.

The Butterworth–Kota Bharu Highway: The third and perhaps most thrilling highway to the East Coast is in the far north of the country, at times touching the Thai border, and crossing a wild and deserted landscape. From **Butterworth**, pass Bukit Mertajam and take the north road to **Keroh** on the Thai border. The road is sprinkled with small settlements all along this road. These diminish in number on the road between Keroh and **Gerik**, 160 kilometres (100 miles) from Butterworth. This is an *Orang Asli* settlement area, and for those wishing to explore the surrounding wilderness, there is a Government Rest House at Gerik and a few small Chinese hotels. East of Gerik is the huge Temenggor Reservoir, and the Banding Fishing Resort on its shores.

Here there are opportunities for fishing, trekking, hiking and picnicking. There is also a campsite and a rest house

In Malaysia, the forest is ever-present.

for those who wish to experience the feeling of spending the night in one of peninsular Malaysia's least populated areas. Indeed, traffic on this highway is not yet a problem, and for many kilometres you will have the road almost to yourself.

After Gerik, you will pass an army checkpoint. The army has a very large presence in this area, for it was here that the communist guerillas had their last hideout in Malaysia. Since this is a desolate place, there are still fears that this would be the area that they would return to, should they inspire an uprising in the future. The highway on this section, between Gerik and Tanah Merah in Kelantan state, is closed between 6 p.m. and 6 a.m. for the same reason, so make sure you set out early enough to be on this road section by 4 p.m.

The landscape is at its most extravagantly wild here, and it is worth stopping to drink in the fresh cool air. The road crosses **Lake Temenggor**, a reservoir of great and mysterious beauty. One hundred and thirty-three kilo-metres (83 miles) from Gerik, the Thai border is touched for the second time near Kampong Nibong.

Twenty-nine kilometres (18 miles) later, you reach the town of **Tanah Merah** (Red Earth) on the Kelantan River, and once again you are in civilisation. But it is immediately apparent that the villages and countryside are very different from those on the west coast.

From Tanah Merah, you can head south to **Kuala Krai** on the Pahang River. It is possible to take boats from here to Kota Bharu at the mouth of the river, passing picturesque Malay villages, where many of the state's arts and handicrafts are produced. Or you can carry straight on to **Pasir Puteh**, an area blessed with numerous waterfalls. From there it's a short drive to the coast at Kuala Besut, the jumping-off point for the exquisite **Perhentian Islands**, and equipped with its own beaches and rest house.

Turning north from Tanah Merah, the road ploughs through quiet little vil- **Long distance travel is the norm.**

lages, crosses the Kelantan River and brings you to **Kota Bharu**, the capital of Kelantan, and a centre for East Coast arts.

These three routes are certainly the most used, and take you past many interesting sights on the way. However, if you have a penchant for out-of-the-way places and the rarely-trodden roads, there are several other possibilities, mostly optional routes leading off from the main ones.

More options: One of these leads from **Batu Pahat** on the west coast of Johor, crossing the north-south highway at **Ayer Hitam** and continuing on a smaller road through **Keluang** on the railway across a plain of little rivers and small villages to meet the Johor Bahru to Mersing road at **Jemaluang**.

Another larger road runs from **Melaka** (Malacca) to **Segamat** in the north of Johor state. From here you can either turn south or head steeply north passing into a remote village area in the south of Pahang.

A side road follows the **Rompin**

A kite for sore eyes: rural backroads scene.

River to the coast at Kampong Leban Chondong north of Kuala Rompin. Otherwise you can continue northwards, passing the turnoff to **Lake Chini** and finally joining the Kuala Lumpur to Kuantan highway.

Another route from Malacca is to drive towards **Gemas**. Just before Gemas, take the turnoff which leads northwards to **Temerloh**, which is situated at the crossroads of the Jungle Railway and the main Kuala Lumpur to Kuantan road.

Passing the town of **Bahau** in eastern Negri Sembilan, a turnoff to the right not far out of town takes you to **Tasek Dampar**, a large body of water attached to the more famous **Tasek Bera**, Malaysia's largest natural lake.

Tasek Bera is more easily reached by continuing along the Temerloh road and turning down a rough road at **Triang**.

Five *Orang Asli* villages nestle on the lake's shore, and at **Pos Iskandar** village, there is a Government Rest House for those wishing to extend their stay in this remote countryside. Permits are required to visit the villages on Tasek Bera, and these can be obtained either by post from, or by direct application at the Temerloh police station. A passport-sized photograph must be attached to the permit, which is issued free of charge.

On the Kuantan/Kuala Lumpur highway, you can turn north at Mentakab for the **Taman Negara**. After a visit to that splendid park, you can take a small road which follows the western boundaries of the park. At **Gua Musang**, the road widens and carries local traffic northwards through the Kelantan countryside to **Kuala Krai**, and eventually to Kota Bharu.

The final option is to take the remote road that pursues its lonely course through the **Upper Perak** region, from **Kuala Kangsar** through *Orang Asli* villages to **Gerik**, and from there you can join the east-west highway to **Kota Bharu**.

On the main highways, filling up your car with petrol is no problem, but if you are taking one of the small road options, start with a full tank, just to be sure.

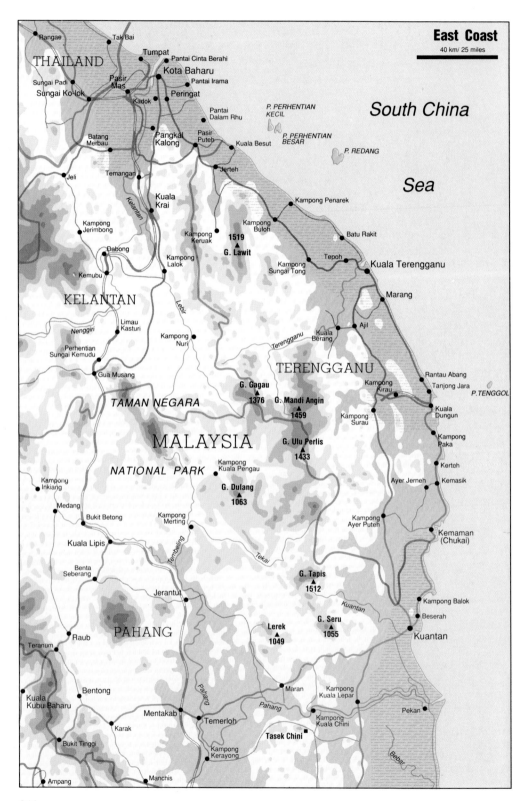

FAR FROM THE MADDING CROWD

To discover the soul of Malaysia, one should visit the East Coast. Bordered by Thailand on the north, isolated from the west by a chain of rugged mountains and separated from the south by swamps and rivers, the East Coast has retained its own identity through the ages. Its relaxed villages and *kampong*, where leisure nurtured its arts, have survived more or less unchanged. The Sultan of Johor has a birthday celebration, and the dancers are imported from Kota Bharu. The University of Malaya puts on a cultural show and they recruit the *Mak Yong* actors from Kelantan. Foreign dignitaries are being entertained and the *Wayang Kulit* shadow play comes from Terengganu.

The East Coast's exquisite silver artisans, its cloth weavers and batik makers are renowned throughout the country. And where else but on the East Coast can you see farmers competing in top-spinning and kite-flying and watch 3½-metre-long, 750-kilo turtles lay their eggs on a particular stretch of beach.

Peaceful, timeless fishing villages, palms bending out over a blue sea, colourfully painted fishing boats pulled up on the shore waiting for the tide to carry them to their fishing grounds, islands floating upon an unattainable horizon – these are the scenes on the quieter side of the Malay peninsula.

Oily operations: The East Coast is still unsophisticated in the most natural sense of the word. But the modern world is beginning to intrude. Offshore oil installations in the South China Sea off Terengganu have converted the state from one of the poorest in the federation to one of the richest. Over the last few years Kuala Terengganu has transformed from a place "slipped past by time" into a rapidly expanding modern city, while farther down the coast huge new oil refineries and depots, modern bungalows and houses are springing up where palm trees had waved in golden solitude over deserted beaches.

Malaysia's East Coast embraces the states of Kelantan, Terengganu and Pahang and the eastern half of Johor. Kelantan and Terengganu are two Malay states which have retained much of their traditional character, cut off as they are by the jungle-clad peaks of the Main Range from the rest of the peninsula. Until the end of the 19th century, these two states were the most heavily populated in the peninsula and their inhabitants remain predominantly Malay till today.

An annalistic rubdown: Kelantan has a long story of independent existence going back to the dawn of history. Important traces of New Stone Age men have been found at various places in the state, which emerged as an important kingdom in the days of the Malaccan sultanate and was ruled by the legendary beauty, Puteri Sa'adong, in the 17th century. But in more modern times Kelantan was under the shadow of Thailand and Thai influence did not come to an end until a treaty signed in 1909 between the Thais and the British, placed Kelantan under British protec-

tion instead. However Thai influence can still be seen in the Kelantan architecture, dialect and art forms of today.

The sultans of Terengganu are direct descendants of the Johor and Malacca royal families, and the state itself was once a fief of Malacca and then Johor before it came under Thai suzerainty. Although sending "golden flowers" to Bangkok as a token of tribute, Terengganu was largely left to its own devices until finally in 1909, when it was transferred along with Kelantan to British overlordship.

Pahang's past does not differ much from its northern neighbouring states. It was part of the kingdom of Malacca and later came under the control of Johor. Its rulers, the *bendahara*, maintained a precarious independence for centuries and as late as the 1880s, one of them finally shook off the Johor connection and converted his state into a sultanate. But the new sultan was not able to enjoy his new status for long before the British took over.

Until this century the East Coast states possessed no roads. Travel along the coast was by boat, and inland transportation was made on rivers or jungle tracks. During the monsoon season from November to January, the states were entirely cut off from the rest of the world as the northwest monsoon flooded the countryside and closed the beaches. Even today the monsoon season is not the time to visit the East Coast.

The East Coast is a place to explore. Do not hesitate to travel off the beaten track to a small fishing village. A friendly gesture will be the return of a smile, or perhaps an invitation to tour the village where the soothing rhythms of Malay life have endured for centuries. Only then, does one come to know the soul of Malaysia.

River mouths of Pahang: Numerous rivers spill their bubbling waters into the sea along the coast of the state of Pahang. Coming from Johor, the state boundary is marked by the **Endau River** which curls its way into *Orang Asli* country. Only a few kilometres northwards are several more rivers: the **Lobster, anyone?**

Anak Endau (child of the Endau), the **Pontian River** opening out into the sea at Kuala Pontian, and the end of the Rompin River at **Kuala Rompin**. Nearby is a comfortable **Government Rest House**. In the town of Kuala Rompin, you can rent a four-wheel drive vehicle and drive inland 10 kilometres (6 miles) to **Iban** and to **Kampong Aur** (25 kilometres/15 miles inland) where there are *Orang Asli* settlements of the *Jakun* tribes.

Other interesting rivers moving northwards include **Sungai Merchong** and **Bebar**, but there are no roads here: you must rent a boat if you wish to explore further.

Islam, royalty and polo: **Pekan** occupies the southern end of the estuary of the Pahang River, the longest in the peninsula. The river is gentle and sylvan at this point and with its tidy little houseboats, reminds one of the Thames at Henley. Pekan was the former capital of Pahang and is still a royal town, being the residence of the sultan. It is a small and unremarkable town but on the way

to the **Istana Abu Bakar** (the Abu Bakar Palace), visitors pass a new mausoleum and two handsome, white marble mosques with a riot of golden domes. One of the mosques is newly built and attests to the vitality of Islam in this part of the country – and also to the population boom. The sultan's *Istana* (palace), further on, has an enormous polo ground which when not in use for that sport provides what must be the flattest golf course in the world.

The town houses the **State Museum** of Pahang, which displays many items of historical interest; the most recent acquisitions are the treasures recovered from a Chinese junk lying at the bottom of the South China Sea. Pekan also boasts a silk-weaving centre, situated at **Kampong Pulau Keladi**, 5 kilometres (3 miles) from Pekan.

Forty-four kilometres (27 miles) north of Pekan is **Kuantan**, the capital of Pahang and its commercial centre. There is not much here to detain the visitor except for the handsome new stadium, a pleasant children's play-

ground alongside the Kuantan River or the one kilometre of river esplanade where there are some good eating stalls. There are also several shops selling regional handicrafts along Jalan Besar. However, there is a great deal to see and do around Kuantan.

There is accommodation available in Kuantan but most visitors will prefer to stay at the beach. Drive through town for 3 kilometres (2 miles) and a cross-road is reached at the corner of which is a small villa belonging to the sultan. Drive straight on for one kilometre to reach **Telok Chempedak Beach**, once pleasant but now rather overcrowded with hotels and tourist development. Here are the Hyatt and Merlin hotels, as well as a good selection of cheaper accommodation. Alternatively, turn right and after one kilometre the **Government Rest House** is reached. This *chengai* and tiled building is one of Malaysia's finest rest houses and is a far cry from the days when travellers showered with a dipper in a Shanghai jar and kept cool with a ceiling *punkah* fan. It

has hot tubs and showers, piped-in music and a beach that is sheltered by a sandbar and is ideal for children. Alongside it is the clubhouse of a sporting 18-hole golf course and a splendid 50-by-30 metre (165-by-100 foot) public swimming pool. About 200 metres (220 yards) away is an excellent children's playground.

The Tourist Bureau will make arrangements – although it may take two or three days – for performances of *Silat* and *Wayang Kulit* (for description of these art forms, see Cultural section in Travel Tips at the back), as well as two of the local dances – *Olek Mayang* and *Rodat*. The latter is a traditional fishermen's dance in which hand movements feature prominently. *Olek Mayang* is a remarkable trance dance in which one of the villagers clutches a bunch of betel nut flowers and is lulled into a trance by his fellow dancers chanting a song, inviting the spirits of seven princesses to cast a spell upon the dancer. This forces him to dance the steps and movements of their choice. At

The Hyatt Kuantan is a top holiday spot.

250

the conclusion of the chanting the dancer collapses and so tightly does he clutch his bouquet that it takes half a dozen men to pull it from him.

Naturally, the best time to see these happenings is during a festival. The alternative is to have the Tourist Bureau hire an entire village to stage a festival. The charges are moderate if divided among several patrons.

Kuantan and its surroundings are noted for authentic craftsmanship – wood carving, brocade, batik and weaving. Places where handicrafts are made or the arts performed are marked by a board with green, yellow and red circles and a ten-point red star. However, most of the signs are dilapidated and should not be taken too seriously. The **Brocade Weaving Center** at **Selamat** village (part of Kuantan town), where silk *sarong* are handwoven with intricate designs in gold and silver, and where one of the block printing shops on Jalan Selamat, still using primitive methods in preparing designs, can readily be visited. There is also a **Batik Centre** at **Be-serah**, a pretty little fishing village just north of Kuantan. Kite-flying and top-spinning can also be seen here.

Of lake monsters and crocodiles: Some excellent side trips can be made from Kuantan. One unusual journey is to **Lake Chini**, actually a conglomerate of 12 connecting lakes. The lake is large and from June to September, is covered by a brilliant carpet of red and white lotuses which contrast sharply with the surrounding green hills.

The *Jakun* tribes live along the shores of this lake. The *Jakun* use blowpipes to catch monkeys and other jungle animals, and to supplement their diet, collect lotus seeds when the flowers on the lake wilt. When ripe, the cream-coloured seeds, slightly smaller than quails' eggs, taste distinctly nutty and are a good source of protein.

The *Jakun* peoples have lived long by this lake, and their oral traditions are alive with the legends surrounding the area. Of the origin of the lake, the headman will relate the experiences of his ancestors, who while clearing a section

This reclining Buddha near Kota Bharu is the largest in the region.

of forest one day, met an old woman with a stick. She claimed that the area was hers, and to make her point clear, stuck her stick firmly into the ground there before vanishing.

A barking dog distracted the hunters, and running to where the dog was, they found a large black log. Overcome with curiosity, one man plunged his spear into it. Others followed suit and blood began to spurt out of the log, the sky grew dark, and thunder and lightning added to their panic. In the pandemonium that followed, the old woman's stick was uprooted and from the hole, water poured forth, flooding the whole area, and thus creating Lake Chini.

Other tales tell of *nagas*, dragons or monsters, living in the lake. Two of these mythical creatures are said to have become the islands of Tioman and Daik. British officials, possibly recalling the famous Loch Ness, have claimed to have seen mysterious beasts swimming in the lake. Crocodiles have certainly been spotted here and on the shores of the lake lives an old woman who is legendary for her friendship with these reptiles. It is said that she has saved them from being hunted and they have saved her from being drowned by pushing her to the shore with their noses. Now over a hundred years old, her memory is a little confused about events, but she certainly remembers her friends with fondness.

Another tale tells of a lost city beneath Chini's waters, and archaeological examination of the site has proved that there are remains of a civilisation to be found 12 metres (40 feet) below the lake's surface, possibly the ruins of a Khmer settlement, verified by historical descriptions of one in the vicinity.

Tasek Chini lies on a rough road off the Kuantan to Segamat road. There you can hire a boatman and a guide for the tour which takes you down the Pahang River and out into the lake. The entire trip can be done in one day, but if you wish to linger in this myth-filled place, there are camping grounds and chalets. A rest house lies further away. For those patronising Club Mediterranée at Cher-

The beach at Tanjong Jara is wide, windy and wonderful.

ating Beach (north of Kuantan), accommodation is available here. Besides floating on this beautiful lake, you can also go trekking and catch fish – 5 kilo bites are said to be nothing here.

Cliffs, caves and caverns: Another interesting side trip is northwest along the road to **Sungai Lembing**. Near the 24-kilometre mark, a turning to the right leads through dusky rubber estates and lush green oil palm plantation until suddenly, without warning, travellers find themselves under the lee of a towering limestone cliff, known as the Charah Caves. At its foot are a couple of small shops, and when you look upwards there seems to be no top. But far above are a ledge and a railing, and right in front is a steep and rickety stairway. You are at the foot of **Gua Panching**.

Until about 25 years ago, the fact that this huge limestone outcrop contains great deep caverns was unknown, except to a few locals. Then a Thai Buddhist monk chanced by and made the caves his home. In the deepest of them, he laboriously built a massive reclining Buddha, carrying the building material up the rugged rock face by himself with the aid of a handful of acolytes. He devoted the rest of his life to this project and by the time he died a few years ago, the task of devotion was completed.

The climb up to the ledge is taxing, the view exhilarating. The path leads up further into the main cave. A guide will take you through the entrance and into its recesses to the innermost cavern where the Buddha lies. The path which leads downward is slippery. It takes a while for your eyes to adjust to the darkness. Suddenly the guide stops and points upward. Unbelievable! It is not a cave but a cathedral. Thin shafts of light filter down through cracks hundreds of metres above. In the half-light distances are deceptive. Bats flutter away. The guide starts a generator for lights and leads you to a second cave, almost as big as the first. Here is the work of a lifetime, a giant statue of the sleeping Buddha, measuring 9 metres (30 feet) long. There are more caves, and more exploring to do. If you wish, arrange-

Turtle-watching is a prime attraction. Far right, mending the nets.

ments can be made to venture deeper.

If you continue driving on the same road to Sungai Lembing, and if you have made prior arrangements with the Manager of Pahang Consolidated Ltd, you can tour the world's second largest and deepest tin mine. Tin mines, however, can be dangerous and most supervisors are hesitant about allowing visitors on the premises and will certainly not allow them underground. Travellers must obtain special permission in advance before they are allowed a close-up view of one of West Malaysia's most valuable exports.

About 16 kilometres (10 miles) away inland from Sungai Lembing is the **Gunung Tapis** mountain and nature park. A conservation area, the park offers exciting activities such as shooting rapids in nearby rivers, fishing for the delicious *ikan kelah*, going on wildlife walks, or simply bathing in the various hot springs scattered around the park. Arrangements to visit and stay in the park can be made at the Tourist Information Centre in Kuantan, or through the local outbounders' society.

Chalets by the coast: Moving northwards out of Kuantan, the road follows the coast with its delightful palm-fringed beaches. Chalets are scattered on the various beaches, beginning at the 15-kilometre marker and continuing into the state of Terengganu. Forty kilometres (25 miles) from Kuantan is the **Titik Inn**, one of the first of this kind of accommodation, started by an Englishman who lived here with his wife, a Malay princess. The chalets are surrounded by trees, green lawns and a profusion of flowers.

At the 45-kilometre marker, you arrive at the friendly and relaxed village of **Cherating**. If you haven't tried staying in simple beach accommodation in Malaysia yet, this is definitely the best place to start. Nowhere could be more relaxed than the homely **Coconut Inn**, where Ilal and his Dutch wife Marina keep meticulously clean huts and chalets. The beach is close by, and the huts and chalets are cooled by coconut palms. In the evenings the family will

Marang is a well-known fishing village.

254

cook you a slap-up dinner on their barbecue, while travellers sit waiting at the tables, exchanging travel news.

The family will also arrange river trips for you, and a tour taking you to **Pulau Ular**, a small island 1 kilometre (½ mile) offshore, which is ideal for a day trip and picnic.

At the other end of the accommodation scale is Asia's first **Club Mediterranée**, situated between Kemaman (called Chukai on the road signs) and Cherating village. The club only caters for members but membership can be immediate. Viewed from the sea, the club can be seen to be walled off from the outside world, and within are the reddish brown buildings with their peaked roofs, surrounded by olive casuarina trees. Excellent French and local food, free wine with lunch and dinner, as well as the usual fun and games are all part of this exclusive and somewhat expensive establishment. Because of its emphasis on outdoor activities, the club closes during the monsoon.

Further along the road to Kemaman is some more accommodation at the **Chendor Motel**, with chalets and dormitories. Turtles can be seen in season at Chendor Beach, but these are a smaller species than their Terengganu cousins.

Crossing boundaries: Crossing the border into Terengganu, the road continues north through the town of **Kemaman** (also known as Chukai) and through the fishing village of **Kemasik** and follows the sea to **Kampong Paka**. There is little traffic. Waves break along the beaches. Inland there are rice fields, where imaginative farmers have animated the landscape with lifelike scarecrows, some dressed in regal splendour. At Paka, the road leads over a bridge, offering a striking view of the village nestled on the bank of the Paka River. The road now turns inward to Dungun.

Kuala Dungun, a dreamy little seaside town and port, was once an outlet for the state's great ore mining industry at Bukit Besi. But most of the mines have closed down and once again the town has reverted to its ancient trade of

From Marang, Pulau Kapas is a short boat ride away.

fishing. From here you can get boats out to **Pulau Tenggol**, 29 kilometres (18 miles) offshore. Thirteen kilometres (8 miles) north of Dungun is the government-run **Tanjong Jara Beach Hotel**, especially attractive for its traditional Malay style of construction, which uses only timber. Most appealing are the spacious rooms on the second floor with their wide verandahs facing the sea. For the energetic, cycling, tennis, squash and water sports are offered.

From Tanjong Jara the road follows the sea along a 65-kilometre (40-mile) stretch of exquisite shoreline. It is dotted with houses and willow casuarina trees, which the Malays say grow only near the sound of the surf. During good weather the houses are on the east side of the road near the beach, since the folk are fishermen. However, during the monsoon season the fishermen carry their houses further inland. Pulled high up the beach are the elegantly designed *prahu*, many of which still display bows called *bangau*, elaborately carved in the shape of mythical birds or demons,

forming an art in their own right. Fishing nets hang to dry on trees. Swimming is excellent and you can stop almost anywhere along the road to take a dip.

Turtle watching: A popular entertainment on the East Coast is turtle watching. On a stretch of beach 35 kilometres (22 miles) north of Kuantan, all seven known species of turtles struggle ashore, lay their eggs in the sand and then depart, never to see their young. If the eggs survive the attacks of predators, they will hatch after six to eight weeks, depending on the species.

There can be no doubt that the star of this attraction is the giant leatherback turtle and, like any great performer – it may be the largest reptile in the world – it is determined not to be upstaged. Although on occasion they do put in an appearance at Chendor Beach, leatherbacks are best seen at the turtle watchers' "Mecca". At **Rantau Abang**, 160 kilometres (100 miles) north of Kuantan and 56 kilometres (35 miles) south of Kuala Terengganu, you can witness the miraculous spectacle of the arrival

Sekayu Waterfalls is the place for a refreshing dip.

of the giant leatherback turtles coming ashore to lay their eggs once a year at the very same beach where they themselves were born, and to which their offspring will return when fully mature and laden with eggs. Seldom do other species use Rantau Abang for their accouchement. There is a **Visitors' Centre** at Rantau Abang where you can rent self-contained wooden chalets and visit the turtle museum. Other places to stay in while waiting for the turtles to put in an appearance include the **Merantau Inn** and many small huts and chalets built right on the beach itself.

The leatherback grows, it is claimed, to a length of 3½ metres (11½ feet) and may weigh up to 750 kilos (1650 pounds). Like the other species, it lays eggs from May through September, the last two weeks of August being the peak of the laying season. During these months visitors come from the world over to await the turtles. The best time to see them is at night, especially at high tide. All that is needed is a flash lamp and patience. Industrious village folk at Rantau Abang have built shelters along the beach in which travellers can pass the night dozing on a simple bed or drinking coffee. Youngsters with flash lamps scan the sands and at the first sighting of a turtle give the signal.

The subject of turtle watching is controversial. Observers are often appalled by the way local people gather up the eggs, ride on the backs of the turtles, flash lights in their eyes and even molest them. It might appear that the magnificent leatherbacks are on the road to extinction, since turtle eggs bring good prices at the marketplace. But a short walk down the beach during daylight would prove otherwise. Here members of the Department of Fisheries keep close tabs on turtles and record their habits and migrations across the seas. Even more important is their systematic collection of eggs.

A great leatherback usually lays about a hundred eggs in a large hole it digs in the sand with its rear flippers. The gestation comes not so much from man as from certain predators, such as crabs and various insects. Even more

critical is the period after the eggs are hatched when young turtles must make their way to the sea, usually across several hundred metres of open, hostile beach. Many fall prey to the flocks of birds circling overhead. When the young turtles hatch, they crawl to the surface. Each morning before dawn inspectors collect and release them in the sea. Only after about 40,000 young have returned to the sea each year are people allowed to collect the eggs. Leatherbacks have been sighted in waters as far from Malaysia as the Atlantic Ocean, yet the huge turtles return to lay their eggs only on this one stretch of beach. To watch their laborious and brief sojourn on land is reason enough to visit the East Coast. In spite of local efforts to protect the turtles, their numbers are fast diminishing, and fewer and fewer of them return. Alarmed scientists are at work to determine the cause of this, and sea pollution and the changing of sea currents are two reasons cited.

River mouths and islands: The picturesque fishing village of **Marang** lies

just south of Kuala Terengganu and is well worth a visit, if only to hire boats from there to the islands of **Pulau Kapas** and **Pulau Raja**. Both are a delight for coral lovers and sun worshippers. The **Beach House** in Marang has boats which can zip you out to Kapas in 45 minutes. Pulau Raja is about the same distance, and you can either hire your own boat or take the one from the Beach House. Pulau Raja has been designated a marine park because of its beautiful waters alive with multicoloured corals and fish.

Pulau Redang and **Pulau Bidong** are more accessible from **Merang** (not to be confused with Marang) just north of Kuala Terengganu.

Setting its own pace: Over the last four or five years, **Kuala Terengganu** has developed from a timeless fishing port and a marketplace of yesteryear into a bustling modern town, that owes its growing affluence to Terengganu's offshore oil. But enough of the old charms remain to set it apart from the contemporary worries of an urban town. Terengganu (and its neighbouring state Kelantan) is also set apart from other states by its weekends, which occur, not on Saturday and Sunday, but on Thursday (half-day) and Friday.

The pulse of Kuala Terengganu is felt in the **Central Market** alongside the river in the early morning when fishermen bring in their catch. They come directly to the market with their boats and soon the scene is alive with heated haggling over prices. The market is a modern concrete building with fresh food stalls downstairs in the courtyard and numerous general merchandise shops on the first floor.

This early morning hustle and bustle spills out into the neighbouring streets; in **Jalan Sultan Ismail**, batik and handicraft stores open their doors early to Malay housewife and tourist alike. The activity spreads to **Kampong Dalam Kota**, a place whose name means Village inside the City, and that's just what it is.

Just beyond the market in the direction of the river mouth is a broad espla-

Mat weaver and her wares.

nade which faces the **Istana Maziah**, the official residence of the Sultan of Terengganu, who actually lives in another palace a few miles away. The Istana resembles a French country house and was built at the beginning of the century to replace an older palace destroyed by fire some years before. The Istana is located at the foot of a small hill called Bukit Puteri, literally, The Hill of the Princess. Behind the Istana is the new **Zainal Abidin Mosque**, built on the site of a much older mosque constructed in wood during the reign of Sultan Zainal Abidin.

The road from the market runs on into what was, until only recently, Kuala Terengganu's main thoroughfare – **Jalan Bandar** (Main Street), a narrow, congested crescent-shaped street lined with Chinese shophouses whose architecture dates back several generations to when Terengganu was still an independent sultanate. Stroll down this street (or take a trishaw, still the most popular means of transport in downtown Kuala Terengganu) and peek into the narrow doorways: the houses seem to stretch back forever, through dark rooms, and at the back Granny can be seen sipping tea. Better shopping, however, can be found in the modern premises beyond Jalan Bandar.

The small jetty at the end of Jalan Bandar is the place to hire a boat to cruise along the island-studded estuary of the Terengganu River and get a close look at typical Malay villages by the shore. **Pulau Duyung**, the largest of the islands, is immediately opposite the jetty and is renowned as a shipbuilding centre. Once upon a time its master craftsmen were responsible for building the unique junks with fore- and main-masts, and bowsprits called *Bedor*. These fine boats were used to fish off Terengganu's shores. Today, only a couple of shipyards survive by building yachts for Australian, American and other foreign boating enthusiasts who know that a Terengganu shipbuilder is without peer in the region. Fishing further upriver is excellent and 10-kilo bites are not uncommon.

Kite-flying is a competitive sport.

Fine examples of local artistry and craftsmanship are displayed at the **State Museum**, off Jalan Air Jerneh. The museum, tucked away in a couple of rooms in a corner of the State Assembly Building also houses a wealth of exhibits relevant to Terengganu's past.

On the way to Marang, about 7 kilometres (4 miles) out of town, you will notice a fine timber Malay house on the right. This is the **Istana Tengku Nik**, a traditional house in which the aristocracy of Kelantan and Terengganu once lived. This palace used to stand near the Istana Maziah at the foot of Bukit Puteri and was originally built in the 1880s as a temporary palace for the sultan. It was moved at the expense of a foreign mining company to its present site to make way for an extension to the Istana Maziah, and to save it from destruction. Each wooden panel adorning the Istana has entwining patterns which form Koranic inscriptions. The MARA Centre in town will assist travellers who want to see any of the cottage industries at work. Good buys of batik from the Terengganu area can be had at the centre, which has on display many of the state's arts and crafts.

Kuala Terengganu offers the usual Chinese town hotels as accommodation and the international class hotel, the **Pantai Primula**. Situated close to the town centre, this hotel has fine views of the sea and a full programme of seasports is available to hotel guests.

The adventurous traveller may want to visit the picturesque **Sekayu Waterfall** near Kuala Brang, 56 kilometres (35 miles) west of Terengganu. Getting to the falls entails a 3-kilometre (2-mile) hike from the end of the road at Kampong Ipoh. A refreshing swim is the reward. Accommodation (two rest houses and some chalets) is also available here and may be booked through the District Forest Office at Kuala Brang (tel: 09-811259). **Kuala Brang** is famous as the place where a 14th-century Muslim inscription, the oldest in the whole of Malaysia, was found. The stone is now preserved in the National Museum in Kuala Lumpur.

On the way to school.

260

Though village life in Terengganu and Kelantan has changed, many of the traditional arts it fostered are as lively as ever. Seasonal fishing and farming brought village folk leisure and from leisure came time to devote to their arts. Folk dances, shadow plays and traditional games such as kite-flying and top-spinning were celebrated during festivals after a harvest. Many processions and rituals were related to the spirit of the rice, a carry-over from ancient animistic beliefs. Today village festivals are rarer occasions, since farmers are busy planting rice twice a year instead of once, and the Islamic doctrine discourages customs connected with spirit worship. Yet the fun-loving Terengganu Malays have not forgotten the good old times and all the song and laughter that went with them. This is a legacy that lives on.

Handicrafts have also flourished in Terengganu; once for sale in the town market and for local use, but nowadays also patronised by the tourist trade. At **Kampong Tanjong** almost every house has a loom which engages the time of mother and daughters in weaving the richly coloured cloth known as *kain songket*.

At **Rusila**, there is a handicraft centre for visitors to look around, or wander around the village to watch mat and basket weaving taking place. These are woven from the *pandanus* or *nipa* palm leaves, with two or three colours combined. Typical handicrafts include mats, multi-shaped boxes and containers, fans, hats, dishcovers, and baskets of all shapes and sizes. Other handicrafts to be found in and around Kuala Terengganu are traditional brasswork and handmade batik.

Remote and unspoiled: From Kuala Terengganu the road runs north for a distance of 171 kilometres (106 miles) to Kota Bharu and soon loses sight of the sea. About midway at Pasir Puteh there is a turnoff that leads to **Kuala Besut**, a remote and unspoiled fishing village on the coast. Twice daily, at dawn and at dusk, fishing boats make a dramatic show as they arrive from

Waiting for a fare in Kuala Terengganu.

across the sea and unload their catches at the jetty, where some tough bargaining takes place between fishermen and merchants. Visitors go about completely unnoticed, and photographers can snap away without anyone paying attention. For those who want to stay over, there is a rest house, situated on the south side of the river. Kuala Besut is also a jumping-off place for the idyllic **Perhentian Islands**, only 21 kilometres (13 miles) offshore.

Weather permitting, fishermen will willingly ferry visitors across to these lovely, unspoiled islands. Perhentian consists of two islands, **Perhentian Kecil** and **Perhentian Besar**.

Although some villagers will take visitors into their homes for a small fee at Pulau Perhentian Kecil, most travellers head for the larger island. The only village is at the smaller island, which you can visit should you wish to buy foodstuffs to do your own cooking. Just grab a boat to take you across the narrow channel. The villagers sometimes have traditional dance and music festivals which you may be invited to watch.

On the large island is the **Perhentian Island Resort**, situated in an exquisite little bay with searingly clear waters. Accommodation is in the form of chalets, some on the beach and some half-hidden in the jungled slopes behind. There is also a dormitory. A simple restaurant serves up good local food and western-style breakfasts.

On the bay facing the smaller island are several simple huts and chalets, owned by the villagers from the other island. Life is slow and relaxed here. You can walk over several beaches and with the help of a guide, penetrate some of the dense jungle that covers the whole island right down to the beaches. A bath involves drawing water from a well; a shower can be formed by pouring the contents of the bucket over your head! Basic cooking facilities are positioned outside each chalet, or you can walk to the next bay and eat at a small café, where you can sample some of the day's catch.

During the day, you may be able to

Fruits and vegetables to boggle the mind at Kota Bharu's Central Market.

stop an old man and his wife, who wander the beaches with their tame monkey, trained to climb up palm trees and bring down young coconuts for visitors to drink their delicious milk. The Government Rest House is no longer open to the public, but the choice of places to stay is wide enough to suit most tastes. The island, however, is still unspoilt, and it can be hard to leave this South China Sea paradise.

South of the Thai border: **Kota Bharu**, the capital of Kelantan, is the northernmost city on the East Coast, only a few kilometres from the Thai border. It is the residence of the Sultan of Kelantan. It has one of the best-known markets in Malaysia, where in the early morning, fishing folk arrive with their produce from the countryside. The market is also a good shopping place for East Coast crafts, particularly batik and silverwork for which the state is famous. Intricately designed beach mats are a good bargain and craftsmen can work up your own design in a day or two.

Another early morning pastime is the training of *burong ketitir*, the *merbok*, a jungle bird greatly prized for its sweet song. The *merbok* enthusiast takes immense pains to train his birds for the dawn competitions. But the highlight of the year is the great bird-singing competition held in Kota Bharu in June. Contending *merboks* are hoisted aloft on 9-metre (30-foot) poles whilst an entourage of judges determines the champion on the basis of loudness, pitch and the melody of its song.

Beyond the **Central Market** and the taxi rank is a vacant lot, which at night is transformed into a fascinating array of food stalls. The food here is almost exclusively Malay, with a few stalls selling food with Thai overtones. Walk around the stalls and choose your food; then take a table near the drinks stalls, where the servers will provide you with tea, coffee, cold drinks and cutlery. Improvised shows of medicinal wares or magic tricks sometimes spring up here. Music and chatter is all around, and listening to the latter, you will find that the Kelantan Malays have a dialect

Kelantan fishing boats are sturdy and colourful.

all of their own, barely comprehensible to Kuala Lumpurans.

Just beyond the market is **Padang Merdeka** (Liberty Square) on one side of which is the **state mosque**, and on another the old **Istana**. The mosque exhibits a syncretism of architectural styles and looks, at first glance when approached from certain directions, more like a house of Christian worship than one of Muslim prayer. But there are few in Kelantan who are not Muslim and even many Chinese have accepted the word of the Prophet.

The old Istana, which stands within a large compound, is called **Istana Balai Besar** (Palace with the Large Audience Hall). It was built in 1884 by order of Sultan Mohamed II and has recently been restored. At the first ceremony ever held there the sultan received a letter from the King of Thailand, recognising him as ruler. The building, which can be viewed with permission, contains the Throne Room, the State Legislative Assembly Hall and the enormous, multi-columned Hall of Audience.

On another side of the square next to the Istana Balai Besar stands another smaller palace, the **Istana Jahar**, which has now been converted into the state museum. Though quite small, the museum is well worth a visit for an introduction to Kelantan's life and culture. Outside the front entrance is a *wakaf*, one of the wooden platforms with tiled roofs, which not only serve as resting places but also adorn the otherwise plain Kelantan countryside.

Kota Bharu is the centre for Malaysian arts, sports and pastimes, and regular cultural shows are held at **Gelanggang Seni**, or Court of Arts, on Jalan Mahmood. Patrons can also arrange festivals from here, or even better, you may chance upon such a festival in Kota Bharu or in its surrounding villages.

Here, in the afternoons and evenings, you can watch a variety of art forms, sports and games. *Wau* or kites of Kelantan float above you in the sky. In a small *wakaf* or rest hut outside the main hall of the Court of Arts, old men tune up their instruments, drowned by the

The museum at Istana Jahar is a cultural bonanza.

sound of the *rebana*, huge drums fashioned out of logs, and requiring a great deal of energy and enthusiasm to play. On the green, the *gasing* (spinning top) experts are twisting themselves round, ready to spin down their prized tops onto a concrete square. From here they are removed with a wooden palette onto dowels sheltered by a hut. Hundreds of tops are spinning, and their owners watch anxiously to see how theirs are competing with the others in length of spinning time.

Other arts to be seen here include *Wayang Kulit* (shadow puppet plays), *Kertok* (wooden drums), *Silat* (the Malaysian form of self-defence) and *Mak Yong*, which combines theatre, dance, opera, drama and comedy. (See Cultural Section in Travel Tips for details of all of these). The Court of Arts produces a leaflet giving details of the times and locations of its performances. This can be picked up at hotels or at the **Tourist Information Centre** on Jalan Sultan Ibrahim.

Ten kilometres (6 miles) south of Kota Bharu, on the road to Kuala Krai, is **Kampong Nilam Puri**, the home of an Islamic college. Opposite the college is a regular four-square building of timber with a pyramidal two-tiered tiled roof, typical of a Javanese mosque. Known as the **Old Kampong Laut Mosque**, it is reputed to be the oldest surviving mosque in Malaysia (although the Malaccans might dispute that). It indeed dates back to the 18th century and is built of stout *chengal* wood. The mosque used to be located at Kampong Laut River on the banks of the Kelantan River opposite Kota Bharu. But since the mosque was threatened by the encroaching river, it was removed to its present site with funds raised by the Malaysian Historical Society.

Intriguing itineraries: Kota Bharu has many other delights to offer. It is the most "Malay" town in the whole of the peninsula and it is a thrill to simply wander along its streets, or to be wheeled around in a hired trishaw. Hunt out an antique shop – there are three or four in town – and get lost amongst

traditional Malay games, wonderfully graceful bird traps, handmade Chinese lanterns, wavy Malay daggers, musical instruments, mythical birds, masks and puppets and exotic coins of a bygone age. The prices quoted are outrageous. Or are they? It depends on your purse, your mood and your scale of values.

Kota Bharu is surrounded by a patchwork of little villages set between rice fields and orchards and linked to one another by little roads akin to twisting English country lanes. Explore them and you'll come across all sorts of surprises; a Thai *wat* (temple) – for the Thai border is not far away – is one of them, hidden by thick laurels and tall palms back from the road. A fishing village is another, where you can watch the boats go down to the sea in the cool of the morning and see them return laden with the catch in the afternoon. If you are keen to see more of the Thai Buddhist temples, venture off the road to **Tumpat**, Kota Bharu's port. Or to **Kampong Perasit**, near Pasir Mas, a few kilometres south of Kota Bharu, where you

Pounding the grain is a communal affair.

will find the **Wat Putharamaram**.

The traditional centre of the silver-smiths' craft in Kelantan is at **Kampong Sireh** (at Jalan Sultanah Zainab). It may be possible to see some of the smiths at work, fashioning a filigree butterfly brooch or an embossed cosmetic case. Designs show both Thai and Indonesian influence, as well as the motif of the Indian lotus blossom. These items are sold throughout Malaysia and also in Singapore.

Kota Bharu also has a 20th-century claim to fame; **Pantai Dasar Sabak**, 13 kilometres (8 miles) north of the town, is a pleasant, wide, casuarina-shaded beach which is popular with the locals. It was here, at 4.55 p.m. on 7 December 1941 (Greenwich Mean Time), that the Japanese started World War II in the East and began their march southward to Singapore. (The attack on Pearl Harbour was not to take place until 95 minutes later.) There are many other beautiful beaches in Kelantan, among them – **Pantai Dalam Rhu** (also known as Pantai Bisikan Bayu, the Beach of the

Whispering Breeze) near the fishing village of Semerak to the south of Kota Bharu; **Pantai Irama** (Beach of Melody), 25 kilometres (15½ miles) south of Kota Bharu near Bachok; and **Pantai Kuda** (Horse Beach), 25 kilometres north of the city near Tumpat.

Inland adventurers will find beautiful waterfalls feeding natural swimming pools in the midst of the tropical jungle in the region of **Pasir Puteh**. **Jeram Pasu** is frequented most by local students during the weekend (remember this is Thursday and Friday in Kelantan, as it is in Terengganu, and not Saturday and Sunday) and school holidays. It can be reached by an 8-kilometre (5-mile) hike along a jungle path from Kampong Padang Pak Amat. More waterfalls are to be found at **Jeram Tapah**, **Jeram Lenang** and **Cherang Tuli**.

Back on the seashore, Kota Bharu's most famous beach, **Pantai Cinta Berahi** (The Beach of Passionate Love) attracts Kota Bharu's citizens at weekends. In spite of the fact that the setting is marvellous, with yellow sands, warm sea and coconut palms, the vision with its romantic name is rather marred by untidy development and litter. Needless to say, since this is a Muslim country, passionate love is not to be seen here.

On the way to this beach are a number of small *songket* weaving "factories" which are open to the public. These are usually simple rooms with a few girls sitting behind huge looms, turning fine balls of silk and cotton into finished fabric. There are also several handmade batik shops.

Despite its contacts with the Thais and the Japanese, life in Kota Bharu follows the gentle rhythms of the Malay countryside, with the muezzin's call to prayer from the mosque's minaret from morning to evening. Kota Bharu is a place of the past, but since the building of the highway between here and Butterworth, it has become a crossroads for travellers and news. Kota Bharu is also the terminus for the eastern railway line, also known as the **Jungle Railway**. A few kilometres away, across the border in Thailand, begins the line that whisks travellers all the way to Bangkok.

Sitting on the dock by the bay.

SABAH, IN AN ISLAND OF LEGENDS

The mystery of Borneo spun a golden thread through the history of the "civilised" world. It glittered with those unrealities on which all rumours thrive. For centuries, no one knew its shape or size, other than that it was a seemingly boundless island. Buckles of "golden jade" adorned the imperial belts of the Son of Heaven, yet none of the audacious Chinese merchants who bartered Sung porcelain for golden jade had ever seen the sacred hornbill from which it came. The merchants discreetly resigned that privilege to the jungle dwellers, who disappeared back into sunless forests. At the turn of the century, the world was still mystified. Western outsiders had populated the coasts in scattered settlements, claiming to govern vast tracts of land they had never seen. Impressionable British officials wrote strange stories in which the hero was held captive by head-hunting savages and published them in leading magazines back home. Their tales were half-truths and half-fiction, just as Borneo has always been.

Out of this eerie heritage emerged the state of Sabah in 1963, the year British officialdom ended and north and northwest Borneo became part of the Federation of Malaysia. Sabah covers the

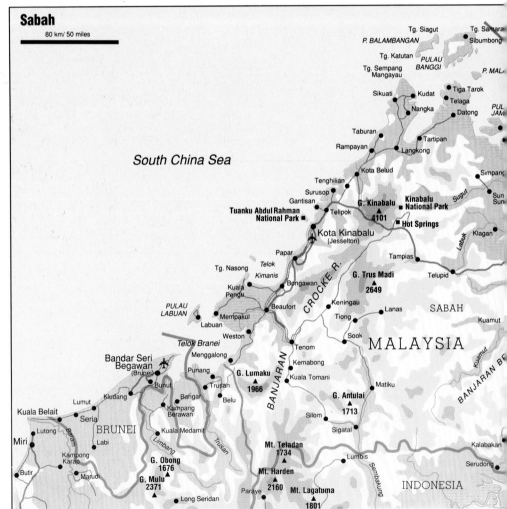

northern tip of the world's third largest island with Sarawak to the south. Together they bridge 1,000 kilometres (600 miles) of sea to join the Malay peninsula as a nation. Though Sabah and Sarawak occupy only the north and northwest coast of Borneo, together, they are larger than peninsular Malaysia, and on an island with footprints dating from the Ice Age, their nationhood is newer. In colonial days, Sabah was known as British North Borneo.

Kota Kinabalu, the state capital on the northwest coast, has the cumbersome and orderly grace of the 1950s, except perhaps for Kampong Ayer, a neighbourhood standing 6 metres (20 feet) above water on stilts. Yet even some of

Preceding pages: majestic Mount Kinabalu; *Rafflesia* – nature's largest flower – in full bloom.

Kampong Ayer's seaworthy sidewalks have come tumbling down in the rapid wake of progress. Sabah's capital city changes swiftly. Not far from the settlements of the *Bajau* boat people, the secretariat and six-metre- (20-foot) high Silver Kris stand as symbols of modern national unity. The state mosque which stands nearby is a recent addition to the skyline. New government buildings gracefully introduce onion-shaped domes and windows to Kota Kinabalu's contemporary scene.

Outside the city, in a never-ending landscape, freshly-cut roads tentatively feel their way through the Crocker Range to the far side of Mount Kinabalu and beyond to the other coast at Sandakan. The newly laid asphalt goes only as far as Ranau, after which gravel surfaces follow, but vast trucks and diggers are at work to change this.

The native people of Sabah have ancestors who practised the most diverse trades. The *Kadazans* were farmers, the *Muruts* were blowpipe hunters, the *Bajaus*, sea gypsies and the *Illanuns*, freebooters. Sabah's Brunei Malays belonged to a sultanate that once ruled all Borneo and then sold most of it piecemeal to ambitious and adventurous Europeans. Its Chinese have ancestors who sailed over in quest of kingfishers' feathers and bezoar stones (stones extracted from the stomachs of monkeys, and with supposed medicinal values) before the days of Kublai Khan. Now, the offspring of all these people are the citizens of the state. On big occasions – a visit by the king, National Day, or travel agent conventions – they don the ceremonial dress of their forefathers and parade their traditions. In daily life, they toil the rice fields, build the roads, man the factories and control the trade – timber, palm oil, copra, prawns and cocoa – on which Sabah's economy depends.

To visitors, Sabah's people are congenial, informal and polite, treating each foreigner as a stranger and guest simultaneously. When requested they seldom hesitate to help a traveller by giving directions, advising one on where to stay, and sometimes even booking you a room if they have access to a telephone. The word "Tourist" with a capital "T" has not filtered down through the ranks to the point where he wears a dollar sign on his lapel. This is not to say Sabah is inexpensive – in fact, hotels are quite the opposite. Most merchandise are imported, and hotel and transport prices are higher than they are on the peninsula. But accommodation is easily found at small Chinese hotels or government rest houses found in almost all of Sabah's small towns.

The small tourist trade works on a personal level. Exploring Sabah with a flexible itinerary leaves visitors open to unexpected "tips for travellers" which local citizens may volunteer in a coffee shop, a mountain retreat, a riverboat or a hotel lobby. The "tips" go on, offering new directions and old memories of Sabah. They can take you to the little island of Labuan, diamond and sapphire centre and a free port over many centuries; to a pearl station in the timeless town of Semporna set down on a picturesque peninsula in a sea strewn with enchanting islands; or to the furthest southeast corner where Tawau lazes away each peaceful tropical day. They can lead way up north to Kudat town, near where the *Illanun* and *Rungus* tribes meet at the Sunday fair and where the unspoilt beaches spread wide and desolate. Or they can lead deep into the interior, past the *Murut* settlement of Pensiangan, where the legends of Borneo still sleep in the trees.

"Where the eye lingers": Kota Kinabalu, the capital of Sabah, is a sprawling, relaxed town on the west coast of the state, affording a splendid view of the beautiful sunsets over the offshore islands. The fiery sunsets reflect Kota Kinabalu's history most fittingly, for although the state capital is now a peaceful and easy-going place compared to the bustling streets of cities on the peninsula, it has had a past long connected with fires. Indeed, at one time it was named "*Api! Api!*" (Fire! Fire!) because it was several times burned to the ground, only to rise again, like a phoenix from its ashes. Pirates from north

Kota Kinabalu has undergone rapid change.

Borneo were several times responsible for this.

When the British Chartered Company arrived in Borneo, they settled on Gaya Island in the bay of the present city, following a British colonial penchant for offshore island bases. But the famous rebel Mat Mohamad Salleh attacked and destroyed the settlement in 1897. Moving to the mainland, the Chartered Company then set up Jesselton, named after the company's vice-chairman, Sir Charles Jessel, and so it remained until 1968, when with independence came a new Malay consciousness. For a short time, the town was called "*Singgah Mata*" or "Where the eye lingers", before becoming Kota Kinabalu, in honour of the great mountain whose craggy peaks in the early morning and towards sunset, give a magnificent backdrop to the city. As a trading post Jesselton grew to be important enough to be bombed to ruins in 1945, in order to prevent the Japanese from setting up a base in this strategic position.

Over the next decade Kota Kinabalu grew into a gentle, unimposing town, occupied with covering up the scars of World War II. Within the past decade, the town has literally mushroomed with some of the most striking buildings in all Malaysia, as befits the capital of one of the fastest growing states.

Amongst the most impressive of these, standing alone in a devastated landscape is the great tower of the **Sabah Foundation**, an institution created out of the timber royalties of the state. It is one of the few "hanging" structures in the world, a 72-sided polygon rising up some 30 storeys.

There is also the monumental **State Mosque**, well worth a visit to see its fine contemporary Islamic architecture. Nearby is the new **State Museum**, built in the longhouse style of the *Rungus* and *Murut* tribes. White concrete structures point upwards the length of the roof, like modernistic hands held together in prayer. The museum has a wealth of historical and tribal treasures, as well as a good section on Sabah's fascinating flora and fauna. The complex also has a

Science Centre with a large exhibition on the oil and petroleum industry. At the **Art Gallery** is a multi-vision theatre, which holds regular slide shows, including one on Sabah called "The Land Below the Wind", once the name by which Sabah was known (referring to the fact that it lies beneath the cyclonic belt of the Philippines). A restaurant, coffee-house, well planned gardens with man-made lakes and a souvenir shop complete the complex.

The town itself is a mixture of ultra-modern structures in between typical Chinese shophouses, with a shanty water village known as **Kampong Ayer** along the seafront, between steep hills and the shore.

In front of the Hyatt hotel is the bustling **Central Market**, best seen early in the morning. Here fishermen unload their catch directly onto market tables, and *Kadazan* tribal women display their fresh fruit and vegetables, brought down from the hills surrounding Mount Kinabalu that same morning. Here are also small foodstalls which produce

Ceremonial costumes evoke elegance and grace.

tasty snacks and quick meals.

At the other end of the day, Kota Kinabalu's restaurants come alive, and some of the best food of the state is served in small coffeeshops dotted around the town. As with towns in peninsular Malaysia, night markets are to be found, selling clothes and curios, as well as local culinary delicacies. On Sundays is the very popular **Gaya Street Fair**, where bargains in local handicrafts can be had.

To get a good idea of what the town looks like as a whole, visitors can climb **Signal Hill** (by car or on a tour bus) situated at the eastern end of the city. From here one can see, beyond the city, a pleasant stretch of beach on the airport road with a park right next to it. This is **Tanjong Aru**, Kota Kinabalu's most popular beach, located next to **Prince Philip Park**. The sea here is clear and the beach clean. For the hungry, food stalls sometimes set up right on the sands; or sample the seafood restaurant nearby. Moving further upmarket, the **Tanjong Aru Beach Hotel** has western and local food in its restaurants.

The large international airport lies at the end of the road that runs behind the beach, with its fleet of 747s and 12-seater aircraft which fly passengers to remote outposts of civilisation in the jungles of Sabah and Sarawak.

From Signal Hill, one can also see beyond the city coastline to a group of islands not far offshore, surrounded by azure-blue waters. These islands together form the **Tunku Abdul Rahman Park**, protected from coral collectors and other industries.

The Park Headquarters are to be found on the most developed, **Gaya Island**. Gaya has a population of island Malays and Filipino refugees, living on a village built on stilts over the water. **Pulau Sapi** is organised with nature trails as is Pulau Gaya. Wildlife abound here: look for the amusing monkeys who cautiously make their way down to the beach to look for crabs, the *pangolin* (scaly anteaters) and the strange bearded pig. The sea eagle is also a visitor to these islands.

Sidewalk on stilts in Kampong Ayer.

276

The other three islands that make up the park are **Manukan**, **Mamutik** and **Sulug**. Snorkelling is good on all of these, especially on remote Sulug. Camping is possible on all the islands; Pulau Mamutik has a rest house with cooking facilities and sleeping space for 12 persons; accommodation on Pulau Manukan is at present under construction.

To book the rest house and to get permission for camping, you must first visit the National Parks office in town. Boats run to the islands from Tanjong Aru Beach Hotel, or you can charter a boat from Kota Kinabalu. The islands are well worth a visit, if only to view the spectacular sight of Mount Kinabalu rising up from behind Kota Kinabalu, its peak often visible at sunrise and sunset. And there is nothing quite like a Pulau Mamutik sunset.

South-East Asia's highest mountain: Everyone in Malaysia knows about the mysterious **Mount Kinabalu**. The closer one journeys towards its famous jagged profile wreathed in feathery clouds, the better one understands the meaning it has for the local *Kadazan/Dusun* people. To them its name derives from *"Aki Nabalu"* or "Revered Place of the Dead". On the forbidding peaks were said to be the spirits of the tribe's dead ancestors, and no-one dared climb to the top to disturb them.

Another origin given to the name seems less likely, and is probably more recent. *"Kina Balu"* was thought to mean "Chinese Widow", *"kina"* being a corruption of China, and *"Balu"* a dialectical word for widow. The story goes that a Chinese prince came to Kinabalu in search of a giant pink pearl guarded by a ferocious dragon. He married a local *Kadazan* woman, but finding himself homesick for his native land, deserted her and left for China. For the rest of her life, the unhappy widow wandered aimlessly on the mountain until she turned into a stone. You will see her if you climb to the peak.

In spite of the taboos and myths surrounding the mountain, Hugh Low, a young British officer, was still keen to

Sunsets in Kota Kinabalu are legendary.

reach the top. Climbing Kinabalu in 1851, Low was accompanied by a *Kadazan* chief and his guides. The summit was soon reached. Low climbed a small peak at the top and placed a bottle with a note in it to mark his success. The small peak, actually the highest of all Kinabalu's peaks at 4,101 metres (13,450 feet), was named **Low's Peak** after its first climber. He was standing on top of South-East Asia's highest mountain, and the highest mountain between the Himalaya and Papua New Guinea.

The mountain is still said to be growing at a rate of half a centimetre a year. It is relatively young, its jagged crown being sculpted by the last ice age, around 9,000 years ago. Although Kinabalu's peak is below the snow line, it still grows cold enough here in August for ice to form in the rock pool at the base of the summit, and snowflakes have been known to fall.

Falling away 1,800 metres (5900 feet) straight downwards is the terrifying **Low's Gully**, its name being a typical piece of British understatement. On ascending the mountain and reaching the peak, one can still imagine Low's exhilaration at being the first man here.

Nowadays, to get to the top, one does not, like on Low's first ascent, have to spend days cutting through tropical rain forest before getting to the granite slopes. Well-laid trails with steps and rails made of branches and wood collected from the mountain slopes, help today's climber ascend and descend the mountain in just two days.

Accommodation is available both at Park Headquarters and also on the mountain slopes. The latter are mostly basic huts with sleeping bags for hire and cooking facilities, with the exception of Laban Rata, which has a restaurant and private centrally-heated rooms. At the Headquarters, there is a great variety of accommodation ranging from hotel to chalet to dormitory style sleeping. There are also two restaurants, and a shop selling basic food supplies for climbers. In the main ad-

Granite slabs are much in evidence near the peak.

ministration building (not to be confused with the reception building) there is an exhibition on mountain flora and fauna, and in the basement, you can watch a film about the Park. A recreation centre will open soon at Headquarters, as well as a private Country Club, for use by government ministers.

Transport can be had from Kota Kinabalu to the Kinabalu National Park. Before leaving the city, you should book your accommodation at the **National Parks Office**. Also stock up on food and cooking items, as the shop at the Headquarters is mainly limited to noodles and chocolate. Kerosene cannot be obtained at the Park either. Other useful equipment includes a hat and gloves, as it can be extremely cold on the summit, and some kind of waterproof garment to protect you from the frequent rainfalls. If you can, leave the majority of your luggage at a hotel and take a light pack only, or use the luggage store at Headquarters. The air is thinner up on the mountain, and even the lightest pack can feel heavy after a while. A torch is also useful for the final ascent at three in the morning.

Park Landrovers take visitors from the capital to Park Headquarters. You can also join the minibuses which head for Ranau, making a detour to the Park entrance on the way. Package tours can be booked from Kota Kinabalu. If you miss all the buses and do not like to be restricted by a tour, you can rent a car and drive there, or take an expensive taxi from town.

On the way you pass through **Tamparuli**, 47 kilometres (29 miles) north of Kota Kinabalu, where bus drivers stop for their cup of morning coffee.

So far the trip has been a mellow roll through tropical green landscapes, studded with small farmhouses and grazing water buffalo. But less than a kilometre past Tamparuli, you say goodbye to the level ground, and begin to ascend the foothills of the great mountain. Although the landscape is often swathed in cloud and you cannot see the mountain, you know it can't be far away when your ears begin to pop.

Looking down at the world from John's Peak.

On cloudy days you are at the Park Headquarters before you have had a single glimpse of the peaks, but on a clear day, you recognise the unforgettable peaks, their silhouette now incorporated into the state's flag.

On arrival, visitors proceed to reception, where the *Kadazan* rangers will confirm bookings, which include the huts on the mountain. Maps and books are available here too. You will not climb the same day you arrive, so make yourself comfortable in your accommodation, acclimatise yourself to the cool air, check out the library with books and magazine articles on the Park and the mountain, and prepare yourself for the feat ahead.

Although Kinabalu has to be one of the easiest mountains to climb, it is difficult to rise from your office desk, jump on a plane and run up the trail. Some regular exercise is recommended before climbing, so that you don't come off the mountain a wreck of cramps, headaches and fatigue.

Just before you get on the trail, there is a rather forbidding notice placed there by the Park Authorities, giving a list of ailments with which they do not recommend you climb. Among these are: hypertension, diabetes, obesity, chronic asthma, heart disease, arthritis, anaemia, ulcers, hepatitis, muscular cramps and epilepsy.

Climbing 1,500 metres (4950 feet) in one day – from the power station above Headquarters to Panar Laban hut – does take inordinate reserves of strength and zest for those who have a sedentary life. But this is when the mountain is approached as a "rush job" which it need not be. Some competition does crop up around the fireplace at Headquarters. Experienced and intrepid climbers have "done the whole thing" in a day, but if your interest lies not just in getting there, but in the full experience of exploring the flora of the mountain slopes, and stopping to admire the spectacular views, then relax. There is much to see.

Attached to Headquarters, but not directly employed by them are a team of *Kadazan* guides, who for a fee will ac-

Sure-footed *Kadazan* women act as porters.

company you up the mountain. If you are interested in the mountain flora, make sure your guide is knowledgeable in this: many of them are amateur botanists and geologists!

One of the personalities of Kinabalu is Awok, a Kadazan woman barely 1.5 metres tall, who chews betel nut, rolls her own cigarettes and presides over no less than 15 grandchildren. She is one of the mountain's porters, her size belying her strength. Into her *burong* basket slung on her back, she stuffs a heavy knapsack, camera equipment and cans of food, and strides up the mountain trail, while the knapsacks' owners straggle puffing and empty-handed far behind.

Porters like Awok are hired at Park Headquarters, and will carry your luggage as far as Panar Laban hut. Here they stop, build fires, and await for your exhilarated but exhausted faces to appear the following morning before beginning the descent. Fees depend on how heavy your luggage is; anything over 10 kilos will require a higher price.

The climb begins at 7 a.m. the following morning; make sure you have a bar or two of chocolate in your pocket, not a luxury but a necessity here, giving you instant energy for the climb and the cold. Also in your pocket should be some headache tablets, as some climbers suffer from headaches because of the altitude. You will be climbing to a great height very quickly.

Passing the welcoming gate at the power station (with the slogan *"Selamat Mendaki"* – Happy Climbing! written over the arch), your first steps lead you downward into a small, lush valley with a waterfall. After the waterfall, the climb begins, at first gently, later steeply through tropical rain forest.

All around you are some of the Park's 1500 species of orchids, clinging to mossy tree trunks and surrounded by swinging vines. Steep and arduous stairs directing you ever upwards, are happily spaced out between gentler paths. Small rest huts and viewpoints are positioned all the way up the trail to give the out-of-breath climber an ex-

Mist-shrouded trees on Kinabalu's slopes.

cuse to stop and admire the view. Don't forget to bring some water with you: although the air is cool, perspiration while walking will deplete your water level.

At 1,300 metres (4260 feet), the vegetation on either side of the trail begins to change from lowland rain forest into an oak and chestnut forest, displaying more temperate plants, such as the ferns and small flowering plants.

As you proceed up to the next level of vegetation, you have the feeling of growing larger, the higher you climb. The trail began with huge trees towering over you; now the trees have shrunk and you are almost the tallest thing in the landscape. At 2,600 metres (8500 feet), are these small gnarled tree, twisted and bent and wrinkled by the harsh mountain air. Although small, some of them are believed to be more than 100 years old. The soil is poor here, and lichens cling desperately to the little trees.

The soil disappears altogether at 3,300 metres (10,800 feet) and the granite body of the mountain reveals itself.

Here sedges, grasses and tiny alpine-looking flowers cling to the rocky crevices where a scrap of soil might remain.

Just when you thought you must have left all civilisation far below you on the trail, now obscured by the afternoon mist, you arrive at a series of huts – the camp where you will spend the night.

A leisurely climb should get you here by around 2 p.m. Here at **Panar Laban**, you can retreat to the **Laban Rata Rest House**, whose electrical cables you will have passed all the way from the power station. There is a simple restaurant here, or you can cook your food in the hostel just down the path. A little further up the slope is **Gunung Ladagan Hut**, with simple four-bed rooms, sleeping bags for hire, and a basic kitchen equipped with cooking utensils.

Once you've stopped climbing, you will begin to feel the cold, so even if you don't feel like it, have some hot soup and filling food. You will now be able to rest and think about your achievement so far – but alas! – the path you so strenuously climbed has been lost in the

The mountain forest takes on a dream-like quality.

mountain mists.

If it is not raining, many climbers only rest here, and climb for another one and a half hours to **Sayat-Sayat Hut**, allowing for a later rising time the following morning.

Many climbers find it hard to sleep on the mountain because of the thin air and the headaches caused by the altitude. You also need to go to bed extra early to be able to struggle out of bed at 3 a.m.! Only Laban Rata has electricity, so candles are needed at the other huts.

Your guide will wake you long before dawn. If you have a thermos flask, heat some water and fill the flask with sweet tea for a reviving drink at the summit. Don't forget to stuff some chocolate into your pocket too, and bring your raincoat. Other than filming equipment, everything else can be left at the hut to be collected on the way down.

With night rain, the granite slopes can be slippery, and it is doubly difficult because of the pitch black. Soon you are climbing rockfaces of granite, how steep the incline you're not sure in the dark, holding onto the rope systems that guide your way to the top. With an early start, you will be labouring up the slabs of granite with the peak in sight just as the skies begin to lighten. Here the granite rock, bared to the winds, is crumbling and broken. At last you reach **Low's Peak**. Harsh wind whips round and cuts into you.

The sun lips over the horizon like a brilliant apricot and you begin to see the landscape you have been walking in blindly for the last few hours of the night. On a clear day, the lights of Kota Kinabalu and the coast and then the outlines of the Tunku Abdul Rahman islands can be visible.

Venturing to look down into the depths of Low's Gully, the view is awe-inspiring. This does indeed seem a place for spirits, for no-one else could endure the harsh weather that sweeps away the offerings of sacrificial chickens, eggs, tobacco, betel nut, sirih leaves, limes and rice left here by the *Kadazan*. Depending on your guide and the strength of his beliefs, he may decide to make offerings while you are "oohing

Along the Summit Trail.

and aahing" over the landscape. Or you may not see the charms that he carried, amongst them perhaps special pieces of wood, human teeth and other items with "protecting" properties.

The descent can be more leisurely: you are still glowing with the feat of having reached the summit. After collecting your belongings from Panar Laban, you will be heading downwards, intent on seeing some of the vegetation, such as the pitcher plants, you may have missed in your rush to get to the top. Many climbers find the way down harder than the climb up, for the relentless steps leading ever downwards soon turn firm legs into jelly!

On arrival at Park Headquarters, you can rightfully claim your badge commemorating your ascent, only for sale to those who have made it to the top (your guide can act as witness).

World's largest flower: Many climbers leave the Park the same day or the day after they have made the climb, but if you have more time on your hands, stay in the area a couple of days more, both

to rest and to explore the jungle around the Headquarters, which is neatly laid out in trails for nature lovers. A guide here can introduce you to Kinabalu's magnificent flora and some of its fauna.

Amongst the rare plants found here, some species unique to this region, is the famous *Rafflesia*, largest flower in the world, measuring up to over a metre across, and nine species of pitcher plants. In 1858 the explorer Spencer St John chanced upon a huge specimen of the latter which contained 4 litres of rain water, as well as a dead rat!

The 750 square kilometres (300 sq miles) of the Park is unique in the world of flora, in that it contains plants from almost every area on earth: here are plants of the Himalayan and Chinese genera, species from Australia, New Zealand, alpine Europe and even America. There are 1500 species of orchids, from the world's largest to the world's tiniest, 26 kinds of rhododendron and 60 types of oak and chestnut, as well as 80 species of fig trees.

Animals found here include the

famous *orang-utan*, gibbons, leaf monkeys, tarsiers, *pangolin* (scaly anteaters), wild pig and deer; and a whole host of "flying" animals; many of them very rare indeed in other parts of Malaysia. These latter include "flying" squirrels, lemurs, snakes and lizards. Reported to be found here but seldom seen are the very rare clouded leopard and the even rarer Sumatran Rhinoceros.

The 518 species of birds include several kinds of hornbills, the scarlet sunbird, the mountain bush warbler, the pale-faced bulbul, the mountain blackeye, and the mountain's own Kinabalu friendly warbler. Around the area's waterfalls, look for the lovely butterflies, some as large as birds, and the less easy-to-see stick insects, well camouflaged to the human eye. You may also catch sight of squirrels, lizards, treeshrews and bats. All this a veritable feast for the naturalist!

Ranau and hot springs: Although the park holds all these fascinating sights, and more besides, many ex-climbers will be too tired to appreciate the beauty of a "pleasant stroll" through the forest. After perhaps taking a quick look at the **exhibition hall** and the **herbarium** close to Headquarters, they may charter a minibus to take them to **Poring**, 45 kilometres (28 miles) away to the east beyond Ranau. The motive? Natural hot sulphur springs to soothe those aching muscles.

The area around **Ranau** and the **Kundasong** region is *Kadazan/Dusun* country and also the market garden of Sabah, being situated on Kinabalu's cool foothills. At the weekly *tamu* (market) in Ranau, one sometimes sees wild-looking rural peoples, half in traditional dress (black *sarong* and long earrings), and half in modern western attire (fake Rolex watch and Coca Cola tee shirt).

The road beyond Ranau is rough, and the asphalt has yet to arrive (although road construction is underway). Driving to Poring, you have to drive through a couple of rivers – some motorists stop and wash their vehicles!

At Poring there are pleasant chalets and a hostel to stay in, but few visitors rest long before making straight for the

Pitcher plants are a part of the Kinabalu experience.

baths – the outdoor ones that is. To get there descend some steps (climbers of Kinabalu groan!), and cross a wire and wood suspension bridge over the river. The baths themselves are rather ugly, but are set in pretty grounds with hibiscus bushes and frangipani trees, with the untamed jungle above and beyond. The baths were built during World War II by the Japanese, with their love of communal bathing giving them the impetus to tame the jungle. The baths provide both hot and cold water, the latter to temper the furious heat of the volcanic water. Nothing could be nicer than to bathe here at night, with the jungle sounds all around.

For those who recover quickly from their mountain ascent and descent, the jungles here have trails to follow, and all the wildlife in Kinabalu Park can be found here, including *Rafflesia* and pitcher plants. You are still high up on the central plateau.

At present, there is no restaurant in Poring; visitors must drive to Ranau for food supplies, or those without a vehicle of their own should bring their foodstuffs with them. There is one small shop opposite the Park entrance, but it is expensive and its range is limited. Both chalets and hostel provide cooking facilities.

In the Park is a friendly sign, a reminder from the Park Ranger: "Please: Take nothing but photographs. Leave nothing but footprints."

Kadazan tamus and whitewater rafting: Twenty kilometres (12 miles) south of Kota Kinabalu is **Papar**, situated on the mouth of the Papar River. Padi fields lie all around and on the coast is a pleasant beach called **Pantai Manis** (Sweet Beach). The Sunday *tamu* (market) is a lively scene of *Kadazan* traders, bringing their wares in from the surrounding hills. Coconut wine (*tapai*) is also made here, and if you visit a house, you will no doubt be offered some of this potent liquid. Tours run by Api Tours in Kota Kinabalu will bring you here for whitewater rafting, an experience well worth trying, but be prepared to get wet! Or you can simply take leisurely boat trips

Wild orchids to catch any botanist's fancy.

up the smooth areas of the river, which runs down from the main Crocker Range.

From Papar, you can head southwards to Beaufort, Tenom and Labuan (Sabah's port), or eastwards to Tambunan, Sapulut and from there, along the Kalimantan border on a logging road to Tawau and Sandakan.

Taking the southern road first, the route takes you down the west coast of the state on rather rough road to **Beaufort**, situated on the Padas River, which regularly floods the small provincial town. Transportation suddenly improves between here and Tenom: for here is a small and romantic funicular railway – the only one in Borneo.

The train starts from Tanjong Aru but the best stretch to take is that between Beaufort and Tenom. A funny little railcar, shaped like a three-dimensional trapezoid, zips along a diminishing track, stringing small towns together as it cuts through the Padas gorge.

The *Muruts*, or "Men of the Hills" as the *Bajau* call them, have always lived in this region. Although many young people of the tribe have adopted the fast-encroaching western civilisation creeping inland from the capital, there are still some who prefer the life in the jungle, armed only with a *parang* (large sharp knife) and a blowpipe. Others have turned to cultivating the countryside and growing crops.

Tenom is at the centre of the *Murut* community, and the small hilly town is surrounded by *Murut* longhouses, where young "warriors" still take their blowpipes and hunting dogs out for a "stroll" in the jungle to catch supper. A popular pastime in the longhouse is the *lansarang*, a huge trampoline-like structure supported by a wooden platform. The largest can hold 40 people – perhaps the entire population of the longhouse!

South of Tenom, close to the village of **Tomani**, are Sabah's only **rock paintings**. Strange distorted faces and enigmatic figures are painted on massive boulders; they are not thought to be more than one thousand years old, but

The KK-to-Tenom railway slices through Sabah's wilderness.

are impressive all the same. Tenom also has an **Agricultural Research Station**, complete with orchid garden and rest house. One must apply in advance for permission to visit the station. Tenom's one classy hotel sits on the hill overlooking the town.

From Tenom, you can travel through Keningau and Tambunan, completing a round trip to Kota Kinabalu.

Keningau is the centre of the interior timber industry of West Sabah, and possesses many sawmills and log-holding depots. The town has grown from its timber industry and has several hotels and a sports complex for the managing directors visiting their logging sites.

From Keningau, you can travel with four-wheel drive southwards into *Murut* country, or northwards to Tambunan and the coast. It is worth taking the southward route if you are adventurous, and details of what to see are given in the next section. However, for those heading back to civilisation, the road heads out of the Keningau plain up into and across the Crocker Range to **Tam-**

bunan. There an old stone on a grassy plain marks Mat Salleh's (famous hero of old) last fort.

The tall, strikingly featured rebel built the fort completely underground in the middle of the jungle, supplying his dug-out with water through a sophisticated bamboo system which carried water from a river 6 kilometres (4 miles) away. He might have survived longer than 1900 had not a villager betrayed his location to British Chartered Company forces, who promptly cut off Mat Salleh's water supply, surrounded the fort and waited. The rebel and his thirsty followers were all shot down when they emerged, and the rebellion launched by a native lord who refused to pay tax to foreigners of his land ended.

Padi terraces are ranged around Tambunan and the little village of **Sinsuran**, with its *Dusun* houses made of bamboo. A tourist village with all the modern amenities, but externally looking like a traditional village has been built and is now being promoted as "the real thing".

Family life is simple in the more remote regions.

On the way back from Tambunan to Kota Kinabalu, the visitor passes through **Penampang**, a pretty *Kadazan* village, where the Sumazau Harvest dance is performed. **St Michael's Church** in Penampang is the oldest church in Sabah. Memories of a previous religion can be found in the *Kadazan* graveyards, where there are still some ancient burial jars. The road now heads for the capital and the coast.

Hidden limestone outcrops: Visitors intending to explore southern Sabah should equip themselves with a four-wheel drive vehicle, food supplies and gifts for the inhabitants of the longhouses who provide accommodation for them on the way.

Driving southeast of Keningau, you come to Nabawan, last outpost of government administration, and then further on to the settlement at **Sapulut**. From here you can take a rough track to **Agis**, or if you prefer, hire a native canoe (and its driver!) along the Sapulut River encountering rapids and staying at longhouses along the way. **Tetaluan**

is the village furthest up this river. A half-hour boat journey from here takes you to **Batu Punggul**, a large limestone outcrop soaring from the encircling jungle to 150 metres (500 feet). The climb to the top is possible but dangerous, and it is very much recommended that you hire a guide in Tetulan or a village further downriver. The caves and the nearby forest are also worth exploring.

Another half hour's walk through deep jungle brings you to **Batu Tinahas**, almost entirely obscured by the forest. This limestone massif was only recently discovered by a Sabah Museum team. Although it is not as high as Punggul, its cave and tunnel system is enormous and rivals the Gomantong Caves in the east of Sabah.

The river flows southwards past Agis and eventually into northern Kalimantan. There is an immigration checkpoint at **Pegalungan**, but it is doubtful that you will be allowed to cross the border, unless you have already obtained an Indonesian visa, and even then you may

Eye to eye with a Wreathed Hornbill.

be turned down.

At this point the Sapulut River joins the **Tagal River**. Turning down the latter river, you reach **Pensiangan**, the former centre of district administration, transferred to Nabawan three decades ago because the latter town was far more accessible. Here there is a rest house and several shops where everything is twice the price of goods in the city.

Just 4 hours will take you on a most adventurous trip from Pegalungan to Kalimantan. Traditional longhouses lie on the riverbanks, where boats are built and the women engage in cloth weaving, making rattan mats and elaborate beadwork.

You will be most welcome to stay the night, and the *Muruts* are renowned for their hospitality. Remember though, that it is polite to accept a drink when it is offered to you, as it is a host's duty to please his guests with a cup of *tapai*. If you do not drink alcohol, simply touch the cup with your lips or fingers and get the guide to explain that you don't wish to partake of the fiery liquid.

Gifts of food for the adults and toys for the children are customary, and items from your own country will be even more welcome than a product available in Kota Kinabalu.

Lands of cocoa and timber: Flights from Kota Kinabalu and Sandakan arrive at **Tawau** on the southeast coast of Sabah, connected to these cities because it is an important area for timber and cocoa. It is also the home of a reforestation programme situated at **Kalabakan**, with 30,000 hectares (71,400 acres) planted with fast-growing trees such as *Albizia Facalaria*, the fastest growing of which is said to have soared 30 metres (100 feet) in just 5 years.

But Tawau's pride is the cocoa plant, which thrives in the region's volcanically rich soils, making Sabah the largest cocoa-producing state in all Malaysia. It is also the present timber capital of the state, taking over from the now devastated area around Sandakan. Oil palm is being planted here too, following Sandakan's example.

Nature leaves much to admire in Sabah.

Tawau also boasts an international-standard hotel, a recreation park, hot springs and waterfalls.

The Tawau district can be reached from Sapulut in the interior, travelling along logging tracks skirting the Kalimantan border, but permission to do this must first be obtained in Kota Kinabalu. The drive from Sapulut to Tawau takes around 5 hours, passing first long-houses and then logging concessions.

Malaysia's only oceanic island: The road from Tawau now travels up the coast on the way to Lahad Datu and Sandakan, arriving first at **Semporna** town, which is situated on a tip of land. Semporna is a small settlement of *Bajau* and *Suluk* tribespeople and Chinese shopkeepers.

But Semporna is best known for **Pulau Sipadan**, Malaysia's only true oceanic island rising up 600 metres (1970 feet) from the seabed. In 1978 the World Wildlife Fund voted this one of the best coral areas in the world. This international interest has made the locals proud of their treasure and regular

boats run to the island, carrying professional scuba-divers and simply curious tourists. Scuba-diving instruction is given here and equipment is available for hire. A tour operator in Kota Kinabalu may be able to help you arrange this trip.

On another island, **Pulau Bohey Dulang**, closer to Semporna is a pearl farm, and the island can be visited for its beautiful and deserted beaches.

The rich marine life around Semporna yields delicious fish and seafood, which can be bought at the town's market. Local restaurants will cook it for you, any style and serve it together with locally grown vegetables. There is a good seafood restaurant floating on stilts over the sea near the harbour. Attached to this is a motel, and other simple accommodation can be found in the town.

Birds' nests for Chinese cuisine: An hour's drive northwest of the town will bring you to **Madai** where there is a limestone outcrop with large caves. The outcrop lies just 2 kilometres (1½ miles) off the main road. Outside the caves is a village which may be deserted save for one or two persons when you arrive. The village is inhabited when twice a year birds come to build nests in the caves, nests much coveted by the villagers who come here to climb the network of ladders and bamboo platforms to collect these much-prized "bird homes".

The kinds of edible birds' nests are the black and the white – the latter fetching up to $1000 per kilo in Hong Kong's markets. The nests are used as the main ingredient to a famous Chinese soup, considered a delicious delicacy throughout the Chinese world. A torch is necessary for exploring the caves, for although sunlight filters down through crevices in the limestone roof in some caves, many of the deeper caves are pitch black. Remains found at Madai prove that man has been in the area for the last 15,500 thousand years.

Eighteen kilometres (11 miles) west of Madai is **Baturong**, another limestone structure situated in the middle of an area that was once a lake called

Marine life abounds off the northeast coast.

Tingkayu Lake, which drained away 16,000 years ago. Man was also here at about the same time as the settlement at Madai. With a guide from Lahad Datu or Kunak, you can visit this fascinating massif. The journey involves an hour's drive through cocoa and oil palm plantations to a mud volcano.

From here another hour's trek takes you through virgin jungle to the limestone outcrop. Few visitors make it to these parts, but the experience is exhilarating. To complete the adventure, set up camp here and spend the night in the Sabah jungle.

The road northwards from Semporna takes you to **Lahad Datu**, Sabah's "cowboy town". At **Silam**, just south of the town is an area known as the **Danum Valley**, where the Upper Segama River and its tributaries, the Bole and the Danum rivers run. In the valley is a 440-square-kilometre (170-square-mile) forest reserve, set up by the Sabah Foundation, for conservation and research. The area is totally unlogged and has walking trails, a Science Research

Sepilok houses the world's largest *orang-utan* community.

Centre and hostel. With prior permission, you may be allowed to visit the park.

Sabah's one-time Hong Kong: In **Sandakan**, Sabah's busy boom town, people call the logs bobbing in the Sulu Sea "floating money". They float down the Segama River from timber forests near and far, pass through the hands of Chinese entrepreneurs at the harbour, and are lifted onto massive freighters bound for Japan. So prosperous was Sandakan that many investors thought the town would become another Hong Kong, with its largely Cantonese population, but the speed of deforestation of the Sandakan division has slowed down its progress.

Once the capital of North Borneo, Sandakan was completely razed to the ground during the bombings of World War II, and the modern town was built on these ruins. The original town started life as a gun-running settlement run by the Spanish; the gun-runners were mostly Germans, and they are remembered by local people who still refer to

all white foreigners as "*Orang Jerman*" (German man) rather than the usual "*orang putih*" (white man).

The town was at one time highly cosmopolitan with traders from all over the world: Europeans, Arabs, Japanese, Dusun, Javanese, Bugis, Chinese and even Africans. An interesting census of 1891 classes 75 Japanese out of 90 as either prostitutes or brothel keepers! The Chartered Company also had its main settlement here, as the harbour was one of the finest in Borneo and the town was guarded by hills from behind. The capital was transferred to Kudat in 1881.

Pulau Selingan is the largest of three islands now designated a protected turtle park, off the coast at Sandakan. Green and hawksbill turtles come here to lay eggs, reputedly every single night of the year, but the best time is between July and September. A turtle hatchery was set up here in the 1960s. The other two islands are known as **Pulau Bakin-gan** and **Pulau Gulisan**. Accommodation is available on Selingan, but must be booked first.

For the locals the most popular island in the area is **Pulau Berhata**. Although it is a pleasant island with a fine beach, clear waters and splendid limestone outcrops, it has a somewhat lurid past – having been formerly a leper colony and then a prison camp during World War II.

Across the harbour from Sandakan are the **Gomantong Caves**, some of the largest in Borneo. Thirty-two kilometres (20 miles) south of Sandakan, it is the home to 1 million swiftlets, whose nests are collected to furnish the tables of the many Cantonese restaurants in town. Collectors scale the bamboo ladders up to heights of 90 metres (295 feet) in the vast caves to collect these treasures. Bats are also in evidence, and their huge *guano* pile is gradually raising the cave floor level. If you wish to visit these caves, it is advisable to bring a torch with you.

A 20-minute drive westwards from Sandakan brings you to the **Sepilok Park**, an *orang-utan* rehabilitation **Market day at Kota Belud.**

292

centre. In 1964, 4,000 hectares (9880 acres) were awarded to these magnificent and intelligent primates. The centre helps *orang-utans,* who have lived long in man's captivity or company, gradually adjust to a return to the wild. Instruction to the animals includes encouraging them to climb, build nests in trees (something wild *orang-utans* do naturally) and forage for food in the jungle. They are gradually weaned off expecting food to appear from the centre's kitchen and after some time return but infrequently.

Besides being able to make friends with these gentle creatures, visitors can explore the nature trails set around the park, look round the nature centre and watch slide-shows on the life of the *orang-utan* in the wild. Other animals here include the amusing proboscis monkey. There is also a crocodile farm close to Sepilok which is open to visitors.

Kota Belud: On the road from Kota Kinabalu to Kota Belud and the north, visitors will pass through Tuaran and its famous pottery factories. **Mengkabong Water Village** can be reached by a side road just before Tuaran. Mengkabong is a pretty coastal *Bajau* village built entirely over the water on stilts. Transport around the village is by sampan or canoe, and some houses are connected to one another by precarious-looking plank walks. Handicrafts can be purchased here as well as in Kota Belud. And if you wonder where the village puts the growing population, they simply add on more houses out onto the sea!

Kota Belud is one and half hour's drive north from Kota Kinabalu and has two claims to fame. Firstly it is renowned for the *Bajau* "cowboys", famed for their rearing and handling of horses. Secondly, it is the scene of Sabah's most colourful *tamu. Bajau* market woman, their faces crinkled by the harsh sun and hours of laughter, squat beside tobacco wrappers and sugary doughnuts for hours on end, forever chewing the omnipresent betel nut which stains their gums and teeth a macabre red.

Bajaus are Muslims originally from the Philippines.

There is always more on sale at the *tamu* than mundane necessities, even if those necessities include such remarkable things as buffalo and ponies. A Pakistani medicine man, complete with white moustache, strikes up his one-man-band accompanied by a histrionic sales chatter in four languages, while his assistant busies himself with the products – pink bottles filled with a sticky liquid.

Of course an entire row of market displays is devoted to the art of betel nut chewing, which every saleswoman unconsciously and continually demonstrates. These women use the *tamu*, not just to sell their wares, but also for a chance to catch up on what's what.

Ever since the days of the Chartered Company, which much favoured countryfolk coming together to meet at the main settlements, *tamus* have been popular with old and young, the favourite day being Sunday. The word *tamu* actually means "meeting place", and even today it is as much a picnic as a marketplace. Visitors will find many of Sabah's tribal handicrafts here, muddled up with betel nut stalls and electrical items from Taiwan. Plus there are the taste treats to be found at any market throughout Malaysia.

Longhouses and deserted beaches: In the northmost tip of Sabah is **Kudat**, the state's first capital, once an important port in the trade between China and Europe. The East India Company took advantage of this position and set up a trading post on Belembungan Island in 1773. However, they were much deterred by lack of water and constant pirate raids. Local chiefs enraged by the Company's meagre payment to them, sacked the post and the area was abandoned for less troubled waters.

Kudat is still an area of trouble, as, since it has a long history connected with the Philippines, the Philippine government still refuses to recognise this region as part of Malaysia. There is a large and long-established Filipino population in the area.

More peaceably settled are the *Rungus* people, a sub-group of the *Dusun/Kadazan* group. Many still live around Kudat in their traditional longhouses and hold spiritualistic and animist beliefs. They have managed to hang on to their traditions much longer than other tribes of Sabah. Their architectural style of building (with outwardly leaning roofs) is mirrored in the state's museum in Kota Kinabalu. They are also famous for the long brass coils that the women use to decorate their necks, arms and legs with. Nowadays this practice has been discontinued, although forearm coils may still be spotted. The women still work on their distinctive mat-weaving and beadwork, much prized items in Sabah's Sunday *tamus*.

There is also a large Chinese Hakka community living here, Kudat being the first area to be inhabited by Chinese in the 1880s; many of them are Christians and traditionally farmers by trade. On the island of **Banggi** is a small tribe long thought to be of *Dusun* extraction, but their dialect contradicts this ancestry. They remain apart, remote and living much as they have done for the last several hundred years.

The Kudat region has not yet prepared itself for tourism, and although there are several tours from the capital to touristic longhouses, the state offers no accommodation save that of small Chinese hotels for tired business travellers. Most of these are basic but good as a base from which to explore the region. Some supply maps to the area, and on this appear the thin lines of dirt tracks, connecting one settlement to a longhouse to a fishing village.

With your own vehicle (preferably with four-wheel drive, as Kudat's roads are not good), you can explore the villages and seek out the empty and beautiful beaches hidden down small side-roads.

If you ask where the beach is, you will be directed to **Bak Bak**, a rather plain little beach past Kudat's tiny airport. To the locals, only this can have the title of a beach for tourists, as it is equipped with toilets, showers and picnic tables. But venture beyond here and you will find yourself alone, save for a *Rungus* tribesman strolling along with his blowpipe hoisted over his shoulder.

Jogging along the famous beach at Tanjong Aru.

294

TALES FROM THE LONGHOUSE

Sarawak is still a name that evokes more romance than reality. White *Rajahs* and Borneo headhunters ring more bells than 125,000 square kilometres (48,260 sq miles) of hills, jungle and swampland just north of the Equator, a land of abundant rainfall and innumerable rivers that weave their way over the state's boundaries into Indonesian Kalimantan, and provide routes into remote jungle areas.

Borneo is also a *Kelabit* agricultural centre, a Malay fishing village, an *Iban* longhouse, a *Penan* jungle camp, a *Melanau* sago factory and a Land Dayak rice field all at once.

The days of the reign of the White *Rajahs* and head-hunting have now passed. Since 1963 Sarawak has been a member of the Federation of Malaysia, and traces of colonialism soon began to disappear under the struggle to form a modern state. With colonialism, some of the old serenity went too, with the advent of the oil industry, Kuala Lumpur's interest in developing the state, and the logging disputes in recent years. Without a doubt, Sarawak is destined to undergo great changes in the next decade.

Sarawak's long tradition of open hospitality is what makes city or jungle

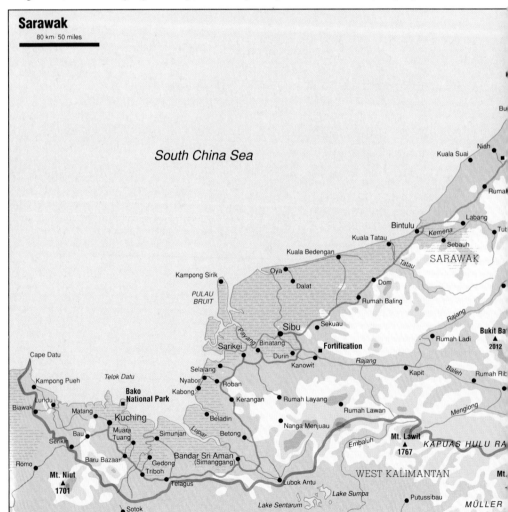

Sarawak

80 km 50 miles

South China Sea

travel so genuine. A traveller can find himself made welcome in a Kuching market where Chinese women offer free samples of their wares, and also at an *Iban* longhouse, where he may sit with the chief over a glass of the heady, home-brewed *tuak*, the ubiquitous palm wine of Sarawak.

Tourism has begun to grow up in a somewhat disorganised and unpredictable fashion in the state. While some tour operators offer a genuine experience, taking you inland to visit caves, longhouses and national parks in small intimate groups, others with little understanding of tribal pride and dignity will take you to commercialised longhouses close to the capital, where the

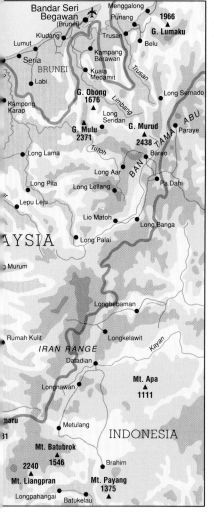

inhabitants will perform dances and "exhibit" their way of life for you. The experience is demoralising, and smacks of the clumsy explorations of tourism in the 1950s and 1960s.

Far better to strike out on your own, or visit some of the reputable tour operators recommended at the back of this book. The real challenge of Sarawak is a trip upriver to visit the "real" longhouses and settlements of the *Kayan*, *Kenyah*, *Murut*, *Iban*, *Kelabit* and *Penan* people, some of whom have been in this part of the world for perhaps forty thousand years.

Two weeks is a minimum for a trip taking you upriver to areas far from the commercial and touristic world. You can start first at the **Tourist Information Centre** in Kuching, but probably the best sources of information will be people you meet on the river or at small river towns such as Kapit and Belaga. Most likely they will be from the *Iban* or other tribes, many of whom have a tradition of going on "walkabouts" and may decide to join you. You'll need a guide to take you to the smallest and most interesting little riverlets, as well as foodstocks and gifts for your longhouse hosts. Food items and things for the children are most acceptable.

This kind of trip can become rather expensive, with many people wishing to "tag along" as paid "guides", so be prepared for some bargaining. All those who have done it with good preparation claim that there is nothing like weaving your way through the jungle on Sarawak's highway – the river.

Although there is a fairly good network of roads in and around Kuching, these disappear as you head inland. A road has been cut between Sibu and Kuching but it is as yet a very rough ride indeed. So most of your travel around the state will be by boat, canoe and Fokker 27. MAS has an extensive network around Sarawak (see Transportation section in the Travel Tips at the back of this book) and there are also small missionary planes which may accept you on board. Travelling to a place in Sarawak is certainly more than half the fun!

Preceding pages: the Niah Caves contain traces of Early Man.

It seems extraordinary that a white man once ruled in this land of jungles and tribal traditions, yet this came about, unusually for colonial history, not by force but by invitation.

The young debonair James Brooke, whose admiration for Sir Stamford Raffles lured him to the East, forsook the cocktail parties and fashionably dressed women of Singapore for a trip to Borneo.

Aside from a brief stint in the Indian Army, James held no titles among the British foreign legion, but his charisma embodied the romance of a cultured Englishman in search of adventure, and what he lacked in rank, he made up for in personality. He was also a diplomat and a strategist, assets which aside from his awe-inspiring appearance, earned him almost by accident the sole rule of Sarawak.

When James Brooke's ship *The Royalist* wound its way upriver to Kuching in 1839, Sarawak was suffering. Rebellions against the brutal extortions demanded by the Brunei overlords, as well as struggles between Malays and Land Dayaks were everywhere. Returning a year later, Brooke was asked by the Sultan of Brunei to help settle these disputes.

To the amazement of all, Brooke managed to talk both sides into agreeing upon a truce, but even more incredible to the Brunei overlords was his insistence that the lives of the rebels be spared and that they be allowed to return to their villages. Thus, Brooke gained the friendship of the Dayaks, the Malays and the Chinese.

In return, the Sultan offered him the title of Governor and Rajah of the Sarawak region. So the rule of the White Rajahs began, and with the novelty that became the essence of his rule: justice without favouritism.

If the peculiar genius of James Brooke conceived Sarawak as a state where a handful of Europeans should guide numerous Eastern races to a life of harmonious peace, it was his nephew, Charles Brooke, who succeeded him, who sealed its reality.

All smiles from a Dayak native.

Unlike James, who lived in a nimbus of international glamour, Charles was reserved in manner and difficult to approach. He had accustomed himself to months of loneliness as a district officer in the jungle where he lived among Dayak friends. Throughout his reign, he cultivated a betel nut plantation at the back of the *Astana* (palace) which provided gifts for his Dayak chief guests. He was in fact more relaxed in their presence than at a stiffly formal gathering of European officials.

Typical of his taciturn nature, Charles Brooke proposed marriage to the young Margaret de Windt by handing her a note while she was playing the piano. It read:

"With a humble demean
If the King were to pray
That you'd be his Queen,
Would you *not* say nay?"

Golden hues of the Sarawak River at dusk. To her parents' horror, Margaret agreed to become Ranee of Sarawak. Margaret wrote several books about her life there and accompanied her husband on journeys upriver where her gentle kindness to her native hosts did much to create goodwill. Living with Charles Brooke can't have been easy, but *he* held great respect for Margaret, and when a fort was built in Kuching, he named it after her.

Charles Brooke was a benevolent despot who insisted on having his hand in every affair, right down to choosing the marble slabs which were to be used for the fish stalls in Kuching Market. He commissioned the design of all public buildings, supervised the construction of the *Astana*, chose the paint colour for Fort Margherita and the uniforms for the Sarawak Rangers. He even sailed all the way to the Philippines to select a conductor for the municipal band and determined all of its music. Missives were directed by him to his district officers in the outback, insisting among many other things, that they should never be caught sitting in an easy chair.

Until his last years, Rajah Charles Brooke would rise with the five o'clock gun, dress in white trousers and a blue serge coat, with a sprig of honeysuckle

in his buttonhole, proceeding ceremoniously to the court house across the river, where he had the last word. He also spent some time in the Treasury, and though the accountants quivered beneath his sharp eye, Sarawak had never been so prosperous. Nor was it ever peaceful for so long. During his reign too, the first oil was found at Miri in 1895, and the Sarawak Oil company set about exploiting it in 1910. Rubber was also introduced as Sarawak's first real cash crop.

At 86, Rajah Charles Brooke still oversaw national affairs in the morning and took a three-kilometre walk in the afternoon. When he died in 1917, a significant era of white rule ended.

Several years later, his eldest son Charles Vyner Brooke, some European officials, Malay aristocrats, Dayak chieftains and Chinese merchants congregated outside the old Court House to honour the man who had devoted 65 years of his life to the rule and care of Sarawak, 49 of them as *Rajah*. As the *Iban* chief Penghulu unveiled the obe-

lisk memorial, the first airplane ever sighted in Sarawak appeared. Several of the guests were sure that the spirit of the old Rajah had returned.

Charles Vyner Brooke's rule was to be short-lived, as the state of Sarawak was handed over to the British Crown in 1945. With the formation of the Federated States of Malaysia in 1963, Sarawak left behind its White Rule past, save for the stories which are still retold at night in the longhouse.

Catching the midtown sampan: Memories remain too in Sarawak's capital city, **Kuching**. The Brooke era buildings make the city a town with a past. Amidst the noisy traffic and the bustling markets, scenes of every Malaysian centre of commerce, these edifices rise up to give the now modern capital an elegant and dignified air.

Charles Brooke's **Astana**, built in 1870 for the newly married *Rajah*, still stands, although it has undergone several renovations since it was first built. It consists of three bungalows, supported by square brick pillars, with the

Kuching still retains a small-town atmosphere.

low, spreading roof giving shade to the interior. The *Astana* is now the official residence of Sarawak's Head of State.

Fort Margherita (named after Charles Brooke's wife, the Ranee Margaret) still commands a position on the long stretch of the Sarawak River next to the town. However, by the time it was built in 1879, Sarawak was enjoying a period of calm and peace without attacks from outside powers, and the fort was never used for the purpose for which it had been intended. The only time that the fort came under fire was after the end of the Brooke era, when the Japanese took Kuching in an air raid. No severe damage was caused to the fort. Since the war, the fort has been used mainly by the police force, and today it houses the Police Museum.

Charles Brooke's **Courthouse** is a rather plain colonial building, but Brooke obviously had functionalism in mind here. Built in 1874, the building later had the addition of a clock tower in 1883. The **Charles Brooke Memorial** stands facing the building, erected there

Fort Margherita is now a police museum.

in 1924.

The **General Post Office**, with its Corinthian columns is a more decorative building, built in 1931. Another older and more imaginative building is the **Square Tower**, built in 1879, the same year as the Fort. Its architecture harks back to the Victorian's fascination with mediaeval culture. Although equipped with a real dungeon for prisoners, the tower later came to be used as a popular dancing hall. In 1886, the odd-looking **Round Tower** was built in Carpenter Street to house the town dispensary. Brooke seems to have had a predilection for fort structures, as the Round Tower was also meant to double up as a fort in times of attack. Nowadays, the building has yet another use, being offices attached to the Judiciary Department.

Other old buildings of interest abound in Kuching. One of the oldest is the **Bishop's House** of 1849, built by James Brooke, for the reverend Thomas Francis McDougall and his wife. With his typical astuteness, Brooke selected

McDougall for the position of Bishop of Kuching because he had previously been a surgeon. **The Pavilion**, close to the Round Tower and the Courthouse, is of an uncertain date and its elaborate frontage is very different from other colonial buildings in Kuching. It was built as Kuching's medical headquarters, but is now occupied by the Ministry of Education.

Along the Main Bazaar Road is the **Chinese Chamber of Commerce**, close to where the town's earliest Chinese shophouses were located and also near the first Chinese Temple, the **Tua Pek Kong**. Its construction in 1912 marked the firm establishment of the Chinese community in Sarawak. Now they are ubiquitous; rising from the handful that James Brooke found in 1839, they trade not only on the main towns and cities, but also upriver, attached to remote longhouses as suppliers of goods from downriver and building up a network of trade and news wherever they go.

Indian traders followed the Chinese

example in the last century, headed for Sarawak to set up cloth shops and money-lending facilities. The **Indian Mosque** hidden in between India Street and Gambier Road and dating from 1876, is a mark of their success here. The streets around the mosque are a labyrinth of small Indian shops and restaurants.

Images charged with intensity: But perhaps the most important and enthralling building for the visitor is the marvellous **Sarawak Museum**, set in its grounds between Jalan McDougall and Jalan Tun Haji Openg. The naturalist and co-founder of the theory of evolution along with Charles Darwin, Alfred Russell Wallace, spent many years in Borneo, and became a particular friend of Rajah Charles Brooke. With Wallace's encouragement, Brooke built the museum to house a permanent exhibition of native arts and crafts, as well as specimens from Wallace's extensive collection, many of which Wallace shot and preserved himself while exploring the jungle.

The facade of the building, however, betrays another influence. Its architecture was inspired by the Rajah's French valet after a house in Normandy. But the interior of the building is dedicated to the soul of Borneo, and its exhibits take one far beyond the paved streets of Kuching into the land's heart.

The Brookes were steadfast in their sense of justice. They suppressed crime and established peace in the state. But they wisely refrained from imposing any "civilised" versus "primitive" comparisons upon the native cultures. The *Rajahs* insisted upon capable curators, whose Western expertise was to serve only to illuminate the ethnological richness of Borneo and the vivid expressions of the societies it nourished.

The museum is packed with exotic fineries of the country's tribes, and it is possibly the best laid-out museum in Malaysia – set aside a good chunk of a day to go through it.

One display case is devoted to the bead-conscious *Kelabit* people, who have names for 60 varieties of ancient glass beads, each one with a special

There is no age limit on praying to the gods.

price. Another case houses figurines carved 2,000 years ago by the now-extinct *Sru Dayaks*. An entire corner of the museum has been transformed into a walk-in replica of an *Iban* longhouse, with simulated fires burning, genuine human skulls hanging from the rafters, as well as a warrior's headdress and finely shaped weaponry resting near his bedside, as if the warrior was about to walk in and sound the battle cry. Smaller models of other styles of long-houses are also found in this section.

The Sarawak tribespeople's great love of adornment is reflected in the high walls of the interior painted with flowing designs. A museum employee found one end of a Kenyah longhouse at Long Nawang completely covered with a majestic mural celebrating "The Tree of Life", and he returned to Kuching and commissioned painters to reproduce it inside the Museum.

Past rituals that lent a somewhat brutal aspect to tribal societies remain here on record. Giant handcarved burial poles with the ashes of the dead en-shrined in lofty niches were carried from upriver graveyards and placed impressively on the front lawn of the new Museum Annexe. In days gone by, slaves were sometimes crushed to death at the foot of the pole, if the family was in dire need of a sacrifice to appease the deceased.

Another strange tradition can be imagined inside the longhouse display – the *Anak Umbong* (the Secluded Daughter) was a tradition whereby the Dayak chief refused to allow anyone to catch sight of his daughter until a heroic warrior claimed her as his bride.

The old part of the museum has an eclectic character that recalls a succession of spirited curators, as well as the great diversity of Sarawak. There is a human dental plate on display that was found in the stomach of a 6-metre crocodile. A rhinoceros horn cup that can detect poison is another item. If the drink was contaminated, the liquid bubbled up to the top, and since princes were always trying to poison one another, rhinoceros horn was in high de-

Built in 1876, Tua Pek Kong is Kuching's oldest temple.

mand during the days of the dynasties.

Over in the Invertebrate Gallery, visitors can discover that the Damsel fly has been on earth for 300 million years, that the long-horned beetle was Wallace's favourite insect, and that the flea is the world's strongest jumper, leaping as much as 200 times the length of its body, which is roughly equivalent to a midget jumping 300 metres (as explained by the write-up).

If the museum is the storage of a wealthy heritage, it is also a living museum. The old museum is joined by a footbridge over the road to the new **Museum Annexe** completed in 1983. Here, besides more galleries devoted to the ways of life and industries of the various tribes, Chinese porcelain, and a reconstruction of the Niah caves where man lived 40,000 years ago, there are contemporary exhibitions – one entirely devoted to the study of cats, most suitable for Kuching which means cat – and films, videos and slide-shows in various rooms. These are on such Sarawak topics as the great golden hornbill

(Sarawak is often known as the land of hornbills), the *orang-utan*, life in the jungle, and popular tribal dances. Schoolchildren are driven round in well-ordered droves and at weekends families come here for a cultural half hour.

Outside the museum is a pleasant garden with an outdoor **Aquarium** and a small teashop run by two elderly Chinese ladies. The Annexe also has a good shop which is non-profitmaking and aims to help encourage local craftsmen. Although some of the exhibits you fell in love with back in the Iban or Kenyah sections might not be for sale here, there is still a good selection of handicrafts produced far away on the verandah of a longhouse.

Kuching's treasures: Along **Wayang Street**, some of the "antique" handicrafts you might have admired in the museum are for sale in small shops – for a price. Outrageously fanciful and symbolistic renditions of the sacred hornbill are carved on a large scale and painted with vivid reds and greens.

Sarawak Museum links the present with the past.

Behind in a case is a human skull, which makes you catch your breath – but the proprietor grins, and explains it is a plastic replica. If you are much disappointed, he will lead you to his display of charms, bundles of human and animal teeth, Chinese coins and special pieces of wood, wound together to protect the owner from evil spirits.

In **Temple Street** is the small and unassuming **Sarawak Batik Art Shop**, owned by artist Mr Pang Ling. You will find him amongst *Iban* and *Kelabit* artefacts: baskets, bamboo water-holders, and mats all with distinctive designs; and not forgetting Mr Pang's own collection of batik paintings. He will tell you how he met Queen Elizabeth in 1972 at the Sarawak Arts Council Exhibition. In his free time, Pang Ling makes trips to longhouses from where he says he derives most inspiration. His customers come from all over the globe and his paintings have even been exhibited in New York. Yet his success has not gone to his head, and he continues to work in a quiet and unostentatious way.

There is a good sampling of native art on display.

He will also make you feel very welcome at his shop, even if you come simply to admire and not to buy.

Markets and temples: Like many other Malaysian towns, Kuching has its share of ornate temples. Apart from the Tua Pek Kong, there is the **Kuek Seng Ong Temple** on Lebuh Wayang, built in 1895. Henghua fishermen pray here for good catches and a safe return from the sea. The temple is dedicated to the god Kuek Seng Ong, whose figure is placed on a sedan chair on the 22nd day of the second moon, and carried through the town's main thoroughfare.

The popular **Sunday Market**, which attracts Dayak tradesmen from the surrounding countryside, is situated on the outskirts of town at Jalan Satok. The stallholders actually arrive on Saturday night and the market begins on Saturday night continuing on till Sunday morning. All manner of strange foodstuffs – wild boar, bats, lizards, monkeys and turtles – are for sale here, alongside fruits, vegetables and fish.

Sarawak's beaches: Kuching's sun

worshippers and beach lovers head for the **Damai Beach Resort**, just 30 minutes from Kuching by boat, near Santubong. There the Sheraton Damai Beach Hotel commands the shores, offering hotel and chalet accommodation. Or you can stay at the **Government Rest House** by booking first at the Kuching District Office (242-533).

The fishing village of **Santubong** is also worth a visit. For those interested in history, the village's past dates back to the Tang and Sung dynasties (between the 7th and 13th centuries A.D.) when it was an important trading centre. Ancient Hindu and Buddhist-influenced rock carvings have been discovered around the river delta.

Other beach resorts further south along the coast include the **Santin Resort**, hidden amongst mangroves west of Kuching. Tour buses leave the capital and take you to the jetty where a boat zips you to the resort, which is inaccessible by land. The resort has been built for the needs of government ministers and wealthy Sarawakites, and water and land facilities are only available if you book long in advance and are a member of a sizeable group. There are, however, boats to take you snorkelling, but if you've been to the peninsula's East Coast, you'll be somewhat disappointed. With prior permission you may be allowed to visit the **Pulau Satang turtle sanctuary**, where turtle eggs are carefully guarded.

If you have wheels, you can get to **Sematan** in the far west of the state. In this sleepy relaxed little fishing village, accommodation is in the form of self-contained chalets. Book first from Kuching. From there you can visit several turtle sanctuaries situated on the nearby islands, a crocodile sanctuary near the village, and a jungle park at **Samunsan**.

Tours from Kuching: Tour companies arrange many trips from the capital to the surrounding points of interest. Not all of them are good, so choose carefully. The Tourist Information Office may be able to help you select one to suit your interest.

Shopping in Kuching can be an adventure.

Semmongok is Sarawak's *orang-utan* sanctuary, 22 kilometres (13½ miles) from Kuching. Rehabilitation services are offered there not just for the *orang-utans* but also for hornbills, monkeys and honey-bears.

Serian, a town just southeast of the capital, is popular with the locals for its waterfalls. Other trips may take you up the **Skrang River** where your tour may include a visit to a "longhouse". The experience may not be very genuine, as the inhabitants are used to seeing the tour buses roll in. Some tour companies even offer wedding tours for those who wish to tie the knot in a Sarawak long-house. Needless to say, if you want to see "real" longhouses, you'll have to venture further up the river and inde-pendent of tour companies. **Segu Be-nuk**, just 35 kilometres (22 miles) from Kuching and accessible by road, is one of the most frequently visited.

Bako National Park: A bus ride and a boat trip away from Kuching brings you to **Bako National Park**, situated on a peninsula at the mouth of the Sarawak River. Bako's relatively small area of 27 square kilometres (10 sq miles), has primary rainforest bounded on one side by a picturesque coastline of sandy bays and steep cliffs, and is uniquely rich in both flora and fauna.

The rainforest is home to beautiful insect-eating flowers and plants, and also to small animals such as the long-nosed monkey, the long-tailed ma-caque, pigs and *sambar* deer, some of which find their way down to the beach-es. Within the park is a good system of well-marked paths, and on arrival you will be handed a guide map.

One of these trails will take you to the **Lintang salt lick**, and a small observa-tion hide allows you, if you are enor-mously patient, to see animals come here to drink.

Another path takes you across several trails, first along the Lintang path through thick jungle, then up to **Bukit Tambi** to get a view of the park. A side-trail from here takes you across a pla-teau landscape, where the vegetation and geological formations look dis-

These Muslim girls see the lighter side of a situation.

tinctly Australian. Then, after this hot and vigorous walk, what could be better than to stumble across two perfect little bays, at **Telok Pandan Besar** and **Telok Pandan Kecil**, where you can refresh yourself by diving into the sea.

Bako National Park is an easy day trip from Kuching, but should you wish to stay in the park, there is accommodation at the **Rest House**, dormitories and chalets at the Headquarters at **Telok Assam**. There is a small shop where you can buy provisions, or visit the market before you leave Kuching. A restaurant is planned. Beware of the overfriendly long-tailed macaques who may find their way into your chalet kitchen! To book accommodation, apply at the National Parks office in Kuching.

Journey up the Rejang River: Beyond Kuching, cosmopolitan city life fades away and the innumerable rivers that mark Sarawak's green interior claim the status of being the highways to the centre of inland settlements. **Sibu**, capital of Sarawak's third and largest division, is an easy-going predominantly

Chinese town where trishaws are still in service and where fish markets overflow with gigantic freshwater fish such as the carp and the much-prized *kolong* which finds its way to the dining tables of Hong Kong.

Although it's possible to take a bus from Kuching to Sibu, you'll have your bones considerably rattled by the time you arrive and the trip takes two days. Pleasanter ways are by boat via Sarikei, or by small plane, the latter giving you a wonderful view of the never-ending jungle with its silver rivers snaking their way through the landscape. The flight takes only forty minutes. Flights also go further up the Rejang River to Kapit and Belaga, so you have the choice of taking the boat one way and flying the other.

From Sibu, the express boats, long and narrow and with interesting names, depart regularly and take you up to Kapit, and also to Belaga if the river level is high enough.

You tumble aboard with an assortment of other passengers: Chinese merchants taking their wares to distant

longhouses, river and inland officials (usually *Ibans*) off to attend a longhouse festival, and schoolchildren who learn their lessons in Sibu but return for holidays to their family longhouse.

On the way the boat stops at **Kanowit** and **Song**, or more regularly, if the boat is not full, at the tiniest of settlements. On the river, boats and canoes struggle up or fly downriver, and suddenly a huge floating raft comes into view. Sarawak's longest river is also the conveyor belt for the timber industry, and massive logs on rafts float downstream. Should one of these hazards become waterlogged, they present considerable danger to outboard motors. But the express boats have their bellies lined with steel with that very danger in mind.

To those who live far up the Rejang River, **Kapit**, the little town where the express boat will drop you, is London. Kapit has electricity 24 hours a day, shops selling goods at considerably higher prices than back down the river at Sibu, a market and several small hotels.

The cinema at the back of town has closed down, and now the nightly entertainment is to find someone who's been upriver recently, and maybe even over the border into Kalimantan, and to hear his tales. You can also work at finding someone who is returning to his longhouse in the next few days and who is willing to take you along. Although this is by far the best way to get a boat, you will still be charged even though he is going there anyway. Boat prices depend (even for the locals) on the level of the river, the weather, time of day, strong river currents and how willing the boatman is to hurry the journey to fit your tight schedule. For foreigners, prices will naturally be much higher and some bargaining is in order.

Kapit lies in the heart of *Iban* country, Sarawak's largest indigenous population. Ibans were once the headhunters who gave Borneo its romantic and primitive reputation. But some understanding of their culture will help the visitor to see that they were not merely bloodthirsty in an anarchic way.

Fruit stall, left, and food stall, below, in downtown Kuching.

To bring good fortune to the long-house and fame and a bride for themselves, young *Iban* warriors would (and some still do) set out from home to travel "the world". Heads of a few enemies were brought home to imbue the longhouse with protective spirits. Only warriors of equal strength, and never women, the old or sick, were killed. Sadly, these traditions have been much misunderstood by the 19th-century writers who revelled in writing lurid stories about the *Iban* tribes.

Ibans are in truth a proud and democratic people, sharing a communal way of life in their longhouses, honouring the supernatural forces recognised by their religion, and remaining loyal to their heritage and to their heroes. If they have been converted to Christianity, as many have, they take up hymn-singing in the evenings with as much gusto as in the days of tribal chanting and sacrificial ceremonies, and there is still much overlap between the old and the new faiths.

One early leader of the Iban was the

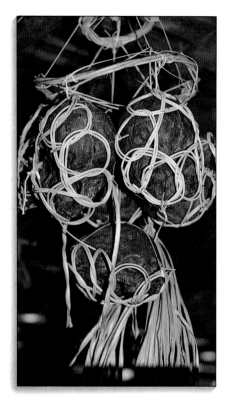

warrior Rentap, whose name in Iban means "one who makes the world shake". Tribal wars were common in Rentap's days when neighbouring tribes competed for favourable soils in which to plant their rice. Sarawak is an infertile land once the jungle has been removed, and the thin topsoil quickly erodes after a monsoon or two. For many years, longhouse dwellers were forced to resettle, even if it meant destroying another community's chances to do so.

Rentap, being a powerful and dauntless Iban chief, did not want James Brooke or any other foreigner to rule over his people. He fought so fiercely against the *Rajah*'s foot soldiers that it took five years and a 4.4-kilo (10-pound) cannon to defeat the chief. Rentap eventually surrendered, but not before letting the *Rajah* know that *Ibans* could not be pushed around.

The *Iban* gradually grew to respect the Brookes, even if their ideas conflicted with the traditions of head-hunting and piracy. The second *Iban* to rise to fame was Penghulu Koh, reputedly tattooed from head to toe. Tattoos are given to warriors for their great deeds, and Penghulu Koh had obviously done quite a few. However, he reformed to become one of the *Rajah*'s staunchest supporters, and was later conferred the title of Master of Peace Ceremonies, and paramount chief of all *Ibans*.

The spirit of Penghulu Koh still lingers in many *Iban* longhouses. Faded photographs of the *Rajah* Brookes and Queen Elizabeth in her twenties reverently hang alongside those of the great Iban chief.

But life is slowly changing in the longhouse. Along with these photographs may be found newspaper clippings of Asian beauty queen competitions, racing cars and Mr and Mrs Elvis Presley cutting their wedding cake. The "secluded daughter" tradition has lapsed. Many longhouse heirlooms – beautiful antique swords and silver belts – have been sold to Chinese jewellers from the big towns. Children who once enjoyed carefree days frolicking in the longhouse and the rice fields are

Reminder of head-hunting days hangs in Iban long-house.

now in school studying *bahasa Malaysia* and physics.

Tourism has a mixed effect on the longhouses. On the one hand, the virile and difficult dance of the warrior, and the chants and gongs accompanying it, are being revived because of touristic interest. On the other, the traditional handicrafts made by the women in the olden days with such loving care are now being churned out at a fantastic rate to meet the demands of the tourist shops in Kuching, casting aside much of the quality on the way. Without a doubt, further changes are on the way.

On the optimistic side, many young Ibans, even though they may have ignored the tradition of tattooing, are becoming more and more interested in their heritage, and in protecting their traditional homes from the onslaught of modernism and from the threat of logging. Of all the tribes the *Ibans* have been one of the most vociferous opposers of the latter problem, mainly because many of them have had foreign education and greater contact with the modern world than such tribes as the nomadic *Penan* and *Punan*.

To get an idea of what is afoot in the way of changes in longhouse communities, make the effort to spend at least one night in a longhouse. Remember to bring the customary gifts, which, you may find after your stay there, are mean recompense for the warm hospitality offered to you.

Boom towns and inland rivers: Bintulu and Miri lie on the coast of Sarawak and are the towns that mushroomed with the oil industry. **Bintulu** has to be one of the most expensive places to stay, and hotels and restaurants are all there to burn holes in the pockets of those drunk with oil wealth.

On top of **Canada Hill** overlooking **Miri** is Sarawak's first oil well. Constructed by the Shell oil company in 1910, the well was the forerunner of a further 623 oil wells drilled in the area known as the "Miri land field". It also survived longer than most of the other 623. After over 6 decades of an estimated extraction of 600,000 barrels, its

Ibans live in a close-knit community.

productivity and that of the wells around it ceased in the early 1970s. Oil drilling has now moved southwards to Bintulu where the main oil activity is still producing steadily.

From Miri, several exciting and adventurous trips can be made inland up the rivers to longhouses scattered from the coast all the way to the *Kelabit* district and over into Kalimantan. By road you can get as far as **Kuala Baram**, from where boats depart down the Baram river for Marudi. You can also enter the oil state of **Brunei** from that point. **Marudi** is the the starting point for the long river trips that take you down first large and then increasingly smaller rivers into the cooler *Kelabit* valleys. Permits to Bareo on the Kalimantan border can also be obtained from Marudi, which is also the place to come to should you wish to visit the Gunung Mulu National Park.

Bareo is situated in the cool valleys of *Kelabit* country. After the long journey from Marudi, several days walking and travelling down small rivers, you will be made welcome at a *Kelabit* longhouse. It is also possible to fly there from Marudi, Miri and Long Lallang in one of MAS' Twin Otters (12 seaters).

The *Kelabit* community is split in two by the border between Sarawak and Kailmantan, but such formalities seem not to trouble the *Kelabit* people who travel over it frequently without ever seeing an immigration point. Unfortunately it is not nearly so easy to do this trip, as a visitor must first hunt around for someone to stamp his passport on the Malaysian end, and then do the same thing all over again in Kalimantan.

From Bareo, and with the help of *Punan* guides, it is possible to climb **Gunung Murud.** At 2,423 metres (8000 feet), it is the highest peak in Sarawak, and you need five clear days to ascend and descend the mountain – a memorable experience. *Punan* guides and porters will also take you on a 6-day walk back to **Long Lallang**, from where you can fly back to civilisation. For those who are adventurous and fit, one of these expeditions is definitely

The Niah Caves were inhabited by man some 40,000 years ago.

worth experiencing.

Secrets from the Stone Age: Back in Miri, there are a couple of side-trips for which most travellers find themselves here in the northwest of Sarawak. The **Lambir Hills National Park** just south of Miri makes a pleasant day trip. The park's highlights are waterfalls with natural swimming pools and a climb up **Bukit Lambit**.

Much more famous, and perhaps with more to offer is the **Niah Caves National Park**. The limestone caves and their past inhabitants are the attraction here. In the 1870s, animal collector and adventurer A. Hart Everett came across the caves – already well-known and protected by the local people – only to dismiss them as "rather dull".

It was not until the 1950s that the Sarawak Museum heard of its being an archaeologist's goldmine. Sure enough, when the curator dug down 5 metres (16 feet) he found the skull of a young *Homo sapiens* who had lived here some 40,000 years ago. The "Deep Skull" as it was known was what remained of the earliest known community of modern man in the East. It disproved the haughty theories which insisted that man's true ancestor originated on the west side of the Middle East and only later "wandered" over to this part of the world.

As the archaeologists probed deeper, they found haematite paintings, featuring stick figures with strange little boat-like objects. The objects were in fact the canoe-shaped coffins of the culture, and this cave (now known as the Painted Cave) was once a burial chamber. Other discoveries revealed that this man worked with instruments made from bone and shell, and that he cut stone adzes and carved wooden coffins or burial boats. Many agreed that this discovery was as significant as the unearthing of Java Man.

When the Iron Age reached Borneo in A.D. 700, the Niahans were trading hornbill ivory and edible birds' nests for Chinese porcelain and beads. They decorated enormous earthenware urns **Out on a limb** and placed them beside the graves of **near Niah.** special men. Then in A.D. 1400, they seem to have entered a tropical Dark Age which forced them to desert the caves. They then vanished from history.

The Niahans may have been the forefathers of the nomadic *Punan* whose elders still maintain beliefs and rituals that allude to those in the prehistoric graveyards of the Great Caves. The *Punan* rediscovered the caves in the 19th century and found them to be unbelievably rich in edible birds' nests. Millions of swiftlets inhabit the bowels of the Niah Caves. Their glutinous saliva with which they build their nests is reputedly very tasty and their nests are the most expensive delicacy in Borneo.

The cost of these nests must have much to do with the markets they attract – China, Hong Kong and Singapore – but perhaps most of all because of the way they are collected. A typical day's work entails scurrying up 60 metres on a slender bamboo pole, scraping nests off rock ceilings and from deep crevices, and keeping balance where any fall could be fatal. You could say that the high cost of nests take a man's life insur-

315

ance into consideration.

Naturally, nest collectors guard their trade jealously, and pass their inherited territory only to their sons. The hundreds of chambers, chimneys and sub-caves where the tiny swiftlets nest are divided into sectors, each privately owned. Some yield but a few hundred nests, others several thousand. The cave owners live in villages and longhouses situated in the park area and during birds' nest season – normally two or three times a year, sometimes more – they bring the entire family along to help gather up the riches.

To get there, you must drive or take a bus or a taxi from either Miri or Bintulu, the former being much closer. At **Batu Niah village** a short trip across the river will bring you to the Niah Caves Visitors' Centre at Pangkalan Lubang.

Although there are a few hotels at Batu Niah, it is 13 kilometres (8 miles) back down the river, and it is much pleasanter to stay right in the park at the hostel. The hostel is a friendly and relaxed place, providing cooking facili-ties, bedding, toilets and showers, and electricity till 10 p.m. You will need to bring food supplies with you as there is no restaurant here; if you have forgotten something, you can "go shopping" at the little store just across the river from the Visitors' Centre.

From Pangkalan Lubang, just next to the Visitors' Centre, the plankwalk to the caves begins. The 3-kilometre (2-mile) plankwalk is built of the mighty *belian* wood, a wood that is reputedly so dense that it will not float. Forty-five minutes should get you to the caves if the planks are dry. Sensible shoes are preferable to sandals both for the plankwalk and the caves. Other necessities include a strong torch with spare batteries and some waterproof clothing.

Although the trip can be done in forty-five minutes, it is well worth stopping to absorb the atmosphere of the forest and listen to the jungle's "chorus". Down one of the forks in the plankwalk, you can visit a collectors' longhouse, although they may charge you to have a look around their home.

A breeding colony of Black-nest Swiftlets.

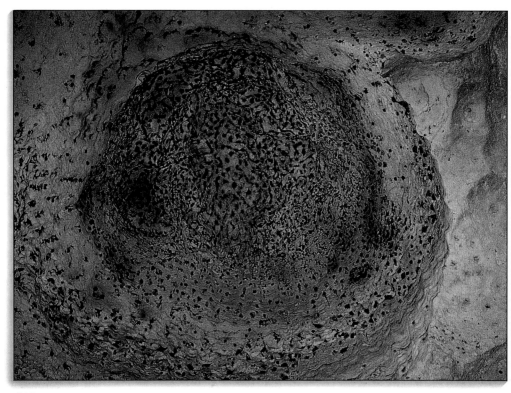

At the end of the plankwalk you will arrive at the caves. The **Great Cave** is the main area for birds' nest collection – and also for another interesting substance. Besides the three species of swiftlets of which there are said to be around 4 million, there are twelve species of bats, also countable in the millions. Their slimy, strong-smelling *guano* lines the cave floor and is collected almost as avidly as the birds' nests – for a rich fertiliser. In fact, you may have given way to some of the *guano* collectors on the plankwalk up to the caves. It is carried manually to Pangkalan Lubang, where it is weighed and then sent downriver to Batu Niah and to markets beyond.

With a strong torch, you will be able to pick out the creatures that inhabit the caves. Only two of the caves are open to visitors without a guide, and the second, the **Painted Cave** can only be entered with a permit issued by the National Parks Office in Kuching.

The most spectacular sight of all at Niah is worth taking camping equip-

ment along for. At 6 p.m., the swiftlets return into the caves to sleep in their nests, while the bats, being nocturnal animals, sweep past them out of the entrance of the cave into the night. This great flurry of activity is a wonderful sight, and in spite of their numbers, the bats and birds never collide. The reverse "shift" takes place at daybreak. It is a sight that man must have watched and wondered at 40,000 years ago.

Largest cave in the world?: A trip to **Mulu National Park**, together with a visit to a longhouse, must be the crowning glory of a visitor's stay in Sarawak – provided he be of the adventurous and intrepid sort. The Mulu Caves are not easy to get to, and yet their popularity, due to their reputation of housing the largest cave in the world, is on the rise.

A trip to the Park involves a long journey of a series of boat trips down several rivers. Even though you can fly to Long Lallang, you are still not at the Park's doorstep, and the trip via the river is certainly worth experiencing, if only done one-way and flying back the other. Several family travel agents in Miri operate good tours to Mulu, arranging all the river trips and boats for you in advance. As you can be vastly overcharged for the boats if travelling independently, it is recommended you take a tour. Your group might be the only ones taking it when you go, and the tour can be small and intimate. Whichever way you go, the trip will be fairly expensive, as boats and compulsory guides within the park must also be paid for. But it is the trip of a lifetime.

The Park was reopened in 1985, and is Sarawak's largest park, covering 52,866 hectares (130,580 acres). It is home to many interesting flowers, fungi, mosses and ferns, as well as eight species of the fabulous hornbill. Pitcher plants of ten kinds also flourish here. But the centre of attraction for all are the magnificent caves. One hundred and fifty kilometres (95 miles) of caves have already been surveyed, but specialists feel they may have only scraped the surface of this giant cave system.

The **Sarawak Chamber** is reputed to be the largest cave in the world, but its size is not readily described in metres, only in fascinating comparisons that set the imagination working – it is big enough "to hold 16 football fields" or "to house 40 Jumbo Jets".

The other cave with a claim to fame is the **Clearwater Cave**, definitely the longest cave passage in the world stretching 51 kilometres (32 miles). Comparisons for this passage suggest that "it could hold St Paul's Cathedral 5 times over". Visitors can get an idea of how true the boasts are about the Clearwater Cave, but unfortunately the Sarawak Chamber is at present only accessible to scientists and museum experts, much of it being far too dangerous to allow curious tourists into.

The 51-kilometre (32-mile) Clearwater Cave is an experience indeed and visitors wishing to enter it require a good torch and a willingness to get wet – up to the waist. The 355-metre (1165-foot) deep cave is very dark inside, but with a strong torch, you'll be able to see the marvellous limestone formations and the cave's inhabitants which in-

clude scorpions, frogs and centipedes. At times you'll have to wade through rivers which cross the cave.

Another cave the explorer has access to is the **Gua Payau** or **Deer Cave**. This underground "hall" is 2,160 metres (7090 feet) long and 220 metres (720 feet) deep. Thirty minutes is all it takes to walk from one end to the exit at the other, where the bats are pouring in. With some illumination as well as your own torch and crevices in the ceiling, you should be able to get a good view of the magnificent stalacmites and stalactites, still growing, as water cascades down through the roof crevices. It is possible to camp here to watch the nightlife around the cave entrance.

The other attraction, apart from pleasant walks along jungle trails, meeting *Punan* hunters along the way, are the two peaks **Gunung Mulu** and **Gunung Api**. Gunung Api is of special interest, being the highest limestone mountain in Malaysia, and possessing **the Pinnacles**, strange limestone spikes, like figures watching the park below, with some standing 45 metres (148 feet) high. The steep ascent to these marvels involves a 2-day trip, camping out overnight at a simple hut near the Melinau River.

Gunung Mulu is a much harder and longer trip. Expert mountain climbers have "done it" in one and a half days but the average modest climber should aim at doing it in a leisurely five. You have to take all your goods and chattels with you: cooking utensils, tins of food, water, a sleeping bag, a raincoat, good walking shoes and a strong torch. There are camps all the way up, but these are simply glorified shelters, and your pleasure must derive from travelling in this wild landscape, far away from cities, deep in an ancient jungle.

At the peak, you might stop and survey the landscape, folding away into a green carpet below, split only by limestone outcrops. You have seen Sarawak, you have seen the changes taking place in the city and longhouse alike. But this final experience confirms what you have believed all along. Borneo is still Borneo.

Left, nomadic *Punans* help to transport goods. **Right**, bats take flight in Mulu.

TRAVEL TIPS

GETTING THERE

Malaysia is well connected by airlines to all continents, and if you are coming from Europe or North America, you will enter the country by Subang Airport, Kuala Lumpur. If you are arriving from a nearby Asian country (Thailand, Indonesia or Singapore), it is possible to fly to some other Malaysian cities either directly or by connecting flights through Kuala Lumpur. Penang, Langkawi and Tioman can be reached directly from Singapore. For details of flights, contact your airline or travel office.

For details on other destinations in Malaysia, see the "Getting Around" section, where there is a full list of Malaysian Airline (MAS) services.

BY SEA

Cruise liners call at Malaysia on round-the-world trips, but most ports harbour cargo ships. There are boats to Penang from Phuket in Thailand and from Medan in Sumatra, Indonesia, to Penang. The latter operates twice weekly and details are available at travel agents in Penang. Another interesting route is with the Greek-built *MV Vigneswara* of the Greenseas Shipping Company, which plies the waters between Madras in South India, and Penang and Singapore twice a month. The ship is equipped with air-conditioning, casino, bar, TV lounge and a duty-free shop. Ask at travel agencies in Madras or Penang.

BY RAIL

An extensive railway network runs through Malaysia (for information on trains, see "Getting Around" section) from Singapore, with connections to Bangkok. The Thai-owned International Express leaves daily from Bangkok for Butterworth, and trains from Haadyai in the south of Thailand connect to trains on the Eastern Malaysian railway. The trip from Bangkok takes about two days, and you can travel in a first-class air-conditioned sleeper, a second-class non-air-conditioned sleeper, or in upright seats in third class. For reservations, contact the railway station in Bangkok (Hualamphong) or a local travel agent. Trains from Singapore to Kuala Lumpur and Kota Bharu run several times daily and take from 7 to 10 hours (Kuala Lumpur) or 12 to 15 hours (Kota Bharu) respectively.

BY ROAD

From Thailand, it is possible to get buses from Bangkok or Haadyai that cross the border at Padang Besar and travel to Penang or Kuala Lumpur, or at Sungei Golok on the East Coast. From Singapore, there are many buses which travel to all parts of peninsular Malaysia from the bus station at New Bridge Road, Singapore. Other buses run from Beach Road in Singapore. New Bridge Road buses may be booked by calling 221-6603. Long-distance taxis also run from Queen Street in Singapore, although you will get a better bargain by taking the bus to Johor Bahru across the Malaysian causeway and taking a taxi from there.

TRAVEL ESSENTIALS

VISAS & PASSPORTS

Valid passports and a health certificate of vaccination against yellow fever are required if travelling from an infected area. Citizens of Commonwealth countries, Ireland, Switzerland, the Netherlands and Liechtenstein do not need a visa to visit. The following countries do not need a visa for a visit not exceeding three months: Austria, Italy, Japan, South Korea, Tunisia, the

United States, West Germany, France, Norway, Sweden, Denmark, Belgium, Finland, Luxembourg and Iceland.

Citizens from communist countries are granted visas from 7 to 14 days. Citizens from Israel and South Africa are not able to visit Malaysia, and Chinese, Kampuchean and Vietnamese citizens are only able to visit on an official basis.

Immigration requests that your passport be valid for at least 6 months. Bear in mind that Sabah and Sarawak are treated like other countries, and you will have to go through customs again there, both from peninsular Malaysia and between the two states.

On arrival, the most common visa will be for 30 days. If you wish to extend your stay, and are from one of the countries enjoying diplomatic relations with Malaysia, then you may do so at any of the following immigration offices:

Federal Territory
Blok 1, Tingkat 2-3, Pusat Bandar
Damansara, Bukit Damansara,
50490 Kuala Lumpur
Tel: 03-7579063

Kuala Lumpur
Headquarters Office, Blok 1,
Tingkat 4-7, Pusat Bandar Damansara,
50490 Kuala Lumpur
Tel: 03-757-8155

Johor
Wisma Persekutuan Johor, Blok B,
Tingkat 1, Jln. Air Molek,
80550 Johor Bahru
Tel: 07-244255

Kedah
Tingkat 2, Wisma Persekutuan,
0500 Alor Setar, Kedah
Tel: 04-723302

Kelantan
Tingkat 2, Wisma Persekutuan, Jln. Bayam,
15550 Kota Bharu, Kelantan
Tel: 09-741644

Melaka (Malacca)
Tingkat 2, Bangunan Persekutuan,
Jln. Hang Tuah, 75300 Melaka
Tel: 06-224958

Negri Sembilan
Tingkat 2, Wisma Persekutuan,
Jln. Datuk Abdul Kadir,
70675 Seremban, Negri Sembilan
Tel: 06-727707

Pahang
Tingkat 1, Wisma Persekutuan,
Jln. Gambut, 25000 Kuantan, Pahang
Tel: 09-521373

Perak
Bangunan Persekutuan, Jln. Dato' Panglima
Bukit Gantang, 30000 Ipoh, Perak
Tel: 05-540394

Perlis
Tingkat 1, Menara Kemajuan PKNP,
Jln. Bukit Lagi, 01000 Kangar, Perlis
Tel: 04-753535

Pulau Pinang (Penang)
Jln. Leboh Pantai, 10550 Pulau Pinang
Tel: 04-610678

Sabah
Tingkat 4 & 5, Bangunan Penerangan,
88550 Kota Kinabalu, Sabah
Tel: 088-51752

Sarawak
Peti Surat 639, 93908 Kuching, Sarawak
Tel: 082-20895

Selangor
Kompleks PKNS,
40550 Shah Alam, Selangor
Tel: 03-506061

Terengganu
Tingkat 1, Wisma Persekutuan,
Jln. Paya Bunya,
20200 Kuala Terengganu, Terengganu
Tel: 09-622457

MONEY MATTERS

Currency and Exchange: The Malaysian currency note is the *ringgit* or Malaysian Dollar, which is divided into 100 *sen*. The amount of Malaysian dollars you are allowed to bring in or take out of Malaysia is unlimited. At the current exchange, US$1 will give you M$2.70, A$1 – M$2.03, and £1 – M$4.24. Singapore and Brunei dollars are worth about 30 percent more than the Malaysian *ringgit*, and no longer circulate freely in Malaysia. You may be able to use Singapore dollars in the state of Johor, but they are counted as having the same value as the *ringgit*.

Banks and licensed money changers offer better rates than do hotels and shops, where a service charge may be levied (usually 2-4 percent). Make sure that you have enough cash before you leave for smaller towns or remote areas.

Travellers' Cheques and Credit Cards: In the more flashy quarters of the larger towns, in department stores, shops, first-class restaurants and hotels, travellers' cheques change hands easily. Have your passport ready when changing cheques. Off the beaten track, you may find it harder to change travellers' cheques. Established credit cards – Diners Club, American Express, Visa, Mastercard and Carte Blanche – are honoured in the major cities. Several hotel chains maintain their own credit card system. But when travelling extensively through Malaysia, nothing could be better than the coin of the realm.

Costs: Bear in mind that accommodation, transportation and food costs tend to be higher in East Malaysia than on the peninsula. But in general, costs in Malaysia are considerably lower than in Europe or North America (except for some imported goods), and higher than in neighbouring countries such as Thailand and Indonesia. Approximate prices for accommodation and some transportation are offered in this guide to give a general idea of costs. It is advisable to carry a mixture of monies, local and foreign currencies, as well as travellers' cheques and credit cards, and to store these separately in your luggage in case of theft.

Below is a budget guide published by the Tourist Corporation of Malaysia (TDC); you will find that you may possibly be able to exceed it or even undercut it!

HEALTH & EMERGENCY

Travellers have few worries in a country where the health standards are ranked amongst the highest in Asia.

Water in cities is generally safe for drinking, but it is safest to drink it boiled. Bottled drinks are also widely available. Avoid drinking iced water from roadside stalls. It is important to drink sufficiently to avoid dehydration; drink more than you would normally if you're coming from a cold country.

The sun is deceptively strong here: one

Hotel accommodation – room only

	Single	Double
International Hotel	From M$100.00++	From M$120.00++
Budget Hotel (20 to 50 room hotel)	From M$ 30.00++	From M$ 35.00++

Meals

Breakfast	Price per person in M$
Continental (in hotel coffee shop)	8.50++
Full breakfast	12.00++
Local coffee shop	5.00
Local stall	2.00

Lunch	
Hotel	18.00++
Modest local restaurant	10.00
Local stall	4.00

Dinner	
Hotel	20.00++
Modest restaurant	12.00
Local stall	4.00

++ A 5 percent government tax and 10 percent service charge is added to hotel and restaurant meals.

hour of sunbathing a day for the first few days will get you a lasting tan without giving you sunstroke.

If you are visiting remote jungle areas, it is advisable to take malaria tablets; your doctor will know which type is suitable for the region. To help keep mosquitoes at bay, use insect repellents, mosquito coils and nets at night. If you intend to travel to Borneo, ask your doctor about outbreaks of cholera in the region. These are rare, but should there be any, you would be wise to have a vaccination before leaving home.

Treat open cuts and scratches immediately as infection in humid climates can delay healing, and at worst, cause tropical ulcers. If you are swimming in the sea near coral reefs, do not touch any of the interesting shells, snakes and other creatures you find there. Many of them are poisonous, but if you don't threaten them, you will be quite safe. To avoid getting sea urchin prickles in your feet, it is a good idea to wear plastic shoes while exploring the coral reefs.

Medical supplies are widely and readily available in Malaysia, and all large towns have government polyclinics as well as private clinics. Bring a small first-aid kit, or buy one from Kuala Lumpur or another large city. French and German-speaking doctors can be found by contacting the relevant embassies. Travel and health insurance, as well as documents concerning allergies to certain drugs should also be carried.

In an emergency, the charge-free number to call is 999 for ambulance, fire or police services. Most hotels have security services and many of them have safes for valuables. Never carry too much cash on your person, and keep travellers' cheque numbers apart from the cheques. In the event of loss, you can call the Tourist Police Unit at the following numbers:

Johor Bahru	07-232222
Kuala Lumpur	03-241-5522
	03-243-5522
Melaka	06-222-2222

WHAT TO WEAR

In the delightful tropical climate of Malaysia, informal wear is most suitable and comfortable. However, since this is a predominantly Muslim and conservative country, observance of local customs is important. Men may wear tee-shirts or cotton shirts with short sleeves, and open sandals. Women should not wear dresses, skirts or shorts that are too short, and topless sunbathing is frowned upon. In cities, towns and villages, shorts are not a good idea – save them for the beach. In mosques, the legs should be covered to below the knee, and some mosques will provide scarves for the head and arms. When visiting government offices and passing through immigration points, long trousers and skirts are looked upon favourably.

WHAT TO BRING

There is very little need to worry about leaving something important behind when you visit Malaysia. Toiletries, medicines, clothes, photographic film, suntan lotion and straw hats are all readily available in most towns, and definitely in the large cities. In fact, the best advice is to take as little as possible so that you can travel lightly and comfortably.

If you are planning to visit the hill stations, a light sweater would be a good idea for the cooler evenings. If you're embarking upon the Mount Kinabalu climb, a lightweight plastic raincoat is a must, as are a warm hat and gloves, but all these items can be found in Kuala Lumpur, Singapore, or Kota Kinabalu. Camping gear is often available for hire in national parks, but it is also under heavy demand; so it may be best to bring a lightweight tent with you. If you intend to go jungle-trekking, the Taman Negara National Park issues a list of contents for the average backpack (see "Where To Stay" section).

In more remote areas, you will not have the luxury of a shaving point, but disposable razors are sold widely in towns and cities, or you can buy a battery-operated razor at reasonable prices. Sanitary protection for women is also available in larger centres. Cheap clothes are everywhere – batik shirts are colourful and cool, and tee-shirts with interesting slogans are also a good buy. You may even decide to adopt the multi-purpose sarong as skirt, towel or sheet! So...just bring your camera. Or buy one in Singapore!

TAKING THE FAMILY

Malaysia holds pleasures for all age groups, and having small children or elderly parents should not prevent you from coming to Malaysia. The younger members of the family will be well looked after as Malaysians have a great fondness for children and *kampong* mothers will take them in as their own. Most hotels have baby and child beds, and baby products are found everywhere. If you have older members in your group, you will have to decide whether they are fit enough to venture into the national parks. Tour operators provide tours suitable for those less agile on their feet, and air-conditioned hotels will give them relief from the tropical sun.

CUSTOMS

Import duties seldom affect the average traveller, who may bring in 250 grammes of tobacco or cigars, or 200 cigarettes, and a one-quart bottle of liquor duty-free. Other duty-free items include food items not exceeding $75, 3 pieces of clothing (shirts, scarves, ties etc.), one pair of shoes, and any gift item not exceeding $25. Used portable articles are normally exempted from import tax. Pornography, weapons and walkie-talkies are strictly prohibited. Possession of narcotics and other illegal drugs carries the death sentence, and firearms are subject to licensing.

The above duty-free items are not available to you if you are travelling on a domestic flight, or from Singapore.

ON DEPARTURE

Departure Tax: Airport tax is collected at all airports. For domestic flights, the tax is $3; for flights to Brunei and Singapore, $5; for all other international flights, the departure tax is $15.

GETTING ACQUAINTED

GOVERNMENT & ECONOMY

Malaysia is the official name of the former British protectorates of Malaya, British North Borneo and Sarawak. Independent since 1957, the Malaysian government is regulated by the Parliament comprising the *Yang di-Pertuan Agong*, King or Supreme Sovereign, and two Houses: the House of Representatives and the Senate. The executive functions of the government are carried out by the Cabinet, led by Dato' Seri Mahathir Mohammed who became Prime Minister in 1981.

The population of 17.36 million comprising of Malays, Chinese, Indians, Pakistanis and other indigenes, is spread over 13 states. The capital city of Kuala Lumpur alone has a population of approximately 1 million.

Petroleum oil, natural gas, tin, timber, pepper, palm oil and rubber are the main exports. Its main trading partners are Japan and the United States.

TIME ZONES

Malaysia's standard time is 8 hours ahead of Greenwich Mean Time (or 7 hours ahead of British Summer Time). When it is noon in Malaysia, it is:

4 a.m. in London
(or 5 a.m. British Summer Time)
5 a.m. in Paris, Rome, Madrid and Bonn
7 a.m. in Athens, Cairo and Johannesburg
8 a.m. in Moscow
9.30 a.m. in Bombay
11 a.m. in Bangkok and Jakarta
noon in Singapore
1 p.m. in Tokyo
2 p.m. in Sydney
6 p.m. (previous day) in Hawaii
8 p.m. (previous day) in San Francisco and Vancouver

The Bank Who Cares for your business.

BANK DAGANG NEGARA
(STATE COMMERCIAL BANK)

HEAD OFFICE : Jl. M.H. Thamrin No. 5, Jakarta   Phone : 321707, 3800800,
P.O. Box : 338/JKT Jakarta 10002, INDONESIA
Telex : 61628 BDNULN IA, 61649 BDNULN IA, 61621 BDNLN JKT, 61640 BDN FX IA.

OVERSEAS OFFICES :

NEW YORK (AGENCY) &
CAYMAN ISLANDS (BRANCH)
45 Broadway Atrium 30th floor
New York, N.Y. 10006,
USA
Telex :   226698 BDN NYUR
226690 BDN NYUR

LOS ANGELES (AGENCY)
3457 Wilshire Boulevard
Los Angeles, C.A. 90010
USA
Telex :   3716724 BDN LA USAG
3716705 BDN LA USAG

HONG KONG (REPRESENTATIVE) &
STACO INTERNATIONAL FINANCE LTD
6/F Admiralty Centre Tower II
Queensway, Victoria
Hong Kong
Telex :   60322 BDN – HX
60323 BDN FX – HX

SINGAPORE (REPRESENTATIVE)
50 Raffles Place 13-05
Shell Tower, Singapore 0104
Telex : DAGANG RS 24939

THE PROBLEMS OF A

HEAVY TRAFFIC.

You'll come across massive Thai jumbos at work and play in their natural habitat. In Thailand, elephants are part of everyday rural life.

FALLING MASONRY.

A visit to the ruined cities of Sukhothai or Ayutthaya will remind you of the country's long and event-filled history.

EYESTRAIN.

A problem everyone seems to enjoy. The beauty of our exotic land is only matched by the beauty and gentle nature of the Thai people.

GETTING LOST.

From the palm-fringed beaches of Phuket to the highlands of Chiang Mai there are numerous places to get away from it all.

OLIDAY IN THAILAND.

GETTING TRAPPED.

In bunkers mostly. The fairways, superb club houses and helpful caddies make a golf trap for players of all standards.

HIGH DRAMA.

A performance of the 'Khon' drama, with gods and demons acting out a never-ending battle between good and evil, should not be missed.

EXCESS BAGGAGE.

Thai food is so delicious you'll want to eat more and more of it. Of course, on Thai there's no charge for extra kilos in this area.

MISSING YOUR FLIGHT.

In Thailand, this isn't a problem. Talk to us or your local travel agent about Royal Orchid Holidays in Thailand.

Thai
We reach for the sky.

A CLASS OF ITS OWN

11 p.m. (previous day) in New York and Montreal

CLIMATE

A tropical sun and clouds laden with the makings of a sudden downpour compete for the skies of Malaysia, with the odds on the sun. Malaysia's seasons follow the monsoon winds, which splash rains inland from September to December on the west coast of the peninsula, only to be overtaken by sunshine within the hour. Rains arrive later, between October and February, on the east coast of peninsular Malaysia and in Sabah and Sarawak. Malaysia's weather, however, is generally warm, humid and sunny all year round, with temperatures wavering between 32°C during the day and 22°C at night. The highlands, both during the day and at night, and the lowlands in the evening, are comfortably cooler, which is why Malaysia's nightlife is liveliest outdoors.

CULTURE & CUSTOMS

The customs, religions and language of many nations converge in Malaysia. With everyday etiquette relaxed and straight-forward, visitors behaving courteously stand little chance of unintentionally giving offence. It is beneficial, however, to learn something of how Malaysians behave towards one another so that you will become more integrated in the culture.

Seniority is much respected. The oldest male member of a family is greeted first, often sits in the best and highest seat, and is consulted first on any matter. Pointing with the finger is considered very rude and a whole hand is best used to indicate a direction (but not a person). For those interested in learning more about Malaysian customs, have a look at the Times Editions guidebook *Culture shock! Malaysia and Singapore* (see "Books section"). The following is a brief guide to customs appropriate to certain places and ceremonies.

TEMPLES & MOSQUES

Removing one's shoes before entering a mosque or an Indian temple has been an unspoken tradition for centuries. Within, devotees do not smoke. Neither of these customs generally apply to Chinese temples where more informal styles prevail. Visitors are most welcome to look around at their leisure and are invited to stay during some religious rituals. While people pray, it is understood that those not participating in the service will stand quietly to one side. A polite gesture would be to ask permission before taking photographs; unless there is a sign indicating otherwise, this request is seldom if ever refused. Moderate clothing, rather than short skirts or shorts should be worn. Most temples and mosques have a donation box for funds to help maintain the building. Contributing a few coins before leaving is customary.

PRIVATE HOMES

The hospitality of a Malaysian friend is a good feeling. In private homes, visitors are received as honoured guests. Without hesitating, the host or hostess will prepare some drinks. Women especially pride themselves in serving good food whenever a guest arrives, and when returning the visit, they will bring a small gift of fruit or cakes. You would do well to bring a similar small gift with you, and a modest present from your own country, especially at a longhouse, will be very welcome. Do not be offended if the hostess immediately places your gift to one side; excessive expression of pleasure in receiving a present is not customary. Although not everything served in a home is expected to be eaten, nothing pleases a hostess more than knowing her guests enjoy her cooking. All Malays, Indians and Chinese remove their shoes at the door to keep the house free from dust. No host would insist his visitors do so, but it is the polite way to enter a home. One can always tell if there is some kind of get-together happening at someone's house – by the number of shoes and sandals scattered around the front door!

SHARING A MEAL

As every dish has its own flavour, every food has its own style. Chinese food is generally eaten with chopsticks and deep spoons, while most Malays and Indians eat with the right hand (never the left, which is considered unclean). However, forks and spoons are more commonly used now, especially in restaurants.

Asian meals are usually served in large bowls or dishes placed in the centre of the table, with each diner helping himself to a little at a time from each bowl. Piling up your plate is not only impolite but also unwise. With possibly more dishes to follow, it is best to take a small amount and later help yourself to more if you find the dish irresistible. Local people are inwardly pleased if you join them in practising their style of dining, for a simple reason: they know it tastes better that way.

If you have been invited out to a restaurant by a Malaysian, do not expect to pay the bill at the end, for that is his honour. Malaysians are extremely courteous over this, no matter what their income bracket is, and sometimes, even if you invite them out, they will insist on paying. Settling the bill may require some craft on your part!

WEDDINGS

A gift of money – from $10 upwards – is customary at weddings of all races. The gift is generally used as a contribution to the cost of the wedding banquet, often a lavish affair with hundreds of guests invited. The money should be placed inside an envelope with your name written on the back, and given to the bride or groom (except at Sikh weddings where it is given to the bride's mother). The Chinese present gifts of money in an *ang pow,* a small red envelope obtainable at banks or stationers. Traditionally an even number of notes or coins is considered lucky.

TIPPING

Tipping is not common in Malaysia, especially in more rural areas. In most hotels and large restaurants, a 10 percent service charge is added to the bill along with 5 percent government tax. In large hotels, bellboys and porters usually receive tips from 50 *sen* to $2 depending on the service rendered. Outside these international establishments, however, simply a thank you (*terima kasih*) and a smile will do.

WEIGHTS & MEASURES

Malaysia is fast converting from the English Standard System to the metric system, though it will be some time before it is complete. Road distances are always given in kilometres, but if you ask a *kampong* dweller for directions, he will give distances in both miles and kilometres. There is a similar confusion over weights.

ELECTRICITY

Do not expect to plug an American electric razor into the communal circuit of a clapboard coconut palm-shaded *kampong* house. The Malaysian current is 220 volts, 50 cycles, although most first-class hotels can supply an adaptor for 110-volt, 60 cycles appliances. Bargains in electrical appliances can be found in Singapore.

BUSINESS HOURS

In an Islamic nation with a British colonial past, weekly holidays vary. In the former Federated States which were united under the British – Selangor, Melaka, Penang, Perak, Pahang and Negri Sembilan – there is a half-day holiday on Saturday and a full-day holiday on Sunday. The former unfederated states, which remained semi-autonomous under British rule – Johor, Kedah, Perlis, Terengganu and Kelantan – retain the traditional half-day on Thursday and full-day holiday on Friday; Saturday and Sunday are treated as weekdays. The workday begins at 8 a.m. and ends at 4.30 p.m. with time off on Friday from noon until 2.30 p.m. for communal *Jumaat* prayers at the mosque. Most private businesses stick to the nine-to-five routine. Shops start to close at 6 p.m., unless they are attached to a night market, and department stores like *Klasse* and *Metrojaya* in Kuala Lumpur keep their cash registers ringing past 9 p.m.

Banking: The nationwide network of 42 commercial banks has all the facilities to cope with simple as well as more complex transactions. The various banks operate more than 550 offices throughout the country and have connections with the major financial centres of the world. Banking hours are Monday through Friday 10 a.m. to 3 p.m., and Saturday 9.30 a.m. to 11.30 a.m.

HOLIDAYS

JANUARY

Jan 1   New Year's Day – except Johor, Kelantan, Terengganu, Kedah and Perlis
Jan 21   Birthday of the Sultan of Kedah – Kedah only

FEBRUARY

Feb 1   Federal Territory Day – Federal Territories of Kuala Lumpur and Labuan only
Feb 8   Thaipusam – Negri Sembilan, Penang, Perak and Selangor only
Feb 12   Hari Hol Almarhum Sultan Ismail – Johor only

MARCH

Mar 5   Ishak and Mikraj – Kedah and Negri Sembilan only
Mar 8   Birthday of the Sultan of Selangor – Selangor only
Mar 10   Birthday of the Sultan of Terengganu – Terengganu only
Mar 11   Official Opening of the State Mosque, Shah Alam – Selangor only

APRIL

Apr 8   Birthday of the Sultan of Johor – Johor only
Apr 13   Good Friday
Apr 19   Birthday of the Sultan of Perak – Perak only

MAY

May 1   Labour Day
May 7   Hari Hol Pahang – Pahang only
May 9   Vesak Day – except for Federal Territory of Labuan
May 29   Dayak Day (Hari Gawai) – Sarawak only
May 30 & 31   Harvest Festival – Federal Territory of Labuan and Sabah only

JUNE

June 6   Birthday of *Yang di-Pertuan Agong* (King)

June 14   Birthday of the Yang di-Pertua Negri Melaka – Melaka only

JULY

July 16   Birthday of the Yang di-Pertua Negri Pulau Pinang – Penang only
July 16   Birthday of the Yang di-Pertuan Besar of Negri Sembilan – Negri Sembilan only
July 23   Maal Hijrah
July 31   Birthday of the Sultan of Kelantan – Kelantan only

AUGUST

Aug 23   Birthday of the Rajah of Perlis – Perlis only
Aug 31   National Day

SEPTEMBER

Sept 16   Birthday of the Yang di-Pertua Negri Sabah – Sabah only
Sept 16   Birthday of the Yang di-Pertua Negri Sarawak – Sarawak only

OCTOBER

Oct 26   Birthday of the Sultan of Pahang – Pahang only

DECEMBER

Dec 25   Christmas Day

The following holidays are moveable feasts depending on the Christian, Muslim, Buddhist or Hindu calendar:

Chinese New Year (2 days; except Kelantan and Terengganu – 1 day)
Hari Raya Puasa (2 days)
Hari Raya Haji (1 day; 2 days in Kedah, Kelantan, Pahang, Perlis)
Deepavali (except Sabah, Sarawak and the Federal Territory of Labuan)
Prophet Mohammed's Birthday
Awal Ramadan
Birthday of the Sultan of Terengganu (Terengganu only)

If a holiday falls on a weekend or a Friday, the following day becomes a holiday.

It is difficult to say which is the most exciting spectacle – a blowpipe's bull's eye in the Borneo interior; a top that spins for 50 minutes under a makeshift canopy on peninsular Malaysia's east coast; an imperial howl at Penang's Chinese opera; or an Indian dancer with bells on her toes. In Malaysia, not only do all these occur, but several may be going on at the same time. The country has a public holiday nearly every month, not counting the market feasts, regal birthdays and religious processions that sprinkle calendar pages like confetti. The only problem is distance. Malaysia spreads out over 5,000 km and so do its festivals.

The Muslim calendar consists of 354 days in a year. The Chinese and Hindu calendars, unlike the Gregorian calendar, use the lunar month as their basic unit of calculation. Hence dates vary widely from year to year. These festivals and celebrations with variable dates probably include some of Malaysia's more exciting events. For immediate events, read the daily newspapers and *Kuala Lumpur This Month*, distributed free at leading hotels.

RELIGIOUS SERVICES

Minarets, spires, domes and steeples adorning the skyline of Kuala Lumpur reflect a rich diversity of faiths in Malaysia. Below is a small selection of places of worship in Kuala Lumpur. Hotels and travel agents provide the times of services and can help arrange transportation. (Also see under "Temples and Mosques".)

Kuala Lumpur Baptist Church
70 Jln. Hicks, KL

Mar Thoma Church (Syrian)
Jln. Ipoh, KL

National Mosque
Jln. Sultan Hishamuddin, KL

See Yeoh Temple (Taoist)
14A Leboh Pudu, KL

Seventh Day Adventist Mission
166 Jln. Bukit Bintang, KL

Sikh Temple
Jln. Bandar, KL

Sri Mahamariamman Temple (Hindu)
163 Jln. Bandar, KL

St Andrew's Presbyterian Church
31 Jln. Raja Chulan, KL

St Francis Xavier Church (Jesuit)
Jln. Gasing, Petaling Jaya

St John's Cathedral (Roman Catholic)
Bukit Nanas, KL

St Mary's Church (Anglican)
Jln. Raja, KL

Wesley Methodist Church
off Jln. Hang Jebat

Zion Church
21 Jln. Abdul Samad, KL

COMMUNICATIONS

MEDIA

Television: This is the most popular communication medium in Malaysia, watched in international hotel rooms and longhouses with the same enthusiasm! Programmes are highly cosmopolitan and British and American sit-coms and documentaries are shown alongside Indonesia's hottest film and Koran reading competitions from Kuala Lumpur. British football is also given wide coverage, and sports in general have a generous slot of transmission time. The news is given in English on Channel RTM 1 at 6 p.m. and on TV 3 at 6.30 p.m.

Radio: Radios can also be heard everywhere, blaring out a wild assortment of different sounds; a flick of the dial will tune you into Indonesian pop, Malay rock and heavy metal, Indian pop or classical music, Chinese theatrical, John Williams sci-fi music scores or the number one sound in Britain or America. Soap operas and programmes of daily events around the country will also familiarise you with the Malay culture. For the news in English, tune into Blue Network (280 MW) at 7 a.m., 8 a.m., 1.30 p.m., 5 p.m. or 7 p.m., or to "Beautiful Malaysia" (97.2 FM) between 6 and 7 p.m.

The Press: Malaysia's newspapers come in a variety of languages, from *Bahasa Melayu* (Malay, the national language), English and Chinese, to Tamil, Punjabi and Malayali. The *New Straits Times* and the *Star,* masters of the English press, arrive every morning crammed with national and world news, occasional eye-opening letters to the editors, and "Peanuts" and local cartoonist Lat comic strips. The *Malay Mail*, an afternoon paper, is less formal and more chatty, and entertains its readers by focussing more on local news and entertainment. The *Sabah Times, People's Mirror, Sarawak Tribune* and *Borneo Post* hail from East Malaysia with international news appearing next to events from the remote jungle. Foreign newspapers and magazines can also be purchased in large cities.

POSTAL SERVICES

Malaysia has one of the most efficient postal services in Asia. There are post offices in all state capitals and in most cities and towns. Except for the General Post Office in Kuala Lumpur, which opens from 8 a.m. to 7 p.m. (Monday to Saturday), all post offices are open from 8 a.m. to 5 p.m.

An aerogramme to any country costs 40 *sen*. Postcards to other Asian countries cost between 20 and 25 *sen*, to Australia and New Zealand 30 *sen*, to Europe 40 *sen* and North America 55 *sen*. Most international hotels provide postal services; and stamps and aerogrammes are often sold at the small Indian sweet and tobacco stalls on street corners. Malaysian stamps are very attractive, often picturing the country's beautiful flora and fauna.

TELEPHONE & TELEGRAM

Local calls in Malaysia cost 10 *sen*, and public phones can be found in most towns, often located in front of restaurants. Long-

distance and international calls can be made from the post office or from a hotel.

On Penang Island, different area codes have been given to each suburban district – Balik Pulau 898, Batu Ferringhi 811, Batu Uban 883, Bayan Lepas 831, Penang Hill 892, and Tanjong Bungah 894. Inter-state calls require the following prefix codes:

Ipoh	05
Johor Bahru	07
Kota Bharu	09
Kota Kinabalu	088
Kuala Lumpur	03
Kuala Terengganu	09
Kuantan	09
Kuching	082
Melaka	06
Penang	04
Seremban	06
Sungai Petani	04
Taiping	05

For international calls, dial "108" to book the call. If you dial "104", an operator will take your telegram dictation over the phone. International Direct Dialling is available in most international hotels, as are secretarial and facsimile services.

Other useful numbers include:

Trunk Calls Assistance	101
Connection difficulties	102
Directory Enquiries	103
Fault reporting	100
Time signal (KL and Klang only)	1051
Weather Report	1052
Emergency (Police/Fire/Ambulance)	999
Tourist Police	
Kuala Lumpur	03-241-5522/
	03-243-5522
Melaka	06-222-222
Johor Bahru	07-232222

GETTING AROUND

ORIENTATION

Malaysia is one of the easiest Asian countries to travel around in. Transportation ranges from an Orang Asli dugout canoe up remote rivers, to a trishaw in Kuala Terengganu, to funicular railways and fast modern jets. There are almost always several alternatives to travelling to a place. Travelling in Malaysia can be as exciting and as adventurous as you want to make it. To get a feel of the country, you should try several of the different modes of transport.

FROM THE AIRPORT

Buses, public and private, taxis and even limousine services operate from major airports in Malaysia. Many airports have a taxi desk, where taxis can be booked and paid for and where the price is fixed. Where there is no such service, inquire at the information desk about how far the town is from the airport, and how much you should pay a taxi driver. Otherwise, you might fall prey to an unscrupulous taxi driver who takes advantage of you by overcharging you for a very short distance. Taxi fares from airports are in general much higher than around the town. Distances to towns from airports are given in the following airfares table.

DOMESTIC TRAVEL

By Air: Malaysian Airlines System (MAS) runs an extensive network of airways over the entire nation. In remote jungle areas, the Fokker 27s and Northland Islanders operate buses linking out-of-the-way places to national centres. Singapore Airlines, Royal Brunei and Thai International have flights to Malaysian destinations other than Kuala Lumpur. Inquire at the appropriate offices. Below is a list of MAS offices in Malaysia for bookings and confirmations:

Alor Setar
1543 Jln. Sultan Badlishah,
05000 Alor Setar, Kedah
Tel: 711186, 711187

Bandar Seri Begawan
144 Jln. Pemancha, P.O. Box 72,
Bandar Seri Begawan, Brunei Darussalam
Tel: 24141/2

Bario
c/o Bario Co-Operative Society Ltd., Bario,
Fourth Division, Sarawak

Belaga
c/o Syarikat Awang Radin, 4 Belaga Bazaar,
Sarawak

Bintulu
P.O. Box 932, 97008 Bintulu, Sarawak
Tel: 31554

Ipoh
G01 Bangunan Seri Kinta,
Jln. Sultan Idris Shah, 30000 Ipoh, Perak
Tel: 514155, 514886

Johor Bahru
G/F Orchid Plaza, Jln. Wong Ah Fook,
80000 Johor Bahru, Johor
Tel: 220888, 220709

Kapit
c/o Hua Chiong Co., 6 Jln. Temenggong
Koh, 96800 Kapit, Sarawak
Tel: 96344, 96484

Kota Bharu
Kompleks Yakin, Jln. Gajah Mati,
15000 Kota Bharu, Kelantan
Tel: 747000, 743346

Kota Kinabalu
10th Floor, Kompleks Karamunsing,
Jln. Tuaran/Jln. Selatan,
88300 Kota Kinabalu, Sabah
Tel: 51455, 53560

Kuala Lumpur
33rd Floor, Bangunan MAS,
Jln. Sultan Ismail, 50250 KL
Tel: 2610555

Ground Floor Menara Utama UMBC,
Jln. Sultan Sulaiman, 50000 KL
Tel: 2305115

Lot 157, 1st Floor Complex Daya Bumi,
Jln. Sultan Sulaiman, 50000 KL
Tel: 2748734

Lot 7A, 3rd Floor Pan Pacific Hotel Kuala
Lumpur, Jalan Putra, 50746 KL
Tel: 4426759

Shop Lot No. 15/16 Menara Majlis Perban-
daran Petaling Jaya, Jln. Tengah,
46200 Petaling Jaya, Selangor
Tel: 7550770

Kuala Terengganu
Ground and Mezzanine Floors,
No. 13 Jln. Sultan Omar,
20300 Kuala Terengganu, Terengganu
Tel: 621415

Kuantan
Ground Floor, Wisma Persatuan Bolasepak,
Jln. Gambut, 25000 Kuantan,
Pahang Darul Makmur ·
Tel: 521218, 522020

Kuching
Bangunan MAS, Lot 215 Song Thian Cheok
Road, 93100 Kuching, Sarawak
Tel: 246622

Kudat
c/o Lo Cham En, P.O. Box 10,
89057 Kudat, Sabah
Tel: 61339

Labuan
Lot No. 1, Wisma Kee Chia (1st & 2nd
floor), Jln. Bunga Kesuma,
87008 Wilayah Persekutuan Labuan
Tel: 412042, 412137

Lahad Datu
Ground Floor, Mido Hotel Bldg.,
P.O. Box 299,
91108 Lahad Datu, Sabah

Langkawi
Langkawi Island Resort, Kuah,
0700 Langkawi, Kedah
Tel: 788209

Lawas
c/o Eng Huat Travel Agency,
No. 2 Jln. Liaw Siew Ann, P.O. Box 45,
98857 Lawas, Sarawak
Tel: 5570, 5368

Limbang
c/o Mah Moh Hin, No. 15 Cross Street,
98700 Limbang, Sarawak
Tel: 21881, 21834

Long Lellang
c/o Koperasi Serbaguna Long Lellang Berhad, Long Lellang, Sarawak

Long Pa Sia
c/o Puan Runang, Long Pa Sia, Sabah

Long Semado
c/o Co-Operative Multi-purpose Society
Ltd., Long Semado, Sarawak

Long Seridan
c/o Yami Kota, Long Seridan, Sarawak

Long Sukang
c/o Co-Operative Society, Long Sukang,
Sarawak

Marudi
c/o Tan Yong Sing, 57 Queen's Square,
Marudi, P.O. Box 57, Sarawak
Tel: 55240, 55480

Melaka
No. 238 Taman Melaka Raya, Bandar Hilir,
75000 Melaka
Tel: 235722/3/4

Miri
Lot 239, Beautiful Jade Centre,
P.O. Box 180, 98007 Miri, Sarawak
Tel: 414144

Mukah
c/o Wee Lam Hai, 6 Main Bazaar,
94600 Mukah, Sarawak
Tel: 62204

Pamol
c/o Pamol (Sabah) Ltd., P.O. Box 203,
90007 Sandakan, Sabah
Tel: 3155, 3893

Penang
Tun Abdul Razak Complex, Penang Road,
10000 Penang
Tel: 620011

Sandakan
Ground Floor, Sabah Bldg.,
Lorong Edinburg, P.O. Box 190,
90007 Sandakan, Sabah
Tel: 273963

Semporna
c/o Today Travel Services, 1st Floor,
Lot 7 B111, P.O. Box 6,
91307 Semporna Sabah
Tel: 781077

Sibu
No. 61 Jln. Tuanku Osman,
96000 Sibu, Sarawak
Tel: 326166

Tawau
Lot 1A, Block 34, Tawau Extension II,
Fajar Complex, 97008 Tawau, Sabah
Tel: 772703/4

Tomanggong
c/o River Estate Sdn. Bhd., P.O. Box 1209,
90008 Sandakan, Sabah
Tel: 2130

Guide to Domestic Airfares: The fares stated in the table on pages 334-335 are correct at the time of going to print. Special fares are available between certain destinations as well as for multi-destination tickets. Check at any MAS office or at a reputable travel agent in Malaysia. Return airfares are normally double the one-way fare. If you are coming from Singapore, buy your air tickets for travel around the country in Malaysia, as prices, being the same in Singapore as in Malaysia, are cheaper in Malaysian dollars.

	Distance from destination airport to its town (km)	One-way Fare M$
From Kuala Lumpur to		
Ipoh	10	55
Johor Bahru	30	77
Kota Bharu	10	86
Kota Kinabalu	21	380
Kuala Terengganu	18	80
Kuantan	15	61
Kuching	10	231
Melaka	10	39
Penang	13	86
Singapore	20	130
From Penang (Tel: 04-830811) **to**		
Ipoh	10	41
Kota Bharu	10	72
Kuala Terengganu	18	80
Singapore	20	150
From Kota Kinabalu (Tel: 088-52553) **to**		
Alor Setar	11	94
Bandar Sri Begawan (Brunei)	8	65
Bintulu	1	110
Keningau	–	38
Kudat	4	50
Lahad Datu	1	88
Labuan	3	43
Lawas	2	47
Miri	8	90
Ranau	–	38
Sandakan	15	84
Singapore	20	346
Tawau	2	80

	Distance from destination airport to its town (km)	One-way Fare M$
From Sandakan (Tel: 089-660525) **to**		
Kudat	4	54
Lahad Datu	1	57
Pamol	3	40
Semporna	4	50
Tawau	2	78
Tomanggong	4	42
From Tomanggong to		
Lahad Datu	1	35
Semporna	4	40
Tawau	2	55
From Kuching (Tel: 082-454255) **to**		
Bandar Sri Begawan (Brunei)	8	192
Bintulu	1	97
Kota Kinabalu	21	198
Miri	8	150
Mukah	4	90
Sibu	5	60
Singapore	20	170
From Sibu (Tel: 084-330831) **to**		
Belaga	1	48
Bintulu	1	64
Kapit	2	48
Miri	8	75
Mukah	4	30
From Lawas to		
Bekelan	–	46
Labuan	3	31
Limbang	6	25
Long Semadoh	1	40
Long Sukang	1	25
From Marudi (Tel: 085-55635) **to**		
Bario	4	55
Long Lellang	1	46
Long Seridan	1	42
Sibu	5	100
From Miri (Tel: 085-33884) **to**		
Bario	4	70
Bintulu	1	57
Labuan	3	57
Lawas	2	59
Limbang	6	45
Marudi	1	29
Mukah	4	55

From	To	Distance from destination airport to its town (km)	One-way Fare M$
Alor Setar (Tel: 04-744021)	Kota Bharu	10	59
Bintulu (Tel: 086-31073)	Mukah	4	44
Johor Bahru (Tel: 07-241985)	Kota Kinabalu	21	301
Kuantan (Tel: 09-581291)	Johor Bahru	30	77
Lahad Datu (Tel: 089-81747)	Tawau	2	40
Long Seridan	Long Lellang	1	35

PASSENGER FARES BETWEEN PRINCIPAL STATIONS
Single Journey Fare

From Station	Butterworth			Kuala Lumpur			Singapore		
	1	2	3	1	2	3	1	2	3
To Station	$	$	$	$	$	$	$	$	$
Alor Setar	12.40	5.60	3.50	58.30	26.30	16.20	105.70	47.60	29.30
Bangkok	81.10	37.70	–	125.40	57.70	–	174.00	76.60	–
Butterworth	–	–	–	48.60	21.90	13.50	96.00	43.30	26.60
Gemas	69.20	31.20	19.20	21.90	9.90	6.10	28.00	12.60	7.80
Haadyai	24.60	11.40	–	68.90	31.40	–	117.50	53.30	–
Ipoh	22.50	10.20	6.30	25.50	11.50	7.10	74.10	33.40	20.50
Johor Bahru	93.50	42.20	25.90	46.20	20.80	12.90	3.20	1.50	0.90
Kluang	82.60	37.20	22.90	35.30	15.90	9.80	14.00	6.30	3.90
Krai	122.70	55.30	34.00	75.30	34.00	20.90	81.40	36.70	22.60
Kuala Lipis	97.20	43.80	26.90	49.80	22.50	13.80	54.70	24.70	15.20
Kuala Lumpur	48.60	21.90	13.50	–	–	–	48.60	21.90	13.50
Padang Besar	21.30	9.60	5.90	65.60	29.60	18.20	114.20	51.50	31.60
Segamat	72.90	32.90	20.20	25.50	11.50	7.10	23.70	10.70	6.60
Seremban	57.10	25.80	15.80	9.30	4.20	2.60	40.10	18.10	11.10
Singapore	96.00	43.30	26.60	48.60	21.90	13.50	–	–	–
Taiping	11.90	5.40	3.30	36.50	16.50	10.10	85.00	38.30	23.60
Tampin	63.20	28.50	17.50	15.20	6.90	4.20	34.00	15.40	9.50
Tapah Road	29.20	13.20	8.10	19.50	8.80	5.40	68.00	30.70	18.90
Tumpat	133.60	60.20	37.00	86.20	38.90	23.90	91.10	41.10	25.20
Wakaf Bahru	131.20	59.10	36.30	83.80	37.80	23.20	89.90	40.50	24.90

FARE – EKSPRES RAKYAT/SINARAN (XSP)

From Station	Butterworth				Kuala Lumpur				Singapore			
	1	2	2	3	1	2	2	3	1	2	2	3
	AFC	ASC	SC	TC	AFC	ASC	SC	TC	AFC	ASC	SC	TC
To Station	$	$	$	$	$	$	$	$	$	$	$	$
Butterworth	–	–	–	–	55.00	28.00	25.00	17.00	–	50.00	47.00	30.00
Bukit Mertajam	8.00	7.00	4.00	4.00	53.00	27.00	24.00	16.00	–	49.00	46.00	20.00
Ipoh	29.00	17.00	14.00	10.00	32.00	18.00	15.00	11.00	–	40.00	37.00	24.00
Johor Bahru	–	49.00	46.00	29.00	53.00	27.00	24.00	16.00	10.00	8.00	5.00	4.00
Kampar	33.00	19.00	16.00	11.00	28.00	16.00	13.00	9.00	–	38.00	35.00	23.00
Kluang	–	44.00	41.00	26.00	42.00	22.00	19.00	13.00	20.00	13.00	10.00	7.00
K. Kangsar	22.00	14.00	11.00	8.00	39.00	21.00	18.00	13.00	–	23.00	40.00	26.00
K. Lumpur	55.00	28.00	25.00	17.00	–	–	–	–	55.00	28.00	25.00	17.00
Segamat	–	39.00	36.00	24.00	32.00	18.00	15.00	11.00	30.00	17.00	14.00	10.00
Seremban	–	32.00	29.00	19.00	16.00	11.00	8.00	6.00	48.00	25.00	22.00	15.00
Singapore	–	50.00	47.00	30.00	55.00	28.00	25.00	17.00	–	–	–	–
Taiping	18.00	12.00	9.00	7.00	43.00	23.00	20.00	14.00	–	45.00	42.00	27.00
Tampin	–	35.00	32.00	21.00	22.00	13.00	10.00	8.00	40.00	22.00	19.00	13.00
Tapah Road	36.00	20.00	17.00	12.00	26.00	15.00	12.00	9.00	–	37.00	34.00	22.00

Notes

AFC: Fare first class air-conditioned
ASC: Fare second class air-conditioned
SC: Fare second class ordinary
TC: Fare third class ordinary by Ekspres Rakyat only.

Supplementary Charges:

Berth Charges KTM
1st class – $20.00 air-conditioned
1st class – $10.00 ordinary
2nd class – $8.00 lower
2nd class – $6.00 upper
(Singapore/K. Lumpur – K. Lumpur/
Butterworth – K. Lumpur/Tumpat –
Tumpat/Singapore)

International Express Berth Charge
1st class – $19.00 air-conditioned
1st class – $11.80 ordinary
2nd class – $9.10 lower
2nd class – $6.40 upper
Express train charges $2.80
(Butterworth/Bangkok – Bangkok/Chiengmai)

By Rail: Malaysian Railways or Keretapi Tanah Melayu (KTM), runs right from the heart of Singapore's business centre, through the Malay peninsula and on into Thailand in the north, calling at major cities and towns including the capital Kuala Lumpur. Another line, the East Coast line, branches off the main one at Gemas, plunges through the central forests and emerges eventually at Tumpat, near the border to Thailand. Malaysian trains are generally comfortable, and travelling by train gives one an excellent idea of Malaysia and its varying countryside. Passengers can choose from air-conditioned first class coaches on the day trains and first-class air-conditioned twin berth cabins on the night trains. In the second class are fan-cooled sleepers, and sleeperettes are in the third class coaches. First and second class tickets may be purchased 30 days in advance, third class tickets 10 days in advance. Passengers holding tickets for distances over 200 kilometres are allowed to "break journey" at any station – one day for every 200 km or part thereof, in addition to time occupied by the journey. Passengers taking advantage of this scheme must remember to have their tickets endorsed by the station master at the alighting station immediately upon arrival.

For foreign tourists, KTM offers a railpass which entitles the holder to unlimited travel in any class and to any destination for a period of 10 or 30 days. The Railpass costs M$85 for 10 days and M$175 for 30 days. The cost of the pass does not include sleeping berth charges, and for these you would be wise to book in advance.

There are a number of different train services available. The passenger can either choose the normal train which stops at most stations, or the express which only stops at major towns. For more information, charts are provided on pages 336 and 337.

Most stations have left luggage services. Charges are a reasonable 50 *sen* a day.

SCHEDULES OF EXPRESS TRAINS

Butterworth/Kuala Lumpur /Butterworth
(Air-conditioned, 1st & 2nd Class)

Station	XSP 7	XSP 3	XSP 4	XSP 8
Butterworth	0730	1500	1355	2130
Bt. Mertajam	0746	1516	1330	2104
Taiping	0856	1626	1223	1952
K. Kangsar	0936	1706	1144	1913
Ipoh	1027	1757	1050	1818
Tapah Road	–	1850	0956	–
K. Lumpur	1405	2125	0730	1500

Kuala Lumpur/Singapore /Kuala Lumpur
(Air-conditioned, 1st & 2nd Class)

Station	XSP 5	XSP 9	XSP 10	XSP 6
K. Lumpur	0730	1500	1420	2135
Seremban	0838	1606	1256	2020
Tampin	0923	1649	1213	1937
Segamat	1047	1812	1045	1809
Kluang	1212	1937	0919	1645
Johor Bahru	1341	2106	0800	1528
Singapore	1420	2145	0730	1500

Note XSP: Express Train No.

WATER TRANSPORT

Traditionally, transport in Malaysia, particularly in the west, was by water. In Pahang, on the Endau River, and of course, in Sarawak, water transport still has some importance, but in general, roads have taken over as the main means of transport.

On rivers in peninsular Malaysia, you may find boats for hire, but often the best way is to find out which boats are going where and hitch a ride. Boat rental can sometimes be phenomenally expensive, especially, for example, if you want a ride downriver. The boatman will be reluctant, because he has to motor all the way upriver again afterwards. He might prefer to sell the boat to you!

In Sarawak, there is a lot of traffic on the rivers inland throughout most of the year as roads are still few and far between and mostly in a poor condition. On the Rejang River, regular boats run between Sibu and Kapit, and if the waters are high enough, all the way to Belaga. Boats to smaller rivers and to remote longhouses can be fearfully expensive, and it is best to go down to the jetty and see where all those women with baskets are heading for and change your plans accordingly.

Other regular ferry and boat services include boats to the islands Pangkor, Penang and Langkawi. Boats to Pangkor stop running at 7 p.m., but ferries to Penang run 24 hours, and boats to Langkawi till 6 p.m.

Boats out to islands on the east coast are slightly less regular, especially in the monsoon season when several services may stop altogether. There are services to the Perhentian Islands, Kepas, Redang and Tenggol in the north, and many boats run out to the islands off Mersing. Mersing boats can be a little confusing as there is a wide choice. Boats to Tioman range from fishing boats that charge $15 per person, or catamarans and ferries that cost $25-$30 and take 2½ hours, to the hydrofoil which takes 75 minutes and costs around $25. Some of the other islands also have ferries (e.g. Rawa and Sibu) or you can hire a fishing boat to get there. The price of the boat is the same whether you are one person or twelve (maximum capacity).

Besides ferries to Penang, there are several leisurely cruises which allow one to see Malaysian shores on the peninsula and also in Borneo. Introduced in August 1986, Feri Malaysia operates cruise *Muhibah*, a holiday cruise ship, between Singapore, Kuantan, Kuching and Kota Kinabalu. The ship offers air-conditioned cabins and comfortable suites, as well as facilities such as restaurants, a discotheque, gymnasium, cinema, swimming pool and golf putting green.

Stopover packages and shore excursions are available and further information can be obtained at Feri Malaysia Sdn. Bhd., Ground Floor, Menara Utama UMBC, Jln. Sultan Sulaiman, 50000 Kuala Lumpur, Tel: 03-238-8899, Telex: FM KUL MA 50055. For cruise schedules and fares, see the table below.

PUBLIC TRANSPORT

By Taxi: Taxis remain one of the most popular and cheap means of transport, especially on a shared basis. You can hail them by the roadside, hire them from authorised taxi stands, or book them by phone, in which case, mileage is calculated from the stand or garage from which the vehicle is hired.

Although most taxis are fitted with meters, they are only used in major towns such as Kuala Lumpur, Johor Bahru and Ipoh.

At the start of the journey, the meter reads $1.00 and turns over in 10 *sen* lots every 200 metres. Check that your driver turns his meter on only when you have got into the car. Apart from the amount stated on the meter, you also have to pay 30 percent of the price extra for air-conditioning, regardless of whether you want it or not! If you are travelling in the early morning or late at night, taxi drivers are reluctant to use their meters and prefer to fix a price for the destination: this is where you'll need your bargaining skills! You can also negotiate a day

CRUISE SCHEDULE

Port	Arrival	Departure	Day	Voyage No
Kuantan	0900	1430	SAT	FM 101
Kuching	2030	0200	SUN/MON	FM 101
Kota Kinabalu	0800	1400	TUES	FM 102
Kuantan	1200	1800	THURS	FM 102A
Singapore	1000	1800	FRI	FM 101A

Note: Check in 2 hours before departure.

CRUISE FARES

	Standard Cabin		Deluxe Cabin		Suite	
	One Way	Return	One Way	Return	One Way	Return
Ex Kuantan						
Kuching	$160	$320	$235	$470	$350	$700
Kota Kinabalu	$265	$530	$380	$760	$550	$1100
Singapore	$99	$198	$140	$280	$210	$420
Ex Kuching						
Kuantan	$160	$320	$235	$470	$350	$700
Kota Kinabalu	$140	$280	$195	$390	$300	$600
Singapore	$200	$400	$270	$540	$355	$710

price with town taxis.

Outstation taxis are a popular way of getting to another city or town, and if your bargaining powers are good, it can be very economical. The taxis usually operate on a shared cost basis, with four passengers, and many drivers will not leave until that quota has been reached. If you want to pay four times as much, then you can charter a taxi, which will mean you don't have to wait around for other passengers to turn up.

Below is a guide to some of the journeys you might take in peninsular Malaysia. Prices quoted are per person for a taxi shared by four persons.

Johor Bahru to Mersing	$11
Johor Bahru to Melaka	$16
Johor Bahru to KL	$30
Melaka to KL	$12
KL to Penang	$30
KL to Ipoh	$15
Ipoh to Penang	$15
Kuantan to KL	$19
Kuantan to Kota Bharu	$29
Kuantan to Kuala Terengganu	$16
Kuala Terengganu to Kota Bharu	$12

There are no meters in taxis in Sabah or Sarawak. Find out how much other transport cost to your destination and calculate accordingly. Transportation costs are generally much higher in East Malaysia than on the peninsula.

By Bus: There are three types of buses that operate in Malaysia: the non-air-conditioned buses plying between the states, the non-air-conditioned buses that provide services within each state, and the air-conditioned express buses connecting major towns in Malaysia. All prices are reasonable though bus departures do not always adhere to the schedule. Some of the bus fares are indicated in the table below.

By Trishaw: If you want to see the city at your own pace, you can still find trishaws at your service. These are very popular in cities such as Melaka, Kota Bharu, Kuala Terengganu and Georgetown, Penang. For short trips, they are better than taxis as their slow pace allows you to see points of interest along the way.

Except in Penang, where passengers sit in a sun-hooded carriage in front of the cyclist, a trishaw is a bicycle with a side carriage. In Penang, trishaw drivers will warn you to hold on to your bags firmly for fear of snatch-thieves on motorcycles. Incidences of this kind, however, are rare nowadays.

It is important that you fix the price before proceeding in a trishaw. A little bargaining is necessary, and you should inform the peddler if you wish to stop somewhere along the way, as stopping time also has to be calculated. In some places, especially in Penang, you can rent trishaws by the hour, which can be economical should you wish to see several places.

BUS SCHEDULES AND FARES

Routes: From Kuala Lumpur to	Departure Times At Bus Terminal	FARES Air-conditioned	Non-Air-conditioned
Alor Setar	9.30 a.m./9 p.m./9.30 p.m.	$19.50	$16.20
Batu Pahat	8.30 a.m./10 a.m./2.30 p.m./3.30 p.m.	$10.00	$8.40
Butterworth	8 a.m./10 a.m./12 a.m./10 p.m.	$15.50	$13.00
Cameron Highlands	8.30 a.m.	–	$7.75
Dungun	10 a.m./9.30 a.m.	$16.50	$13.50
Grik	9.00 a.m.	$13.60	$11.50
Ipoh	8.30 a.m./10.30 a.m./1.30 p.m.	$8.50	$6.70
Johor Bahru	9.30 a.m./11 a.m./1 p.m./10.30 p.m.	$15.20	–
Kangsar	9. a.m./9.30 p.m.	$21.00	$18.00
Kota Bharu	8.30 a.m./8.30 p.m.	$25.00	$21.00
K. Kangsar	9 a.m./11.30 a.m./3 p.m.	$10.50	$8.50
K. Terengganu	9 a.m./9.30 a.m./10 p.m.	$20.00	$16.70
Kuantan	8.30 a.m./9.30 a.m./2.30 p.m./4.30 p.m.	$11.00	$9.00
Muar	8 a.m./10 a.m./1 p.m./5 p.m.	$7.90	$6.55
Singapore	9 a.m./10 p.m.	$17.00	–
Taiping	8 a.m./11.30 a.m./3 p.m./10.30 p.m.	$12.00	$10.00

N.B. Children are charged 50 percent of the normal fare.

Car Rental: Having your own transport gives you the freedom to explore places off the beaten track at your leisure. The principal car rental firms are listed here. Most have branches in the main towns throughout Malaysia including those in Sabah and Sarawak. Check at the main office.

Cars are usually for rent on an unlimited mileage basis. The daily rates vary from $125 for economy cars per day to $300 for cars in the super luxury class. Weekly rates are also available. Four-wheel drive is advisable in Sabah, Sarawak, and the central regions of the Malay peninsula.

Avis Rent A Car
40, Jln. Sultan Ismail, Kuala Lumpur
Tel: 03-241-0561

Budget Rent A Car
Ground Floor, Wisma MCA, 50450
Tel: 03-261-1122

Hertz Rent A Car
4th Floor, Ming Building
Tel: 03-232-9125
Lot 11, 4th Floor, KL Hilton
Tel: 03-243-3014
Airport: 03-746-2091

National Car Rental
Lot 9, Mid-Level Floor, Equatorial Hotel, Kuala Lumpur
Tel: 03-261-9188
Airport: 03-746-2025

Olympic Rent A Car
54A Jln. Bukit Bintang
Tel: 03-243-8519

Distance chart locations (diagonal headers, left to right):
Alor Gajah, Alor Setar, Ayer Hitam (Johor), Bagan Serai, Bahau, Baling, Muar (Bandar Maharani), Batu Pahat (Bandar Penggaram), Batu Gajah, Bukit Fraser, Butterworth (Ferry), Cameron Highlands, Gerik, Ipoh, Johor Bahru, Kajang, Kampar, Kangar, Port Kelang (Malaysia & Indonesia Less), Keluang, Kota Bharu, Kota Tinggi, Kuala Dungun, Kuala Kangsar, Kuala Kerai, Kuala Kubu Baharu

599																									
148	747																								
451	148	599																							
66	607	163	459																						
570	114	718	122	576																					
66	667	82	517	108	636																				
118	716	32	573	158	686	50																			
343	291	489	124	348	245	407	,457																		
225	454	348	306	185	423	291	343	192																	
506	97	654	55	514	87	572	623	182	367																
343	377	491	229	351	346	409	460	118	198	283															
489	169	638	161	497	68	555	605	175	343	155	267														
341	258	489	109	349	229	407	459	21	196	164	119	148													
242	840	93	692	256	799	175	124	578	467	747	584	731	583												
101	499	240	349	109	469	169	219	242	124	404	242	388	240	343											
303	296	451	148	311	267	369	420	37	156	203	97	187	39	544	201										
642	43	791	192	650	156	708	760	320	497	140	420	213	301	884	541	341									
156	515	303	367	167	485	221	270	229	143	422	259	404	258	394	60	196	559								
169	768	21	620	175	739	103	53	510	361	675	512	658	510	105	270	472	811	324							
667	1085	765	937	602	1055	708	732	832	646	992	829	976	828	706	679	789	1129	697	776						
251	850	103	702	266	819	185	134	618	451	778	594	741	592	42	353	554	890	431	98	658					
430	847	526	699	364	816	472	520	592	406	753	594	737	589	620	441	551	890	459	539	243	422				
391	208	539	60	399	177	459	509	64	246	114	169	111	50	633	291	100	251	308	560	877	663	639			
679	1098	776	948	613	1067	721	745	842	658	1003	840	987	839	719	692	800	1141	708	803	71	675	256	890		
187	417	336	267	196	386	254	304	156	37	322	159	306	158	430	87	119	459	95	357	670	459	431	209	681	
287	543	394	394	230	514	338	388	283	105	449	287	433	285	478	204	246	586	221	406	641	496	402	335	652	127
124	475	272	327	132	444	192	242	217	101	382	219	365	217	365	24	179	518	40	293	657	396	419	267	668	65
50	583	188	433	26	552	118	167	322	190	488	325	472	325	282	84	285	625	143	201	617	291	378	375	628	171
195	488	341	253	201	465	259	309	164	122	403	240	385	238	433	92	200	539	53	362	724	443	486	288	737	85
502	931	599	771	436	890	544	594	668	481	826	663	810	662	540	515	623	963	531	612	169	497	79	713	182	504
283	702	382	554	217	671	325	375	449	262	609	446	591	444	320	296	404	745	312	393	383	279	147	494	396	287
375	274	539	126	399	246	459	509	71	246	180	172	203	85	633	291	92	317	308	560	877	642	639	92	890	209
24	623	124	475	90	594	42	93	365	250	503	367	514	365	217	126	327	667	179	145	691	227	452	415	702	213
274	876	126	726	270	845	208	158	615	456	781	618	765	616	134	378	564	918	436	105	572	92	334	668	583	464
465	134	615	14	473	106	533	583	138	320	40	243	172	124	707	364	163	177	543	634	952	716	713	74	964	283
309	734	267	581	243	696	349	299	477	292	636	472	633	472	283	332	433	791	340	246	427	235	188	522	438	316
190	791	69	641	232	760	124	74	531	417	696	533	679	531	60	293	493	832	345	80	832	93	517	583	845	459
68	575	214	425	93	544	132	182	317	201	481	319	480	317	308	77	279	618	106	235	691	317	452	367	702	164
224	481	332	332	169	451	277	327	222	42	388	225	370	224	445	142	185	525	158	345	630	435	393	274	642	66
97	675	93	526	69	646	79	103	423	254	581	419	565	417	187	177	378	718	233	105	671	195	431	467	684	264
56	541	206	393	66	512	124	175	285	167	448	285	431	283	299	43	245	584	100	227	657	309	419	333	668	130
269	868	121	720	283	850	203	151	605	494	774	612	758	610	27	370	572	911	422	132	736	69	647	660	897	457
541	58	689	90	549	55	607	658	217	396	37	319	124	200	782	440	238	101	396	710	1027	813	789	150	1038	357
428	184	576	35	436	143	494	544	90	282	90	206	138	87	670	327	126	227	343	597	913	699	676	37	926	245
13	591	161	443	53	562	79	130	335	227	497	335	481	333	254	93	295	634	150	182	654	264	415	383	665	180
206	393	356	245	214	362	274	324	134	61	299	137	282	135	448	105	97	436	113	375	692	457	454	185	705	24
283	317	431	167	291	287	349	399	58	137	224	60	206	58	523	182	19	361	198	452	768	533	531	109	781	100
312	303	460	156	320	430	379	68	167	211	98	224	85	554	211	47	348	229	481	799	584	560	113	810	129	
156	575	254	427	92	546	200	250	322	137	481	319	465	317	384	171	279	618	187	259	510	357	272	367	522	159
132	731	18	581	145	700	64	27	480	330	638	475	620	473	111	233	435	774	285	39	747	121	509	523	758	319

San's Tours and Car Rental
Lot 1, 34 Wilayah Shopping Centre
Tel: 03-292-2024

Sintat Thrifty Rent A Car
Lobby Floor, Holiday Inn on the Park
Tel: 03-124-8238

SMAS Rent A Car
Lot 12, UBN Office Tower,
Shangri-la Hotel Annexe,
Jln. Sultan Ismail
Tel: 03-230-7788

Toyota Rent A Car
Federal Hotel, Jln. Bukit Bintang
Tel: 03-243-8142

MOTORING ADVISORIES

An international driving licence is required by visitors who wish to drive in Malaysia. National driving licences are only acceptable upon endorsement by the Registrar of Motor Vehicles. Travel insurance must also be taken out.

From the causeway connecting Singapore and peninsular Malaysia, the main trunk road runs up the west coast to the Thai border. From this road, two main highways cross the peninsula to the east coast. In the north, the East-West Highway connects Butterworth with Kota Bharu, while in the central part of the peninsula, the Kuala Lumpur-Karak Highway cuts through the Main Range and joins a road leading to Kuantan on the east coast. In Sabah and Sarawak, motorways run along the coast connecting major towns. The distances between towns in kilometres is given in the chart below. Roads leading to more remote areas inland are often unpaved or rough, and a four-wheel drive is advisable for these routes.

Driving is on the left-hand side of the road. International traffic signs are used, along with a few local ones such as *"Awas"* meaning "caution", *"ikut kiri"* meaning "Keep left", *"kurangkan laju"* meaning "slow down", and *"jalan sehala"* meaning "one-way street" in the direction of the arrow. Where compass points are given, *"Utara"* is north, *"Selatan"* south, *"Timur"* east, and *"Barat"* west.

The speed limit in towns is 50 km/h. Outside towns, the familiar speed limit signs are displayed where limits have been imposed. The wearing of seat belts by drivers and front seat passengers is compulsory. Monsoon rains can cause hazards for motorists. Drive slowly and be prepared for delays on smaller roads as whole roads are sometimes washed away entirely.

For safety, local drivers have developed a few signals of their own. There are individual variations on these, so watch to see what the other motorists do. If the driver in front flashes his right indicator, he is signalling to you not to overtake. This is usually because of an oncoming vehicle or a bend in the road, or he himself might be about to overtake the vehicle in front of him. If he flashes the left indicator, this means to overtake with caution. A driver flashing his headlamps at you is claiming the right of way. At roundabouts or traffic circles, the driver on the right has the right of way.

Petrol is inexpensive and petrol stations are to be found in or on the fringes of towns. Very few of them

From \ To	Kuala Lipis	Kuala Lumpur	Kuala Pilah	Kuala Selangor	Kuala Terengganu	Kuantan	Lumut	Malacca	Mersing	Parit Buntar	Pekan	Pontian Kechil	Port Dickson	Raub	Segamat	Seremban	Singapore	Sungai Petani	Taiping	Tampin	Tanjung Malim	Tapah	Teluk Intan
Kuala Lumpur	180																						
Kuala Pilah	237	108																					
Kuala Selangor	211	68	175																				
Kuala Terengganu	475	491	451	560																			
Kuantan	258	274	232	341	219																		
Lumut	335	267	375	288	713	494																	
Malacca	311	148	74	219	525	308	415																
Mersing	501	401	296	469	406	187	668	246															
Parit Buntar	409	341	449	362	787	568	140	489	742														
Pekan	283	306	269	383	264	45	538	333	142	609													
Pontian Kechil	462	316	241	383	668	449	583	166	185	657	327												
Port Dickson	280	100	74	150	525	306	367	90	340	441	338	256											
Raub	63	119	174	187	465	246	274	248	440	348	262	401	219										
Segamat	301	200	95	269	507	288	402	97	200	541	312	161	153	238									
Seremban	246	66	40	134	491	274	333	82	333	407	306	248	34	185	134								
Singapore	514	393	309	460	570	351	660	245	161	734	311	87	335	452	214	327							
Sungai Petani	485	417	523	438	861	644	216	565	816	76	675	731	517	423	617	483	810						
Taiping	372	304	411	325	749	530	103	452	704	50	547	618	404	309	504	370	697	126					
Tampin	274	116	37	185	488	270	383	37	283	465	296	203	69	211	84	50	280	533	420				
Tanjung Malim	150	82	190	103	528	309	185	230	483	259	341	398	182	89	282	148	475	335	222	198			
Tapah	227	158	266	179	609	385	109	308	559	184	417	473	258	164	359	225	551	258	145	275	76		
Teluk Intan	256	188	295	97	633	415	92	336	588	171	441	502	288	195	388	254	581	246	132	304	108	39	
Temerloh	182	147	106	214	344	127	367	180	362	441	155	324	180	121	161	147	375	517	404	143	182	259	288
Yong Pang	375	256	182	324	581	362	523	106	143	597	285	87	196	314	74	190	138	673	559	145	338	414	604

operate 24 hours (24 *jam*), so be sure to fill up your tank by 6 or 7 p.m. if you intend to drive at night.

The Automobile Association of Malaysia (AAM) is the national motoring organisation and has offices in most states. Tourists who are members of motoring associations affiliated to AAM are given free reciprocal membership. The head office is located at: 22/23 The Arcade, Hotel Equatorial, Jln. Sultan Ismail, KL, Tel: 03-242-0042.

HITCHHIKING

Hitchhiking is fairly common in Malaysia, and Malaysian students and budget travellers use this form of transport. Malaysians are helpful people, and will sometimes offer to take you where you want to go. This is another good way of getting to know the Malaysians.

WHERE TO STAY

Accommodation in Malaysia encompasses many different styles. You can choose anything, from youth hostel and crash pads to top-class international hotels with saunas, jacuzzis and tennis courts. To sample all of Malaysia, it may be well worth your while to try out accommodation from several different categories. The smaller and more homely establishments will be more likely to bring you closer to the Malaysians.

Most small Malaysian towns, in any case, do not offer the cosmopolitan facilities of a worldwide hotel chain; instead, they provide the personal touch, simplicity and cleanliness of a wayside inn. A typical urban street is dotted with small budget hotels renting simply furnished rooms for between M$10 and M$40 (depending on whether the room has air-conditioning or a simple ceiling fan).

If you intend to visit one of Malaysia's national parks, it is necessary to go to the national park's office in the nearest town in order to book accommodation. In some cases, a deposit must be paid towards the accommodation and permit.

The following list of hotels is by no means exhaustive, but will give the visitor some idea of what is available. A cross-section of prices is given wherever possible. Bear in mind that the prices given here were correct at the time of going to print, and should therefore be used as a guide only.

PENINSULAR MALAYSIA

KUALA LUMPUR
(Federal Territory)

Apollo Hotel
106-110 Jln. Bukit Bintang
Tel: 03-242-8133
42 rooms, air-conditioned; from $51 to $133

City Hotel
366 Jln. Raja Laut
Tel: 03-441-4466
90 rooms, air-conditioned, centre of town, 30 minutes from rail terminal, room service, telephone, music; from $42 to $63

Coliseum
100 Jln. Tun Perak
Common bath facilities, famous old planters' restaurant and cafe; from $13 to $19

Colonial
43 Jln. Sultan
Air-conditioned; from $17 to $25

Cylinman
110 Jln. Raja Laut
Air-conditioned, hot water; from $20 to $30

Dashrun Hotel
285 Jln. Tuanku Abdul Rahman
Tel: 03-292-9314
41 rooms, air-conditioned; from $45 to $65

Federal Hotel
35 Jln. Bukit Bintang
Tel: 03-248-9166
450 rooms, air-conditioned, revolving lounge, 3 dining rooms serving Western and Chinese cuisine, 5 bars, 2 banquet halls, 6 international rooms, 2 supperclubs with international shows nightly, 24-hour coffeehouse, swimming pool, bowling alley (18

lane), 15 shops, sauna, massage and beauty parlour, barber's shop, air-conditioned limousine service; rooms from $125 to $1000

Fortuna Hotel
87 Jln. Berangan
Tel: 03-241-9111
100 rooms, bar, restaurant, nightclub, TV on request, coffeehouse, grill; from $95 to $140

Furama Hotel
Kompleks Selangor, Jln. Sultan
Tel: 03-230-1777
100 rooms, health centre, coffeehouse, grill; from $60 to $300

Grand Central
Jln. Putra/Jln. Raja Laut
Tel: 03-441-3021
142 rooms, coffeehouse, health centre; from $55 to $121

Grand Pacific Hotel
Jln. Tun Ismail/Jln. Ipoh
Tel: 03-442-2177
110 rooms, telephone, coffeehouse, nightclub, health centre, colour TV available on request; from $70 to $102

Holiday Inn City Centre
Jln. Raja Laut
Tel: 03-293-9233
30 minutes from airport, 15 minutes from railway terminal, 45 minutes from seaport, 5 minutes from downtown. 584 rooms, air-conditioned, Melaka Grill (local and Western), Planters' Inn (24-hour), Chinese restaurant, The Paddock rooftop supperclub, Gazebo with nightly barbecue and movie theatre. Tin Mine Disco, 2 bars, swimming pool, squash courts, steam bath, sauna, massage, beauty and barber shops, 86 shops, travel and airline agencies. Nightly cultural shows with Malay dinner; from $95 to $185

Holiday Inn on the Park
Jln. Pinang
Tel: 03-248-1066
32 km from airport, 8 km from railway station, 48 km from seaport. 200 rooms, Malay and Western restaurants, beauty and barber shops, car rental; from $120 to $185

Hotel Equatorial
Jln. Sultan Ismail
Tel: 03-261-7777
300 rooms, 3 speciality restaurants, 2 bar lounges, 24-hour coffeehouse, swimming pool, shopping arcade, convention and conference facilities; from $145 to $180

Hotel Grand Continental
Jln. Belia/Jln. Raja Laut
Tel: 03-293-9333
328 rooms, Chinese restaurant, coffeehouse, poolside barbecue, 2 bars, swimming pool, health centre, snooker club, shops, travel agent, beauty and barber shops; from $37.50 to $95

Hotel Imperial
76/78/80 Jln. Hicks
Tel: 03-242-2377
90 rooms from $56 to $110

Hotel Malaya
Jln. Hang Lekir
Tel: 03-232-7722
Air-conditioned, private baths, Chinese dining room, nightclub, coffeehouse, lounge bar, health club, disco; from $79 to $220

KL Hilton
Jln. Sultan Ismail
Tel: 03-242-2122
589 rooms, full room facilities and services, restaurants, grill, coffeehouse, bar and cocktail lounge, swimming pool, tennis, squash, health centre, disco, night club, shops, beauty salon, business centre, car rental; from $160 to $450

KL International
Jln. Raja Muda
Tel: 03-292-9133
90 rooms, room facilities and services, restaurant, grill, coffeehouse, bar and cocktail lounge, health centre, business centre; from $72 to $250

KL Mandarin
2-8 Jln. Sultan
Tel: 03-230-3000
150 rooms, 24-hour room service, TV, coffeehouse, Chinese restaurant, bar lounge, beauty and barber shops, health centre, travel service; from $78 to $210

KL Station Hotel
Bangunan Stesen Keretapi, Jln. Sultan Hishamuddin
Tel: 03-274-7433
30 rooms, 70 years old and a regular charmer! Victorian bathtubs, balcony, air-conditioned, restaurant, pub, coffeehouse, hawkers' corner; from $30 to $40

KL Youth Hostel
9 Jln. Vethavam, Batu 3¾, Jln. Ipoh
Tel: 626-0872

Lodge
Jln. Sultan Ismail
Tel: 03-242-0122
50 rooms, full room facilities and services, restaurants; from $88 to $195

Malaysia Hotel
67-71 Jln. Bukit Bintang
Tel: 03-242-8033
30 minutes from airport, 10 minutes from railway terminal, centrally located. 60 rooms, air-conditioned, steak house, Continental and Chinese restaurant, cocktail lounge, room service; from $75 to $140

Merlin Hotel
Jln. Sultan Ismail
Tel: 03-248-0033
32 km from airport, 10 minutes from railway terminal, 45 minutes from seaport, located in residential area, 5 minutes walk from commercial and shopping centres. 700 rooms, full room facilities and services, 5 restaurants, disco, 24-hour coffeehouse, 2 bars, 2 nightclubs, swimming pool, bowling alley, tennis and squash, beauty and barber shops, shopping arcade, travel offices, car rental; from $135 to $650

Ming Court Hotel Kuala Lumpur
Jln. Ampang
Tel: 03-261-8888
447 rooms, full room facilities and services, restaurants, coffeehouse, recreation, swimming pool, shops; from $160 to $229

Miramar Hotel
Jln. Maharajalela
Tel: 03-248-9122
88 rooms, air-conditioned, restaurant, grill, coffeehouse, health centre, beauty salon, car rental, room service; from $88 to $195

Oriental Kuala Lumpur
126 Jln. Bukit Bintang
Tel: 03-248-9500
Centrally located. 300 rooms, full room facilities and services, restaurants, coffeehouse, swimming pool, health centre and sports facilities, shops, beauty and barber shops, travel service; from $150 to $600

Palace Hotel
46-1 Jln. Masjid India
Tel: 03-298-6122
64 rooms, air-conditioned; from $39 to $43

Pan Pacific Kuala Lumpur
Jln. Putra
Tel: 03-442-5555
571 rooms, full room facilities and services, restaurants, grill, 24-hour coffeehouse, cocktail lounge, bar, swimming pool, gymnasium, tennis, squash, health centre, water sports, disco, beauty and barber shops, business centre, car rental; from $150 to $600

Plaza Hotel
Jln. Raja Laut
Tel: 03-298-2255
160 rooms, air-conditioned, restaurants, health club, shops; from $50 to $130

Prince Hotel
Jln. Imbi
Tel: 03-243-8388
300 rooms, full room facilities and services, restaurant, coffeehouse, bar, swimming pool, health centre, disco, shops, beauty salon, car rental; from $145 to $205

Puduraya Hotel
4th Floor Puduraya Station, Jln. Pudu
Tel: 03-232-1000
200 rooms, restaurants, coffeehouse, health centre; from $145 to $205

Regent of Kuala Lumpur
Jln. Sultan Ismail
Tel: 03-242-5588
30 minutes from airport, 10 minutes from railway, ½ hour from seaport, centrally located. 400 rooms, full room facilities, Chinese and Malay restaurants, grill, cocktail lounge, nightclub, disco, swimming pool, shopping arcade, sauna and steambaths, massage and beauty shops, medical and secretarial services; from $160 to $210

Shangri-La Hotel
Jln. Sultan Ismail
Tel: 03-232-2388
722 rooms, full room facilities and services, restaurants, grill, coffeehouse, bar, cocktail lounge, swimming pool, tennis, squash, health centre, disco, beauty salon, business centre, car rental; from $160 to $200

Shiraz Hotel
1 & 3 Jln. Medan Tuanku
Tel: 03-292-0159
56 rooms, air-conditioned, bar, restaurant, TV and fridge for hire; from $35 to $110

South-East Asia Hotel
69 Jln. Haji Hussein,
off Jln. Tuanku Abdul Rahman
Tel: 03-292-6077
30 minutes from airport, 10 minutes from rail terminal, 45 minutes from seaport. 204 rooms, Chinese and Muslim restaurants, bar, coffeehouse, health centre, movie theatre, shopping arcade; from $76 to $190

Sungei Wang Hotel
74-76 Jln. Bukit Bintang
Tel: 03-248-5255
60 rooms, room facilities and services, restaurant, coffeehouse, bar; from $84 to $180

Wisma Belia
40 Jln. Lornie
Tel: 03-232-6803
30 minutes from airport, 5 minutes from rail terminal. 115 rooms, restaurant, shops, badminton; from $20 to $40

YMCA of Kuala Lumpur
Jln. Brickfields
Tel: 03-274-1439
60 dormitories and rooms; from $10 to $50

SELANGOR

Merlin Subang
Jln. 12/1 Subang Jaya
Tel: 03-733-5211
162 rooms from $140 to $240

Mimaland
11th Mile Jln. Gombak
Tel: 03-232-9813
Lodge, $13 per person; motel rooms, $89 per room; bagan cottages, $150 per cottage.

Subang Airport Hotel
Kompleks Airtel Fima
Tel: 03-774-6122
162 rooms from $95 to $135

Subang View Hotel
Subang Jaya
Tel: 03-535211
162 rooms, restaurants, bars, swimming pool, gymnasium, putting green

• **Petaling Jaya**

Dayang Hotel
Jln. Barat
Tel: 03-755-5011
54 rooms from $125 to $250

Hyatt Saujana Hotel and Country Club
Subang International Airport Highway
Tel: 03-746-1188
230 rooms from $120 to $1005

Petaling Jaya Hilton
Jln. Barat
Tel: 03-755-9122
398 rooms from $160 to $500

Shah's Village Hotel
3 & 5 Lorong Sultan
Tel: 03-756-9322
44 rooms from $80

NEGRI SEMBILAN

• **Seremban**

Carlton Hotel
47 Jln. Tuan Sheikh
Tel: 06-725336
2 hours from airport, 10 minutes from railway terminal, 2½ hours from seaport, downtown. 38 rooms, air-conditioned, dining room, bar, entainment on request, 1 shop; from $20 to $50

Hotel Tasik Sdn. Bhd.
Jln. Telamu
Tel: 06-730994
41 rooms from $80 to $100

International New Hotel
126 Jln. Veloo
Tel: 06-714957
22 rooms from $14 to $25

Rest House Bahau
Jln. Taman Bunga, Jempul Bahau
Tel: 06-843322

Ria Hotel
Jln. Telamu
Tel: 06-287744
From $85 to $95

Ruby Hotel
39 Jln. Leman
Tel: 06-75201
34 rooms from $20

Tong Fong Hotel
Birch Road
Tel: 06-73022
From $12

• **Port Dickson**

Blue Lagoon Village
16 km south of Port Dickson; has 6 beach cottages

Holiday Inn Port Dickson
9th Milestone

Lido Hotel
8th Mile Telok Kempang
Tel: 06-405273
22 rooms from $25 to $45

Milo Hotel
22-24 Wilkonson Street
Tel: 06-723451
25 rooms from $18 to $24

Ming Court Beach Hotel
11 km Jln. Pantai
Tel: 06-405244
165 rooms from $50 to $350

Pantai Dickson Resort
Batu 12, Jln. Pantai
Tel: 06-405473
200 bungalows; from $180 to $210

Pantai Motel
9th Mile
Tel: 06-405265
22 rooms, bar, restaurant, beach location; from $20 to $35

Port Dickson International Youth Hostel
Batu 3⅓, Jln. Pantai

Sea View Hotel
841 Batu 1, Jln. Pantai
Tel: 06-471818
20 rooms from $25 to $35

Si Rusa Inn
Batu 7, Jln. Pantai
Tel: 06-405233
3¼ hours from Subang Airport, 11 km from Port Dickson, beach location. 160 rooms, air-conditioned chalets and rooms, dining room, cocktail lounge, dance band Saturday evenings, Sunday luncheon music, deep sea and inshore fishing boats, sailboats, ski boats, local golf club, laundry service, babysitting; from $50 to $350

Sunshine Rotary Club
3¼ miles from Port Dickson; on beach
Rooms from $7 per person

MELAKA STATE

• **Melaka**

Admiral Hotel
Jln. Mata Kuching
Tel: 06-226822
36 rooms from $50 to $120

Cathay Hotel
100-105 Jln. Munshi Abdullah
Tel: 06-223744
Rooms from $14

Cheng Hoe Hotel
26 Jln. Tokong
Tel: 06-222-6102
Rooms with and without air-conditioning; from $10 to $21

City Bayview Hotel
Jln. Bendahara
Tel: 06-239888
182 rooms from $80 to $200

Hotel Midtown Melaka
20 Jln. Tun Sri Lanang
Tel: 06-240088
84 rooms from $68 to $98

Lotus Inn
Jln. Semabok
Tel: 06-227011
30 rooms, air-conditioned, coffeehouse;
from $28 to $44

Malacca Hotel
27A Jln. Munshi Abdullah
Tel: 06-222325
From $20

Malacca Straits Inn
37A Jln. Bandar Hilir
Tel: 06-21211
45 rooms, air-conditioned, 24-hour coffeehouse, La Famosa Grill, Straits Club, disco,
beer garden; from $95

Merlin Inn
Jln. Munshi Abdullah
Tel: 06-240777
243 rooms from $85 to $400

Old City Hostel
332 Jln. Kilang
From $2.50 to $15

Palace Hotel
201 Jln. Munshi
Tel: 06-225329
48 rooms, air-conditioned, dining room,
cocktail bar; from $45 to $68

Plaza Inn
Jln. Munshi Abdullah
Tel: 06-240888
142 room from $100 to $140

Ramada Renaissance
Jln. Bendahara
Tel: 06-248888
295 rooms, air-conditioned, Chinese restaurant, grill, Ramada Club, squash courts,
poolside bar, disco; from $95 to $160

Regal Hotel
66 Jln. Munshi Abdullah
Tel: 06-222433
30 rooms, air-conditioned, restaurant, bar;
from $36 to $51

Sentosa Hotel
Jln. Tun Razak
Tel: 06-228222
30 rooms, air-conditioned; from $35 to $52

Tan Kim Hock Hostel
153 Jln. Laksamana
Tel: 06-315322
40 rooms from $75 to $120

Wisma Hotel
114A Jln. Bendahara
Tel: 06-228311
39 rooms, air-conditioned, coffeehouse;
from $30 to $70

• **Tanjong Keling**

Chalet El-Kundor
Pantai Kundor
Tel: 06-511015
Bungalows with living room, bedroom,
kitchen, bathroom, hot water, verandah and
stereo; from $35

**Melaka Beach Bungalows and
Youth Hostel**
7379C Spring Gardens
Tel: 06-512935
Dormitories and air-conditioned rooms;
from $3.50 to $35

Shah's Beach Motel
6th Mile Tanjong Keling
Tel: 06-226202
50 chalets, air-conditioned; from $50 to $85

Westernhay Hotel
114A Jln. Bendahara
Tel: 06-28311
39 rooms, air-conditioned coffeehouse;
from $30 to $60

Yashica Traveller Hostel
Tanjong Keling
Rooms from $6 to $10

• **Ayer Keroh**

Ayer Keroh Country Resort
Tel: 06-32521
50 motel rooms at $46; and 15 chalets at $70

Malacca Village Resort
Tel: 06-323600
147 rooms from $140 to $800

• Butterworth

Ambassadress Hotel
4425 Jln. Bagan Luar, 12200 Butterworth
Tel: 04-342788
27 rooms from $22 to $37

Apollo Hotel
4475 Jln. Kampung Benggali,
12200 Butterworth
Tel: 04-342955
14 rooms from $21 to $31

Capital Hotel
3838 Jln. Bagan Luar, 12200 Butterworth
Tel: 04-344822
10 rooms from $8 to $15

City Hotel
4591 Jln. Chain Ferry
Tel: 04-340311
12 rooms from $20 to $30

Federal Hotel
4293-4294 Kg. Benggali
Tel: 04-341911
10 rooms from $13 to $15

Government Rest House
Bukit Mertajam, 229 Jln. Kulim
Tel: BM-0122

Hotel Kuala Lumpur
4448 Lorong Bagan Luar Satu,
12200 Butterworth
Tel: 04-345166
45 rooms from $36 to $52

Merlin Inn Butterworth
4802 Jln. Bagan Luar
Tel: 04-343322
87 rooms, restaurant, bar, swimming pool,
shops; from $60 to $80

Metro Hotel
4226 Kg. Benggali, 12200 Butterworth
Tel: 04-343833
16 rooms from $18 to $25

Paris Hotel
4382 2nd Floor, Jln. Bagan Luar
Tel: 04-344822
25 rooms from $26 to $30

Travel Lodge
No. 1 Lorong Bagan Luar
Tel: 04-348899
50 rooms from $50 to $110

• Georgetown

Ambassador Hotel
55 Penang Road, 10000 Penang
Tel: 04-24101
78 rooms, bar restaurant, TV on request, 24-
hour coffeehouse; from $75 to $85

Asrama Belia Youth Hostel
Lebuh Farquhar, next to E & O Hotel
Dormitories at $4.50

Bellevue Penang Hill Hotel
11300 Penang
Tel: 04-892256
12 rooms, on Penang Hill overlooking town,
old-fashioned elegance, dining room, cocktail lounge; from $60 to $80

Cathay Hotel
15 Lebuh Leith, 10200 Penang
Tel: 04-626271
40 rooms, private bathroom, old-fashioned
elegance, health centre; from $25 to $35

City Bayview Hotel
25A Lebuh Farquhar, 10200 Penang
Tel: 04-368722
160 rooms, full room facilities, coffeehouse,
lounge bar, business centre, swimming pool,
tennis, squash, car rental; from $90 to $265

Eastern and Oriental Hotel
10 Lebuh Farquhar, 10200 Penang
Tel: 04-375322
100 rooms, old-fashioned elegance, swimming pool, waterfront views, 1885 grill, bar,
E & O ballroom with twice weekly ballroom
dancing and buffet, one of Somerset Maugham's favourite hotels; from $125 to $185

Eng Aun Hotel
389 Lebuh Chulia
Tel: 04-372333
40 rooms from $9 to $15

Gallant Hotel
6 Transfer Road, 10050 Penang
Tel: 04-379584
64 rooms, health centre; from $35 to $49

Garden Inn
41 Anson Road, 10400 Penang
Tel: 04-363655
60 rooms, air-conditioned, restaurant, coffeehouse, car rental; from $72 to $160

Hotel Central
404 Penang Road
Tel: 04-21432
20 minutes from airport, 10 minutes from rail terminal and seaport, free airport transfer service, centrally located. 140 rooms, air-conditioned, Chinese restaurant, 24-hour coffeehouse, lounge, bar, nightclub, bank, barber shop, health centre; from $45 to $50

Hotel Continental
5 Penang Road, 10000 Penang
Tel: 04-26381
116 rooms, bar restaurant, nightclub; from $66 to $180

Hotel Embassy
12 Jln. Burma
Tel: 04-23145
27 rooms, air-conditioned, 24-hour room service, telephone, hot water, bath/shower, coffeehouse; from $23 to $33

Hotel Equatorial Penang
Close to Penang Bridge, hill location
5 minutes from the airport. 460 rooms, Chinese, Japanese and French restaurants, coffeehouse, lounge and terrace bar, 18-hole golf course, tennis, squash, gymnasium and jogging tracks

Hotel Fortuna
406 Penang Road, 11600 Penang
Tel: 04-24301
32 rooms, air-conditioned, telephone, piped-in music, hot water, bath/shower, health centre; from $40 to $72

Hotel Golden City
12 Kinta Lane, 10400 Penang
Tel: 04-27281
124 rooms from $41 to $57

Hotel Macalist
7 Penang Road, 10000 Penang
Tel: 04-29401
96 rooms, air-conditioned, 24-hour room service, telephone, colour TV, hot water, bath/shower; from $40 to $65

Hotel Malaysia
7 Penang Road, 10000 Penang
Tel: 04-363311
126 rooms, coffeehouse, health centre, nightclub, disco, bar; from $52 to $72

Hotel Metropole
46 Northam Road
Tel: 04-23317
24 rooms, restaurant; from $26 to $30

Hotel Mingood
164 Argyle Road, 10050 Penang
Tel: 04-373375
52 rooms, air-conditioned, telephone, piped-in music, hot water, bath/shower, restaurant; from $34 to $60

Hotel Pathe
23 Lebuh Light, 10200 Penang
Tel: 04-620195
14 rooms, air-conditioned, telephone, baby cots, hot water, shower; from $26 to $33

Hotel Waldorf
13 Lebuh Leith, 10200 Penang
Tel: 04-26141
57 rooms, air-conditioned, coffeehouse, telephone, room service; from $30 to $42

Hotel Waterfall
160 Jln. Utama
Tel: 04-27221
35 rooms, coffeehouse, restaurant, bar; from $41 to $53

Merlin Inn
126 Jln. Burma, 10050 Penang
Tel: 04-376166
295 rooms, fully air-conditioned, restaurant, grill, coffeehouse, bars, swimming pool, health centre, indoor games, disco, shops, beauty salon, business centre, tourist information, car rental; from $95 to $800

Ming Court Hotel
202A MacAlister Road
Tel: 04-26131
110 rooms, full room facilities, restaurant, coffeehouse, bar; from $110 to $130

New China Hotel
Lebuh Leith
From $5.50 to $15

Oriental Hotel
105 Penang Road
Tel: 04-242116
94 rooms, air-conditioned, restaurant, cocktail lounge, shops; from $59 to $66

Paramount Hotel
48F Northam Road
Tel: 04-363649
33 rooms, air-conditioned, dining room, bar, shops; from $23 to $40

Peking Hotel
50A Penang Road, 10000 Penang
Tel: 04-366191
73 rooms, air-conditioned, restaurant; from $28 to $35

Penang Youth Hostel
Lebuh Farquhar
Tel: 04-60553

Shangri-La Inn Penang
Jln. Magazine, 10300 Penang
Tel: 04-622622
442 rooms, full room facilities, coffeehouse, Chinese restaurant, lobby lounge, poolside bar, disco, business centre, health club, swimming pool, beauty salon, travel office, tours, car rental; from $115 to $1260

Swiss Hotel
31F Lebuh Chulia, 10200 Penang
Tel: 04-620133
34 rooms, telephone, refrigerator, hot water, shower; from $11 to $15

Town House Hotel
70 Penang Road
Tel: 04-362211
45 rooms, air-conditioned, 24-hour coffeehouse, restaurant, bar, cocktail lounge, beauty salon; from $50 to $140

Tye Ann Hotel
282 Lebuh Chulia
10 rooms, restaurant downstairs, bicycles for hire; from $4.50 to $11

United Hotel
101 Jln. MacAlister
Tel: 04-21361
118 rooms, air-conditioned, restaurant, bar, 24-hour coffeehouse, health centre; from $40 to $50

YMCA of Penang
Jln. MacAlister
Tel: 04-366-2211
35 rooms, some with air-conditioning, dormitories, rooms with shower and toilet, $1 membership charge; from $7 to $29

YWCA Penang
8A Green Lane
Women only; dormitories and rooms from $7 to $26

BEACH HOTELS IN PENANG

Bayview Beach Hotel
Batu Ferringhi, 11100 Penang
Tel: 04-811311
74 rooms, restaurant, coffeehouse, swimming pool, bar, tennis; from $80 to $170

Casuarina Beach Hotel
Batu Ferringhi, 11100 Penang
Tel: 04-811711
175 rooms, boating, tennis, water sports, restaurant; from $140 to $380

Ferringhi Beach Hotel
12.5 km Batu Ferringhi Road, 11100 Penang
Tel: 04-805999
136 rooms, full room facilities and services, restaurant, grill, coffeehouse, bar, swimming pool, disco, shops, travel centre, beauty salon; from $130 to $180

Golden Sands Hotel
Batu Ferringhi Beach
Tel: 04-811911
310 rooms, full room facilities, sea views, restaurants, barbecues, swimming pool, sea sports, trekking, tennis; from $140 to $400

Holiday Inn Penang
Batu Ferringhi Beach
Tel: 04-811601
152 rooms, full room facilities and services, 24-hour coffeehouse, Baron's Table Steakhouse, bar, rock garden, swimming pool, water sports, shops, travel service; from $130 to $360

Lone Pine Hotel
97 Batu Ferringhi
Tel: 04-811511
54 rooms, air-conditioned, cocktail lounge, fishing, tennis; from $45 to $65

Motel Sri Pantai
516G Jln. Hashim, Tanjong Bungah
Tel: 04-895566
21 rooms, water-skiing; from $70 to $80

Orchid Hotel
Tanjong Bungah
Tel: 04-803333
323 rooms, full room facilities, 24-hour coffeehouse, Continental restaurant, 5 bars, disco, business centre, swimming pool, private beach, health club, jacuzzi, sauna, gymnasium, squash, tennis, arrangements for golf and sailing, shops, beauty salon, watersports, travel service, tours, car rental; from $125 to $1800

Palm Beach Hotel
105A Batu Ferringhi
Tel: 04-811833
145 rooms, full room facilities and services, restaurants, bars, swimming pool, terrace, water sports, tennis; from $90 to $140

Rasa Sayang Hotel
Batu Ferringhi Beach
Tel: 04-811811
320 rooms, full room facilities and services, Western, Chinese and Japanese restaurants, swimming pool, tennis, squash, croquet, putting green, water sports, health centre, shops; from $130 to $2200

White House Hotel
Batu Ferringhi
Tel: 04-23485
Rooms with bathroom, restaurant; from $15

PERAK

• Ipoh

City Hotel
79 Chamberlin Road, 30250 Ipoh
Tel: 05-512911
67 rooms, air-conditioned; from $26 to $52

Excelsior Hotel
Clarke Street, 30300 Ipoh
Tel: 05-536666
133 rooms, air-conditioned, bath/shower, mini-bar, TV, video, restaurant, coffeehouse, bar, disco, travel service, car rental; from $118 to $280

Hollywood Hotel
72-76 Chamberlin Road, 30300 Ipoh
Tel: 05-515322
38 rooms, shower, laundry; from $24 to $34

Hotel Eastern
118 Jln. Sultan Idris Shah
Tel: 05-543936
30 rooms, coffeehouse, Chinese restaurant; from $69 to $95

Hotel Fairmont
10 Kampar Road, 30250 Ipoh
Tel: 05-511100
58 rooms, coffeehouse; from $45 to $52

Hotel French
60-62 Jln. Raja Ikram
Tel: 05-513455
40 rooms from $69 to $100

Hotel Mikado
86/88 Jln. Yang Kalsom, 30250 Ipoh
Tel: 05-515855
44 rooms, air-conditioned, bath/shower, video, TV, business centre; from $65 to $105

Lotte Hotel
97 Jln. Raja Ikram, 30300 Ipoh
Tel: 05-542215
30 rooms, air-conditioned; from $65 to $100

Merlin Hotel
92-98 Clare Street, 30300 Ipoh
Tel: 05-541351
35 rooms from $28 to $50

New International Hotel
23-25 Jln. Toh Puan Chah
Tel: 05-512699
29 rooms from $27 to $35

Royal Casuarina
24 Jln. Gopeng, 30250 Ipoh
Tel: 05-505555
217 rooms, full room facilities, Italian restaurant, coffeehouse, cocktail lounge, disco, beauty shop, health centre, sauna, spa, pool, car rental; from $130 to $800

Station Hotel
Club Road, 30000 Ipoh
Tel: 05-512588
34 rooms, air-conditioned, old-fashioned elegance, restaurant, bar; from $40 to $300

Tambun Inn
91 Tambun Road, 30350 Ipoh
Tel: 05-552211
100 rooms, full room facilities, restaurant, coffeehouse, bar, heath centre, disco, travel service, car rental; from $75 to $320

Winner Hotel
32-38 Jln. Ali Pitchay, 30250 Ipoh
Tel: 05-515177
54 rooms from $28 to $79

YWCA Ipoh
211 Jln. Raja Musa Aziz
Tel: 05-540809
Dormitories and rooms from $7 to $36 (air-conditioned rooms)

• **Lumut**

Government Rest House
Lumut
Tel: 05-935938
7 rooms, museum; from $12 to $15

Lumut Country Resort
331 Jln. Titi Panjang, 32200 Lumut
Tel: 05-935009
44 rooms, air-conditioned, room service, restaurants, bars, swimming pool, disco, shops; from $70 to $80

Wilderness Adventure Camp
Teluk Batik, 32200 Lumut, Perak
Tel: 05-93559 (Lumut) or 03-930-0325 (Kuala Lumpur)
$35 per day for accommodation, food and forest activities

• **Sitiawan**

Hotel Mutiara
1 Taman Intan, Jln. Hj. Mohd. Ali, 32000 Sitiawan
Tel: 05-914904
12 rooms from $21 to $32

• **Pangkor Island**

Beach Huts Hotel
Pantai Pasir Bogak
Tel: 05-939159
40 rooms, air-conditioned, restaurant, bar, water sports, boat trips, car and bicycle rental; from $30 to $80

Government Rest House
Pasir Bogak
Tel: 05-951236
2 chalets, 1 longhouse; from $15

Mini Camp & Youth Hostel
Pasir Bogak
Tel: 05-939164

Pangkor Anchor
Pasir Bogak coconut huts, garden, breakfast, restaurant next door; from $11.50 to $16

Pan Pacific Pangkor
Telok Belanga
Tel: 05-939091
161 traditional style rooms and chalets, full room facilities and services, swimming pool with sunken bar, tennis, 9-hole golf course, hiking treks, jogging paths, games room, water sports, boat trips, restaurants, bars, barbecue on beach, disco, private beach; from $200 to $350

Pansea Resort
Pulau Pangkor Laut
Tel: 05-951372 (Pangkor Laur) or 03-242-1589 (Kuala Lumpur)
94 rooms, full room facilities, water sports, boat trips, private beaches; from $70 to $100

Sam Khoo's Mini Camp
Pasir Bogak
Tel: 05-951164
Coconut huts from $4 to $5 per person

Sea View Hotel
Pasir Bogak
Tel: 05-951605
37 rooms, some air-conditioned, chalets, bar, lounge, restaurant, water sports, boat trips; from $55 to $75

• **Taiping**

Government Rest House
1 Jln. Residensi Taman Tasik
Tel: 05-822044
12 rooms, overlooking Taiping Lake Gardens; from $26 to $47

Lake View Hotel
Taiping
Tel: 05-822911
From $15

Old Government Rest House
Taiping Town
From $12

• Kampar

Oriental Hotel
9 Jln. Kuala Dipang
Tel: 05-651288
15 rooms from $13 to $17

• Kuala Kangsar

Double Lion Hotel
74 Jln. Kangsar
From $8

Government Rest House
Tel: 05-851699
16 rooms, air-conditioned; from $17.50

• Maxwell Hill (Bukit Larut)

Maxwell Hill Bungalows
Tel: 05-886241
8 bungalows from $18

• Telok Intan

Government Rest House
868 Jln. Daly
Tel: 05-611724
17 rooms from $16 to $32

• Upper Perak

Government Rest House
Jln. Haji Meor
Tel: 05-891086 GRIK
16 rooms from $23 to $36

Government Rest House
JKR 548 Jln. Pejabat Pos, Pengkalan Ulu
17 rooms from $13 to $35

• Tapah

Bunga Raya Hotel
Main Road, Tapah
Tel: 05-641436
12 rooms from $11 to $22

Government Rest House
Tapah
From $4

Rumah Rekat Rest House
Selim River (outside Tapah)
Fan, bedding, towels and soap, mosquito
coils, bath; from $4 to $6

KEDAH

• Alor Setar

Government Rest House
75 Pumpong
Tel: 04-722422
15 rooms from $12 to $24

Hotel Putra Jaya
250B Jln. Putera
Tel: 04-730344
62 rooms, air-conditioned; from $24 to $40

Kedah Merlin Inn
Lot 134, Jln. Sultan Badlishah
Tel: 04-735917
130 rooms, full room facilities and services,
restaurant, coffeehouse, bar, disco, business
centre, car rental; from $105 to $360

Mahawangsa Hotel
449 Jln. Raja
Tel: 04-721835
54 rooms, full room facilities and services,
restaurant; from $32 to $80

Station Hotel
74 Jln. Langgar
Tel: 04-723855
53 rooms from $14 to $20

• Gunung Jerai

Gunung Jerai
c/o 427 Jln. Kolam Air, Sungai Petani
12 rooms from $50 to $103

• Pulau Langkawi

Hotel Asia
1A Jln. Persiaran Putra, Kuah
Tel: 04-788216
15 rooms from $21 to $50

Hotel Langkawi
Kuah
Tel: 04-788248
13 rooms, from $12 to $40

Langkawi Island Resort
Pantai Dato Syed Omar, Kuah
Tel: 04-788209
220 rooms, water sports; from $95 to $800

Mutiara Beach Hotel
Tanjong Rhu Beach
Tel: 04-788488
Beach location, 68 rooms; from $70 to $120

Pelangi Beach Resort
Pantai Cenang
Tel: 04-789799
300 traditional style bungalows and chalets, full room facilities, restaurants, sunken bar, swimming pools, games room, gymnasium, sauna, conference facilities (Queen Elizabeth stayed here in 1989 after the CHOGM meeting in KL), disco, water sports, snorkelling and diving trips, island trips, tours, jeeps (four-wheel drive) for hire, transport to town and airport; from $130 to $800

Sandy Beach Motel
Pantai Cenang
20 chalets from $36 to $46

Semarak Resort
Pantai Cenang
Tel: 04-7173650
32 chalets, air-conditioned, traditional open-air restaurant on beach, barbecues, transport to town; from $44 to $180

PERLIS

• **Kangar**

Federal Hotel
104A & B Jln. Kangar
Tel: 04-766288
35 rooms, air-conditioned, bath, room-service, restaurant; from $35 to $50

Hotel Ban Cheong
76A Main Road
Tel: 04-761184
22 rooms, air-conditioned, hot water, restaurant; from $10 to $21

Hotel Malaysia
67 Jln. Jubi Perak
Tel: 04-761366
26 rooms, air-conditioned, telephone, TV, hot water, shower; from $20 to $33

Sri Perlis Inn
Jln. Kangar
Tel: 04-767266
50 rooms, full room facilities, restaurant, coffeehouse, shops; from $49 to $103

• **Kuala Perlis**

Soon Hin Hotel
Opposite taxi stand
Rooms from $10

KELANTAN

• **Kota Bharu**

Berling Hotel
826 Jln. Temenggong Petra Semerak
Tel: 09-785255
37 rooms, air-conditioned; from $14 to $50

Ideal Traveller House
Jln. Padang Garong
Dormitories and rooms with breakfast; from $4 to $10

Indah Hotel
236A Jln. Tengku Besar
Tel: 09-785081
44 rooms, air-conditioned, restaurant; from $48 to $80

Irama Bahru Hotel
3180A Jln. Sultan Ibrahim
Tel: 09-782722
20 rooms, air-conditioned, restaurant, bar; from $35 to $60

Kencana Inn
Lot 177-181 Jln. Padang Garong
Tel: 09-747944
36 rooms, air-conditioned, full room facilities, restaurant, bar; from $58 to $145

Kota Bharu Stadium Corporation Youth Hostel
Jln. Mahmud
Tel: 09-781123

Milton Hotel
5471A Jln. Pengkalan Chepa
Tel: 09-782744
27 rooms, air-conditioned; from $20 to $32

Murni Hotel
Jln. Dato Pati
Tel: 09-782399
38 rooms, air-conditioned, room facilities,
restaurant, coffeehouse; from $52 to $150

Perdana Hotel
Jln. Mahmud
Tel: 09-785000
136 rooms, full room facilities, restaurants,
coffeehouse, bars, swimming pool, tennis,
squash, water sports, golf course, disco,
beauty salon, car rental; from $75 to $320

Rex Hotel
Jln. Temenggong
Tel: 09-781419
34 rooms from $6 to $15

Suria Hotel
Jln. Padang Garong
Tel: 09-746477
24 rooms, air-conditioned; from $30 to $50

Temenggong Hotel
Jln. Tok Hakim
Tel: 09-783130
36 rooms, air-conditioned, restaurant, disco,
coffeehouse, bath/shower; from $55 to $80

• **Pantai Cinta Berahi**

Long House Beach Motel
Tel: 09-740090
Huts, rooms (some air-conditioned) and
chalets, restaurant; from $10 to $40

Pantai Cinta Berahi Resort
Tel: 09-781307
21 chalets, sea sports; from $55 to $85

• **Gua Musang**

Government Rest House
From $16

Kesedar Inn
Tel: 09-901229
21 rooms, air-conditioned; from $25 to $42

• **Kuala Krai**

Kiew Shi Hotel
Near railway station
From $9

TERENGGANU

• **Kuala Terengganu**

Bunga Raya Hotel
105-11 Jln. Banggol
Tel: 09-621166
39 rooms, some air-conditioned, hot water,
coffeehouse; from $16 to $36

City Hotel
97-99 Jln. Banggol
Tel: 09-621481
34 rooms from $12 to $30

Meriah Hotel
67 Jln. Paya Bunga
Tel: 09-622655
41 rooms, air-conditioned; from $24 to $32

Motel Desa
Bukit Pak Apil
Tel: 09-623438
20 rooms, air-conditioned, room service, hot
water, bath/shower, swimming pool, restaurant, bar; from $90 to $100

Motel Sri Marang
Kampong Pulau Kerengga
Tel: 09-632566
29 rooms from $40 to $140

Pantai Primula Hotel
Jln. Persinggahan
Tel: 09-622100
264 rooms, full room facilities, restaurants,
coffeehouse, ballroom, disco (topfloor),
bars, swimming pool, grill, tennis, horse-
riding, tours, watersports, island trips, turtle
watching, fishing, handicraft shop, trips to
Sekayu Waterfalls, shops, travel service,
business centre; from $115 to $300

Seri Hoover Hotel
49 Jln. Sultan Ismail
Tel: 09-624655
61 rooms, air-conditioned, TV, restaurant,
bar; from $20 to $62

Sri Terengganu
120A & B Jln. Sultan Ismail
Tel: 09-634622
20 rooms, air-conditioned, restaurant; from
$20 to $48

Terengganu Hotel
12 Jln. Paya Bunga
Tel: 09-622900
35 rooms (some air-conditioned), telephone, shower; from $16 to $32

Warisan Hotel
65 Jln. Paya Bunga
Tel: 09-622688
36 rooms, air-conditioned, TV, hot water, bath/shower, restaurant; from $40 to $58

• **Kuala Besut**

Government Rest House
Close to beach and boats for Pulau Perhentian; from $8 to $16

• **Pulau Perhentian**

Perhentian Beach Resort
Pulau Perhentian Besar
Dormitory, huts and chalets, restaurant, boat trips, snorkelling; from $20 to $50

Razali's Beach Chalets
Pulau Perhentian Besar
Huts and chalets, cooking facilities, water from well; from $10. Other huts on the beach are $8 per person.

• **Kemaman (Chukai)**

Duin Hotel
K355 Jln. Kg. Tengah
Tel: 09-591801
32 rooms, shower; from $16 to $29

Muni Hotel
K312 Jln. Che Teh
Tel: 09-592366
40 rooms, air-conditioned, telephone, restaurant; from $70 to $120

• **Kerteh**

Parpel Lodge
Bandar Bahru, Kerteh, 24300 Kerteh
Tel: 09-861155
48 rooms, air-conditioned, telephone, hot water, bath/shower; from $50 to $120

• **Dungun**

Sri Dungun Hotel
K135 Jln. Tambun
Tel: 09-841881
27 rooms, air-conditioned, telephone, bath/shower; from $16 to $38

Tanjong Jara Beach Hotel
8th Mile off Jln. Dungun
Tel: 09-841801
100 rooms, air-conditioned, full room facilities, sailing, water skiing, fishing, tennis, golf park, squash, swimming pool, sauna, restaurants, bars; from $140 to $350

• **Tanjong Jara**

Tanjong Jara Beach Resort
Tel: 06-531201
80 rooms from $70

• **Rantau Abang**

Awang's
Rantau Abang Beach
Tel: 09-842236
Huts and chalets, restaurant, turtle watching; from $5 to $10

Merantau Inn
Kuala Abang
Tel: 09-841131
17 chalets, turtle watching, restaurant; from $44 to $66

Rantau Abang Visitors' Centre
13th Mile, Jln. Dungun
Tel: 09-841533
10 chalets, turtle watching; from $80 to $90

• **Marang**

The Beach House
Tel: 09-682516
Beach location, huts and chalets, some with air-conditioning; from $7 to $70

Zakaria Guest House
2 km south of Marang
Tel: 09-682328
Family homestay, dormitories and rooms, home-cooked meals and snacks, island trips; from $5 to $10

• Pulau Kapas

Call 09-681044 to book and arrange transport. Boats leave from Marang. 4 chalets from $10 to $28

PAHANG

• Kuantan

Annexe Rest House
Jln. Telok Sisek
Tel: 09-521043
16 rooms, restaurant; from $19 to $25

Beserah Hotel
2 Jln. Beserah
Tel: 09-526144
45 rooms, air-conditioned; from $40 to $65

Champagne Emas Hotel
3002 Jln. Haji Ahmad
Tel: 09-528820
50 rooms, air-conditioned, room service, restaurants, bar; from $70 to $120

Embassy Hotel
60 Jln. Telok Sisek
Tel: 09-524844
27 rooms, air-conditioned; from $11 to $26

Hotel Raya Bahru
134 Jln. Besar
Tel: 09-522344
26 rooms from $20 to $34

Jaafar's Place
Kampong Beserah
Beach location; pretty fishing village, dormitory accommodation including breakfast and snacks; from $9

Ming Hong Hotel
22 Jln. Mahkota
Tel: 09-524885
10 rooms, restaurant and bakery; from $11

Pahang Hotel
7 Main Road
Tel: 09-521614
33 rooms, air-conditioned; from $24 to $34

Ramada Beach Resort
Tel: 09-587544
162 rooms, full room facilities, restaurants, bars, shops, water sports, travel service, car rental, swimming pool; from $110 to $350

Samudra Hotel
Main Road
Tel: 09-522688
75 rooms, full room facilities and services, restaurant; from $70 to $125

Simgifa Hotel
9th Mile Kuantan Port
Tel: 09-587254
51 rooms, air-conditioned; from $40 to $50

• Telok Chempedak Beach, Kuantan

Asrama Bendahara Hostel
Telok Chempedak
Tel: 095-527091

Hyatt Kuantan
Telok Chempedak
Tel: 09-525211
185 rooms, full room facilities and services, squash, tennis, beauty salon, health centre, business centre, swimming pool, restaurant, bar, coffeehouse, disco; from $130 to $200

Kuantan Hotel
Tel: 09-524755
22 rooms from $30 to $70

Merlin Inn Resort
Telok Chempedak
Tel: 09-522388
106 rooms, full room facilities and services, swimming pool, golf club, restaurant, disco; from $100 to $170

Telok Chempedak Rest House
Tel: 09-521711
Rooms from $25; public pool nearby

• Cherating

Chendor Motel
29th Mile Kuantan-Kemaman Road
Tel: 09-591369
59 rooms and chalets; from $54 to $120

Cherating Holiday Villa
Lot 1303, Mukim Sungei Karang
Tel: 09-508900
94 rooms with full facilities, restaurant, bar, tennis, squash, sauna, gymnasium, swim-

ming pool, island excursions, horse-riding, golf, fishing, water sports; from $65 to $120

Club Mediteranée

For reservations and membership, apply at Bangunan MAS 1st Floor, Suite 1, 1 Jln. Sultan Ismail, 50250 Kuala Lumpur, or apply at the resort itself at Pantai Cherating, Tel: 09-591131

The usual Club Med facilities, fun and games. Membership fee $50; from $150 to $180 per person per night; weekly package including flight from KL from $1530.

Coconut Inn

Cherating Beach
Clean huts and chalets with verandah, home-cooked meals, pub nearby, river and island trips, barbecues; from $10 to $14

Mak Long Teh Hostel

Main Kuantan-Kemaman Road
Chalets, meals and snacks included; from $10 to $15

• Kuala Rompin

Government Rest House

(Rumah Persinggahan Dara) Bandar Ibam
Tel: 09-565245
12 rooms, air-conditioned; from $14 to $30

• Pekan

Pekan Hotel

60 Jln. Teng Ariff Bendahara
Tel: 09-571378
12 rooms from $10 to $12

Pekan Rest House

Tel: 09-571240
Rooms from $10

• Tasek Chini

Club Med have chalets here if you're staying with them. Other accommodation include two rest houses and chalets from $40

• Jerantut

Hotel Picadilly

312 Sungei Jan
Tel: 09-562895
18 rooms from $12 to $18

Jerantut Hotel

36 Jln. Besar
From $14

• Temerluh

Ban Hin Hotel

40 Jln. Tengku Besar
Tel: 09-291250
17 rooms, bath; from $14 to $30

Government Rest House

Tel: 09-291254
From $27 to $60

Hotel Tropicana

A73 Jln. Sultan Ahmad
Tel: 09-451095
45 rooms, bar, coffeehouse, restaurant; from $28 to $45

Swiss Hotel

Tel: 09-451324
20 rooms, bar; from $10

Temerluh Hotel

29 Jln. Kuantan
Tel: 09-451499
22 rooms, bar, restaurant; from $16 to $30

Titik Inn

Batu 25 Jln. Kuantan
Tel: 09-531329
16 chalets, air-conditioned, restaurant, cooking facilities, bar, lounge, turtle watching, fishing, jungle trips; from $45 to $90

• Mentakab

Cosy Inn

10 Jln. Bahru
Tel: 09-271977
19 rooms from $15 to $27

London Cafe and Hotel

71 Jln. Temerloh
Tel: 09-271119
21 rooms from $15 to $23

Walto Hotel

66 Jln. Temerloh
Tel: 09-271262
12 rooms from $10.50 to $17

• Kuala Lipis

Government Rest House
Tel: 09-312599
17 rooms, some air-conditioned, telephone,
TV, video, shower, ; from $16 to $50

Sing Sing Hotel
From $8

Mee Chew Hotel
From $10

• Raub

Government Rest House
13 Jln. Manson
Tel: 09-351455

Raub Hotel
57-58 Jln. Lipis
21 rooms, bath/shower; from $10

• Bentong

Cheong Aik Hotel
49 Jln. Ah Peng
Tel: 09-221133
15 rooms, shower; from $12 to $14

Union Hotel
50 Tingkat, 1 Jln. Ah Peng
Tel: 09-721088
26 rooms, bath/shower; from $10 to $13

• Cameron Highlands
(accessible from Perak State)

The Lakehouse
30th Mile Ringlet
Tel: 05-996152
16 rooms, Tudor architecture, antique furnishings, restaurant, fishing, jungle walks, waterfalls and lakes; from $130 to $300

Lake View Bungalows
Ringlet
Tel: 05-941630
Chalets and bungalows from $50

Federal Hotel
44 Main Road, Tanah Rata
Tel: 05-941777
31 rooms, telephone, bath/shower, hot water, restaurant; from $18 to $45

Garden Hotel
Tanah Rata
Tel: 09-941911
46 rooms, telephone, bath/shower, restaurant, bar, room service; from $60 to $70

Golf Course Inn
Tanah Rata
Tel: 05-941214
30 rooms, restaurant, golf and badminton by arrangement; from $90 to $150

Golf View Villa
Tanah Rata
Tel: 05-941624
6 bungalows; from $80

Government Rest House
Tanah Rata
From $15 to $28; olde world charm

Hollywood Hotel
38 Main Road, Tanah Rata
Tel: 05-941633
12 rooms, hot water, bath/shower, restaurant and bar; from $18 to $80

Merlin Inn Resort
Tanah Rata
Tel: 05-941205
64 rooms, telephone, full room facilities, restaurant and bar, tennis, golf course, disco, shops; from $80 to $270

Strawberry Park Resort
P.O. Box 81, Tanah Rata
Tel: 05-941166
172 rooms, full room facilities, restaurant, coffeehouse, grill, bar, tennis, squash, health centre, golf course, horse-riding, disco, shops, travel service; from $120 to $250

Town House Hotel
41 Main Road, Tanah Rata
Tel: 05-941666
12 rooms, hot water, bath, car rental, travel service; from $12 to $22

• Berinchang

Bala's Holiday Chalets
Berinchang
Tel: 05-941660
Restaurant and cooking facilities; rooms from $5 to $40

Berinchang Hotel
36 Berinchang Town
Tel: 05-941755
28 rooms, restaurant; from $30 to $45

Highland Hotel
29-32 Berinchang
Tel: 05-941588
60 rooms, bath; from $25 to $40

Kowloon Hotel
34-35 Berinchang
Tel: 05-941366
12 rooms, bar, restaurant; from $18 to $80

Wong Villa Youth Hostel
113 Jln. Besar, Berinchang
Tel: 05-911145

Ye Olde Smokehouse
Berinchang/Tanah Rata
Tel: 05-941214
Tudor architecture with English country garden, log fires, 20 family suites, dining and tea rooms, bars, 18-hole golf course, jungle walks, cream teas; from $60 to $300

• **Genting Highlands**

Genting Hotel
Tel: 03-211-1118
51 km from Kuala Lumpur, 15-minutes' helicopter flight from KL or airport. 700 rooms, full room facilities, restaurants serve Western, Malaysian and Chinese cuisine, Malaysia's only casino, coffeehouse, bars, health centre with jacuzzi and sauna, beauty salon, flower nursery, cable car, nightclub, bowling alley, golf course, heliport, shops, lake and boating, swimming pool, squash, revolving disco, car rental/limousine service; from $125 to $2000

Highlands Hotel
Tel: 03-211-2812
Sister to Genting hotel. 244 rooms, all room facilities and services, restaurants, coffeehouse, bars, grill, swimming pool, use of facilities at Genting Hotel; from $80 to $110

Pelangi Hotel
Tel: 03-211-3813
150 rooms, all room facilities and services, restaurants, bar; from $50 to $70

• **Fraser's Hill**

Corona Nursery Youth Hostel
Tel: 09-382225
20 minutes' walk from tourist office, rooms with bathroom; from $7 per person

Fraser's Hill Bungalows/Chalets
c/o Fraser's Hill Development,
Corporation Fraser's Hill
Tel: 09-382201
69 rooms, dining room, tennis, 18-hole golf course, squash, sauna, barber shop, skating rink, swimming pool; from $25 to $55

Merlin Hotel Fraser's Hill
Jln. Lady Guillemard
Tel: 09-382274
109 rooms, full room facilities, restaurant, games room, horse-riding, 9-hole golf course, tennis, squash; from $80 to $300

Puncak Inn
Tel: 09-382201
Rooms from $25 to $45

Seri Berkat Rest House
Tel: 09-341026
Rooms from $30

• **Tioman Island**
(in Pahang state but accessible
from Johor at Mersing)

ABC Huts
Ayer Batang
Basic huts from $4

Ben's Diving Centre
Pantai Salang
Chalets from $5

Coral Reef Chalets
Pantai Tekek
12 chalets on the beach, restaurant with seafood, barbecues, jungle treks; from $35 to $45; packages from Mersing

Hussein's Chalets
Pantai Juara
Chalets, cafe; from $16 to $46

Nazri's
Ayer Batang
Close to jetty, cafe; chalets from $8

Samudra Swiss Cottages
Pantai Tekek
Tel: 07-242-2829
Longhouse and beach chalets, restaurant, snorkelling and diving gear for hire, barbecues; from $25 to $42

Tekek Rest House
Kg. Tekek
Fan and attached bathroom; from $10 to $18

Tioman Island Resort
185 Seaview
Tel: 04-44544
Hillview, chalet and standard rooms, air-conditioned, full room facilities and services, restaurants, cocktail lounge, picnic packs, all water sport including scuba diving, boat trips, glass-bottom boats, jungle treks; from $90 to $450

• **Taman Negara**

Head Office
260-H 2nd Mile, Jln. Ipoh, KL
Tel: 03-291-5299

Branch
10th kilometre Jln. Cheras, 56100 KL
Tel: 03-905-2872

Entry Permit: $1; Camera Licence: $5; Fishing Licence: $10; Return boat fare to Park Headquarters: $30; Park Deposit: $30.
Gunung Tahan Climb: $400 per guide per week, and $50 for every subsequent day. Camping and fishing equipment for hire, 2 restaurants at Headquarters, cooking facilities at hostel; 5 percent Government tax on all accommodation, cash payment only at the Park.

Accommodation

Rest House: $38 per room per night (double)
Chalet: $30 per night (double), mosquito net, bathroom
Hostel (dormitories): $10 per person per night
Camping: $1 per person per night
Fishing Lodge: $8 per person per night
Jungle Hides: $5 per person per night.

JOHOR STATE

• **Johor Bahru**

First Hotel
Jln. Station
Tel: 07-222888
42 rooms, air-conditioned; from $18 to $80

Holiday Inn Johor Bahru
Jln. Dat Sulaiman
Tel: 07-322800
200 rooms, full room facilities and services, swimming pool, health centre, disco, shops, travel service; from $110 to $850

Johor Hotel
69 Jln. Sultan Ibrahim
Tel: 07-224395
33 rooms, bath/shower; from $18 to $28

Merlin Inn
Lot 5435 Jln. Bukit Meldrum
Tel: 07-228851
104 rooms, air-conditioned, full room facilities; from $65 to $180

Peninsula Hotel
6J ABIAD Taman Tebrau Jaya
Tel: 07-323277
38 rooms, air-conditioned; from $31 to $38

Regent Elite Hotel
1 Jln. Siew Nam
Tel: 07-223811
76 rooms, air-conditioned, restaurant, disco, nightclub; from $52 to $95

Tropical Inn
15 Jln. Gereja
Tel: 07-221888
160 rooms, air-conditioned, TV, hot water, bath/shower, restaurant, coffeehouse, bar lounge, health centre, beauty salon, disco, nightclub, car rental; from $110 to $450

Wato Inn
15R Jln. Bukit Meldrum
Tel: 07-221328
22 rooms, air-conditioned, bath/shower, TV, bar, car rental; from $31 to $47

• Kota Tinggi

Waterfall Chalets
Kota Tinggi Waterfall
Tel: 07-241957
Chalets with hot water, some self-catering, restaurant; from $27 to $42

• Desaru Resort

Desaru Beach Resort Camping Ground
Tanjong Penawar
Tel: 07-821202
Camping grounds, with water and cooking facilities, dormitories, private rooms, 10 "*dangau*" huts; from $5 to $27.50

Desaru Beach Resort Chalets
Tanjong Penawar, Kota Tinggi
Tel: 07-821240
35 chalets on beach, from simple 3-bed chalets with sitting room and verandah (TV on request), to family chalets with cooking facilities, all chalets with air-conditioning; restaurant, water sports, golf by arrangement, cycling; from $70 to $220

Desaru Golf Hotel
Tanjong Penawar, Kota Tinggi
Tel: 07-821101
100 rooms, full room facilities, swimming pool, restaurant, bar lounge, billiards, video games, boardgames, horse-riding, cycling, jogging, jungle treks, scuba diving instruction (PADI), tennis, table tennis, volleyball, 18-hole golf course; from $95 to $380

Desaru View Hotel
Tanjong Penawar, Kota Tinggi
Tel: 07-838221
134 rooms, full room facilities and services, restaurant, grill, bar lounge, disco, shops, swimming pool; from $150 to $650

• Mersing

East Coast Hotel
43A-1 Jln. Abu Bakar
Tel: 07-791337
Rooms from $8.50 to $14

Mersing Hotel
Jln. Dato Mohd Ali
Tel: 07-791004
19 rooms from $13 to $28

Mersing Merlin Inn
1st Mile Endau Road
Tel: 07-791311
34 rooms, air-conditioned, TV, hot water, bath/shower, room service, restaurant, swimming pool, disco; from $70 to $90

Rest House Mersing
490 Jln. Ismail
Tel: 07-791101
17 rooms, air-conditioned, telephone, hot water, bath/shower, beach location, restaurant, golf course; from $33

JOHOR ISLANDS

(accessible from Mersing; for Tioman, see Pahang section)

• Pulau Besar

Besar Beach Club
Tel: 07-793111
Chalets, restaurant, sea sports; from $44

Radin Island Pulau Besar Resort
Bookings from office near jetty, or write to Jln. Abu Bakar Mersing
Tel: 07-793124, 07-416044
Coconut-framed huts, bungalows, sea sports, jungle treks, restaurant, seafood, barbecues on request; family-run business; from $10 to $40

• Pulau Rawa

Rawa Safaris Island Resort
Bookings and boats from Mersing
Tel: 07-791204
Wooden chalets and bungalows, some with attached bathroom, electricity till midnight, lanterns provided, restaurant, seafood, barbecues, windsurfing, canoeing, scuba diving, snorkelling, fishing, equipment for hire, aqua and other shops; from $40 to $60

• Pulau Sibu

Sea Gypsy Village Resort
Sibu Island
Tel: 07-793125
Chalets, private bathroom, restaurant, sea sports, fishing; from $34 to $40

Sibu Island Cabanas
Tel: 07-317216
Chalets, fan-cooled, private bathroom, soap and towels, restaurant, sea sports, indoor games, fishing; from $24 to $70

• **Muar**

Muar Hotel
44 Jln. Ali
Tel: 07-921604
30 rooms from $18 to $26

Muar Rest House
2222 Jln. Sultan Tanjung Mas
Tel: 07-922306
17 rooms, air-conditioned, telephone, bath/shower, restaurant; from $32 to $36

• **Batu Pahat**

De Mandarin Hotel
7 Jln. Zabedah
Tel: 07-444011
71 rooms, full room facilities, coffeehouse, nightclub, beauty salon; from $70 to $115

Dragon Hotel
1 Jln. Putri
Tel: 07-441977
41 rooms, air-conditioned, telephone, hot water, health centre; from $27 to $44

• **Kluang**

Kluang Rest House
Jln. Pejabat Kerejaan
Tel: 07-721567
14 rooms, air-conditioned; from $32

Regal Hotel
42 Jln. Dato Captain
Tel: 07-724922
36 rooms, air-conditioned, telephone, hot water; from $16 to $32

• **Segamat**

Hotel Chempaka
99-101 Jln. Genaung
Tel: 07-911505
45 rooms, air-conditioned, telephone, hot water, TV, bath/shower, restaurant, coffeehouse, restaurant, bar; from $52 to $54

Segamat Merlin Inn
26 Jln. Ros
Tel: 07-914611
85 rooms, full room facilities and services, restaurant, bar; from $65 to $150

Segamat Rest House
JKR 750 Jln. Buloh Kasap
Tel: 07-917199

SABAH

• **Kota Kinabalu**

Ang's Hotel
28 Jln. Bakau
Tel: 088-55433
35 rooms, air-conditioned, telephone, bath/shower, TV, restaurant; from $84 to $96

Asia Hotel
68 Bandaran Berjaya
Tel: 088-53533
28 rooms, some air-conditioned, rustic scenery; from $36 to $50

Hotel Jesselton
69 Jln. Gaya
Tel: 088-55633
27 rooms, full room facilities, restaurant; from $140 to $180

Hotel Kinabalu
59-60 Bandaran Berjaya
Tel: 088-53233
30 rooms, air-conditioned, TV, room service, restaurant; from $84 to $150

Hyatt Kinabalu
Jln. Datuk Salleh
Tel: 088-219888
350 rooms, full room facilities, 24-hour coffeehouse, Chinese restaurant, grill, swimming pool, cruises, business centre, travel service, Avis car rental, shops, beauty salon, health centre, golf course arrangements, tour agency; from $200 to $1250

Kin Fah Hotel
7 Jln. Haji Yaacub
Tel: 088-53833
11 rooms, air-conditioned; from $25 to $40

Likas Guest House
371 Jln. Likas
Tel: 088-31706
Rooms from $15 to $20; breakfast available

Nan Xing Hotel
32-34 Jln. Haji Saman
Tel: 088-51433
35 rooms, air-conditioned, telephone, TV, restaurant; from $47 to $70

Palace Hotel
1 Jln. Tangki Karamunsing
Tel: 088-211911
160 rooms, castle architecture, full room facilities, coffeehouse, Chinese restaurant, bar lounge, business and travel centre, swimming pool, squash; from $69 to $190

Sabah Inn
25 Jln. Pantai
Tel: 088-53322
39 rooms, air-conditioned, telephone, TV, hot water, bath/shower, coffeehouse, bar, beauty salon, car rental; from $58 to $108

Sukan Kompleks Youth Hostel
Likas Bau, Likas
Tel: 088-221721

Tanjung Aru Beach Hotel
Tanjung Aru Beach
Tel: 088-58711
300 rooms, full room facilities, swimming pool, restaurants, bars, fitness centre, water sports, boats to islands, business centre, travel service, shops; from $225 to $975

• Beaufort

Hotel Beaufort
Tel: 087-211911
Air-conditioned rooms, attached bathroom, TV on request; from $42

New Padas Hotel
P.O. Box 147
Tel: 087-211441
22 rooms, air-conditioned, hot water, TV; from $23 to $50

• Tiga Island (near Beaufort)

Government Rest House
For further details, check in Beaufort

• Labuan

Hotel Emas Labuan
27-30 Jln. Muhibbah
Tel: 087-413966
40 rooms, room facilities and services, restaurant; from $90 to $125

Hotel Labuan
Jln. Merdeka P.O. Box 354
Tel: 087-412311
151 rooms, full room facilities and services, swimming pool, restaurants, coffeehouse, bars, shops, beauty salon, health centre; from $160 to $510

Kim Soon Lee Hotel
141-2 Jln. Okk Awang Besar
Tel: 087-42554
18 rooms, air-conditioned; from $50

Victoria Hotel
Jln. Tun Mustapha
Tel: 087-42411
39 rooms, air-conditioned, telephone, room service; from $70 to $100

• Tenom

Government Rest House
Tenom
From $12

Hotel Kin San
Shophouse 58, P.O. Box 192
Tel: 087-735485
10 rooms; from $20

Hotel Perkasa
P.O. Box 225
Tel: 087-735811
63 rooms, full room facilities, Chinese, Muslim and Western restaurants, bar, sightseeing tours; from $50 to $100

Tenom Hotel
P.O. Box 78
Tel: 087-735587
10 rooms from $20 to $30

• Keningau

Government Rest House
Tel: 087-31525
Rooms from $12

Hotel Perkasa
P.O. Box 129
Tel: 087-331045
65 rooms, air-conditioned, private bath-room, TV on request, beauty salon, restaurants, bar, golf course, swimming pool, tennis, and jogging; from $50 to $100

• **Kota Belud**

Hotel Kota Belud
21 Jln. Francis, P.O. Box 21
Tel: 088-976576
6 rooms from $28 to $36

Hotel Tai Seng
P.O. Box 41
Tel: 088-551
20 rooms; from $20

• **Kudat**

Hasba Hotel
P.O. Box 105
Tel: 088-61959
6 rooms, close to town, no air-conditioning; from $15 to $24

Hotel Kinabalu
1, Block C, Sedco Shophouse, P.O. Box 82
Tel: 088-62693
9 rooms, all air-conditioned, TV, private bath, hot water; from $65 to $76

Hotel Sunrise
P.O. Box 237
Tel: 088-61617
16 rooms from $29 to $58

Kudat Hotel
Little Street, P.O. Box 200
Tel: 088-616379
8 rooms, air-conditioned, restaurant downstairs; from $30 to $35

• **Ranau**

Government Rest House
Tel: 088-75534
Rooms from $12

Mount Kinabalu Perkasa Hotel
WDT 11, 89309 Ranau
Tel: 088-889511
74 rooms, full facilities and services, restaurants, bar, tennis, fitness room, shops, indoor games, golf course nearby, climbing tours of Mt Kinabalu; from $75 to $200

Ranau Hotel
P.O. Box 1
Tel: 088-875351
10 rooms, air-conditioned; from $25 to $63

• **Sandakan**

Hong Kong Hotel
P.O. Box 522
Tel: 089-212292
30 rooms, centre of town; from $20 to $50

Hotel Hsiang Garden
Tel: 089-43191
45 rooms, air-conditioned, restaurant; from $100 to $180

Hotel Paris
45 Jln. Tiga, P.O. Box 340
21 rooms, some air-conditioned; $27 to $52

Mayfair Hotel
24 Jln. Prayer 1F, P.O. Box 512
Tel: 089-45191
12 rooms, some air-conditioned, centre of town; from $32 to $42

New Sabah Hotel
P.O. Box 214
Tel: 089-218711
28 rooms, air-conditioned; from $48 to $68

Pulau Selingan Rest House
Enquiries at Sandakan District Office.
Turtle sanctuary. Rest house for 4 persons, cooking facilities and bathroom, $120; cabins (no cooking facilities) from $20

• **Lahad Datu**

De Luxe Hotel
P.O. Box 22
Tel: 089-81500
12 rooms, air-conditioned, central; from $30

Government Rest House
Tel: 089-81177
Near airport; rooms from $12

Mido Hotel
94 Main Street, P.O. Box 45
Tel: 089-81800
61 rooms, full room facilities and services;
from $90 to $180

Ocean Hotel
Jln. Timur
Tel: 089-81700
19 rooms from $40

Perdana Hotel
Jln. Bajau, P.O. Box 72
Tel: 089-81400
21 rooms, air-conditioned, restaurant; from
$35 to $65

• Semporna

Island View Hotel
P.O. Box 126
Tel: 088-781638
8 rooms, air-conditioned; from $40 to $48

• Tawau

Hotel Emas
Jln. Utara, P.O. Box 569
Tel: 089-773300
100 rooms, air-conditioned, centre of town,
restaurant, nightclub; from $105 to $210

Hotel Malaysia
37 Jln. Dunlop
Tel: 089-772800
21 rooms, centre of town; from $32 to $45

Hotel Oriental
10 Jln. Dunlop
Tel: 089-771500
29 rooms, air-conditioned, centre of town;
from $68 to $83

Marco Polo Hotel
P.O. Box 1003
Tel: 089-777615
150 rooms, full room facilities, restaurants,
coffeehouse, bar; from $125 to $1000

Royal Hotel
Jln. Belian
Tel: 089-773100
37 rooms, air-conditioned, coffeehouse,
restaurant; from $110 to $240

• Mount Kinabalu National Park

Head Office
Jln. Tun Fuad Stephens, P.O. Box 10626,
Kota Kinabalu
Tel: 088-211585

Entry Permit: $1; Climbers' Permit: $10

Accommodation

In Park Headquarters
Lodges: sleeps 8, kitchen, dining room,
fridge, lounge, fireplace, hot water; from
$270 to $360
Double Storey Cabin: sleeps 7, 3 bedrooms, kitchen, sitting room, fridge, fireplace, hot water; from $180 to $250
Single Storey Cabin: sleeps 5, 2 bedrooms,
kitchen, sitting room, fridge, fireplace, hot
water; from $150 to $200
Duplex Chalets: sleeps 6, kitchen, sitting
room, fridge, fireplace, hot water; from $150
to $200
Annex Rooms: sleeps 4, 2 bedrooms, no
cooking facilities; from $100 to $160
Twin-bed Cabins: sleeps 2, attached bathroom, hot water; from $50 to $80
Basement Rooms: sleeps 2, attached bathroom, hot water; from $50 to $80
Old Fellowship Hostel: dormitories, kitchen, sitting room, bedding provided, communal bathrooms; from $3 to $10
New Hostel: same facilities as Old Hostel;
from $4 to $15

On Mount Kinabalu
Waras Hut: (3300 metres) bunk beds, cook-
ing facilities and gas, sleeping bags for hire,
no electricity; from $1 to $4
Panar Laban Hut: (3300 metres) same as
Waras Hut
Ladagan Rata Hut: (3300 metres) same as
Waras Hut
Laban Rata Rest House: electricity, hot
water, room heater, bedding provided, res-
taurant; from $25 per person
Sayat Sayat Hut: (3811 metres) same as
Waras Hut

At Poring Hot Springs
Old Cabin: sleeps 6, 3 bedrooms, sitting
room, kitchen, bathroom; from $75 to $100
New Cabin: same as Old Cabin, but sleeps
4; from $60 to $80

Poring Hostel: dormitories, cooking facilities, bedding provided; from $2 to $8
Camping Ground: cooking facilities, bathrooms, bedding for hire; from $1 to $2

• Tuanku Abdul Rahman National Park

Head Office
Jln. Tun Fuad Stephens, P.O. Box 10626, Kota Kinabalu
Tel: 088-211585

Accommodation

Rest House Pulau Mamutik: sleeps 12, kitchen, dining/sitting room, bathrooms; from $160
Camping: Camping on all islands with prior permission

SARAWAK

• Kuching

Anglican Cathedral Hostel
Behind St Thomas' Church
Tel: 082-414027
Rooms from $15 to $25

Borneo Hotel
30C-F Jln. Tabuan, P.O. Box 1265
Tel: 082-244121
37 rooms, air-conditioned, cocktail lounge, nightclub, beauty salon; from $48 to $73

Government Rest House
Jln. Crookshank
Tel: 082-242042
Rooms from $32 to $42

Green Mountain Lodging House
Jln. Green Hill
Tel: 082-415244
Air-conditioned rooms, TV on request, restaurants nearby, quiet street; from $33

Holiday Inn Kuching
Jln. Tunku Abdul Rahman, P.O. Box 2362
Tel: 082-423111
312 rooms, full room facilities, restaurant, bar, swimming pool, entertainment, beauty salon, shops; from $135 to $1000

Kuching Hilton
Jln. Tunku Abdul Rahman
Tel: 082-248200
320 rooms, full room facilities and services, restaurants, bar, grill, beauty salon, health centre, swimming pool, shops, travel service

Kuching Hotel
Jln. Temple
Tel: 082-413985
Rooms from $17 to $21

Long House Hotel
Jln. Abell Pandungan, P.O. Box 1591
Tel: 082-249333
50 rooms, air-conditioned, restaurant, bar; from $45 to $90

Palm Hotel
29 Jln. Palm
Tel: 082-240231
24 rooms, air-conditioned; from $30 to $40

Sheraton Damai Beach Hotel
P.O. Box 2870
Tel: 082-411777
202 rooms, full room facilities, restaurants, bars, disco, business centre, fitness centre, indoor games, tennis, squash, mini-golf, swimming pool with whirlpool, water sports, island trips, jungle treks, bicycles, children's corner with mini zoo, 18-hole golf course, car rental; from $180 to $1100

• Sibu

Capitol Hotel
19 Jln. Wong Nai Siong, P.O. Box 489
Tel: 084-336444
30 rooms, air-conditioned, coffeehouse, room service, TV; from $44 to $120

Federal Hotel
24 Jln. Kampong Nyabor, P.O. Box 899
Tel: 084-333088
30 rooms, air-conditioned; from $17 to $36

Government Rest House
Jln. Pulau Rooms
From $40 to $50

Malaysia Hotel
8 Jln. Kampong Nyabor, P.O. Box 13
Tel: 084-332298
21 rooms, air-conditioned; from $35 to $70

Premier Hotel
Jln. Kampong Nyabor, P.O. Box 1064
Tel: 084-23222
120 rooms, full room facilities and services, restaurants, bars, health centre, golf course, disco, nightclub, shops, beauty salon, travel centre; from $80 to $320

Rex Hotel
32 Jln. Cross, P.O. Box 1031
Tel: 084-330625
30 rooms, air-conditioned; from $13 to $48

Sarawak Hotel
34 Jln. Cross, P.O. Box 227
Tel: 084-333045
24 rooms, air-conditioned; from $26 to $77

• Sematan

Thomas Lai Bungalows
Bookings through Mrs Lai
Tel: 082-45174
7 bungalows, kitchen, bathroom, sitting room; from $40 to $100

• Kapit

Ark Hill Inn
Lot 451, Shop Lot 10, Jln. Airport,
P.O. Box 161
Tel: 084-796168
21 rooms, air-conditioned, river views, boats to Belaga; from $35 to $75

Hotel Maligai ·
34 Jln. Airport, P.O. Box 139
Tel: 084-796611
41 rooms, air-conditioned, restaurant, bar, shop, travel service; from $32 to $90

Kapit Rejang Hotel
28 Main Bazaar, P.O. Box 2
Tel: 084-796709
26 rooms, air-conditioned, TV, hot water and bath; from $24 to $36

Long House Hotel
21 Berjaya Road, P.O. Box 5
Tel: 084-796415
20 rooms from $15 to $30

Methodist Guest House
Next to blue church
From $7 to $12

• Belaga

Belaga Hotel
Belaga Bazaar
Tel: 084-461244
4 rooms; from $15

Huan Kilah Lodging House
Belaga Bazaar
Tel: 084-461259
12 rooms; from $15

Sing Song Hing Hotel
Belaga Bazaar
Tel: 084-461257
6 rooms from $18 to $27

• Bintulu

Aurora Beach Hotel
Jln. Tanjong Batu
Tel: 086-31622
108 rooms, nightclub; from $125 to $260

Kemena Lodging House
78 Keppel Road, P.O. Box 497
Tel: 086-31533
12 rooms, air-conditioned; from $50 to $60

Li Hua Hotel
2½ Mile Miri-Bintulu Road, P.O. Box 191
Tel: 086-35000
90 rooms, air-conditioned, restaurant; from $80 to $280

Sunlight Hotel
7 Jln. Pedada, P.O. Box 94
Tel: 086-32681
36 rooms, air-conditioned; from $60 to $90

• Miri

Fatimah Hotel
49 Jln. Brooke, P.O. Box 107
Tel: 085-32255
54 rooms, air-conditioned, dining room; from $64 to $225

Gloria Hotel
27 Jln. Brooke, P.O. Box 1283
Tel: 085-36499
42 rooms, air-conditioned, TV, telephone, room service, restaurant, coffeehouse, shops, beauty salon; from $86 to $120

Thai Foh Lodging House
18 Jln. China
Rooms from $16 to $20

Thai Tong Lodging House
Jln. China
Rooms from $5.50 to $28

• Marudi

Alisan Hotel
63-65 Queen's Square, P.O. Box 133
Tel: 085-55911
34 rooms from $13 to $37

Government Rest House
For details, contact district officer in Marudi

Hotel Zola
Lot 14-15 Queen's Square, P.O. Box 371
Tel: 085-55991
25 rooms, air-conditioned; from $60 to $84

• Bareo

Bareo Long House
Rooms from $8

• Sri Aman

Alisan Hotel
4 Jln. Council
Tel: 083-2578
Rooms from $34 to $50

Sum Sum Hotel
62 Club Road
Tel: 083-2191
9 rooms from $20 to $33

• Limbang

Bunga Raya Hotel
42-43 Main Bazaar, P.O. Box 33
Tel: 085-21181
15 rooms from $31 to $53

National Inn
62A-69A Jln. Buang Siol, P.O. Box 173
Tel: 085-22922
34 rooms from $98 to $198

South East Asia Hotel
27 Market Street, P.O. Box 21
Tel: 085-21013
10 rooms from $20 to $35

• Mukah

Hoover Hotel
18 Lintang Road, P.O. Box 24
Tel: 084-871251
14 rooms from $20 to $35

Hotel Sri Umpang
29 Jln. Lintang, P.O. Box 10
Tel: 084-871533
6 rooms from $30 to $60

Sea View Hotel
1 Main Bazaar
Tel: 084-871226
9 rooms from $30 to $44

• Sarikei

Ambassador Hotel
54 Repok Road, P.O. Box 52
Tel: 084-51264
38 rooms from $15 to $74

Rajang Hotel
1 Jln. Berjaya
Tel: 084-51096
17 rooms from $11 to $26

• Kota Semarahan

Kee Yong Hotel
Kee Yong Arcade
Tel: 082-73624
6 rooms from $20 to $35

Kota Semarahan Serian Hotel
47B Serian Bazaar
Tel: 082-874118
5 rooms from $15 to $35

• Lawas

Country Park Hotel
Lot 235 & 236, Jln. Trusan, P.O. Box 99
Tel: 085-85522
36 rooms from $75 to $145

Lawas Federal Hotel
8 Jln. Masjid Bahru, P.O. Box 18 .
Tel: 085-85115
9 rooms from $5 to $40

• Bako National Park

Park Headquarters
Jln. Gartak, off Jln. Mosque
Tel: 085-246-6477
Kuching payment for accommodation in
Kuching. Local buses for Bako jetty leave
from bus stop just outside parks office.

Accommodation

Rest Houses: sleeps 6, kitchen, verandah,
bathroom; from $44
Hostel Cabins: sleeps 5 to a room, bedding,
cooking facilities provided; from $1 per
person
Permanent Tents: sleeps 3, no bedding
provided, fireplace for cooking; from $1 per
person
Canteen sells foodstuffs and simple meals
(restaurant planned).

• Niah National Park

Park Headquarters
Jln. Gartak Kuching
Tel: 085-248988

Permits to visit the Painted Cave are obtained from the curator at the Sarawak
Museum, Kuching, or from the Visitors'
Centre at Pangkalan Lubang Park Headquarters. Bookings can also be made at the
forest office in Miri: Forest Office (Pejabat
Hutan), Tel: 085-36637. Guides to caves
cost $30 per day.

Accommodation

Niah Visitor's Hostel: dormitories, cooking facilities and bedding provided, bathrooms, electricity until 10 p.m.; from $2.50.
Shop selling groceries just across the river.

• Gunung Mulu National Park

National Parks Head Office
Jln. Gartak Kuching
Tel: 085-246-6477/248988

Miri office
Tel: 085-33361

Tours from Malang Sisters' Travel
Agency Miri, Tel: 085-38141. Permits must
be obtained at one of these offices, and a
deposit of $20 towards accommodation
paid, unless you are taking a tour.

Accommodation

Dormitories, cooking facilities, no bedding. Small canteen selling tinned and dried
foodstuffs. Hostels are $5 per person per
night. Guide fees from $20 to $30 per day.

NATIONAL PARKS JUNGLE-TREKKING KIT

rucksack (lightweight and waterproof)
tent with flysheet
groundsheet
string/ropes (if climbing)
sheet sleeping bag/sheet blanket
sleeping bag (if climbing)
cooking pots/utensils
Swiss Army knife or similar
plates/cutlery, can opener
parang (local knife for cutting wood etc.)
compass and binoculars
torch and spare batteries
map (if any)
notebook & pens
camera and film
1-litre water container (minimum)
spare set of clothes
sweater
plastic raincoat
sarong
sandals
hat
soap, toothbrush, etc.
insect repellent
salt tablets
First Aid Kit
repair kit
food – rice, noodles, canned foods, packet
soups, dried fish, fresh vegetables, sweets/
chocolate, fat, tea/coffee, powdered milk,
sugar, rolled oats, fruits and nuts.

FOOD DIGEST

WHAT TO EAT

The different people that comprise Malaysia's multi-racial population provide the country with enough flavours to please every palate. Variety in food is not just restricted to taste either, but extends to the many dining environments you can find yourself in. These range from plush restaurants with air-conditioning, a formal setting and attentive waiters, to the Chinese coffee shop, Malay *kedai makan* (eating shop) and Indian *roti canai* (Indian bread), to the open-air foodstalls to be found in every Malaysian village, town or city.

During your stay in the country, you should eat at the roadside stalls at least once, for it is there that some of the country's most famous and tastiest foods are cooked. And very often, you will find the stall holders as attentive as the waiters of the hotels.

The most popular cuisines are those of the Malays, the Chinese and the Indians. Thai food is also well represented, especially in the north-east Malaysian states. Western food is now ubiquitous, and American fast food outlets are springing up in the smallest of towns.

Malay food is generally rich and spicy, though not as scorchingly hot as Thai or some Indian food. Although each state has its distinctive style of preparation and taste, ingredients are common to all. White steamed rice (*nasi*) is the staple grain. Seafood, chicken and meat (except of course, pork) are cooked in a variety of ways. Coconut forms the basis for many dishes. The "milk" is a popular drink, while the meat is usually grated and squeezed to provide the juice for a tasty sauce. Perhaps the best known of all Malay dishes is *satay*, tender slivers of meat on wooden skewers, which are barbecued over charcoal, and served with a peanut sauce. Depending on the re-

gional recipe, the sauce can either be sweet or spicy. *Satay* is traditionally served with sliced onion, cucumber and *ketupat* (rice cakes steamed in woven palm leaf packets).

Nasi Padang is a variation of Malay food which hails from Padang in Sumatra, and which has the reputation of being extremely hot, though it isn't always, if the local cooks favour sweetness. Dishes are usually displayed on stalls, so you can point to what you want. Other tasty dishes include *tahu goreng*, fried cubes of soya bean curd with fresh bean sprouts; *gado gado*, a salad of raw vegetables topped with a spicy peanut sauce; *laksa*, a type of spicy soup made of fine noodles and fish stock; *mee rebus,* boiled noodles, and *mee siam*, Thai-style noodles.

Besides cakes and sweets mostly made of sago and coconut, there is the popular *gula melaka*, a dessert treat of sago swimming in coconut milk which is topped by a syrup of palm sugar, a delight for those with a sweet tooth.

Chinese cuisine is everywhere in Malaysia, and you'll find it has influenced many of the Malay dishes. Therefore Malays cook noodles and the Chinese use chilli – it's a mutual exchange, except for the forbidden pork, so loved by the Chinese. Hainanese chicken rice (rice cooked in chicken stock and served with steamed chicken and chilli, the latter optional) makes a good lunch. Other dishes are Hakka *yong tau foo* (beancurd stuffed with meat), Hokkien fried *mee* (noodles fried with pieces of meat and seafood) and Chinese *laksa*, which differs from the Malay version. Teochew rice porridge should also be tried; often written as *congee*, the porridge is served with numerous side-dishes of meat and vegetables. *Nonya* food spans both Malay and Chinese cuisines, has many delicacies and tends to be sweeter than Chinese food.

Indian cooking is characterised by its complex and generous use of spices, not all of them hot. Spices include cardamom, clove, anise and cinnamon, as well as the hotter chilli, curry leaves, cumin and turmeric. Many claim that Indian food in Malaysia is better than that in India. There are three traditions of Indian food represented here: North Indian food, which has rich, creamy sauces and which uses the *tandoor* oven; Muslim Indian food, which serves spicy foods such as *rojak* (a selection of eggs, cuttlefish, potatoes and prawns served with a sweet and hot gravy); and South Indian Hindu food, which, near the local temple, is purely vegetarian. The banana leaf curry and fish head curry are two Indian favourites. Indian breads served with a spiced gravy make an excellent breakfast. *Roti canai* (an unleavened bread tossed and cooked on a griddle, with or without egg) is the most popular. Others are *naan* and *chapati*.

FRUITS OF THE LAND

Malaysia is a veritable garden of Eden of fruits all year round. There are the usual tropical fruits – golden pineapple, rosy papaya, and endless types of bananas – as well as a host of other fruits you may not have seen before. Many are seasonal so you'll need to find out what's "in". For certain, at least one or two of them will become your favourite fruits, which you will hanker after when you've left Malaysian shores.

Durian is the king of fruits in South-East Asia. Mixed with a very sweet taste and a texture like blancmange is a subtle flavour of onions. You must try it at least once!

Jambu Batu is also known as *guava*. Both the green skin and the apple-like flesh can be eaten.

Rambutans have a marvellous hairy red-tinged skin. The flesh is similar to lychees and is very refreshing.

Mango comes long or rounded, with yellow or white flesh.

Mangosteen is dark purple and somewhat forbidding on the outside. But squeeze the fruit in your palm, and it opens to reveal white, juicy segments of delicious sweetness. Excellent for travelling with to cool you down on the road. The mangosteen ripens at the same time as the *durian*, and they are traditionally eaten together. Chinese believe that the "heatiness" of the *durian* is balanced by the "coolness" of the *mangosteens*. Beware of the purple juice which stains clothes.

Nangka or jackfruit is the huge green/brown fruit which you often see on trees in villages covered with sacks or plastic bags to protect them from the hungry birds and insects. The pulp is juicy and chewy at the same time. The *chempedak* is a smaller, sweeter version. Jackfruit and *chempedak*

are often deep-fried – a delicious snack, and even the nutty seed inside is edible.

Starfruit, yellow and shiny, is a good thirst-quencher. It is cut horizontally into star-shaped slices and dipped in salt before being eaten.

Pomelo looks and tastes like a sweet, overgrown and somewhat dry grapefruit.

Buah Duku. To open a *duku*, just squeeze the top gently. The flesh is sweet and rather like the rambutan, but with a sour tinge.

Buah Susu, literally translated "milk fruit", is better known as passion fruit. There are many different varieties, all equally delicious. Crisp-skinned and orange from Indonesia, purple from Australia, New Zealand and California, but the local ones have soft, velvety yellow skins. The grey seeds inside are sweet and juicy.

Buah Durian Blanda (literally Dutch *durian*) or soursop, resembles a chunky durian without the smell or the prickles. The soft, creamy flesh inside has just the hint of a sour tang to it.

WHERE TO EAT

The list of restaurants below is just to get you started on your taste journey in Malaysia. Restaurants in hotels have generally not been listed, as most large major hotels carry Chinese and Western restaurants. Venture out of the hotels and explore. There are delicious treats ahead. And don't forget the local foodstalls, where you can eat Malay, Chinese and Indian foods all at one meal.

PENINSULAR MALAYSIA

KUALA LUMPUR
(Federal Territory)

Malay

Indahku
3rd Floor Kuwasa Bldg.
Tel: 03-293-2572

Kampong Restaurant
Jln. Pinang
Tel: 03-243-7113

Kenanga Seafood Restaurant
1st Floor Medan MARA, Jln. Raja Laut
Tel: 03-293-3790

Nasi Padang
Jln. Bukit Bintang, 56 Jln. Sultan Ismail

Nelayan Titiwangsa
1st Floor Podium Block, Dayabumi
Tel: 03-274-7496

The Pines
297 Jln. Tun Sambanthan
Tel: 03-248-1066 (row of restaurants serving Malay and Chinese food)

Satay Ria
9 Jln. Tuanku Abdul Rahman
Tel: 03-291-1648;
90 Jln. Bukit Bintang
Tel: 03-243-2090;
11 Jln. Medan Tuanku Satu
Tel: 03-291-2805;
130 Bangunan Baitulmal, Jln. Ipoh
Tel: 03-291-7806

Yazmin Restaurant
2nd Floor Ampang Park Shopping Complex
Tel: 03-261-7377

Yusoof Restaurant
G8 Central Market
Tel: 03-274-6425

Chinese

Choi Yuen Restuarant
F-082 Sungei Wang Plaza
Tel: 03-242-5638

Futt Yow Yuen Vegetarian Restaurant
48A City Tower, Jln. Alor
Tel: 03-238-0491

**Happy Valley Seafood and
Shark's Fin Restaurant**
Menara Promet, Jln. Sultan Ismail
Tel: 03-241-1264

Lee's Curry Noodle House
130 Jln. Imbi
Tel: 03-248-3118

Lee Wong Kee Restaurant
239 Jln. Tuanku Abdul Rahman
Tel: 03-291-2606

Mak Yee Restaurant
3rd Floor Wisma Shaw, 32 Jln. Sultan Ismail
Tel: 03-248-2404/248-6036

Neptune Restaurant
Wilayah Shopping Centre
Tel: 03-291-5780

Overseas Chinese Restaurant
G2 Central Market
Tel: 03-274-6406

Restoran Teochew
272 Jln. Changkat Thambi Dollah,
off Jln. Pudu
Tel: 03-241-6572

Seng Kee Restaurant
100 Jln. Petaling

Szechuan Restaurant
42-3 Jln. Sultan Ismail
Tel: 03-248-2806

Tai Thong Restaurant
51 Jln. Barat, off Jln. Imbi
Tel: 03-248-8621

Yow Kee Restaurant
56 Jln. Silang
Tel: 03-238-6672

Yoke Woo Thin Restaurant
Jln. Petaling
(KL's oldest Chinese restaurant)

Indian

Ala'din Restaurant (North Indian)
Wilayah Complex
Tel: 03-292-6805

Bangles Restoran (North Indian)
60 Jln. Tuanku Abdul Rahman
Tel: 03-298-3780

Bilal Restaurant (Indian-Muslim food)
33 Jln. Ampang
Tel: 03-238-0804;
37 Jln. Tuanku Abdul Rahman
Tel: 03-292-8948

Devi Annapoorna (Vegetarian)
Lorong Maarof, Bangsar

Devi's Restaurant
27 Jln. Travers, off Jln. Sambanthan
(uses banana leaf)

Kassim Restaurant (*Briyani* rice)
53 Jln. Tuanku Abdul Rahman
Tel: 03-291-1016

Lakshmi Vilas (Vegetarian)
57 Leboh Ampang
Tel: 03-283-5233

Moghul Mahal Restaurant (North Indian)
8 Lorong Bunus, 6 Jln. Masjid India
Tel: 03-293-3402

Japanese

Daikoku
G12 Kompleks Antarabangsa
Tel: 03-242-4750

Fima Rantei Japanese Restaurant
260 Jln. Raja Chula
Tel: 03-243-4608

Irrori Japanese Restaurant
Tower Ground Floor, Bukit Bintang Plaza
Tel: 03-242-6009

Shiruhachi Japanese Restaurant
77 Jln. Bukit Bintang
Tel: 03-241-2311

Korean

Han Kang Korean Restaurant
Medan Imbi, off Jln. Imbi
Tel: 03-243-0260

Thai

Sri Siam Restoran
14 Jln. Utara, off Imbi
Tel: 03-241-3007

Western

Bacchus (French)
Basement Bangunan Safuan
Tel: 03-291-5898

Castell Pub and Grill (steaks)
81 Jln. Bukit Bintang
Tel: 03-242-8328

Cock and Bull Steak House
50 Jln. Bulan, off Jln. Bukit Bintang
Tel: 03-248-7407

Le Coq d'Or (mixed menu)
121 Jln. Ampang (housed in Bok House, a
stately old mansion)
Tel: 03-242-9732

SELANGOR

Bangles Restoran (North Indian)
40 Jln. 52/18, Petaling Jaya
Tel: 03-756-9183

Black Forest Restaurant (German)
Jln. 21/19, PJ
Tel: 03-776-7150

Sri Melaka (Nonya, Thai, Chinese
& Western food)
7 Jln. 52/8 Merdeka Square, PJ
Tel: 03-756-9011

NEGRI SEMBILAN

ABC Restaurant (Malay)
4F Jln. Hang Tuah, Seremban
Tel: 06-723335

Bilal Restaurant (Indian Muslim)
100 Jln. Birch, Seremban
Tel: 06-712251

Condong Sayang (Chinese/Western)
54 Jln. Laksamana, Seremban
Tel: 06-725204

New Hong Kong Restaurant (Chinese)
96 Jln. Temiang, Seremban
Tel: 06-712305

PENANG

Dragon Gate Seafood Restaurant
(Chinese)
562 Tg. Bungah
Tel: 04-894945

Kashmir Restaurant (North Indian)
Basement Oriental Hotel

Pearl Garden Restaurant (Chinese)
13 Jln. MacAlister
Tel: 04-368774

Selamat Restaurant (Malay)
85 Bishop St.
Tel: 04-261031

PERAK

Blue Diamond Restaurant (Chinese,
Malay & Western)
King's Hotel, 91 Jln. Tambun, Ipoh
Tel: 05-513211

Fung Lum Restaurant (Chinese)
Jln. Sultan Idris Shah, Ipoh
Tel: 05-510306

KEDAH

Restoran Selera (Malay)
64 Jln. Teluk Wanjah, Alor Setar
Tel: 04-726738

PERLIS

Chahaya Bintang Restoran (Malay)
314 Jln. Mutiara, Kangar
Tel: 04-752250

Maamor Restoran (Malay)
38 Jln. Penjara, Kangar
Tel: 04-755150

KELANTAN

Budaya Restaurant (Malay & Thai)
367 Jln. Temenggong, Kota Bharu
Tel: 09-721185

Lak Kau Hok Restaurant (Chinese)
2959 Jln. Kebun Sultan, Kota Bharu
Tel: 09-723762

Puspa Restaurant (Malay, Western
& Chinese food)
Hotel Kesina Baru, Jln. Padang Garong,
Kota Bharu
Tel: 09-721455

TERENGGANU

Intan Mastura (Malay, Thai & Western)
19C Jln. Tok Lam, Kuala Terengganu
Tel: 09-622259

Kedai Kopi Cheng Cheng (Chinese)
224 Jln. Bandar, Kuala Terengganu

Taufik Restoran (Malay & Indian food)
18C Jln. Mesjid, Kuala Terengganu
Tel: 09-622501

PAHANG

Apollo Restaurant (Chinese, Western)
23 Telok Chempedak, Kuantan
Tel: 09-524452

Restaurant Tiki (Malay, Western)
9 Jln. Haji Abdul Aziz, Kuantan
Tel: 09-522272

Zam Zam Restaurant (Indian-Muslim)
B-1658 Jln. Beserah, Kuantan
Tel: 09-520360

JOHOR

Delima Restaurant (Malay)
1st Floor Bangunan MARA, Jln. Segget, JB

Eastern Palace Restaurant (Chinese)
2nd Floor Wisma Abad Century Garden, JB
Tel: 07-335823

The Wagonner (Western)
1st Floor Tun Abdul Razak Complex, JB
Tel: 07-324282

SABAH

Gardenia (Western)
55 Jln. Gaya, Kota Kinabalu
Tel: 088-52307

Kuala Lumpur Restaurant (Chinese)
Jln. Tiga, Sandakan
Tel: 089-4309

Rama Restoran (Indonesia)
No. 3 (1st Floor) Jln. Tugu, Kota Kinabalu
Tel: 088-51463

Sri Kayangan (Malay)
Revolving restaurant at Sabah Foundation
Bldg., Lakes Bay, Kota Kinabalu

SARAWAK

Anika Restaurant (Chinese)
27 Hock Peng Complex, Bintulu
Tel: 086-31391

Hock Chii Lew Restaurant (Chinese & Western)
38 Blacksmith Road, Sibu
Tel: 084-21254

Kah Hing Restaurant (Chinese)
29 Brooke Road, Miri
Tel: 085-31322

Kinto Restaurant (Chinese)
28 Law Gek Soon Road, Bintulu
Tel: 086-31016

Malaya Restaurant (Indian-Muslim)
Jln. India, Kuching

Metropol Restaurant (Indian-Muslim)
20 Pulo Road, Sibu
Tel: 084-24189

Permata Food Centre
Jln. Padungan, Kuching (foodstalls, Chinese, Malay, Indian, Western, Indonesian & Philippino food)

Roda Restaurant (Muslim)
7A Jln. Merbau, Miri
Tel: 085-31814

Ruby Cafe (Chinese)
Jln. Green Hill, Kuching

DRINKING NOTES

In general, alcohol is expensive in Malaysia. A glass of wine may cost as much as a tot of brandy, and the heat of the tropics does not always guarantee a good flavour. Alcohol is forbidden to Muslims, so if you want to indulge in alcoholic beverages, head for the hotels and the Chinese liquor stores. The latter have a fascinating range of familiar and strange bottles on their shelves. Tiger and Anchor beer and Guinness Stout are the most popular and the cheapest.

But far more refreshing in the steamy atmosphere of the tropics are the fruit juices, to be found at small stalls and night markets. Choose your combination: pineapple and orange, starfruit and water melon. If you don't want sugar, ask them not to add the sugar syrup; in Kelantan, salt is often added to cut fruits and juices, which may not be to your taste – ask them for plain fruit or juice. There are a variety of very sweet coconut and soya bean drinks for sale at small stalls, with alarmingly bright colours added to them. Young coconuts produce a refreshing milk which can be drunk straight from the coconut with ice added and a straw stuck into a hole made in the top. Mineral water is sold in grocery stores and in supermarkets.

CULTURE PLUS

MUSEUMS

Malaysia has a host of museums. Most intriguing and most talked about is the **Sarawak Museum** in Kuching, founded in 1888 by the second white Rajah, Sir Charles Brooke, and the great evolutionist, Alfred Russell Wallace. Their foresight resulted in the finest collection of Borneo artistry yet amassed, and the museum is visited annually by more than 10,000 people.

Other museums that must be visited include Kuala Lumpur's **Musium Negara** (**National Museum**), with its life-size displays of court and *kampong* life, the **Malacca Museum**, crowded with Menangkabau treasures and colonial mementos, and the **Perak State Museum** in Taiping. All museums in Malaysia are documented in Exploring Malaysia in the appropriate sections. Most museums are open from 9 a.m. to 6 p.m. daily, except for Fridays when they are closed between noon and 2.30 p.m. Admission to museums is free. Permission to view archives not on display can be obtained by consulting the curator of the museum.

ART GALLERIES

Paintings on Malaysian art gallery walls mirror the essence of the traditional way of life, and the conflict of the new. Much can be gleaned about how young Malaysian artists envision the future. Current exhibitions are well worth a visit. Batik painting is much favoured, combining an old art with contemporary scenes, such as a youth and his girl-friend on a motorbike. But other media are equally popular, and range from water colours of *kampong* scenes to abstract oil paintings to performance art.

Besides the main public art galleries, there are many small galleries in towns, cities and artists' villages, where you can buy a painting from the artist himself.

MOVIES

Subtle drama never stays on the action-packed billboards long. Most Asians buy tickets for noisy, wild entertainment and the more action the better. Favourite topics are bloody fist fights, mass murder, dope smuggling, opium smoking, prostitution and car chases. Fans flock to see the "good guys" win in the end, in the guise of sword fighters, war heroes, gang leaders, tough detectives and sharp-shooting cowboys.

The Asian cinema, if you can take the gore, is unabashedly explosive and violent. Vampires and dinosaurs shriek across the screen nearly every week. There are, of course, soft moments that linger on young love and family comedy. Indonesian movies are very popular, and often deal with mythological characters fighting the battle of Good versus Evil.

You will be able to sample this kind of cinema if you hop on a long distance bus. Regardless of whether you want to hear and see it, the bus video with the sound at top volume is suspended from the ceiling to alleviate the boredom of the journey. American car chases and *kung fu* fights strike an incongruous note when viewed alongside the passing scenery.

DANCES

Performances of *Wayang Kulit*, *Mak Yong*, *Menora* and *Ronggeng* are most likely to be found on the east coast of the peninsula, unless there is an official occasion such as National Day. Details of these dances and shows are usually documented in the region's Calendar of Events released by the Tourist Corporation (TDC) and can be picked up from their offices. In remoter places, a friendly local may well tell you if there is something on in the vicinity – it's always worth asking if they don't. For a description of these art forms, turn to "The Malays – Sons of the Soil".

NIGHTLIFE

PUBS & DISCOS

All That Jazz
14 Jln. 19/36, Petaling Jaya
Tel: 03-755-3152
Live jazz music.

Bier Keller
24 Jln. 14/14, PJ
Tel: 03-756-0444
Entertainment by keyboardist and singer.

Booze N Ooze Pub & Lounge
50 Jln. SS21/39, Damansara Utama, PJ
Organist entertains nightly except Sunday.

Bottoms Up Pub
SS5B/6, PJ
Tel: 03-775-6940
Daily from 4 p.m. to midnight.

Centrepoint Pub & Restaurant
11 SS2/30, PJ
Tel: 03-775-6790
Serves spicy nonya food.

Chequers Pub & Grill
Jln. Kosah, Medan Damansara,
Kuala Lumpur
Wine bar opens at 5 p.m.; live band entertains nightly with popular hits and country and western numbers; closed on Sunday.

Club Fukiko
Menara Promet, KL
Tel: 03-241-7825
Exclusive lounge with hostesses from 8 p.m.-1 a.m. daily.

Copper Grill
Menara Promet, KL
Tel: 03-241-7790
Live entertainment from 8.30 p.m. to 12.30 a.m. (till 1.30 a.m. on Saturdays); supper of local specialities from 11 p.m. to 2 a.m.

Country Inn Jazz Restoran & Pub
Bangunan MCOBA, Jln. Syed Putra, KL
Tel: 03-274-2501
Favourite haunt of Malaysian Union of Musicians.

El Rodrigo
Damansara Jaya, PJ
Tel: 03-718-8426
Live entertainment from 9 p.m. to 1 a.m. daily except Sunday.

Four Aces Pub & Grill
10 Jln. SS6/3, PJ
Tel: 03-703-0063
Entertainment from 9 p.m. to midnight.

Hard Rock Cafe
Taman Tun Dr Ismail, KL
Live entertainment from 9.30 p.m. to 1 a.m.

Hilton Petaling Jaya
Jln. Barat, PJ
Tel: 03-755-3533
Keyboardist and live band perform nightly at Anggerik Lounge.

Holiday Inn City Centre
Jln. Pinang, KL
Tel: 03-248-1066
Rama Rama Lounge, a comfortable cocktail bar with live music from 8 p.m. to midnight.

Holiday Inn on the Park
Jln. Raja Laut, KL
Tel: 03-293-9233
Kapitan Lobby Bar: 8 p.m. to midnight.

Hollywood East
Ampang Park Rooftop
Tel: 03-261-5130
One of the world's largest disco.

Honky Tonk Saloon
11 SS21/1A, Damansara Utama, PJ
Tel: 03-703-0718
Entertainment from 9.30 p.m. to midnight except Monday.

Hot Beauty Lounge
SS2/24, PJ
Tel: 03-775-0520
Daily entertainment by live band.

Hotel Dayang
Off Jln. Barat, PJ
Tel: 03-755-5155
Cafe Desa offers buffet lunch. My Appointment Disco-Lounge: 8 p.m. to 2 a.m.

House of Ma-Ku-Teh
10 Jln. Yong Shook Lin, PJ
Serves North and South Indian cuisine, clay pot chicken, *ma-ku-teh*, chicken or fish tika and bone marrow mysore. Happy hours from 7 to 11.30 p.m.

Kafe Rendezvous
1st Floor, Wilayah Shopping Complex, KL
Tel: 03-291-0232
Live entertainment daily.

Kuala Lumpur Hilton
Jln. Sultan Ismail, KL
Tel: 03-242-2222/2122
Club Bar; English pub luncheon. Table games and bar service. Open from noon to 1 a.m. Aviary Lobby Bar: open from 11 a.m., with live entertainment. Tin Mine Discotheque; theme nights and showtime.

Kuala Lumpur International Hotel
Jln. Raja Muda, KL
Tel: 03-292-9133
La Rosette Coffee House serves Malaysian buffet lunch and Chinese set lunch.

Kuala Lumpur Station Hotel
Jln. Sultan Hishamuddin, KL
Tel: 03-274-7885
Serves Western set lunch and dinner. Dinner daily 6 to 10 p.m. Pub opens till midnight.

Longhorn
1 Jln. SS21/1A, Damansara Utama, PJ
Tel: 03-719-9508
Music nightly from 9 p.m.

Manhattan Jazz Bistro
Mezzanine Floor, Hotel Fortuna, 50200 KL
Tel: 03-241-9111

Merlin Kuala Lumpur
24-hour coffeehouse; singer and keyboardist entertain nightly from 10 p.m. onwards.

Midway Grill & Lounge
Jln. Setiapuspa, Medan Damansara, KL
Tel: 03-255-5861
Western cuisine from noon to midnight.

Ming Court Hotel
Jln. Ampang, KL
Tel: 03-261-8888
Kencana Lounge opens from 10 p.m. to 1 a.m. (weekdays) and till 2 a.m. on weekends and eve of public holidays. Cafe Boulevard: Paris style sidewalk cafe with Continental and local fare served daily from 11 a.m. to 11 p.m. Ming Palace Chinese Restaurant opens from noon to 3 and 7 to 11 p.m.

New Cabana Pub & Lounge
Jln. Brickfields, KL
Tel: 03-274-9332
Singers entertain daily from 1 p.m. until midnight.

New Fujiya Cocktail Lounge
Jln. Burhanuddin Helmi,
Taman Tun Dr Ismail, KL
Tel: 03-718-9334
Serves Western cuisine. Singer and keyboardist perform daily.

New Moon Raker
Jln. Telawi, Bangsar Baru, KL
Tel: 03-254-0509
Live performance from 9.30 p.m. to 1 a.m.

Ono Supper Club
4th Floor, Wisma Selangor Dredging, KL
From 8 p.m. to 2 a.m. Has a karaoke (with hostess). Live music entertainment.

Olivia Steakhouse
61/2km, Jln. Ampang, KL
Tel: 03-456-7766
Live entertainment daily from 8.30 p.m. onwards.

Paddy's Pub & Restaurant
26 Pesiaran Ampang, KL
Tel: 03-456-3883
Live entertainment: 8.30 p.m. to midnight.

Pan Pacific Hotel
Jln. Putra, KL
Tel: 03-442-5555
Selera Terrace serves authentic northern style *nasi kandar*. Selera Coffee House and Continental Restaurant serve Swiss delights. Hai Tien Lo Chinese Restaurant also offers *tim sum* menu. Keyaki Japanese Restaurant serves *jingiskan*, a speciality which originates from Hokkaido.

Pertama Cabaret Niteclub
Pertama Complex, KL
Tel: 03-298-2533
Entertainment by Hong Kong and Taiwanese starlets.

Pink Coconut Discotheque
Hotel Malaya, Jln. Hang Lekir, KL
Tel: 03-238-7655
Disco opens from 8 p.m. onwards.

Plaza Hotel
Jln. Raja Laut, KL
Tel: 03-298-2255
Keyboardist and singer entertain nightly at Pipers Bar Lounge with popular hits and country and western numbers. Open daily from 5 p.m. to 1 a.m.

Prince Kuala Lumpur
Jln. Imbi, KL
Tel: 03-243-8388
Pianist at Rajah Lounge from 5 p.m. to midnight, Monday to Saturday. Poolside barbecue every Sunday and public holiday.

Pub Wagon Wheel
Jln. Tun Mohd. Fuad 1,
Taman Tun Dr Ismail, KL
Tel: 03-718-2004
Country and western setting with country singers from Monday to Saturday. Lunch, noon to 2.30 p.m.; dinner, 7 to 10 p.m.

Regent Kuala Lumpur
Jln. Sultan Ismail, KL
Tel: 03-242-5588
Live entertainment at garden lounge. Monday to Saturday: 5 p.m. to 1 a.m. Regent Club has live disco band.

Shangri-La Hotel
Jln. Sultan Ismail, KL
Tel: 03-232-2388
Live entertainment at lobby lounge from 8
p.m. to 1 a.m.; till 2 a.m. on Saturday and
holiday eves.

Sapphire Discotheque
3rd Floor, Yow Chuan Plaza, KL
Tel: 03-243-0043
Live disco band with lasers.

Seventh Avenue
2nd Floor, Annexe Block,
Menara Apera-ULG, Jln. Raja Chulan, KL
Tel: 03-261-1041

Stargazer Penthouse Discotheque
20th & 21st Floors (Penthouse),
Semua House, Lorong Bunus 6, KL
Tel: 03-293-1577

Tattlers Grill and Lounge
6 Jln. Telawi·Lima, Bangsar, KL
Tel: 03-254-4117
Entertainment by singer from 9.30 p.m. to
midnight.

Traffic Lights
42 & 44, Jln. Sultan Ismail, KL
Tel: 03-248-1282
Nightly 9 p.m. onwards. No casual wear.

Yuyi Grill & Lounge
Loke Yew Building, KL
Tel: 03-298-0206
Opens 6 p.m. to midnight daily.

SHOPPING

SHOPPING AREAS IN KL

DEPARTMENT STORES

Angel
Ampang Shopping Centre, KL,
Tel: 03-261-1544

Batu Road Supermarket
453 Jln. Tuanku Abdul Rahman, KL,
Tel: 03-298-0539

Calan
Plaza Yow Chuan, KL, Tel: 03-248-3659

Chotirmall
131 Jln. Tuanku Abdul Rahman, KL,
Tel: 03-292-8228

Dyalchands
63 Jln. Tuanku Abdul Rahman, KL,
Tel: 03-292-7033

**Fajar Departmental Store
& Supermarkets**
51 Jln. SS21/37, Damansara Utama, PJ,
Tel: 03-719-1123

Hankyu Jaya Shopping Centre
452 Jln. Tuanku Abdul Rahman, KL,
Tel: 03-442-4866

Lin Ho
15 Jln. Hang Lekir, KL, Tel: 03-238-0261

Malaysia Emporium
38 Jln. Tuanku Abdul Rahman, KL,
Tel: 03-298-3850

Metrojaya
Bukit Bintang Plaza, KL, Tel: 03-242-3277

Mun Loong
113 Jln. Tuanku Abdul Rahman, KL,
Tel: 03-298-7688

St. Michael
9 Jln. SS24/11, PJ, Tel: 03-774-1377

Tang Ling Shopping Centre
187 Jln. Tuanku Abdul Rahman, KL,
Tel: 03-292-9885

SHOPPING CENTRES

Ampang Park Shopping Centre
Jln. Ampang, Tel: 03-261-4311

Bukit Bintang Plaza
Jln. Bukit Bintang, Tel: 03-248-7653

Campbell Shopping Complex
Jln. Dang Wangi, Tel: 03-292-8590

Central Market
Jln. Hang Kasturi, Tel: 03-274-6542

Chinatown
Jln. Petaling

Dayabumi
Jln. Sultan Hishamuddin, Tel: 03-274-8899

Goldsmiths Row
Along Lebuh Pudu and Jln. Bandar

Imbi Plaza
Jln. Imbi, Tel: 03-242-3506

Indian Shopping Area
Jln. Masjid India and Jln. Melayu

Kota Raya Complex
Jln. Tun Cheng Lock, Tel: 03-232-2562

Kuala Lumpur Plaza
Jln. Bukit Bintang, Tel: 03-241-7288

The Mall
Jln. Putra, Tel: 03-442-7122

Pertama Complex
Jln. Tuanku Abdul Rahman,
Tel: 03-292-7457

Sungei Wang Plaza
Jln. Sultan Ismail, Tel: 03-243-0311

Wilayah Centre
Jln. Dang Wangi, Tel: 03-291-5534

Plaza Yow Chuan
Jln. Tun Razak, Tel: 03-242-1566

ANTIQUES & CURIOS

Ahmad Curios Art & Handicrafts
Pasar Minggu Kampong Baru, KL,
Tel: 03-298-4258

Asia Arts & Crafts
Kuala Lumpur Hilton, KL,
Tel: 03-242-3631

Celadon
18 Jln. Utara, KL, Tel: 03-242-1038

Chin Li Fine Arts & Furniture
13 Jln. Tun Mohd. Fuad 3, KL,
Tel: 03-718-1000

Eastern Stamps, Coins & Antiques
Sungei Wang Plaza, KL, Tel: 03-243-5418

H Raby Antiques
16 Pinggiran Ukay, KL, Tel: 03-457-3698

KL Goh Crafts
137 Jln. SS2/24, PJ, Tel: 03-774-3650

Kashmir Arts Pro Sharma
174 Jln. Tuanku Abdul Rahman, KL,
Tel: 03-292-1019

King's Art
Hotel Regent, KL, Tel: 03-242-4554

Man Art Gallery
Kuala Lumpur Hilton, KL,
Tel: 03-243-1724

Peiping Lace
223 Jln. Tuanku Abdul Rahman, KL,
Tel: 03-298-3184

Peking Art Co.
Sungei Wang Plaza, KL, Tel: 03-248-7781

Peking Crafts & Furniture
61 Jln. SS2/64, PJ, Tel: 03-776-1350

Shang Antiquities
Wisma Stephens, KL, Tel: 03-248-2935

Warisan Syarikat (Heritage)
Jaya Supermarket, PJ, Tel: 03-755-3942

CAMERAS & FILMS

Bee Loh Photo Supplies
85 Jln. Bukit Bintang, KL,
Tel: 03-241-3641;
58 Jln. Pudu, KL, Tel: 03-238-9849

Eresindo Jaya Trading Co.
21 Jln. SS2/67, PJ, Tel: 03-776-2928

Foto Jaya
Jaya Supermarket, PJ, Tel: 03-757-3014

Fotokem Sdn. Bhd.
Sungei Wang Plaza, KL, Tel: 03-248-7240

Foto Shangri-La
40-3 Jln. Sultan Ismail, KL,
Tel: 03-242-3088;
Plaza Yow Chuan, KL, Tel: 03-243-7670;
Wisma Lim Foo Yong, KL,
Tel: 03-248-8903;
15 Jln. SS2/64, PJ, Tel: 03-775-7006

Peter Photo Centre
Sungei Wang Plaza, KL, Tel: 03-243-2414

Selangor Photographers
Pertama Complex, KL, Tel: 03-298-0390

Shong Lee Trading (M) Sdn. Bhd.
Ampang Park Shopping Centre, KL,
Tel: 03-261-4828

Wing Wah Photo
212 Jln. Bandar, KL, Tel: 03-238-8700

Y S Photo Studio & Colour Processing
33 Jln. SS2/75, PJ, Tel: 03-776-0373

GIFTS & SOUVENIRS

Al Trade
43 Jln. 2/71, Taman Tun Dr Ismail, KL,
Tel: 03-718-7953

Casey (M'sia) Sdn. Bhd.
Imbi Plaza, KL, Tel: 03-243-2038

Cheong Ying Hong
Arcade Hotel Federal, KL,
Tel: 03-248-3540

Fleur De-Lis
Wisma HLA, KL, Tel: 03-243-5997

G S Agencies
63-D Jln. Sultan, KL, Tel: 03-230-1150

Ginza Store
53 Jln. Petaling, KL, Tel: 03-238-3704

Gladys Gifts Shop
Wisma Stephens, KL, Tel: 03-241-3218

Himawari (M) Sdn. Bhd.
Wisma Stephens, KL, Tel: 03-243-6435

Hongwa Gifts & Crafts Centre
22A Jln. Tun Mohd. Fuad 2, KL,
Tel: 03-718-2027

House of Fragrance & Gift
Kuala Lumpur Plaza, KL, Tel: 03-241-9275

Orient House
Ampang Shopping Centre, KL,
Tel: 03-261-2195

Peking Art Co.
Sungei Wang Plaza, KL, Tel: 03-248-7781

Phoenix Syarikat
16 Jln. Yong Shook Lin, PJ,
Tel: 03-756-9195

Silver Presentation
41A Jln. SS22/19, Damansara Jaya, PJ,
Tel: 03-719-6744

Wanree's Gifts & Novelties
Central Market, KL, Tel: 03-274-6725

Watchcraft
Ampang Shopping Centre, KL,
Tel: 03-261-5176

Woody's Gift Corner
Ampang Shopping Centre, KL,
Tel: 03-261-6630

HANDICRAFTS

Batek Malaysia
Wisma Batik, Jln. Tun Perak,
Tel: 291-8608;
114 Jln. Bukit Bintang, Tel: 243-4054

Karyaneka
Jln. Raja Chulan, Tel: 243-1686

Selangor Pewter Co. Sdn. Bhd.
4 Jln. Usahawan 6, KL, Tel: 03-422-1000;
231 Jln. Tuanku Abdul Rahman, KL,
Tel: 03-298-6244

Selangor Pewter Marketing
54 Jln. SS2/67, PJ, Tel: 03-774-7290;
Kuala Lumpur Plaza, KL,
Tel: 03-243-6419;
Hotel Shangri-La, KL, Tel: 03-230-3070;
Kuala Lumpur Hilton, KL,
Tel: 03-248-5104;
Pan Pacific Hotel, KL, Tel: 03-442-1784

Selex Corpn. Sdn. Bhd.
17 Kawasan Perindustrian Ringan, Setapak,
KL, Tel: 03-423-0341

Tumasek Pewter Sdn. Bhd.
16 Jln. Kanan, Taman Kepong, Kepong, KL,
Tel: 03-634-1249

PASAR MALAM (NIGHT MARKETS)

An integral part of shopping in KL is the
Pasar Malam. Caravan-like traders move
from one spot to another selling their wares,
and for those who like good bargains, jos-
tling and pushing, it's all good fun. Always
try to bargain. Here are the markets you can
go to depending on the days of the week:

Sunday
– Pasar Malam Taman Tun Dr Ismail
  Along Jln. Tun Mohd. Fuad
– Pasar Malam Taman Maluri
  Along Jln. Pria

Monday
– Pasar Malam Jln. Kangsar, Jln. Ipoh
  Along service roads and empty spaces
– Pasar Malam Jln. Wira, Taman Maluri
  Along Jln. Wira

Tuesday
– Pasar Malam Kawasan Rumah Pangsa
  3½ Miles Jln. Cheras
  Along blocks 4, 5 and 6
– Pasar Malam Jln. Cemor,
  off Jln. Tun Razak
  Along Jln. Cemor

– Pasar Malam Sri Petaling
  Along Jln. Perlak 1, Jln. Pasar 5 and 4, and
  Jln. Pasai

Wednesday
– Pasar Malam Bandar Baru Tun Razak
  Jln. Bangsawan, along the stretch between
  Jln. Makmur and Jln. Ikhlas
– Pasar Malan Kawasan Bukit Bangsar
  Along the stretch between Sri Pahang flat
  area and Railway Quarters
– Pasar Malam Setapak Garden
  Along the stretch between the Surau
  (place of worship) and Jln. Serjak
– Pasar Malam Taman Kok Lian
  Jln. Ipoh, 5th Mile, on the vacant area
  directly opposite the shophouses

Thursday
– Pasar Malam Rumah Pangsa PKNS
  Jln. Kuching, the surrounding area of the
  apartments
– Pasar Malam Rumah Pangsa
  Sri Terengganu Sentul
– Pasar Malam Taman Cheras
  Along the stretch between Jln. Kaskas and
  Jln. Chengkeh
– Pasar Malam Overseas Union Garden

Friday
– Pasar Malam Kg. Cheras Baru Sentul
  Along Jln. Sentul
– Pasar Malam Taman Desa
  Along Jln. Desa Utama/Jln. Desa Permai

Saturday
– Pasar Malam Bandar Tun Razak
  (Jln. Jujur)
  Along Jln. Jujur Empat
– Pasar Malam Kg. Pasir, Petaling,
  Jln. Kelang Lama
  Along Jln. Kg. Pasir
– Pasar Malam Setapak Jaya
  Along Jln. Rejang 4/6/7
– Pasar Malam Jln. Tuanku Abdul Rahman
  Along Jln. Tuanku Abdul Rahman

Note: There is a nightmarket every night
(unless it rains) in Petaling Street, KL's
Chinatown, and along Chow Kit Road (further up Jln. Tuanku Abdul Rahman)

MARKETS IN SABAH

The *tamu* is a town market in Sabah that brings farmers and their wives down from the hills to sell their produce. Bajau cowboys come to the *tamu* to buy and sell horses, and there are also buffaloes for sale. A colourful array of fruit and vegetables are sold alongside betel nut, baskets, and household goods. *Tamus* were encouraged by the British colonial government, as they brought people from remote tribes together. If you are travelling in Sabah, you will be bound to come upon the weekly *tamu* in a town centre. It is best to go early in the morning when the most heated selling takes place. Below is a list of the main *tamu* and the days of the week on which they are held:

Babaggon	Saturday
Beaufort	Saturday
Keningau	Thursday
Kinarut	Saturday
Kionsom	Sunday
Kiulu	Tuesday
Kota Belud	Sunday
Kota Merudu	Sunday
Kuala Penyu	1st Wednesday of the month
Kundasang	20th of the month
Mangis	Thursday
Mattunggon	Saturday
Membakut	Sunday
Mersapol	Friday
Papar	Sunday
Penampang	Saturday
Putatan	Sunday
Ranau	1st of the month
Sequati	Sunday
Simpangan	Thursday
Sindumin	Saturday
Sinsuran	Friday
Sipitang	Thursday
Tambunan	Thursday
Tamparuli	Wednesday
Tandek	Monday
Telipok	Thursday
Tenghilan	Thursday
Tenom	Sunday
Tinnopok	15th and 30th of the month
Toboh	Sunday
Topokom	Tuesday
Tuaran	Sunday
Weston	Friday

SPORTS

PARTICIPANT

Malaysia is a land of sports. A visitor can enjoy a game of football at an urban field or witness a top-spinning contest in a rural village. Badminton nets are erected on almost every vacant lot available, and not having the right equipment will never deter the sporty Malays from playing the game with improvised rackets and shuttlecocks. For those wishing to participate in a sport, there are abundant facilities throughout the country.

FISHING

There is good angling to be had in the numerous river tributaries which indent the country's coastline. Marine game fishes such as barracuda, shark and Spanish mackerel may be sighted off the east coast of the peninsula from May to October.

If your trip does not allow you enough time for the trial-and-error process of finding a good fishing hole, contact a local tour agent (see "Useful Addresses") specialising in arranging fishing trips to the Taman Negara (National Park). For inland fishing, a licence is required. The months between March and October provide the most suitable weather conditions.

GOLF

Malaysia has over 50 golf clubs with 9 or 18-hole courses. Some of the more prominent ones are listed below.

PENINSULAR MALAYSIA

• Selangor & Federal Territory

Carey Island Gold Club
Selangor 42700, Carey Island

Tel: 03-318611
Course: 9-hole Private.

Kelab Darul Ehsan KL
Jln. Kerja Air Nama, Taman Tun Abdul
Razak, 68000 Ampang Jaya
Tel: 03-457-2333
Course: 9-hole Proprietory.

Kelab Golf Angkatan Tentera
Jln. Lapangan Terabing Lama,
P.O. Box 12577, 50682 KL
Tel: 03-456-9758
Course: 9-hole Private.

Kelab Golf Diraja Selangor
(The Royal Selangor Golf Club)
Jln. Kelab Golf, P.O. Box 11051, 50734 KL
Tel: 03-242-8433
Course: 45-hole Private.

Kelab Golf Negara Subang
P.O. Box 151, 46710 Petaling Jaya
Tel: 03-776-0388
Course: 36-hole Private.

Kelab Golf Sri Morib
Morib, Banting, Kuala Langat
Tel: 03-867-1732
Course: 9-hole.

Kelab Rekreasi Tentera Udara
c/o Pejabat DCOS (air) Materiel Dept.
Tentera Udara, Kementerian Pertahanan,
50634 KL
Tel: 03-755-4873
Course: 18-hole Private (Armed Forces).

Kuala Kubu Baru Golf and Country Club
Kuala Kubu Baru, Selangor
Tel: 03-804-2258
Course: 9-hole Private.

Royal Kampung Kuantan Golf Club
45700 Bukit Rotan, Selangor
Tel: 03-889-1069
Course: 9-hole Private.

Saujana Golf & Country Club
Batu 3 Jln. Lapangan Terbang,
47200 Subang
Tel: 03-746-1466
Course: 36-hole Proprietory.

Sentul Golf Club KL
No. 84 Jln. Strachen, 51100 KL
Tel: 03-298-9410
Course: 9-hole Private.

• Negri Sembilan

Dunlop Bahau Golf Club
Ladang Bahau, 72109 Bahau, NS
Tel: 03-841126
Course: 9-hole Private.

Port Dickson Garrison Golf Club
71050 NS
Tel: 06-471266
Course: 9-hole Private.

Royal Sri Menanti Golf Club
71550 Sri Menanti, NS
Tel: 06-813600
Course: 9-hole Palace Club.

Seremban International Golf Club
P.O. Box 88, 70710 Seremban, NS
Tel: 06-712787
Course: 18-hole Private.

• Melaka

Ayer Keroh Country Club
P.O. Box 232, 75450 Melaka
Tel: 06-322947
Course: 18-hole Private.

Jasin Golf Club
Jasin, 77000 Melaka
Tel: 06-987234
Course: 9-hole Private.

Kelab Golf Bukit Terendak
c/o Markas III Divisyen Kem Terendak,
66200 Melaka
Tel: 06-223133
Course: 9-hole Private (Armed Forces).

• Penang

Airbase Butterworth Golf Club
RAAF Airbase Butterworth,
12009 Butterworth
Tel: 04-347666
Course: 9-hole Private (Armed Forces).

Bukit Jambul Country Club
c/o Island Golf Property Sdn. Bhd.,
No. 1 Sungei Nibong,
Bandar Bayan Baru, 11909 Bayan Lepas
Tel: 04-838552
Course: 9-hole Proprietory.

Penang Turf Club
(Golf Section) 10450 Batu Gantong, Penang
Tel: 04-67176
Course: 9-hole Private.

• Perak

Idris Shah Golf Club, Telok Intan
28 Jln. Changkat Jong,
36000 Telok Intan, Perak
Tel: 05-621238
Course: 9-hole Private.

Kelab Golf Di Raja Perak
(Royal Perak Golf Club)
Tiger Lane, 31400 Ipoh, Perak
Tel: 05-565560
Course: 18-hole Private.

Kinta Golf Club, Batu Gajah
31000 Batu Gajah, Perak
Tel: 05-761236
Course: 9-hole Private.

The New Club
P.O. Box 42, 34007 Taiping, Perak
Tel: 05-823935
Course: 9-hole Private.

Pangkor Island Country Club
c/o The Manager, Pangkor Island Country
Club, 32300 Pangkor Island, Perak
Course: 9-hole Proprietory

• Kedah

Dublin Club
c/o Ladang Sungai Dingin, P.O. Box 201,
09700 Karangan
Tel: 04-546233
Course: 9-hole Private.

Harvard Club
c/o Harvard Estate, 08100 Bedong
Tel: 04-61026
Course: 9-hole Private.

Langkawi Island Golf Club
07000 Pulau Langkawi, Kedah
Tel: 04-788410
Course: 9-hole Public.

Royal Kedah Golf Club, Alor Setar
Kelab Kedah Diraja, Pumpong,
05250 Alor Setar
Tel: 04-727467
Course: 9-hole Private.

Sungei Petani Golf Club
The Secretary, Sungei Petani Golf Club,
08000 Sungei Petani, Kedah
Tel: 04-412653
Course: 9-hole Private.

• Perlis

Kelab Golf Putra Perlis
Kelab Golf Putra Perlis, 01000 Kangar
Tel: 04-752199
Course: 9-hole Private.

• Kelantan

Kelab Kelantan Diraja
Jln. Hospital, 15200 Kota Bharu
Tel: 09-782102
Course: 18-hole Private.

• Terengganu

Badariah Golf Club
c/o Pejabat Setiausaha Sulit Duli Yang
Maha Mulia Sultan Terengganu,
20500 Kuala Terengganu
Tel: 09-632456
Course: 9-hole Palace Club.

Dungun Country Club
P.O. Box 679, Dungun 23007
Tel: 09-641899
Course: 9-hole Private.

Kelab Golf Diraja Terengganu
c/o Jabatan Kerjaraya, Wisma Darul Imam,
20500 Kuala Terengganu
Tel: 09-622111
Course: 9-hole Private.

Kerteh Golf Club
Rantau Petronas, Kerteh 24000 Kemaman
Tel: 09-671357
Course: 9-hole Public.

• Pahang

Awana Golf and Country Club
Genting Highlands, 9th Floor Wisma
Genting, Jln. Sultan Ismail, 50250 KL
Telex: 32324 or 69000.
Genting Highlands, P.O. Box 11482,
50746 KL
Tel: 03-211-3015
Course: 18-hole Proprietory.

Cameron Golf Course
Majlis Daerah Cameron Highlands,
P.O. Box 66, 39007 Tanah Rata
Tel: 05-941728
Course: 18-hole Private.

Fraser's Hill Golf Course
c/o Fraser's Hill Development Corpn.,
49000 Fraser's Hill
Tel: 09-382201
Course: 9-hole Public.

Kelab Golf Bentong
Batu 2 Jln. Tras, P.O. Box 24,
28707 Bentong
Tel: 09-222585
Course: 9-hole Private.

Kelab Golf Diraja Pahang
P.O. Box 53, 25700 Kuantan, Pahang
Tel: 09-527701
Course: 9-hole Private.

Kelab Golf Raub
Jln. Bukit Koman, P.O. Box 7, 27600 Raub
Tel: 09-351937
Course: 9-hole Private.

Pulau Tioman Island Club
P.O. Box 4, 86807 Mersing, Johor, or
Tioman Golf Management Sdn. Bhd., 17th
Floor Menara Kewangan, Jln. Sultan Ismail,
50250 KL
Tel: 09-445444, 03-230-5266
Telex: MA50279
Course: 9-hole Public.

• Johor

Desaru Golf Resort
P.O. Box 57, Kota Tinggi, 81907 Johor
Tel: 07-838187
Course: 18-hole Proprietory.

Gagak Golf Club, Segamat
P.O. Box 22, Segamat, 85000 Johor
Tel: 07-911442
Course: 9-hole Private.

Kelab Golf Batu Pahat
678, Jln. Dato Mohd. Shah,
83000 Batu Pahat
Tel: 07-222022
Course: 9-hole Private.

Kelab Golf Tanjung Emas, Muar
No. JKR 202, Jln. Timbalan, Muar,
84000 Johor
Tel: 06-922591
Course: 9-hole Private.

Kluang Golf Club
Jln. Mengkibol, 86000 Kluang, Johor
Tel: 07-718840
Course: 9-hole Private.

Royal Johor Country Club
Jln. Larkin, 80200 Johor Bahru, Johor
Tel: 07-228882
Course: 18-hole Private .

Sagil Golf Club
Sagil Estate, Tangkak, 84900 Johor
Tel: 06-932331/2
Course: 9-hole Private.

Ulu Remis GCC
Ulu Remis Estate, P.O. Box 103, 81850
Layang-Layang, Johor
Course: 9-hole Private.

SABAH

Kelab Golf Kudat
89050 Kudat
Course: 9-hole Private.

Keningau Golf Club
P.O. Box 94, 89000 Keningau
Tel: 088-31113
Course: 9-hole Private.

Kinabalu Golf Club
P.O. Box 654, Kota Kinabalu
Tel: 088-55199
Course: 9-hole Private.

Sabah Golf & Country Club
P.O. Box 11876, Kota Kinabalu
Tel: 088-56900
Course: 18-hole Private.

The Sandakan Golf Club
P.O. Box 406, 90007 Sandakan
Course: 9-hole Private.

SARAWAK

Kelab Golf Miri
c/o Sarawak Shell Berhad, 98100 Lutong
Tel: 082-453039
Course: 18-hole Private.

The Sarawak Golf & Country Club
Petra Jaya, 93050 Kuching
Tel: 082-23622
Course: 18-hole Private.

Sibu Golf Club
10½ Mile P.O. Box 1234, 96008 Sibu
Course: 9-hole Private.

HUNTING

Hunting is restricted in many areas and is subject to a licence from the Department of Wildlife and National Parks in Kuala Lumpur, Tel: 03-941272. There are hundreds of protected animal species in Malaysia. Obtain more information from the Parks Office.

KARATE

The popularity of karate with the locals has led to the growth of over 150 karate centres in Malaysia. Visitors who wish to try their hand at it can make special arrangements with the Chief Instructor at the Karate Budokun International (KBI) in Kuala Lumpur (Tel: 03-81470).

SQUASH, TENNIS & BADMINTON

Courts for squash, tennis and badminton are found in most international class hotels, as are gymnasiums. Many hotels have swimming pools.

WATER SPORTS

Scuba-diving is catching on in Malaysia, and you will find scuba centres in most developed beach resorts such as Tioman, Langkawi, and Desaru, to name a few. Some centres also teach scuba-diving and you can gain an internationally recognised certificate. Equipment can be hired for scuba-diving, sailing, wind-surfing, snorkelling and water skiing. Check with a resort by phone first. Snorkelling equipment can be bought cheaply in local shops.

SPECTATOR

Spectator sports include horse racing as well as popular local pastimes such as kite-flying and top-spinning. Other favourite pastimes are mentioned below.

HORSE RACING

Meetings are held on weekends and public holidays, rotating between Kuala Lumpur, Ipoh, Penang and Singapore. In Kuala Lumpur, meetings are held at the Selangor Turf Club in Jalan Ampang. Betting is part of the attraction.

KITE-FLYING

This is not a child's game in Malaysia. Especially along the east coast, adults take pride in flying their kites, which are usually hand-made at home. Regular contests are held to determine which man can fly his kite the highest. Check with the tourist office if there are any kite competitions going on.

TOP-SPINNING (GASING)

This is a favourite pastime among children and adults alike. More popularly known as *main gasing*, this game is usually played during the period of the ripening of *padi* or rice. Legend records that the gasing brings in a good harvest. Whether this is true or not, the game certainly offers fun and relaxation. Competitions are held fairly regularly and are merry occasions which bring the whole village to gather and watch.

SEPAK RAGA/SEPAK TAKRAW

The aim of the game is to keep the rattan ball, made from rattan strips and weighing 170 grammes, in the air as long as possible by passing it from one player to another. Scores are given for the number of kicks made before the ball falls. Except for the forearms and the hands, any part of the body can be used to hit the ball.

SILAT

The Malay equivalent of the Chinese *kung fu*, *silat* is the art of self-defence. The origin of this art is accredited to the famous Hang Tuah of old Melaka, who did not hesitate to draw his sword, and even to strike to kill, for justice's sake. Youths today regard *silat* as a form of physical exercise in an artistic form. Demonstrations at weddings and other feasts are given to the rhythmic beat of gongs and drums. It is also part of the school curriculum for boys.

PHOTOGRAPHY

Professionals working in the tropics have one big suggestion for good results in colour: beware of the heat. Exposure of film or camera equipment to hot sun causes changes in the chemical emulsions of the film, which detract from natural colour. Whenever possible, store your camera and film in a cool place; if not in an air-conditioned room, at least in the shade. Experienced photographers also recommend buying film in the cities rather than in the countryside where proper storage facilities for colour films are not guaranteed. Also, get your films processed as soon as possible, either in Malaysia or in Singapore.

Humidity can be another tropical hazard, particularly with jungle photography. The solution here is to carry equipment and film in a closed camera bag containing silica gel, a chemical that absorbs moisture. For suitable tones and rich colour, the best times to photograph are before 10.30 a.m. or after 3 p.m. Few films take noontime sunlight well. Pictures often lose subtle gradations in colour because the light is too strong. In the early morning or late afternoon, sidelights give softer contrasts and deeper colour density. You perspire less as well!

Most Malaysians are more than amiable about having their pictures taken. It usually takes a gang of schoolchildren about 15 seconds before they merrily begin jabbing peace signs in front of your 20 mm lens. Mosques and temples are rightly more reserved about photographers posing their subjects in front of altars. Whatever the situation, you should always ask first for permission, especially with tribal people, who may have an aversion to having their photo taken. Keep a respectful distance from religious ceremonies. If you can bear to carry one, a zoom lens will enable you to photograph interesting groups of people without interfering with them.

Film processing is offered everywhere in Kuala Lumpur. Komal in Petaling Jaya develops Kodak colour film only. Black and white normally needs 24 hours. Kodakcolour and Ektachrome take one or two weeks, as they are sent off to Australia for developing. General colour film can take as little time as half an hour in a developing booth in major shopping centres in Kuala Lumpur.

LANGUAGE

Malay, mother tongue of more than 150 million Asians, is as ancient as a Grecian urn, and nearly as practical. A man can travel from the tip of the Malay peninsula, through the southern Philippines and all along the island-hopping trail that zigzags across the Indonesian archipelago – speaking Malay. New nations have adopted the old language to their own ends, lending it a variety of sophisticated nuances in grammar, spelling and scientific terms. But all countries with official letterheads in Malay trace them back to the trade fairs of antiquity when merchants bargained over gold dust and rhinoceros horn in a tongue similar to today's "Bazaar Malay", the language of the marketplace.

While Europe droned through the Middle Ages, Malay rulers conversed in an increasingly refined and eloquent "Classical Malay", until, by the time the cosmopolitan Malacca Sultanate had set up its throne in the 1400s, the language had reached the heights of epic grandeur. *The Sejarah Melayu*, "Malay Annals", written by a scribe in the Malacca court "for the greater pleasure of his lord the king", achieved a stylistic grandiloquence that would delight the most venerable of storytellers.

Classical Malay relapsed to the marketplace during the colonial era when the social elite, though retaining Malay as an official language, spoke only English among themselves. Independence in 1957 unanimously changed the conversation back to Malay, stressing its new importance as the national language, symbol of unity among all Malaysians. Posters, banners, car stickers and special badges, exhorting people to speak as the "Ancients" spoke, popped up in schoolrooms and government buildings. Certain theme songs played heavily on Radio Malaysia, such as *Bahasa Jiwa Bangsa* – "Language is the Soul of the Nation" – contributed to the superior status Classical Malay now enjoys. With new words from the age of technology enriching its reserves, and patriotic proprieties making it the language of monarchs and citizens alike, Malay can look forward to a future as functional and refined as its past.

Though formal Malay is a complex language demanding some time of serious study, the construction of "Basic Malay" is fairly simple, with many things about the language conducive to learning. Malay is written in the Latin alphabet and, unlike some Asian tongues, is not a tonal language. There are no articles in Malay – *buku* means "the book" or "a book", *anak* means "the child" or "a child". Plurals are made simply by doubling the noun – *buku-buku* means books. To denote time, a few key adverbs are used: *sudah* (already) shows past time, *be-*

lum (not yet), *akan* (will) for the future, and *sedang* (in the process of doing, e.g. *Saya sedang makan* = I am eating) for a present action, being performed at the moment of speaking.

When speaking Malay, you need a few basic rules. Adjectives always follow the noun. *Rumah* (house) and *besar* (big) together as *rumah besar* means "a big house" and so on. When constructing a sentence, the order is subject-verb-object: *Dia* (he) *makan* (eats) *nasi* (rice) *goreng* (fried). *Dia makan nasi goreng* = He eats fried rice. The traditional greeting in Malay is not "Hello!" but rather *Ke mana?* – "Where are you going?" The question is merely a token of friendliness which does not require a specific answer. One simply returns the smile by replying *Tak ada ke mana* – "Nowhere in particular" – and passes on.

Below are some very general guidelines for the pronunciation of Malay, or *Bahasa Malaysia* as it is known here. No written descriptions of the phonetics can replace the guidance of a native speaker, but once you've tried pronouncing a few words, Malaysians are quick to understand and their response is the best way to pick up a feeling for the language.

a	is pronounced short as in *matter* or *cat*. *apa* – what; *makan* – to eat
ai	is pronounced like the sound in *aisle*. *kedai* – shop; *sungai* – river
au	sounds like the *ow* of *how*. *pulau* – island; *jauh* – far
c	is pronounced like *ch* as in *chat*. *capal* – sandal, *cinta* – love
e	is very soft, hardly pronounced at all. *membeli* – to buy; *besar* – big
g	is pronounced as in *go*, never as in *gem*. *pergi* – go; *guru* – teacher
gg	is pronounced as *ng* plus a hard *g* sound: i.e. sing-ging. *ringgit* – Malaysian dollar; *tetangga* – household
h	is pronounced as in *halt*. *mahal* – expensive; *murah* – cheap
i	sounds like *i* in *machine* or *ee* in *feet*. *minum* – to drink; *lagi* – again
j	sounds like the English *j* in *judge*. *Jalan* – Street; *juta* – million
ng	a single *g* in a word is pronouced like the *ng* in *sing*, not with a hard sound.

sangat – very; *bunga* – flower

ny	is similar to *ni* in *onion* or *n* in *news*.
	harganya – price; *banyak* – a lot
o	is most similar to the *o* in *hop*.
	orang – human being; *tolong* – help
u	is pronounced as *oo* in *pool*.
	tujuh – seven; *minum* – to drink.
y	sounds like *y* in *young*, never as in *why*.
	wayang – opera; *kaya* – rich.

There is no specific syllabic stress in Malay as in English (i.e. **na**-tion, not na-**tion**), nearly all syllables are given equal stress; however, the Malays add to their speech a sing-song intonation which often gives more emphasis to the final syllable of a word, especially the last word in an utterance. This has led to the widespread use of the appendage – *lah* to the important word. This can either charm or irritate the visitor! Its purpose is purely emphatic, and it is now used generally in Malaysia, whether the speaker is talking in Malay, Chinese, Tamil or even English! Perhaps the most famous example of this is the phrase "Cannot-lah!", uttered when you have asked something the speaker considers impossible!

USEFUL PHRASES

Good morning.	*Selamat pagi.*
Good afternoon.	*Selamat tengah hari.*
Good evening.	*Selamat petang.*
Please come in.	*Sila masuk.*
Please sit down.	*Sila duduk.*
Thank you.	*Terima kasih.*
You're welcome.	*Sama-sama.*
Where do you come from?	*Anda datang dari mana?*
I come from...	*Saya datang dari...*
What is your name?	*Siapa nama anda?*
My name is...	*Nama saya...*
Can you speak Malay?	*Boleh anda bercakap dalam Bahasa Malaysia?*
Yes.	*Ya.*
No.	*Tidak.*
Only a little.	*Sedikit sahaja.*
I want to learn more.	*Saya hendak belajar lebih lagi.*
How do you find Malaysia?	*Apakah pendapat anda mengenai Malaysia?*
I like it here.	*Saya suka berada di sini.*

The weather is hot, isn't it?	*Cuaca di sini panas, bukan?*
Yes, a little.	*Ya, sedikit.*
Where are you going?	*Pergi ke mana?*
I am going to...	*Saya pergi ke...*
Turn right.	*Belok ke kanan.*
Turn left.	*Belok ke kiri.*
Go straight.	*Jalan terus.*
Please stop here.	*Sila berhenti di sini.*
How much?	*Berapa?*
Wait a minute.	*Tunggu sekejap.*
I have to get change.	*Saya hendak tukar duit.*
Excuse me.	*Maafkan saya.*
Where is the toilet?	*Di mana tandas?*
In the back.	*Di belakang.*
Where may I get something to drink?	*Di mana boleh saya minum?*
Over there.	*Di sana.*
One cup of coffee.	*Kopi secawan.*
One cup of tea.	*Teh secawan.*
Fried noodles.	*Mee goreng.*
Fried rice.	*Nasi goreng.*
The food was tasty.	*Makanan tadi sedap.*
How much does this cost?	*Berapakah harganya?*
Ten dollars.	*Sepuluh ringgit.*
That's quite expensive.	*Mahal sangat.*
Can you make it less?	*Boleh kurangkan?*
Seven dollars.	*Tujuh ringgit.*
Fine.	*Baiklah.*
I'll buy it.	*Saya nak membelinya.*
Good-bye.	*Selamat tinggal.*
I am sorry.	*Saya minta ma'af.*

USEFUL WORDS

Mr.	*Encik*
Mrs.	*Puan*
Miss	*Puan, Cik*
I	*Saya*
you (friendly)	*awak*
you (formal)	*encik*
he, she	*dia*
we	*kami/kita*
they	*mereka*
what?	*apa?*
who?	*siapa?*
where (place)	*di mana?*
where (direction)	*ke mana?*
when?	*bila?*
how?	*bagaimana?*
why?	*menapa?*

which?	*yang mana?*
how much?	*berapa?*
to eat	*makan*
to drink	*minum*
to sleep	*tidur*
to bathe	*mandi*
to come	*datang*
to go	*pergi*
to stop	*berhenti*
to buy	*beli (membeli)*
to sell	*jual (menjual)*
road	*jalan*
airport	*lapangan terbang*
post office	*pejabat pos*
shop	*kedai*
coffee shop	*kedai kopi*
money	*wang; duit*
dollar	*ringgit*
cent	*sen*

NUMBERS

1	*satu*
2	*dua*
3	*tiga*
4	*empat*
5	*lima*
6	*enam*
7	*tujuh*
8	*lapan*
9	*sembilan*
10	*sepuluh*
11	*sebelas*
12	*dua belas*
13	*tiga belas*
20	*dua puluh*
21	*dua puluh satu*
22	*dua puluh dua*
23	*dua puluh tiga*
30	*tiga puluh*
40	*empat puluh*
58	*lima puluh empat*
100	*seratus*
263	*dua ratus enam-puluh tiga*
1,000	*seribu*

FURTHER READING

Books on Malaysia probe the far reaches of the Borneo wilds, flash back to old Penang when secret societies were on the rampage, linger in the traditional Malay *kampong*, or chase surrealistic tracks of elusive, three-metre jungle "giant men". Historical accounts, in particular are on the rise, but the range of books about Malaysia also covers travel adventures, cartoons, political arguments and wildlife.

BOOKSHOPS

The arcades of large hotels and drugstores sell popular and peculiar paperbacks on Malaysia and the South-East Asian region. There are also bookstore chains such as Berita and MPH in Sungei Wang Plaza, Jln. Bukit Bintang and the Dayabumi Complex. In the grounds of the University of Malaysia, there is the excellent University Cooperative Bookshop which is open to the public.

GENERAL

Alliston, Cyril. *Threatened Paradise: North Borneo and Its Peoples.* London: Robert Hale, 1966. Quick, stimulating reading on native tribesmen, Malays, Chinese and English colonialists in Sabah.

Burgess, Anthony. *The Malayan Trilogy.* London: Penguin Books. Burgess' famous novel on post-war Malaya during the chaotic upheaval of independence.

Chapman, Spencer F. *The Jungle is Neutral.* London: Corgi Books, 1949. Malaysia's classic on the terrible reality of jungle warfare in World War II as told by a British officer who wandered the wilderness for three long years, and survived.

Craig, Jo-Ann. *Culture Shock! Malaysia and Singapore.* Times Books Intl. A guidebook for expatriates and visitors to the region on what not to do in Malaysia and why not to do it. Interesting notes on the cultures and customs of the country.

Customs and Traditions of the Peoples of Sarawak. State Government of Sarawak, 1988. A thorough and academic study of the various tribes and peoples of Sarawak, covering history, religion and culture, and supplemented by interesting photographs.

d'Alpuget, Blanche. *Turtle Beach*. Penguin 1981. Award-winning Australian novel on the plight of the Vietnamese people and their arrival in Malaysia.

Fauconnier, Henrí. *The Soul of Malaya*. Oxford University Press, 1965. The book is sheer mood. No other man has written so powerfully on the seductions of Malaya.

Harrison, Tom. *World Within: A Borneo Story*. Singapore: Oxford University Press, 1985. Harrison has a style of description that makes the inland peoples of Sarawak spring from the pages in three dimensions, cracking jokes and chanting songs as they go.

Kanapathy, Dr. V. *The Mahathir Era: Contributions to National Economic Development*. Malaysia: International Investments Consultants. Essays on Malaysia's fourth prime minister, assessing his successes and failures.

Kratoska, Paul H. *The Penang Guide*. Singapore: Graham Brash, 1989. Kratoska lived in Penang for ten years working at the Universiti Sains Malaysia, during which time he learned a great deal about the island. As well as maps for walking, trishaw and driving tours, there are also sections on culture, history and interesting things to do in Penang.

Lat. *Kampong Boy* and *Town Boy*. Straits Times Publishing, 1979 & 1988. Malaysia's most famous cartoonist, Lat, gives a hilarious account of life in a typical Malay village as seen through the eyes of a child. The drawings and autobiographical text of both books are all done by Lat, who has several other cartoon books on the shelf.

Mohammed, Dr. Mahathir Bin. *The Malay Dilemma*. 1970. Prior to his becoming prime minister, Dr Mahathir outlined his views on the problems facing his country in the next few decades.

Mjoberg, Eric. *Forest Life and Adventures in the Malay Archipelago*. Oxford University Press, 1988. A collection of stories and anecdotes by Swedish naturalist Mjoberg, who spent eight years in the archipelago.

Keith, Agnes Newton. *Three Came Home*. Kuala Lumpur: Eastview Productions, 1982. A sensitive, moving account of the grit and mother-love of a civilian prisoner of war during the Japanese occupation in Borneo. This book has been made into a movie.

Osborne, Milton. *South-East Asia: An Illustrated Introductory History*. George Allen & Unwin, 1985.

Sheppard, Mubin. *Living Crafts of Malaysia*. Singapore: International Press, 1978. An illustrated book on Malaysian crafts, highlighting individuals such as Hashim the kite maker and Sulian Sigo the Sarawak beadworker, and getting them to explain how they go about their crafts.

Turnbull, C. Mary. *A Short History of Malaysia, Singapore and Brunei*. Australia: Cassell, 1980.

Tweedie, MWF and Harrison, JL. *Malayan Animal Life*. Kuala Lumpur: Longman, 1954. In this book on Malaysia's wildlife, the authors present an intriguing cast for a jungle play: from Moon rats to Clouded Leopards to Spider-hunting Sunbirds.

Wallace, Alfred Russell. *The Malay Archipelago*. Singapore: Graham Brash, 1987. Wallace's famous account of his travels in the region. During his time in the East, Wallace formulated the theory of natural evolution, only to find that his contemporary Darwin had beaten him to the press.

Winstedt, Richard. *The Malays – A Cultural History*. Revised and updated by Tham Seong Chee. Singapore: Graham Brash, 1981. A fascinating documentation of the Malay people from pre-history to the present day.

World Rainforest Movement. *The Battle for Sarawak's Rainforests*. World Rainforest Movement and Sahabat Alam Malaysia, 1989. Documents the fight by the natives of Sarawak to save their environment.

USEFUL ADDRESSES

TOURIST INFORMATION

The Tourist Development Corporation (TDC) has various offices throughout Malaysia (see the following list). Offices vary in the amount of literature available, but there are usually brochures on local places of interest and some of the staff (especially in KL) are very knowledgeable. The TDC also has a few offices overseas (addresses given in the following list). In smaller places, there are other tourist offices that service the area. Besides these, it is always a good idea to ask several local people for their opinion of a place. You'll get varying reports and will have to make up your own mind as to whether the place is worth a visit!

TDC OFFICES IN MALAYSIA

Head Office
24-27th Floor, Menara Dato' Onn, Putra World Trade Centre, 45 Jln. Tun Ismail, 50480 KL
Tel: 03-293-5884

East Coast Region
2243 Tingkat Bawah, Wisma MCIS, Jln. Sultan Zainal Abidin, 20000 Kuala Terengganu, Terengganu
Tel: 09-621433

Northern Region
10 Jln. Tun Syed Sheikh Barakbah, 10200 Pulau Pinang
Tel: 04-619067

Sabah
Block L, Lot 4 Bandaran Sinsuran, Mail Bag 136, 88700 Kota Kinabalu, Sabah
Tel: 088-211723

Sarawak
2nd Floor AIA Bldg., Jln. Song Thian Cheok, 93100 Kuching
Tel: 082-246575

Southern Region
No. 1, 4th Floor, Kompleks Tun Razak, Jln. Wong Ah Fook, 80000 Johor Bahru, Johor
Tel: 07-223590

TDC OFFICES OVERSEAS

Australia
65 York St., Sydney NSW 2000
Tel: 294441

Germany
Rossmarkt 11, 6000 Frankfurt Am Main, FRG
Tel: 069-283782

Hong Kong
Ground Floor, Malaysia Bldg., 47-50 Gloucester Rd., Hong Kong
Tel: 5-285810

Japan
2nd Floor, Nichiginmae Kyodo Bldg., 3-4 Nihombashi-Hongokucho Chuo-ku, Tokyo 103
Tel: 03-279-3081

Singapore
10 Collyer Quay, 01-03 Ocean Bldg., Singapore 0104
Tel: 02-532-6321

Thailand
315 South East Insurance Bldg., Silom Rd., Bangkok
Tel: 236-2832

United Kingdom
57 Trafalgar Square, London WC2N5DU
Tel: 01-930-7932

United States
818 West Seventh St., Los Angeles, CA 90017
Tel: 213-689-9702

(A TDC office is scheduled to open in Vancouver, Canada)

TOURIST ASSOCIATIONS

Johor Tourist Association
c/o Tropical Inn Hotel, Jln. Gereja,
80100 Johor Bahru
Tel: 07-225-6789

Kedah Tourist Association
Tunjang Agensi 5 & 7, Bulatan Wan Jah,
Jln. Badlishah, 05000 Alor Setar
Tel: 04-724357/728980

Kelantan Tourist Association
Pusat Penerangan Pelancongan Negeri
Kelantan, Jln. Sultan Ibrahim,
15050 Kota Bharu
Tel: 09-785823

Kuala Lumpur Tourist Association
Kuala Lumpur Visitors Centre,
Jln. Sultan Hishamuddin, 50050 KL
Tel: 03-238-1832/230-1624

Malacca Tourist Association
4A Jln. Hang Tuah, Melaka
Tel: 06-221909

Pahang Tourist Association
Purnama Timor Agency Sdn. Bhd.,
Jln. Haji Abdul Aziz, 25000 Kuantan
Tel: 09-522208/592335

Penang Tourist Association
Penang Port Commission Building,
10 Jln. Tun Syed Sheh, Barakbah,
P.O. Box 444, 10200 Penang
Tel: 04-616663

Perak Tourist Association
Pusat Perkhidmat Bumiputra,
Pelancungan Negeri, Jln. Dewan,
P.O. Box 578, 30000 Ipoh
Tel: 05-532008

Perlis Tourist Association
d/a Sri Perlis Inn, Kangar, 01000 Perlis
Tel: 04-752266

Sabah Tourist Association
2nd Floor, Block L,
Lot 6 Sinsuran Complex, P.O. Box 1718,
Kota Kinabalu, Sabah
Tel: 088-57123/57124

Sarawak Tourist Association
1-3 Temple Street, Ground Floor,
Specialist Centre, P.O. Box 887,
93718 Kuching
Tel: 082-20620/456266

Sarawak Third Division
Travel Agents Association
c/o Sazhong Trading & Travel Service,
P.O. Box 1569, 96007 Sibu

Terengganu Tourist Association
Perpel Terengganu Sdn. Bhd., c/o Syarikat
DME, Wisma DME, Jln. Paya Bunga,
20200 Kuala Terengganu
Tel: 09-621664

TOUR OPERATORS

There are innumerable tour operators and travel companies throughout Malaysia. The reputable ones are all registered with the Tourist Development Corporation of Malaysia (TDC). Below is a short list of registered travel agents. If you wish to check whether a certain travel agent is registered, telephone the nearest TDC office and they will check for you.

PENINSULAR MALAYSIA

• **Kuala Lumpur**

Angel Tours (KL) Sdn. Bhd.
G48 Lower Ground Floor, City Tower,
Jln. Alor, 50200 KL
Tel: 03-241-7018
Services: Ticketing (Reg. No. 0353)

Asian Overland Services Sdn. Bhd.
35M Jln. Dewan Sultan Sulaiman 1,
50300 KL
Tel: 03-292-5637
Services: Ticketing, inbound tours, outbound tours (Reg. No, 0281)

Borneo Travel Bureau Sdn. Bhd.
Lot 36/37, The Arcade, Hotel Equatorial,
Jln. Sultan Ismail, 50250 KL
Tel: 03-261-2130
Services: Ticketing (Reg. No. 0901)

Fairwind Travel & Tours Sdn. Bhd.
Lot T 007, Sungei Wang Plaza,
Jln. Sultan Ismail, 50250 KL
Tel: 03-248-6920
Services: Ticketing, inbound tours (Reg.
No. 0971)

Insight Travel & Tours Sdn. Bhd.
9th Floor, Plaza MBF, Jln. Ampang,
50450 KL
Tel: 03-261-2488
Services: Ticketing, inbound tours, outbound tours (Reg. No. 0199)

Ken Air Services Sdn. Bhd.
62 Jln. Bukit Bintang, 55100 KL
Tel: 03-243-3722
Services: Ticketing, inbound tours, outbound tours (Reg. No. 0391)

Mayflower Acme Tours Sdn. Bhd.
18 Jln. Segambut Pusat, Peti Surant 10179,
50706 KL
Tel: 03-626-7011
Services: Ticketing, inbound tours, outbound tours, limousine services, hire and
drive (Reg. No. 0596)

• **Melaka**

Ace Tours & Travel Sdn. Bhd. (Branch)
Ground Floor, Jln. Munshi Abdullah,
75100 Melaka
Tel: 06-247975
Services: Ticketing, inbound tours, out-
bound tours (Reg. No. 0017)

• **Penang**

Speedy Sdn. Bhd.
388 G. Perak Road, 11600 Pulau Pinang
Tel: 04-888996
Services: Ticketing, outbound tours (Reg.
No. 0373)

Tour East
(licensee Harpers Tours, Reg. No. 0425)
Suite 402, Penang Plaza, Burmah Road,
10050 Penang
Tel: 04-362214, Telex: MA 40438
Services: Inbound tour arrangements, limousine and coach hire, hotel reservations,
incentive travel and convention organising

• **Kelantan**

Blue Moon Travel Sdn. Bhd. (Branch)
No. 9 Tingkat Satu, Kompleks Niagga
Tabong Haji, Jln. Dato Pati,
15000 Kota Bharu
Tel: 09-747361
Services: Ticketing (Reg. No. 0976)

• **Pahang**

**Gold Coast Adventure
Travel & Tours Sdn. Bhd.**
No. 4, Merlin Arcade, Merlin Inn Resort,
25050 Kuantan
Tel: 09-529185
Services: Inbound tours (Reg. No. 0953)

SABAH

Bakti Tours & Travel Sdn. Bhd.
Hotel Arcade, Hyatt International Hotel,
G-02 Ground Floor,
Jln. Datuk Salleh Sulong, P.O. Box 11832,
88820 Kota Kinabalu, Sabah, Malaysia
Tel: 53416, 53854, 216862

SARAWAK

Api Tours & Travel
Ground Floor, Lot 49 Bandaran Berjaya,
P.O. Box 12853, Kota Kinabalu
Tel: 088-221230
Sabah tours including whitewater rafting

**Benarat Tourist and Transportation
Agency**
P.O. Box 205 Marudi
Tel: 085-55329
Tours to Mulu

Borneo Adventure Sdn. Bhd.
12 Padungan Arcade 1st Floor, Jln. Song
Thian Cheok, P.O. Box 2112, Kuching
Tel: 082-245175
Tours around Sarawak

Malang Sisters' Travel Agency
Ground Floor, Ria Fatimah Hotel
Tel: 085-38141
Tours to Niah and Mulu Parks

DIPLOMATIC MISSIONS
IN MALAYSIA

Argentina
Embassy: 3 Jln. Semantan 2,
Damansara Heights, 50490 KL
Tel: 03-255-0176

Australia
High Commission: 6 Jln. Yap Kwan Seng,
50450 KL
Tel: 03-242-3122

Austria
Embassy: 7th Floor MUI Plaza Bldg.,
Jln. P. Ramlee, 50250 KL
Tel: 03-2484277

Bangladesh
High Commission: 204-1 Jln. Ampang,
50450 KL
Tel: 03-242-3271

Belgium
Embassy: 4th Floor, Bangunan Sateras,
152 Jln. Ampang, 50450 KL
Tel: 248-5733

Bolivia
Embassy: 12 Lorong Yap Kwan Seng,
50450 KL
Tel: 03-242-5146

Brazil
Embassy: 22 Persiaran Damansara Endah,
Damansara Heights, 50490 KL
Tel: 03-254-8020

Brunei
High Commission: No. 113 Jln. U Thant,
55000 KL
Tel: 03-261-2860

Burma
Embassy: No. 5 Taman U Thant I, 55000 KL
Tel: 03-242-3863

Canada
High Commission: 7th Floor, MBF Plaza,
172 Jln. Ampang, 50450 KL
Tel: 03-261-2000

China (also for North Korea)
Embassy: 229 Jln. Ampang, 50450 KL
Tel: 03-242-9495

Czechoslovakia
Embassy: 32 Jln. Mesra, off Jln. Damai,
55000 KL
Tel: 242-7185

Denmark
Embassy: 22nd Floor, Bangunan Angkasa
Raya, 123 Jln. Ampang, 50450 KL
Tel: 03-241-6088

East Germany
Embassy: 29 Jln. Ampang Hilir, 55000 KL
Tel: 03-456-2894

Egypt (also for Lebanon and Sudan)
Embassy: 28 Linkungan U Thant,
off U Thant, 50764 KL
Tel: 03-456-8184

Finland
Embassy: 15th Floor, Plaza MBF,
Jln. Ampang, 50450 KL
Tel: 03-261-1008

France (also for Portugal and Senegal)
Embassy: 192-196 Jln. Ampang, 50450 KL
Tel: 03-248-4318

India
High Commission: 20th Floor, West Block,
Wisma Selangor Dredging,
142-C Jln. Ampang, 50450 KL
Tel: 03-261-7000

Indonesia
Embassy: 233 Jln. Tun Razak, 50400 KL
Tel: 03-984-2011

Iran
Embassy: 5 Lorong Mayang,
off Jln. Ampang, 50450 KL
Tel: 03-243-3575

Iraq
Embassy: 2 Jln. Langgak Golf,
off Jln. Tun Razak, 55000 KL
Tel: 03-248-0555

Italy
Embassy: 99 Jln. U Thant, 55000 KL
Tel: 03-456-5122

Japan
Embassy: 11 Persiaran Stonor,
off Jln. Tun Razak, 50450 KL
Tel: 03-243-8044

Kuwait
Embassy: 229 Jln. Tun Razak, 50400 KL
Tel: 03-984-6033

Libya
Embassy: 6 Jln. Madge, off Jln. U Thant,
55000 KL
Tel: 03-241-1035

Netherlands
Embassy: 4 Jln. Mesra, off Jln. Damai,
55000 KL
Tel: 03-243-1141

New Zealand
High Commission: 193 Jln. Tun Razak,
50400 KL
Tel: 03-248-6422

North Korea
Embassy: 11-A Jln. Delima, 55100 KL
Tel: 03-242-3296

Norway
Embassy: 11th Floor, Bangunan Angkasa
Raya, Jln. Ampang, 50450 KL
Tel: 03-243-0144

Oman
Embassy: 24 Lingkunan U Thant,
off Jln. Ru, 55000 KL
Tel: 03-475011

Pakistan
Embassy: 132 Jln. Ampang, 50450 KL
Tel: 03-241-8844

Papua New Guinea
High Commission: 1 Lorong Ru Kedua,
off Jln. Ampang, 55000 KL
Tel: 03-457-4202

Philippines
Embassy: 1 Changkat Kia Peng, 40450 KL
Tel: 03-248-4233

Poland
Embassy: 495 4½ Mile, Jln. Ampang,
68000 Ampang, Selangor Darul Ehsan
Tel: 0-457-6733

Romania
Embassy: 114 Jln. Damai, off Jln. Ampang,
55000 KL
Tel: 03-242-3172

Saudi Arabia
Embassy: 7 Jln. Kedondong,
off Jln. Ampang Hilir, 55000 KL
Tel: 03-457-9433

Singapore
High Commission: 209 Jln. Tun Razak,
50400 KL
Tel: 03-261-6277

South Korea
Embassy: 422 Jln. Tun Razak, 50400 KL
Tel: 03-984-2177

Spain
Embassy: 200 Jln. Ampang, 50450 KL
Tel: 03-248-4868

Sri Lanka
High Commission: 8 Lorong Yap Kwan
Seng, 50450 KL
Tel: 03-242-3094

Sweden
Embassy: 6th Floor Wisma Angkasa Raya,
Jln. Ampang, 50450 KL
Tel: 03-248-5433

Switzerland
Embassy: 16 Persiaran Madge, 55000 KL
Tel: 03-248-0622

Thailand
Embassy: 206 Jln. Ampang, 50450 KL
Tel: 03-248-8222

Turkey
Embassy: 118 Jln. U Thant, 55000 KL
Tel: 03-457-2225

USSR
Embassy: 263 Jln. Ampang, 50450 KL
Tel: 03-456-0009

United Kingdom
High Commission: 13th Floor, Wisma
Damansara, Jln. Semantan, 50490 KL
Passport Office: 186 Jln. Ampang
Tel: 03-248-7122

United Sates of America
Embassy: 376 Jln. Tun Razak, 50400 KL
Tel: 03-248-9011

Vietnam
Embassy: 4 Persiaran Stonor, 50450 KL
Tel: 03-248-4036

West Germany
Embassy: 3 Jln. U Thant, 55000 KL
Tel: 03-242-9666

Yugoslavia
Embassy: Lot 300, Batu 4½, Jln. JPT,
off Jln. Ampang, 68000 KL
Tel: 03-456-4561

MALAYSIAN DIPLOMATIC MISSIONS OVERSEAS

Argentina
Embassy: Room No. 2017 Sheraton Hotel,
Buenos Aires

Australia
High Commission: 7 Perth Avenue,
Yarralumla, Canberra A.C.T. 2600
Tel: 602-731543/5

Austria
Embassy: Prinz Eugen Strasse 18,
A-1040 Vienna
Tel: 651142, 651569, 656323

Bangladesh
High Commission: No. 4 Road,
No. 118 Gulshan Model Town, Dacca 12
Tel: 600291/2

Belgium
Embassy: 414A Avenue de Terveran,
1150 Brussels
Tel: 762-6767, 763-0624

Brazil (and Bolivia, Colombia, Peru and Venezuela)
Embassy: SHIS, QI.5, Characa 62,
Lago Sul, Brazilia DF
Tel: 061-248-5008/6215

Brunei
High Commission: Lot 12-15,
6th Floor Darussalam Complex,
P.O. Box 2826, Bandar Seri Begawan
Tel: 28410

Burma
Embassy: 82 Diplomatic Headquarters,
Pyidaundsu Yeikhta Road, Rangoon
Tel: 20248/9

Canada (and Jamaica, Trinidad & Tobago and Guyana)
High Commission: 60 Boteler St., Ottawa,
Ontario KIN 8 Y7
Tel: 613-237-5182/3/4

China (and Democratic People's Republic of Korea)
Embassy: 13 Dong Zhi Menwai Dajie,
San Li Tun, Beijing
Tel: 522531/3

Egypt (and Sudan)
Embassy: 7 Sharia Wadi El-Nil,
Madinet El Mohandessine, Agouza, Cairo
Tel: 460988, 460958

Fiji (and Tonga, Western Samoa, Tavalu and Kiribati)
Embassy: 5th Floor, Air Pacific House,
Butt St., Suva P.O. Box 356
Tel: 312166, 312617

France (and Portugal)
Embassy: 2 Bis Rue Benouville, Paris 75116
Tel: 455-31185

Germany (and Greece)
Embassy: Mittelstr 43, 5300 Bonn 2
Tel: 0228-376-80306

Hong Kong
High Commission: 24th Floor, Malaysia
Bldg., 50 Gloucester Rd. Wanchai
Tel: 5-270921

India (and Nepal)
High Commission: 50M Satya Marg,
Chanakyapuri, New Delhi 110021
Tel: 601291/2/6/7;
Assistant High Commissioner to India: 287
T.T.K. Road, Madras 600018
Tel: 453580, 453599

Indonesia
Embassy: 17 Jln. Iman Bonjol,
10310 Jakarta Pusat
Tel: 336438, 332864;
Consulates: No. 11 Jln. P. Diponegoro,
Medan, Sumatra Utara

Tel: 25315, 518053, 511567;
Jln. Diponegoro 59, Pekan Bahru, Riau
Tel: 22305;
No. 42 Jln. A. Yani Pontianak,
Kalimantan Barat
Tel: 2986, 6061

Iran
Embassy: No. 21 Golgasht St.,
Agrigha Expressway, Tehran
Tel: 297791

Iraq
Embassy: Hai Babil, Mahallah 923,
Zuzak 13, Bldg. 26, Jadiriyah, Baghdad
Tel: 776-2622

Italy
Embassy: Via Nomentana 297, Rome
Tel: 06-855764, 06-857026

Japan
Embassy: 20-16 Nampeidai Machi,
Shibuya-ku, Tokyo
Tel: 03-770-9331/5

Korea, Republic of
Embassy: 4-1 Hannam-dong, Yongsan-ku,
Seoul
Tel: 795-3032

Kuwait (and Bahrain, United Arab
Emirates, Qatar and Oman)
Embassy: Villa 1, St. 70, Block 7,
Faiha, Kuwait
Tel: 254-6022/6213/6413

Laos
Embassy: Route That Luang, Quartier Nong
Bone, P.O. Box 789, Vientiane
Tel: 2662

Libya
Embassy: 32 Trovato Partition, Kilometre 6,
Gargarish, P. O. Box 6309, Andalus, Tripoli
Tel: 833693/2

Mali (and Senegal, Gambia and Guinea)
Embassy: No. 14 Parcelle E, Badalabougou-
Est., B.P. 98, Bamako
Tel: 222783, 223232

Morocco
Embassy: 20 Zankat Hamzah, Agdal-Rabat
Tel: 70259

Netherlands
Embassy: Rustenburgweg 2,
2517 KE The Hague
Tel: 070-506506

New Zealand (and Niue,
and the Cook Islands)
High Commission: 10 Washington Avenue,
Brooklyn, Wellington
Tel: 852439, 852019

Nigeria (and Ghana)
High Commission: Plot 1092,
Adeola Odoku St., Victoria Island,
P.O. Box 3729, Lagos
Tel: 612741, 612710

Oman
Embassy: Villa H.E. Khalfan, Nasser
Al-Wahibi, P.O. Box 6939 Ruwi, Muscat
Tel: 706116

Pakistan
Embassy: No. 224, Nazimuddin Rd.,
F-7/4 Islamabad
Tel: 820147/8

Papua New Guinea (and Solomon Islands,
Vanuatu)
High Commission: Unit 1 & 3, 2nd Floor,
Pacific View Apartments, Pruth St.,
Korobosea, P.O. Box 1400, Port Moresby
Tel: 252076, 251506

Philippines
Embassy: 107 Tordesillas St.,
Salcedo Village, Makati, Metro Manila
Tel: 817-4581/5

Poland (and Hungary, Czechoslovakia
and German Democratic Republic)
Embassy: ul. Gruzinska 3, 03-902 Warsaw
Tel: 171413, 173144

Romania
Embassy: 30 Blvd. Dacia, Bucharest
Tel: 113801/2/3

Saudi Arabia
Embassy: C11 Main Road, Diplomatic
Quarters, P.O. Box 95335, Riyadh 11693
Tel: 488-7098/7100;
Consulate: No. 100 Sharie AlBaladiah,
P.O. Box 593, Jeddah
Tel: 667-4459/62

Singapore
High Commission: 301 Jervois Rd.,
Singapore 1024
Tel: 235-0111

Spain
Embassy: Paseo de La Castellana 91-50,
Centro 23, 28046 Madrid
Tel: 91-455-0684/0737

Sri Lanka (and Maldives)
High Commission: 87 Horton Place,
Colombo 7
Tel: 94837, 596591

Sweden (and Denmark and Norway)
Embassy: P.O. Box 260 53,
100 41 Stockholm
Tel: 08-145990

Switzerland
Embassy: Laupenstrasse 37, 3008 Berne
Tel: 031-252105/6

Thailand (and Laos and Kampuchea)
Embassy: 35 South Sathorn Rd.,
Bangkok 10500
Tel: 286-1390/7769;
Consulate: No. 4 Sukhum Rd, Songkhla
Tel: 331062

Turkey
Embassy: Koroglu Sokak No. 6,
06700 Gaziosmanpasa, Ankara
Tel: 136-1270/1

USSR (and Bulgaria, Mongolia
and Finland)
Embassy: Mosfilmovskaya Ulitsa 50,
Moscow
Tel: 147-1514/5

United Arab Emirates
Embassy: Block B, 17th Floor (Penthouse)
Ahmed Khalifa Al Suweidi Bldg.,
Zayed the Second St., P.O. Box 3887,
Abu Dhabi
Tel: 338112, 328262

United Kingdom (and Ireland)
High Commission: 45 Belgrade Square,
London SW1X 8QT
Tel: 01-2358033

United States (and Mexico)
Embassy: 2401 Massachusetts Avenue
N.W., Washington D.C. 20008
Tel: 202-328-2700;
Consulates: Two Grand Central Tower,
140 East, 45th St., 43rd Floor,
New York NY 10017
Tel: 212-490-2722/3;
350 South Figueroa St., Suite 400,
Los Angeles, California 90071-1203
Tel: 213-621-2991/4

Vietnam
Embassy: Block A-3, Van Phuc, Hanoi
Tel: 53371

Yugoslavia (and Romania)
Embassy: 8 Cakorska, Dedinje, Belgrade
Tel: 660823, 665892

Zimbabwe
Embassy: Room 909 and 1017, Sheraton
Hotel, Harare

CREDITS

INDEX

D

E

F

G

L

M

R

S

T

U - V

W - X

Y - Z

410